Love and ...

Charlie

WWII LETTERS FROM A JEWISH-AMERICAN SERVICEMAN

Charles L. Fletcher

Compiled and Arranged by

Joshua Gerstein

Advanced Reviews

An intimate look into the details of one Jewish G.I.'s experiences, "Love and Kisses, Charlie" brings the full spectrum of military life into focus, from the quotidian to the political to the personal. It's an absorbing read that takes one back in time when folks still wrote letters to express their feelings and describe their lives.

Dr. Deborah Dash Moore
Professor of History and Professor of Judaic Studies,
University of Michigan
Author of "GI Jews: How World War II Changed a Generation"

What do you write home to your Jewish mother when you're in the middle of fighting a global war unlike anything before or since? If you're Charlie Fletcher, you give near daily updates covering all kinds of the details of life. Fletcher's letters, which were sent to his mother, father and sister, reveal a personal side of life during wartime for one soldier training in the U.S. and then marching through Europe. His devotion to Jewish culture, holidays and community come shining through in this trove of correspondence. The letters show the importance of family to Fletcher.

These letters are a great resource for those of us trying to understand the experiences of the Jewish-American soldier in World War II. It's a pleasure getting to know Charlie Fletcher through his wartime letters home.

Michael Rugel
Director of Programs and Content
National Museum of American Jewish Military History

On a visit to his parents' home, Joshua Gerstein made a wonderful discovery in the attic... A treasure trove of World War II letters written by his Grandfather, Charlie Fletcher, over 70 years ago. Charlie's family is given a wonderful legacy and we, the reader, are able to experience the everyday life of a soldier through his letters.

Charlie Fletcher was a devoted son who wrote to his family practically every day. The result is over 600 letters filled with his Army experiences, his thoughts on the war, the Germans, the people he met and his travels... Charlie's family is given a gift; a window into the mind of the young twenty-year-old who would become their Father and Grandfather. We also journey with Charlie and on the way learn a lot from this affable soldier.

Laura Cantor Zelman
Author of "In My Father's Words – The World War II Letters of an Army Doctor"

CERTIFICATE OF SPECIAL
CONGRESSIONAL RECOGNITION

The Late Charles L. Fletcher

In recognition of

His Service to our Country in WWII and for Outstanding
and Invaluable Service to the Allentown Community

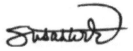

SUSAN WILD
MEMBER OF CONGRESS
7TH DISTRICT, PENNSYLVANIA

AUGUST 1, 2022

Table Of Contents

Foreword

By Dr. Thomas Cragin

The letters of Charles L. Fletcher are not what you might expect from a soldier in World War Two. They provide a fascinating look at the relationship of a young man and his parents and sister as he endeavors to make them a part of his army life and constantly reassure them of his present and future well-being. Charles fills his letters with the little details of his Army life that inspire the most interest for his family, back on the Upper West side of Manhattan where they manage a hosiery boutique. His description of Camp Upton, New York, as "a fine country club resort" and his praise of Basic Training for body building and making "a man out of me" are typical of his exaggerations for their benefit. "We always sing in our barrack while we work, and we have loads of fun and a lot of laughs." Much of these letters is closer to the war's propaganda films than to the harsh realities of Army life. Fine meals he has eaten, movies and shows he has seen or heard (including both USO broadcasts and live performances), friends he makes at Army bases in the U.S. and in France fill his letters. Yet Charles tells them very little about his work and nothing about the fighting.

Consciously or not, Charles employs a series of strategies to assuage his family's anxiety for him. Prior to his assignment to the European Theatre of Operations in September 1944, Charles writes about his efforts to attain "safe" assignments, his work with Army journalism, and his ambitions for promotion. Once he is in Europe, his letters contain a variety or reassurances more and more emphatic. In the midst of the Battle of the Bulge and knowing that his parents were reading about it back home, he writes "There isn't a thing to report." Just after the Battle, he writes of the cold that is remembered by most veterans as one of the most terrible aspects of that winter, "Good ice-skating and sled-riding weather." His optimism is irrepressible. The letters offer us insight into the value of Army "griping." Complaints about dull duties and petty formalities hide the very real dangers that must have troubled soldiers and their families back in the U.S. Charles' letters tell a story that is incomplete, yet replete with details about the side of Army life that would sound good to worried families back home: good, hot food, occasional hot showers, friendships, and advances in the war that promise victory and a return home.

It is evident that his parents' letters (which are not included in the volume) express a desire to help him in any way they can. Charles provides ample opportunities, sending them requests for small conveniences absent from Army life. In the final days of the Battle of the Bulge, he writes, "If there's any Kleenex . . . on sale . . . get me a few boxes please." He tries to make them as present as he can: "Pop . . . could use one of your Sunday breakfasts. How about coming over and serving me one in my pup tent?" In all these areas, the letters offer social historians a valuable source to understand aspects of Army life that were most valued by soldiers and their families. His details about goods and services, their prices and availability is particularly valuable for our understanding of the period.

Only very rarely do the letters offer a glimpse into the real anxieties that soldiers like Charles faced. "I was assigned to the Artillery headquarters. Now I am no longer in the infantry, thank God." As the war progresses, his rhetoric is effected: "Herb Hoffenberg . . . was bumped off recently." But even in this letter of June 1944, he reassures: "We clerks always manage to stay away from the real stuff." Only in the last six months of the war do his letters become less opaque about the war's horrors, but even then he consistently reassures his parents of his physical and psychological well-being. About his unit's discovery of hundreds of dead concentration camp prisoners, he reassures his mother, "I'm not depressed in the least. The sight of those bodies did not make me bitter (except for the first few hours after seeing it) and I'm in excellent spirits. So please don't harp on that in your letters." Only in the last week of the war does Charles indicate how close death was: "Pop, do you know that as a conservative estimate, close to 35 percent of the boys I did Basic with are dead and a good 60 percent have been wounded? . . . You've taken my being away splendidly straight along and I'm sure you'll continue to do so." It is particularly interesting that at war's end, Charles works hard to convince his mother in several letters that "my nerves haven't been affected on bit by the war . . . I'm still the same person who went away September '43."

Charles provides an interesting glimpse of the travails of a young Jewish soldier in an almost entirely Christian Army. He emphasizes his good relations with Christian soldiers of his unit, even attending "Protestant church services" and "singing . . . carols" amidst the Battle of the Bulge. Many of the friends he makes in the Army are Jewish and they join him in dating Jewish girls, attending Jewish services, and even seeking out Jewish delicacies to eat. His knowledge of Yiddish, learned from his father, allows him to communicate with Camp survivors in Germany, providing him with a deeper understanding of the Holocaust than was available to most soldiers of his unit. His letters contain only the vaguest references to this terrible aspect of the war. This knowledge certainly effects his views of Germans and he wants more Americans to know about Germans' "ruthlessness and barbarity."

Charles' letters include observations and thoughts about the conditions of many peoples he encountered in different parts of America and Europe. He decries the attitudes of Germans in the last days of the war and after: their determined faith in the Nazi regime, their refusal to admit responsibility for evident war crimes, and their haughtiness derived from a still rigid class structure. Charles tells us a great deal about American perceptions of the need for re-education in postwar Germany. His letters also indicate the milestones that most penetrate the wall he builds against the war: the D-Day landings, the death of FDR, the atomic bomb.

The letters are expertly annotated by Charles' grandson, Joshua Gerstein. Gerstein's meticulous research provides both details from the military history of World War Two and important aspects of Army culture at that time. Each major transition in Charles' Army life is punctuated by an explanatory preface of the new assignment, one that includes details of his Division and summaries of notable experiences mentioned and unmentioned in the letters.

The letters are a valuable contribution to the American history of World War Two and offer deep insight into soldier-family communications.

Dr. Thomas Cragin
Professor of History
Muhlenberg College

Preface

In Spring of 2017, I visited my parents in Lancaster, Pennsylvania for the holiday of Passover. Together with my wife Devora, and young son Eli, we had made the trip from our home in Jerusalem, Israel to spend much-needed quality time with our extended family. I'd always been a history enthusiast, but after becoming a new father, there was simultaneously born a newfound appreciation and an interest in my learning more about my own historical family roots.

It was this curiosity that found us rummaging through the many boxes in my parent's attic one afternoon during our stay. Box after box of old family photos and mementos were opened and looked through. One of the final boxes of the day became the catalyst for an unexpected yet wonderful four-year journey.

Within the large box were eight smaller shoeboxes, filled with what appeared to be countless old envelopes, stacked together. Devora picked one letter from the box – completely at random – and began to read aloud.

Wednesday, May 16, 1945

> *Hello Folks,*
>
> *Another swell package from you...There are some Polish Jews in this town, and I must have met them all yesterday, about 51. The majority have been in concentration camps for over five years, and they certainly have some stories to tell...God knows what'll become of them. The Poles treated them terribly and none want to go back there. When you see something like this, you begin to realize why Palestine would be such a grand place. These people actually have no place to go. They all speak Yiddish and I understood them, just like hearing my Old Man speak it. A lot came from Warsaw, and they say it was a terrible place for the Jews...*
>
> *That's all now.*
> *Love and Kisses,*
> *Charlie*

We were left speechless, in awe and astonishment. It was not news to me that my Pop-Pop, Charlie Fletcher, had been a serviceman in WWII. I had grown up hearing him repeat the same two or three Army anecdotes, had happily listened while he sang his Unit's song very heartily, albeit off-key. But holding his letters, seeing his handwriting, and reading his short but powerful message written more than 70 years before, was among the most profound experiences of my life.

The next few days of our visit found me carefully unfolding every letter, digitally scanning, and organizing the envelopes according to their respective dates. Though I didn't know at the time what would become of those scans, I knew that these letters and the story within couldn't remain to gather dust. It became my mission to preserve and share the materials that tell of a world through the eyes of my then 20-year-old grandfather. That is how and why the book *Love and Kisses, Charlie* is in your hands today.

While reading through and preparing these letters for print, a few matters quickly became apparent. Firstly, this was no "Band of Brothers" story, in fact it was furthest thing from a soaring Hollywood epic. Like some 39% of all enlisted personnel during WWII, Charlie had an administrative rather than a frontline combat position. Additionally, though thoroughly patriotic and proud of his military service, he was content and grateful for his non-combat role, having no false illusions as to the trials and tribulations of war. Furthermore, Charlie's maturity and inimitable personality take centerstage throughout his correspondence. He was a relatively young man facing a most daunting chapter, yet he maintained his humor throughout and was chiefly concerned not for himself, but for his family, their health, business, and relationships. His letters constantly reassure his parents that everything is "okey-doke" – all while positioned only a few miles from the frontlines while serving in Europe. Finally, Charlie threads a heartwarming and strong cultural and social Jewish identity throughout his correspondence. These foundational characteristics would continue to follow and formulate him on his path in adulthood.

Charlie's letters begin with his arrival to Camp Upton, New York and his induction to the United States Army in September 1943. From there we follow him to training at Fort Benning, Georgia and Camp Swift, Texas, through to his eventual departure to Europe in September 1944. Once in France, Charlie and his Division completed 173 days of combat through Germany until Victory in Europe Day, on May 8, 1945. From May 1945, Charlie is placed on Garrison Duty in Germany until he is honorably discharged in February 1946. All told, Charlie's letters are the personal accounts and reflections of a young man drafted just two months shy of his 20th birthday. They are a slice of Americana, reflecting both the significant historical events as well as the often dull and routine existence of Army life. In short, they describe the "hurry up and wait" maxim, which so powerfully defines the military experience.

At this point, a note regarding the technical structure of this book is in order. The following pages contain upwards of 600 letters, postcards, and telegrams written to his family by my grandfather Charles "Charlie" L. Fletcher between September 1943 and February 1946, while serving in the United States Army in WWII. The letters have been faithfully transcribed, with only small grammatical changes made to the original text. For a more seamless reading experience, the letters have been divided into 13 chapters corresponding to the main events in which Charlie was a participant. The Yiddish and Hebrew terms sprinkled liberally throughout the letters have been italicized, with their English translation footnoted. Additionally, the footnotes added by this author include short definitions of military terminology, explanations of historical events and people.

At the time of the letters' composition, there was a censorship in effect for war correspondence. Therefore, there are many details missing as to Charlie's location at any given time, as well as the military and historical events which served as the backdrop for his letters. To bridge this gap, a brief historical overview concerning the main events of the time as they relate to and affect Charlie's personal experiences can be found at the beginning of each chapter. The accompanying photographs and archival materials are from Charlie's personal collection unless otherwise noted; maps and troop movements were sourced from the Division's war annual published in 1947, *With the 102nd Infantry Division Through Germany.*

The completion of this project has been a poignant journey back to my roots, enhancing both past and present. To view the world through my grandfather's perspective at such a pivotal point in his life helped me to better understand myself, my parents, and the person that he would later become - the man I knew and loved as Pop-Pop. Though he passed away when I was 15 years old, working on this project over the last few years has made me feel that he is still right here beside me. In a truly full circle moment uniting our military journeys, I was privileged to officiate as an IDF Rabbi for a Hannukah candle-lighting ceremony together with US General Mark A. Milley, 20th Chairman of the Joint Chiefs of Staff, during his visit to Israel. It was a profound experience to share Charlie's story at an event which encapsulated the Jewish identity, American patriotism and Zionistic values that he held so dear.

In truth, my grandfather's legacy is the joyful spirit with which he interacted with everyone. Always family oriented, outgoing, good-natured, and one for a good time, I know that he would get a kick out of every bit of fuss being made over him and his letters today. Indeed, he'd think it swell.

Well, Pop-Pop, this one's for you.

Love and Kisses,
Joshua Gerstein
Jerusalem, Israel

Introduction

Charles "Charlie" L. Fletcher was born on November 21, 1923, to Samuel and Pauline (Weisberg) Fletcher and older sister Edith "Eadie" of 585 West 178th Street, New York City. Both of Charlie's parents were Eastern-European Jewish immigrants to the United States, arriving from Warsaw, Poland and settling in New York City in September 1906. Charlie had a typical childhood, attending school as well as helping his parents in their hosiery boutique during his spare time. Among other childhood highlights, Charlie enjoyed waitering at the 1939's New York World's Fair, visiting his maternal grandparents Sam and Anna Weisberg in the Bronx, his paternal grandmother Rose Fletcher (Tishman), as well his Aunt Rose and Uncle Mendel Nelson and their family in Wilkes-Barre, Pennsylvania. During the summer months of his teenage years, Charlie worked as a counselor at Camp Wakonda in Harriman State Park, just an hour outside of New York City.

After graduating from DeWitt Clinton High School in June 1939, Charlie enrolled as a Freshman in NYU's School of Commerce, Accounts, and Finance. From September 1939 - June 1943, Charlie pursued his higher education while serving on NYU's Student Council and writing for the school's *Commerce Bulletin*, first as the Sports Editor and then finally as the paper's Editor-in-Chief. Additionally, Charlie gained real life experience in his field during his college years, working as a Junior Auditor at Marvin Hirsch Accounting. Charlie's responsibilities there included: preparing profit and loss statements, wholesale establishment trial balances and inventory and tax work.

After graduating from NYU with a Bachelor's degree, Charlie began his US Army experience in the Summer of 1943. On July 23, 1943, he was summoned to Local Board No. 27, 201 West 72nd Street, New York; on August 16 he was officially inducted into the military. Like thousands of other young American men, his orders were to report for duty at Camp Upton, New York. It is here at Upton, on September 6, 1943, that his story begins.

Charlie at NYU

ARMED FORCES IN...
GRAND CENTRAL PALACE
480 Lexington Ave., New York, 17, N. Y.

VC-HMK-WW

16 August 1943

Special Orders)
No.   140)   E X T R A C T

* * * * *

Chapter 1:
Induction - Camp Upton, New York

September 1943 - October 1943

Par. No.   10 PAC Par 16b.... 615-... dated.. Sept. 1942, the following
enlisted man, inducted into the ..... ed States this date, is
released from active duty this date, transferred to the ERC and will
proceed to the .... located at
201 W 72nd Street, Rm 207, New York 23, NY

FLETCHER, CHARLES L   ..... 999 0..

Effective 6 September 1943, the above named enlisted man of the ERC is
called i..................... from.... he..been listed Local Board
to Reception Center, CAMP UPTON, NEW YORK, reporting to the Classification
Officer for duty. Should the above named enlisted reservist be found to
be physically disqualified upon reporting for active duty after a post-
induction inactive status or upon recall to active duty, the necessary
steps will be taken to insure discharge under the provisions of Section 11,
AR 615-360, as amended. Under no circumstances will physically disqualified
personnel be transferred back to the inactive Enlisted Reserve Corps.

TIN 1-5020 P 431-02 A 0425-24.

By order of Colonel CHAPPELLE:

H. M. KURTZNER,
Major, Infantry,
Adjutant.

OFFICIAL: *H M Kurtzner*

H. M. KURTZNER,
Major, Infantry,
Adjutant.

N O T I C E

You are now a soldier in th army of the United States!
Congratulations! You have been tr..ferred to the Enlisted Reserve
Corps for twenty-one days, as indicated by the above copy of your
Special Orders. You are directed to report to the Reception Center
in accordance with these orders. If you have not received a notice
from your Local Board telling you of the hour and place of assembly
within 19 days contact your Local Board immediately. Strict
compliance with these instructions is required.

You are not entitled to pay and allowances as a member of the
Enlisted Reserve Corps. Any medical attention or hospitalization which
you may require during this period will be at your own expense. Your
Local Board must be kept informed of your address at all times prior to
your being recalled to active duty.

(over)

The United States declared war on Germany on December 11, 1941, just days after the Japanese assault on Pearl Harbor. Following the surprise attack, the US Army needed to pivot to fighting mode – fast. So began the process of amassing the most pressing military assets, chief among them the soldiers and manpower needed to wage and ultimately win this chapter of global warfare.

In 1939, the US Army only numbered 174,000 soldiers, including the Army Air Forces. At its height during World War II, the Army grew to over 8 million men and women in uniform, plus an additional 3.4 million in the Navy.[1] These ranks were swelled with the induction of new recruits - about 39% of whom volunteered to serve - with the remainder called up through the conscription draft. With the passing of the Selective Training and Service Act in 1940 and the war years that followed, over 10 million men aged 18+ served their country in the European and Pacific theaters.[2]

These fresh recruits were essentially civilians, who had just previously been focusing on their education, careers and social lives. Suddenly, they all needed to be inculcated into the Armed Forces and trained for military duty as quickly and effectively as possible. To achieve this goal, dozens of Induction Centers

[1] https://www.nationalww2museum.org/war/articles/training-american-gi

[2] Ibid.

across the United States served as a central location for recruits from all over the nation to gather and be formed into units. In this environment, the new soldiers received their first taste of Army life, while the military brass assessed those who were qualified for the rigors of training and combat.[3]

A typical inductee arrived at the Induction Center via train or bus, and immediately began the transformation from civilian to soldier. Receiving a military haircut, Army uniform, basic equipment and undergoing a battery of medical examinations were the first item of business. After a short time, these new recruits were then sent to their next location, to commence specialized training in their specific branch of the military.[4]

On September 6, 1943, Charlie Fletcher boarded a bus and arrived at Camp Upton, New York. This Induction Center was built in 1917, its purpose being to train soldiers during WWI. It was deactivated upon that war's end and then reactivated with the military preparation in the United States in the latter part of 1940. After a day of quick initiation at Upton, Charlie settled in and wrote his first letter to Mom and Pop back home.

---

[3] Ibid.

[4] https://ahec.armywarcollege.edu/trail/WWII/index.cfm

1943

Monday, September 6, 1943 - Arrived at General Army Induction Center

I had my tests - it's now 8:30 PM and I'm getting ready for bed. Tomorrow we get our shots. Arrived safely, simply wonderful. Had a nice bite, now I'm off for the races.

Love,
Charles

Tuesday, September 7, 1943

Dear Folks,

Well, I've got all of my clothes now. My clothes are on their way home. I look pretty snappy in them, too. I did very well on my classification test. I got a special typing test also and did okay. But they give you no idea of where you're going to be sent. I won't call anymore.

Love,
Charlie

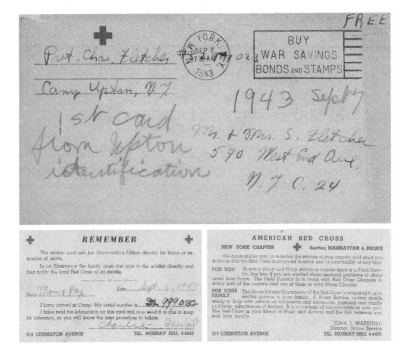

Thursday, September 9, 1943 – Arrived at Camp Upton, New York

Dear Mom and Pop,

Well Folks, this is my first opportunity to write you a letter since I'm at Upton. Yesterday I had my first taste of KP[5] with all the other boys who came in with me. I was a lucky Jew because I was assigned to the latrine. All I had to do was see that there was no loafing in the toilet and keep the sinks and floor clean. So I sat on my can for fifteen hours while the other boys scrubbed pots, floors, dishes etc. I was real lucky and I hope that I get the latrine next time also, but I doubt it.

How come the typewriter? Well, this morning, for no good reason at all, they woke up the whole camp at 4:30. We were called for line-up at 6 and after chow (breakfast) we were all lined up for special detail. Detail includes cleaning the streets, picking up papers, digging ditches, and many other things you connect with a "prison camp." Well, the Sergeant asked for two experienced typists and I stepped out. So here I am in the office sitting on my can while my comrades are walking all over the place. I did a little typing for the office earlier today and now I'm just stalling until I get some more work. This job isn't permanent as they hand out different jobs every day. And then again, a soldier gets shipped out of here on five minutes' notice. I'll probably leave before Sunday.

They usually wake you up for KP at 3:30 but we weren't awakened until 4. The days are real long here because they start so early. When you think you've put in a day's work, it's really only noon. Of course, this place is hard for a new-comer because he's here only for a short stay and must do all the dirty work. The real life in the Army doesn't start until you get to your Basic Training camp but so far I have no kicks coming. It's a fine experience.

Last night I got dressed up in my suntan uniform - that's the summer outfit you see all the boys wear in the city - and went to a show at camp. New selectees performed and they were very good. A Met opera singer, John Elliot, was just drafted and he sang a few songs. The food is fair. This morning I had a pear, oatmeal with a bottle of milk, toast, scrambled eggs, and coffee. Not bad but it's cooked real Army style and that takes away a lot of the real taste. I'm used to all

---

[5] "Kitchen police" or "kitchen patrol" work under the kitchen staff, assigned to junior enlisted military personnel; duties include washing dishes, food prep, and bussing tables.

sorts of food so it won't bother me at all. And then again, food is much better at your permanent camp.

The boys are very nice. Most of the newcomers are married and many have kids. With all the good news from Europe perhaps we'll all be home soon.

Daddy, is Mother still a changed woman? I still can't get over the change that came over her. Take care of yourselves. I hope business picks up. Love to Grandma - tell her I'm enjoying myself and not to worry. With Fletcher fighting for Uncle Sam, how can we lose?

Love and Kisses,
Charlie

P.S. If you don't hear from me for a few days, don't worry. It might mean that I'm being shipped to another camp.

Saturday, September 11, 1943

Dear Folks,

I got a very good night's sleep last night. We went to bed at 9:30 and I slept until 5:45 like a log. I certainly felt refreshed this morning. We had an excellent breakfast; it consisted of cantaloupes, shredded wheat with a little milk, a pancake with bacon and coffee. It was swell.

I'm sitting in the office now not doing a damn thing. There are a few shipments Monday, but I don't know whether I'll be on them.

I feel very well. I do hope you're taking good care of yourselves.

Love,
Charlie

P.S. Just finished delicious lunch - lamb, potatoes, soup, spinach, cabbage, tea and cake.

Monday, September 13, 1943

Dear Folks,

It's a very beautiful day here. The sun is shining and there is a delightful breeze. Well, I wasn't on any shipping list for today so I'll be around some more. I'm in the office again, and as I said, as long as I'm here the job is permanent.

I found out last night that I was working with a well-known celebrity for the past few days; if you recall, the Reader's Digest ran the excerpt of a book called "Out of the Night" and the book was very famous. It was written by Jan Valtin. Well, his real name is Krebs and he's been in the same office as I for three days. He was shipped out this morning. He's wanted by the Nazis - he's an ex-convict - and all in all a very well-known man. Well, your little son was giving him work to do for three days. He is a very nice man and you can see the effects of his beatings by the Nazis. You see, he was in a concentration camp for a period of time before he escaped from Germany. He's been charged as a communist and riot starter in several European countries. He's doing a good job in the Army, though. In fact, once you put on the uniform it doesn't matter who you were. We have two comedians who came in a few days ago. They've been entertaining the soldiers, but they were reported to be unwilling to help clean their barracks, so the Sarge is getting mighty tough with them. I think they'll get KP tomorrow.

Dinner again was excellent. All our noon day meals have been good. Today we had meatloaf, chicken salad, noodles, corn, and canned peaches. I eat first usually, and get everything before they run out. I met a colored boy I graduated with. He's been here for twenty-four days now.

Nothing more right now. Will write soon again.

Love,
Charlie

Tuesday, September 14, 1943

Dear Mother and Dad,

Well, another day has passed and I'm still at Upton. I don't even think of shipping anymore. When the time comes, it'll come. And there is no use worrying or thinking about it.

If you can spare a few dollars, I could use some. I'm sending $15 home each month, so the money you're sending me can be taken out of the money you'll get at the end of the month. I still have half of the $5, but I don't want to leave Upton without some dough.

There were no shipments at all today. Perhaps they'll start shipping again tomorrow. I saw "Heaven Can Wait" Sunday night. It was excellent. There are two movie houses, and one is a beauty. It only costs 15 cents. Everything in fact, is very reasonable for the soldiers.

I'll be writing soon again. Take it easy and do me a great favor and don't worry. Everything is real swell. Things couldn't be better.

Love and Kisses,
Charlie

Wednesday, September 15, 1943

Dear Mom and Dad,

It was raining cats and dogs this morning, but it turned into a beautiful day with the sun shining brightly. I wore my raincoat for the first time, and it gave me adequate protection.

Nothing is new of any importance. I'm having a nice day in the office and there isn't too much doing. I was out in the sun for an hour doing some work for the Sergeant, so I had some sunshine. I'm the old-timer of the selectees in the office because the other fellows shipped out this morning. One of the boys was here 32 days, while the other was here 19. Don't count on that pass on the 21st day. So many boys ship out around 18th day, that it isn't even funny.

Dad, when I left, I told you that I had some pictures in Theresa's Pharmacy. Please take them out right away and mail me one set of the pictures and the call it chow. They served chicken, mash potatoes, string beans, corn, cake and punch. It was very well prepared, surprisingly enough.

It's been a very quiet Sunday. Very little is doing, especially with no shipments going on. The office has been dreadfully quiet and all I did was sit and read the Times.

Upton is receiving all New York State men now, so we have many out-of-town-ers. Many of the boys come from Rochester, Albany and points north. I sure wish I knew where I'm going, but there's no way of telling. I take it as it comes though, and when my time comes to leave, I'll be satisfied. At least I have it very easy while here at Upton.

The army is a little *mashugina*.[9] There are two ways of doing things - the right way and the Army way. There seems to be no purpose to many of the things done around here, but you grin and take it. Sometimes when they wake the boys up at 3:30, they don't call them 'til 6 - things like that make you think the Army is nuts. But I understand that kind of inefficiency exists in reception cen-ters, not at basic training camps.

There was an excellent USO camp show in the outdoor theater last night. There was a lot of good entertainment and I enjoyed it a lot. When you look the camp over, you think what a fine country club resort it would make. It's really quite beautiful. It's spotlessly clean, also. You can't throw cigarette butts on the streets and God help you if you're caught. The streets are policed (Army's word for "cleaned") every day by many men and it's a sight to behold. There's no such thing as an employment problem. If the post exchange needs forty men, they put in a call for them and before you count to ten, they have their men. You see, all men can be put on detail the Sergeant wants them to go on; so you find many guys serving coffee, selling doughnuts, dumping garbage, digging ditches, etc. But your sonny is safe in the office.

That's all now - I'll write soon again.

Love,
Charlie

---

[9] Yiddish: an exclamation to describe something as crazy or bizarre.

Sunday, September 19,1943

Dear Mom and Dad,

Brrrr, it's cold. Just like the weather we have up in the Adirondacks.[10] But with all the stuff I have on, I keep pretty warm.

A fraternity brother of mine came in yesterday and I caught up with him last night. I really didn't know how lucky I was to be in A Company.[11] My friend is in B Company, and I went over to his barrack. It's one small story with very little head room, and no latrine. That means to wash up or use the urinal or bowl you must go out in the bitter cold. Gee, my barrack is paradise compared to that. It's well lit, running drinking water, etc. I felt sorry for the fellow because a nice living place sure lifts your morale.

We slept until 5:50 this morning. Wasn't that nice of them? I think I'll be able to catch a couple of hours this afternoon. Sunday is a regular workday. You hardly know it's Sunday, but I'm able to get away from the office for a while.

Well, that's all the news now. I hope business picks up. Take out my pictures from Theresa and mail me the negatives, Dad. Regards to Grandma and send my best to the family.

Take good care of yourselves now. You have nobody to support but yourselves, so just worry about yourselves. Be good.

Love and Kisses,
Charlie

Sunday Night, September 19, 1943 - Leaving Camp Upton

Dear Mom and Dad,

I'm so glad I spoke to you this morning. It's now 9:30 and I just found out I'm leaving tomorrow. I'm going out with all the ASTP men, so it's a good shipment. All of the men are college men and we'll be trained together.

---

[10] A group of mountains in northeastern Upstate New York.

[11] A military unit, typically consisting of 80–250 soldiers and usually commanded by a major or a captain. Most companies are formed of three to six platoons, with several companies grouped together as a battalion.

I have no idea where I'm going, but I'll be dropping you postcards on my way if it's at all possible.

Don't worry, I'm leaving with a nice bunch of fellas and I'm getting what I signed up for. ASTP stands for Army Specialized Training Program.

It's too bad I couldn't stay another week so I could see you, but I'm glad to be on my way.

I'll write soon.

All my love,
Charlie

Monday, September 20, 1943 - Postcards from the Train - 10:45 AM

Dear Mom and Dad,

I'm on the train now. We're very comfortable and not crowded at all. I'm traveling with two other college men. Altogether, we're about 200. We're headed South; my guess is Georgia, but I'm not sure. Will write soon.

Love,
Charlie

Monday, September 20, 1943 - Postcards from the Train – 3 PM

Hello Mom and Pop,

I'm passing through Trenton now. The trip is very nice. I'm going to Ft. Benning[12] in Georgia. It's a nice camp.

Love,
Charlie

---

[12] Created in October 1918, Fort Benning initially served as a Basic Training site for WWI units. During World War II, Ft. Benning spanned 197,159 acres (797.87 km2) with living space for 3,970 officers and 94,873 enlisted personnel. (https://en.wikipedia.org/wiki/Fort_Benning)

Monday, September 20, 1943 - Postcards from the Train - 6 PM

Dear Folks,

We're in Washington now and we'll be tied up here for 4 or 5 hours.

The food on the train is delicious. They serve us on paper plates, cafeteria style. We're having Virginia ham for supper. I had a nice nap this afternoon. Boy, I'm seeing the country.

Tuesday, September 21, 1943 - Postcards from the Train - 8:30 AM

Dear Folks,

Spent a comfortable night on the train. We left Washington at 11:30 - we went through Virginia during the night. We are now traveling through North Carolina. It's beautiful country. We had delicious eggs for breakfast. I must say that the food on the train is the best Army food I've had. Washed up this morning and feel swell. Take care of yourselves.

Love,
Charlie

Tuesday, September 21, 1943 - Postcards from the Train - 7:15 PM

Dear Mom and Dad,

I've been on the train 34 hours now and we're due in Ft. Benning in three hours. Of course, I don't know much about the camp but from what I hear from the escort party, it's one of the nicest camps in the south. I'll write you all about it as soon as I get a chance.

We're about 100 miles from New York. Boy, I sure saw the eastern part of our country. We went through New York and were in Penn Station for an hour but couldn't get off the train. I would have called if I got off. Then we passed

dents inducted into the Army but kept temporarily in a civilian status; and (3) A-12's, or certain high-school students who by preinduction tests had established their eligibility for the ASTP.[15] Since every inductee with an AGCT of 115 might at some point go to college, it was wasteful to train them except in segregated groups. Beginning in August 1943, all men eligible for ASTP were screened at Induction Centers and given basic training in special battalions, so that all ASTP quotas in the future could be filled from such special battalions only.[16]

Charlie was an ideal candidate for this program, having just graduated from NYU with a degree in Accounting just weeks before his induction to the Army. An active member of college campus and fraternity life, he was eager to apply his academic skills within this new military milieu. However, the critical shortage of infantrymen in the winter of 1943–44 was largely responsible for the closing of the ASTP program in February 1944 and the subsequent transferring of the majority of the men in this program to regular army combat divisions.[17]

---

[15] Ibid, pg. 35

[16] Ibid.

[17] Ibid, pg. 39

Wednesday, September 22, 1943

Dear Mom and Dad,

Everything is swell. Haven't had a chance to write a letter yet, will try soon.

My Address:
Privt. C Fletcher 32999032
14th Co. 4th Bn. 5th Regt.
ASTP—BTC—TIS
Ft. Benning, GA.

Slept very well last night. Our barracks are nice, just like Upton. Food good.

Love,
Charlie

Wednesday, September 22, 1943

Dear Mom and Dad,

Well, I'm finally getting settled in my new camp. It's one of the largest in the US and from what I've seen it's mighty nice.

Our officers and non-com appear to be regular fellows. We eat from our mess kits and the cook sure knows how to beat up a good meal.

The weather was cool during the night. Today is a typical New York summer day. At least I'll be warm this winter.

We're being trained in a special ASTP battalion by special officers. The course will probably last for 13 weeks. A phone call is only $1.35 after 7 PM, so I'll call up soon. Let's make a phone date for Sunday morning.

Love,
Charlie

Wednesday, September 22,1943

Hello Again!

I believe I have a few minutes before chow, so I'll attempt a letter.

Officially, I'm an Army Specialized Training Program candidate. Basic Training will last 13 weeks once we get started. We won't start until a whole battalion is formed. We'll start training on the first Monday we have our completed group. Perhaps we'll start October 4. The 13 weeks starts when actual training begins. So, I hope that it begins as soon as possible.

The past four days have been the most active in my entire life. I practically travelled straight down the Atlantic seaboard on a regular troop train and now, in a few days, I'll begin to learn how to be a soldier.

When we came into camp on trucks from Columbus, it was 12:15 AM. We had to fill out forms and we had some coffee and cake. We got to bed at 2:45. I took a shave and shower before retiring. We got up at 6 AM and felt fresh, surprisingly enough.

We have nice barracks and I have a bed right near the window. It's very comfortable during the night. I have my metal mess-kit and we'll eat out of it for the next 13 weeks. I also have a drinking cup for the drinks at meals. We are on field rations, but so far the food has been good.

Tomorrow we're being interviewed by classifications officers for the purpose of deciding what courses we'll take when we're sent back to school. Enclosed is a page from the Camp's ASTP paper and it might give you a better idea of the set-up. Right now, ASTP is the big thing in the Army and we're being treated as intelligent men. We've got Army IQ of 115 or more and only 110 is required for OCS, so you see we're the "brains of the Army." The basic training will build me up and show me how much my body can really do.

This will be my home for the next four months or so and I could use a few things from home. One package would be fine. Here's what I could use. My moccasins – they're in the hall closet- some (3) face towels - small and whiteish from the drawer - just 3- my hair medicine from Mrs. Gersh, it's the black gooey stuff in the white jar. Face medicine from Gersh, if you can get it. The bottle of peroxide I bought and borax and a small bottle of salt. My good watch from NYU, the gold brown watch; the boys are all good and there's no stealing.

I need the watch for the time I'm off and go to Columbus. I think the watch is in my top drawer. And money, I could use a couple of bucks for incidentals. I won't be able to leave camp for another three weeks or so, so I won't be spending any dough. Stamps, 3 cents and air mail. I won't be able to tell you about camp routine until we start. Then it'll be pretty regular.

If you want my letters Air Mail occasionally, please send Air Mail stamps. I'll just use them for you. The "free" is good enough for others. In fact, once we get going, I won't be able to write more than a postcard. I must be spoiling you now with all this mail. I'll write more about camp tomorrow. So please remember:

1. Moccasins
2. 3 small Turkish towels, must be small
3. Hair medicine - Gersh
4. Clothes Hangers (can't get them here)
5. Face medicine - Gersh, if possible
6. Money - few bucks
7. Borax, peroxide and salt (first 2 are in the house)
8. Air Mail stamps for you
9. Dad, those negatives

When my $15 come home, please pick up my diploma and ring.

Don't worry, I'm really having the experience of a lifetime. It may be a little tough, it'll make a man out of me and serve me in good stead throughout life.

All my love,
Charlie

P.S. I've already eaten chow. I'll take a short walk and then hit the hay early.

Wednesday, September 22, 1943

Dear Folks,

The USO Service Club is very nice and large. We go to the #3 Club so you can imagine how many there are. This camp is the largest in the US. Once we get settled we'll be working real hard and having fine recreation in the evening.

Please add to the list of things I want, my new writing kit. It will come in handy. It's in my top drawer. We're getting up at 5:30 tomorrow morning so I'm going to sleep now— it's 9 PM.

Love,
Charlie

Thursday, September 23, 1943

Dear Folks,

You'll have to get used to less mail now. It'll be impossible to write as much as I'm doing once we start training. Right now, I'm tired and in bed. You'll be getting postcards and big letters once or twice a week. We just haven't time. We're kept busy all the time.

We all have KP once or twice during our 13 weeks' basic. That's not bad at all. I went on tonight at 5 and have it for one day. Then I'll be through with it for 2 ½ months. I'm glad I got it before regular training begins. It's not bad at all. In fact, KP is very easy here. We have a Mess Hall just for the company and the officers, who are swell, get the same chow.

This camp is the largest in the US; we have approximately 200,000 men here, so you can imagine how large the place is. I don't think I'll ever find my way around the whole place.

Columbus is a very bad town for soldiers. Facilities are poor and I understand that very few of the boys go in. So I guess I'll stay in camp over the weekends. We are off on Sunday, so I'll have a day of rest.

The food is marvelous; we could use a little more of it, but what we get is swell. They sure can cook. Lights go out at 10 PM, so I'll close with all my love.

Don't worry and take care of yourselves,

Love,
Charlie

Friday, September 24, 1943

Dear Mom and Dad,

I'm down the service club tonight attending a USO dance. The girls are nice Georgia peaches, but there is so much cutting in that you don't get many dances. And once you start to dance, somebody taps you on the shoulder before you can give the girl your name. So, it's not much fun.

I'm really on my way to becoming a real soldier. Today I got my steel helmet and my rifle and bayonet. I guess we're going to do some shooting pretty soon. All soldiers are now getting this basic training. I'm lucky, though. Regular Infantry goes through 17 weeks, while I'll be done in 13. After that I'll be assigned either to OCS[20] or a specialized branch of the service, finance, quartermaster,[21] etc.

They're not sending college graduates back to school now - except engineers and language majors. We're classified as "over-educated." See, the Army only wants kids for basic or advanced engineering courses and an accounting major doesn't fit in. A month ago, I might have made the foreign language division, but it's filled now except for experts in the languages. But I'm doing my basic, which is necessary, with a select group of men and I'm considered an ASTP program man.

There are many college grads here in the same boat. The area of the camp in which I'm in is the "high class" one. OCS and all the students are in one section and you don't find the real "army" here, but instead a fine educated group. Everybody is swell. This place is so big that it's hard to find the movies, etc. And

---

[20] Officer Candidate School, which trains civilians and enlisted personnel so they may gain a commission as an officer in the military.

[21] Quartermaster refers to the logistical branch of the United States Army.

when you do, it's a big, big walk. I'll have to take the bus to go to the chapel. Nothing more - air mail doesn't help, mail is slow.

Love and Kisses,
Charlie

Sunday, September 26, 1943

Dear Folks,

It was sure nice to speak to you a few minutes ago. It sure is swell to hear your voices. I think I'll call up every Sunday morning, but a little earlier. Say Mom, I thought you were a changed woman. How about letting me speak to Pop for a longer while? Gee, you always interrupt us men when we talk to each other.

If you didn't send out my shoes, please do so soon. This place is enormous. It's a mile walk to the nearest Service Club. This morning I went to services[22] and they were enjoyable. Compared to other Southern camps, Benning is very good. Don't listen to everybody who says they know this or that about the Camp.

Keep well,
Charlie

Monday, September 27, 1943

Dear Mom and Pop,

It's a beautiful day - nice and cool. The weather will be ideal during our basic training. That's one break in our favor. This morning the entire Company went out to the drill field for some preliminary training. We just did some marching, faces and all the elementary drill. We won't start training until next Monday.

Sunday is a complete day of rest. We wash our clothes and just rest. There are movies, too. I took it easy. I hung around for your call and wrote some letters. I got a nice letter from Eadie. I also dropped the Grandfather a big card.

---

[22] Jewish synagogue services, which were headed by Rabbi Samson Aaron Shain, the Jewish Chaplain at Ft. Benning.

Tonight, I'm on guard duty for two hours. I have to challenge anybody who passes after 11 PM if I'm on duty then. Some fun, eh? Just like you see in the movies. We've been getting up at 5:30 but once training starts, we'll arise at 6. Then we'll have to get out in about 10 minutes. Now we have plenty of time.

We had a delicious breakfast and dinner today. We had steak this noon. Boy, it was real good. We had some interviews today and it looks like all college grads who didn't major in engineering or mathematics will be reclassified after our 13 weeks of Basic. So I may still get into Finance or Quartermasters after Basic. The officers are swell and we're really taught a lot. The courses are all prepared in advance, and everything is done on schedule.

We got our new time calls today. We'll get up at 7 instead of 6 as I told you earlier in this letter. Lights are out after 11 PM. That gives me a good 8 hours sleep and 7 AM isn't too bad a time. Nothing more, write soon, send my regards to the family.

Love and Kisses,
Charlie

Tuesday, September 28, 1943

Dear Mom and Dad,

I served guard duty last night. Guard duty is when you walk around the area and see that everything's under control. There are 6 shifts: 7 PM-9 PM; 9-11, 11-1, 1-3, 3-5, and 5-7 AM. I was lucky and got the 9-11 shift. All you do is walk around your post slowly for the two hours. You don't challenge persons until 11 PM. So, I didn't have to yell "Halt!" We didn't use guns last night but the next time we're on guard, we'll walk with guns and fixed bayonets. Wowee! Gosh, if somebody doesn't stop when I yell "Halt!" I'll have to shoot. Don't worry, nothing ever happens around our area. We're all good little boys. You only serve every 16 or 17 days, so it's not bad. Don't let the gun business scare 'ya. you never use them except for practice.

We're getting some more shots today. One will be for typhoid and the other for tetanus. At least we get injections for all the stuff. I'm having my teeth looked after, the dentists are real good.

How are the grandfolks feeling? And yourselves? Please take care of yourselves, that's my only worry. I'm well and contented but I do worry about you both. So, take care and be careful when crossing the streets. Don't daydream and think when walking. Don't fight either, I know you don't because mother is a changed woman. Huh, Pop?

Nothing more,

Love and Kisses,
Charlie

Later the same day, September 28,1943

Dear Folks,

The weather is simply ideal. It really hasn't been too hot since we're here.

We had more drill this morning and some exercise. I'll be in perfect shape mighty soon. They haven't been working us hard at all. We're getting into shape slowly for the start of Basic on October 4. I march pretty well. Just like you did Dad, in the last war.[23] If I'm as good a soldier as you, Pop, I'll be satisfied.

Wishing you a happy New Year,[24] I hope you have everything you desire come true this coming year. May God bless you always.

Love,
Charlie

Samuel Fletcher in uniform, 1917.

---

[23] Charlie's father, Samuel Fletcher, was drafted on September 21, 1917, into the 308th Infantry Division, later transferred due to his age of 32 to Battery D, 1st New York National Guard.

[24] *Rosh Hashanah*, a two-day holiday celebrating the Jewish New Year.

Wednesday, September 29, 1943 - Rosh Hashanah, Day 1

Dear Mom and Dad,

I've just returned from *Rosh Hashanah* services at the Main Post. This camp is so big that all the men from my area had to be transported to the chapel in trucks. The service was held in the children's school where all the officer's kids go and there were at least 600-700 and WAC's and a few civilians.

You both don't realize that I'm perfectly content here. Don't let all that stuff about the Basic get you down. Don't forget, the heat plays a big part and it's not hot at all now. The photographer's boy was here during the summer and then the heat goes up to 130-140 degrees. That makes the training extra tough.

שנה טובה תכתבו
May you be inscribed in the Book of Life for a Happy New Year

Of course, it'll be a little tough but this is the Army. I also know how to take orders. There's a good thing to remember. You don't respect an officer as a man, you just respect the uniform. By practicing this you find you salute all officers without holding any grudges. It's just like a pledge in a fraternity. You remember when I pledged Phi Alpha[25] and had to do all those things for the members. Well, I'm used to all that and I don't have any trouble taking orders. So don't fret. I'm just as good and able as all the other boys here and if they can do it so can I.

Dad, you should forget about that thing you wanted me to do. A doctor knows if that condition effects walking and if I said I got pains when I walked the doctor would know what's what. You may not believe me, but there was a man at Upton in my barrack who had a double hernia and wore a dress - he was still inducted, they are taking everybody - and I was no special case. The mixture for the gums that I have from the dentist is ¼ teaspoon salt, ¼ teaspoon Borax and ½ teaspoon Peroxide and 1 glass hot (warm) water. Rinse your mouth and massage gums. Please try to see the dentist soon.

---

[25] Established in 1914, Phi Alpha was a historically Jewish fraternity. Charlie was a member of the Theta chapter of New York University, founded in 1920.

The Army is real crowded now. Remember that. Chances of advancement are tough, practically impossible. If I came in 3-4 months ago, I would have gotten the language course. Now there are enough experts in the languages that they don't take men with just a fair knowledge of a language. My friend, Al Rosman, is also in the same boat I'm in as to going back to college, and he may remain at his camp as a permanent party man. He's in Alabama so you can never tell what will happen. You can never regret anything you do in the Army. If I didn't join the ASTP I might have been sent to a regular infantry unit and that wouldn't have been so good. The soft jobs are all taken, that's easy to see. First come, first serve. So, I am lucky to have stayed out as long as I did, and we'll hope for the best. Many of the boys who graduated with me are regular infantrymen. At least I have a chance to be transferred or get some sort of office job down the line. So don't worry I'm cheerful - just you be cheerful.

I'm going to services tomorrow night and also *Yom Kippur*[26] (or at least *Kol Nidre*[27]).

Love and Kisses,
Charlie

Thursday September 30,1943 - Rosh Hashanah, Day 2

Dear Mom and Dad,

We got this morning off for services, so I went to the school again. I didn't go tonight, but I'll go to the regular Friday night services. Then next Friday is *Kol Nidre*. I must be getting religious.

We had two good meals today. We did a little drilling and we're learning to handle our gun. I'll be a soldier soon. Dad, remember your pack in the last war? Well, we're practicing making them up now. I'll be able to make up a package when I come home. Gee, wouldn't I like to deliver a package for you to some customers.

---

[26] Considered Judaism's holiest day of the year, *Yom Kippur's* central themes are that of atonement and repentance. Jews traditionally observe a day-long fast and engage in intensive prayer, often spending most of the day in synagogue services.

[27] This Hebrew and Aramaic prayer commences the *Yom Kippur* evening service in the synagogue.

The boys in my barrack are all swell. I sleep right next to a big Irishman who is from a hick-town in New York State, he's loads of fun.

Everything is swell,
Charlie

Friday, October 1, 1943

Dear Mom and Pop,

I received your letter from Upton with a buck and I also got one from the Grannies. I'm all set now until payday.

Aunt Rose sent me a whole chocolate cake and it went over big with the boys. It sure was good to taste her famous cake. Yes, Mom, you can send edibles. Don't send them too often Mom, and nothing fancy, it's really not necessary.

I haven't received the moccasins yet, Dad, so if you have an insurance slip hold on to it. I'll probably get it soon. The mail is very slow, I'm still getting mail from Upton. I'm getting loads of mail from E.[28] One more day and then we get a day of rest in beautiful weather.

Love,
צדוק לייב [29]

Aunt Rose Nelson

---

[28] Eadie, Charlie's older sister. She is often referred to as "E" throughout the letters.

[29] *Tzadok Leib*, Charlie's Hebrew/Jewish name. *Tzadok* is Hebrew for righteous, and was also the name of a biblical figure, Tzadok the first High Priest of Israel, who served during the reigns of King David and King Solomon. *Leib* is Yiddish, translates to lion.

Tell me if you get the $15. When you do, please go down to school for my diploma and ring. Have them mail the ring to me; I'd like to wear it on Sunday.

Pop, go to my drawers and see if I left my bathing trunks in one of the drawers. I don't think I sent them to the basement. If you find the new brown bathing shorts or the blue ones, send them down. There's a pond nearby and we're allowed to go swimming. If you can't find the shorts, don't bother; I'll buy a cheap pair when I go to town.

Mother, I don't know how you're taking me being in the Army. You're not the only mother who has a son in the service. I know how you feel, I'm your son and you don't care about anybody else. Well, you have a lot to be thankful for. I was out of the Army for a mighty long time - I entered when the war was reaching a climax - and it's very unlikely that I'll see action. So don't get blue spells or cry. I hope that you're being brave and thinking that I'm just away for a while. I'd be disappointed to know that you were having crying or emotional spells. Be a good girl and the same goes for you Dad - although I know you have a lot of brains because your head shape is just like mine.

Kiss each other a few times for me.
Love and Kisses,
Charlie

Monday, October 11, 1943

Dear Folks,

It's Columbus Day tomorrow, but we wouldn't know it.

Went through a very interesting day today. We kept packing and unpacking our packs and we practiced pitching tents. We were rushed all the time, but it wasn't tough. The mornings are cool, but it warms up around 10 AM.

We're getting pretty good putting on our gas masks and we're going to go through a gas chamber in a few days. We were out in the field until 7 tonight, so I've been pretty busy cleaning my rifle, etc. Just no time for a letter but I'll write a long one tomorrow night.

With all my love,
Charlie

Tuesday, October 11, 1943

Dear Mom and Pop,

I had a very easy day. We had lectures during our eight-hour class period. See, we work from 8:30- 12:30 and 2-6. That's what we're supposed to, but we're usually busy in the evening fixing up.

We're learning a great deal. For instance, today we had map reading, military courtesy, identification of chemical gasses, a memory test, a discussion about the compass and how to tell direction (north, south etc.) by the use of the sun and a regular wristwatch, a demonstration of camouflage and 2 hours on the tactics of the infantry soldier - that is, how to fight and a lot of theory. So, you can see that we're really getting a lot of information. The more we learn, the better off we are so I'm trying my best to take it all in.

I'm writing from the company's "day room," lights are off in the barracks at 10 PM but we can sit in the day room until 11. One fellow is swinging it out on the piano and two fellows are playing the saxophones, so we're having a jam session. You should see all the boys beat time with their feet.

Tonight, we fixed up our packs for a practice march tomorrow. We always sing in our barrack while we work, and we have loads of fun and a lot of laughs. All of the men in the barracks - 62 - are contributing 5 cents toward a fund to buy little things for the barrack - certain cleaning agent the Army doesn't produce, etc. Well, the Sergeant put me in charge of all the dough, so I'm the treasurer. I have to give a report every time we spend money. Don't worry Daddy, I'll be a good accountant.

I'm feeling fine, I'm getting into great shape and you'd be surprised to see how everyone improves in doing certain things, I'm much faster in many ways now. Well, I guess I'm a real soldier now, I got paid $28 today. Tell me if you get $15. I haven't found out just what deductions they made the first month. I only have one more tetanus shot, and I'll be through. That'll make seven shots in all. I'll call up Sunday morning.

Love and Kisses,
Charlie

Wednesday, October 13, 1943

Dear Mom and Pop,

Went on a 7-mile hike and I felt swell throughout. Two months ago, I couldn't have done it, so you see my physical condition has improved.

The "gas chamber" was simple. They use tear gas, and we wear our masks to show how valuable they are. Then before we go out of the tent, which is called "chamber," we take off our masks to see how the gas affects us. I didn't even tear. This tear gas is supposed to make you cry but I wasn't exposed to enough of it.

How did Murray[48] look? I thought something was funny because I didn't hear from him for a while. Thanks for your letter, Pop. As long as you can get the stuff, it's okay. I know the price is high, but what can you do!

Love and Kisses,
Charlie

Saturday Night, October 16, 1943

Dear Mother and Dad,

Excuse me for being a little lax with my letter writing, but since I knew I was going to speak to you Sunday I took a little vacation from writing for a day or two. We go out on some night work so you may not receive a letter every day, but I'll do my best.

Did I tell you I got $28.60 in pay? I don't think you'll get the $15 until next month.

Dad, you asked me about the difference in Army hats. Well, if I wanted to invest $4 or $5 right now, I could buy the kind of cap that Howard Kane has. There's no difference except the overseas cap you saw in the picture and Artie's[49] is that it's Government Issue and Artie's division doesn't permit him

---

[48] Murray Goldblatt, a childhood friend of Charlie. Murray served in the 15th Finance Battalion, responsible for financial operations, most notably payroll and resource management of the Army. Murray's collection of home movies capturing sights and scenes in Europe during World War II can be viewed online via the United States Holocaust Museum website.

[49] Charlie's brother-in-law. Arthur Irving Marshak, also known as Artie, born May 1, 1919, and married to Charlie's sister Edith in August 1942. Artie served in the 4th Armored Division during the war.

to wear the "garrison" cap. The different types don't signify anything. It's just that some posts allow them, and others don't. When I come home for furlough, I'll probably buy one. But, then again, I may not, because at any time they can forbid you to wear them and there goes $5. I'll see.

We were issued passes for the first time this weekend. No overnight passes yet. Today we were through at 3 and if we went to Columbus you had to be back in camp by 11:30. So I'm going into town tomorrow (Sunday). We must be in by 11:30.

I'll have a good steak dinner, so you should get some *nachas*[50], folks. I heard from Charlie Nelson[51] and got cake and cookies from Aunt Rose.

I hope the building isn't too much for you, Pops.[52] Take care of yourself, please.

Mom, I'm not worried about business. With Daddy's brains, I was confident everything would be okay. I heard from E but nothing about Artie, she'll probably write soon.

All my love,
Charlie

Sunday, October 17, 1943

Dear Folks,

You both sounded very well this morning over the phone. Doesn't the 5 minutes fly by? But it's sure swell to speak with you. Now I'll save a call for Thanksgiving. As I told Dad over the phone, I went to Columbus today. Besides being a little crowded, it's not too bad. After I go there a few times I may tire of it because there isn't too much to do.

This afternoon the Junior Hadassah[53] had a luncheon-dance and I got a ticket – 75 cents. We had a delicious roast beef and a complete dinner - it was very

---

[50] Yiddish: Joy or pleasure.

[51] Charlie's younger cousin, the son of his Aunt Rose and Uncle Mendel of Wilkes-Barre, Pennsylvania.

[52] In addition to their hosiery boutique, Charlie's parents were landlords of a small building with apartments for rent as a secondary source of income.

[53] Jewish Women's organization, the local chapter of Columbus, Georgia hosted receptions each week at Ft. Benning as well as mid-week dances for the soldiers in town. (Historic Columbus, Bnei Israel)

home. Have them mail the ring, also mail me the one picture of the man with the pipe.

Love again,

צודק לייביש

Saturday Night, October 23, 1943

Dear Mom and Dad,

Today marked the completion of my third week of Basic Training, so I'm practically ¼ through. Time sure flies here. We're so busy that the days come and go, and before you know it, the week is over. I'm not going out this weekend, as I plan to make a little trip soon and I'm saving my money. I'll either go to Atlanta or Macon - both are about 100 miles away. We now are allowed out for Saturday night, so you have the weekend from Saturday 3 PM to Sunday midnight.

The weather is still grand. The mornings until 8 are a trifle cold but the days are warm, and the sun is always shining. We haven't had more than one hour of rain since we were here.

The cycle is officially over January 1st. Perhaps I'll be home for your birthday, Pop. Don't count on a furlough, I've met men here who haven't been home for a year. But I'll try, it's too early to think about a furlough yet. Has Grandma come home yet? I hope Riley returns, Grandma sure needs her. Let me know what happens.

I'm feeling very well. In another week or two I'll be in perfect physical condition. We're always exercising, I'll be a tough man when I come home. We're learning hand-to-hand fighting now and how to kill a man by stepping on him with our heel—some fun, eh?

In another week or two we go out on the rifle range. We live in tents for a week and do all our shooting. We still haven't fired our rifles. The food has improved and now we look forward to our noon day meal. This week we had chicken, Swiss steak, meatloaf and roast pork at the meals.

We had a map reading test and I got a 91. See, Dad, I inherited your sharp head and also your brains. I won't write tomorrow. Don't send the letters in Air Mail, it's foolish as it doesn't save time.

Be good and kiss each other for me.
Love and Kisses,
Charlie

Sunday, October 24, 1943

Dear Folks,

No letter for you today,[54] so here's a short line.

Having a good rest today. Stayed in bed until 11 o'clock and took a nap after a delicious fried chicken dinner in the Mess Hall. Most of the boys went to town, so it's nice and quiet.

Wrote quite a few letters and am caught up with my correspondences. I don't get a chance to write during the week. I dropped Mary Walker a card.

We took a company picture yesterday. If it comes out good, I'll buy one. I'm going to take a picture of myself soon and send it home. If there's any mail for me at home, please send it to me.

Love and Kisses,
Charlie

Monday, October 25, 1943

Dear Mother and Dad,

All's well. It was nice and cool. Tomorrow we go on a hike and the weather will be ideal for walking. We're only wearing light packs, so all will be ok.

I don't know if Murray told you, but he will be overseas very shortly. I don't know whether he's told his mother yet so be sure not to say anything. I heard from him today and he told me he goes to a Port of Embarkation very shortly. He's already taken injections for the trip and he's getting new clothing.

---

[54] This "letter" was sent via postcard.

Next week I plan to go to Macon, Georgia. I told you about this girl I met while at camp. Well, she's teaching there and I'm going to see her.

Mom, I'm glad you got a new coat and hat. I'm sure you look sweet. What kind of overcoat did you get, Dad? I'm not kidding when I say it was a real easy week. I hope the sixth week is as easy. From what I hear, it is very easy. Even though the house is in my name, I want you to know it's both of yours. If you can get a little living from it, swell. But remember the two of you get everything it'll bring.

Dad, I'm not keeping anything from you. I'm feeling swell, never felt better.

Be good and all my love,
Charlie

Sunday, November 7, 1943

Dear Mom and Pop,

I got your swell package this morning and boy, it was a real treat. I put most of it away in my trunk (footlocker). I ate a little of everything and it all tasted delicious. My buddies also enjoyed the stuff very much. I'll have stuff left for a few days.

The shoes looked grand and feel fine. Thanks also for the wash rags and the wallet. Don't send me a better wallet. I can't use it. I only use the wallet on Sundays, so the one Dad bought fills the purpose.

I got up at 9 today and missed breakfast. However, one of the fellows in my barracks, an Italian from Rochester, New York, brought me the full breakfast to my bed, so help me. He had eaten and then washed his mess kit and got me grapes, toast, bacon and scrambled eggs and coffee. Boy, did it feel good eating breakfast in bed—who said that a soldier can't get breakfast in bed?

I left camp with the fraternity brother I told you about at 11, and got into Columbus at 11:45. We took the bus; it costs 15 cents.

We came here to the USO and sure enough we got coffee and toast with marmalade, free of charge. The USO sure does a grand job. We're going over to that girl's house in a little while.

It's raining today, the first real rain since I'm here. It's letting up somewhat and should stop soon. I didn't wear the shoes today on account of the rain. I would rather get the big GI shoes wet. I didn't get caught in the rain, as the bus stops near the USO and I have my raincoat with me.

Say, ain't I a good boy? You've heard from me every day this past week. Very few of the other boys write so often, See, I must love you.

Love and Kisses,

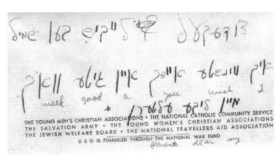

Monday, November 8, 1943

Dear Mom and Dad,

A quick letter before I go to eat. Incidentally, I'm eating some of the stuff you sent me now.

I had a marvelous time yesterday. My fraternity brother took me over to this Jewish girl's house and the hospitality was splendid. It was great to be inside a nice home once again. We came after lunch, so we had some pie (lemon meringue) and milk during the afternoon.

We had supper at 8 and boy, just like you love, Mom. Herring—those fancy sardines, lettuce and tomato salad chopped up like you do, rye bread, salami, chili, coffee and cake, and all we wanted. It was a fine day. I got back in camp at 11:15 and was asleep by 11:45. The people's name is Witt, real Southerners but good Jews. Have a daughter around 18—not too beautiful but a nice personality. They always have a lot of soldiers over and are really good *yids*.[63] The old man owns 6 dry goods stores in Columbus and is pretty well off. So you see, it was nice. A very nice house, piano, good radio and I really had a pleasant day at home. Perhaps I'll get over there some day again, although we only get another weekend off.

It's raining today, so we did our work indoors. Maybe the New York rain is coming our way.

---

[63] Yiddish: Jews.

Nothing more,

Will write again tomorrow.
Love and Kisses,
Charlie

P.S. Important -

Dad, I want to save money, so here's why I'm bothering you. We go out on the Range soon. I have a blue sweater I bought in Macy's a few years ago. The real nice one and there are also 1 or 2 sleeveless sweaters in my drawers. Send me the blue sweater and one of the sleeveless sweaters. That will keep me warm. Don't send the package special delivery, just send it out by Saturday. I don't go out on the range til November 22, so that's plenty of time. If you find my gloves (green woolen) from last year, send them. If you don't, it's okay as I have GI gloves. I'm mainly interested in the sweaters. Don't bother with any food.

Thanks a lot!

Wednesday, November 10, 1943

Dear Folks,

Everything's just fine. We had to attend an interfaith conference last night, so I couldn't write a letter. Dr. Rosenblum (Rabbi) from the synagogue on 78th Street or around there was one of the speakers.

Dad, if you haven't mailed me the sweaters yet I'd appreciate it if you bought me a serviceable olive drab scarf - not a dress one - but a good woolen olive one that I can wear in the field. We're allowed to wear scarves and it will come in handy.

All my love,
Charlie

Wednesday, November 10, 1943

Dear Mom and Dad,

Burr - it's getting chilly. Not too cold, but cold enough. I dress warm so I don't even get chilled and then again, the sun still shines and warms things up.

I told you we attended a religious conference last night. Well, it was a Jew, Catholic and Protestant speaker talking about interfaith ideas and also the peace we have to win after the war. The speeches were all right, but it was hardly the time for it. We were forced to go and it was just another evening we lost for ourselves. But I'm used to that by now.

I received the letter from Paul Bialo this morning and this evening I got a small package from Morris. It was one of Schrafft's servicemen's packages and it was the nuts. I'll write him soon and thank him. All the boys enjoyed the stuff. It was very thoughtful of Morris and Paula.

I am (I hope) going to Macon, Georgia this weekend to meet the girl from New York who is teaching down here. It's our last free weekend for a long while and I want to have a good time.

Say, did you receive the $15 yet? You should have by now. Don't forget the ring and diploma, please.

We had a nice fire in the recreation room and it's nice and cozy with the radio going. Our barracks are well heated. The week isn't hard. Most of the time is spent on "dry" firing in preparation for the rifle range. We practice aiming, positions, etc.

Nothing more-
Love and Kisses,
Charlie

Thursday, November 11, 1943

Dear Mother and Dad,

Things are just about the same. Very little out of the ordinary here, so it's hard to find news to write home. That Rabbi Rosenblum is from Temple Israel on 91st Street. He's speaking again on Sunday, but I plan to be out of camp. We've learned the four positions for shooting: prone, sitting, kneeling and standing. It just requires practice.

We had an easy afternoon. We practiced laying mines in open fields. It was easy; just dig small holes, place the mines in and cover up the holes. I put the bathing trunks away down in my locker. I won't have any use for them until next spring. It's chilled up too much.

How's Grandma? Send her my love.
Love and Kisses,
צודעך לייביש

Saturday, November 13, 1943

Dear Mom and Dad,

I had to cancel my trip to Macon this weekend.

I got a telegram from the girl saying that she couldn't get away from college this weekend. So I saved myself some dough and I'm getting a good rest. It's now 9:30 and I'm in my nice cozy bed. We got through 11:30 this morning, had a short inspection and have been free all day.

We'll only be in our barracks one more week before going out on the rifle range for 2 weeks. We leave for the range on Saturday (November 20th).

We're practically halfway through with our basic now. Today was the end of the six weeks. Seven to go. Gee, Folks, doesn't the time go by fast? The weeks just seem to fly. I suppose that's because we're kept on the go.

I'm getting out of camp one-night next week and I'm going over to that girl's house in Columbus. At least I'll get a good home cooked meal. I've been invited over for Thanksgiving, but we will be out on the range, and I doubt whether we'll get the day off.

I got a letter from Charlie Nelson the other day. I managed to get quite a bit of mail and its sure swell to receive letters. I don't mind writing for that reason.

We've had some warm afternoons lately, although it's still cold in the morning and evenings. It's nice to read both your letters and see what you think of me.

You know I appreciate the things you've done for me and of course, without saying, I love you very much.

I suppose you're used to me being away by now. I hope you are. Don't be like, let's hope we'll all be home soon for good.

Love and Kisses,
Charlie

Sunday, November 14, 1943

Dear Mom and Dad,

It's a beautiful day and I'm soaking in the sun in the big football stadium at the Main Post. There's a very good game here today and I hitched a ride over in a lieutenant's car with a friend. It's now 1. The game doesn't start until 2 but in order to get a good seat you must get in early. I've got a swell seat. It sure is a funny sight, a big football field with all the people dressed in khaki. There are few girls around, so we have some color. Many officers are present, and captains and majors are a dime a dozen.

Slept until 9 today and lounged around until 11. Then I got dressed and came over here. The reason you only received the $15 for November is that they didn't take out a lot meant for the first month, October.

Everything is swell. I'm feeling fine.
All my love,
Loves and Kisses,
Charlie

Monday, November 15, 1943

Dear Mom and Dad,

I received your package today and it wasn't necessary to send it special delivery. That costs dough and it only takes 3 days at the most and to top it all, special delivery doesn't help in the least. Thanks for the stuff. It will certainly come in handy, I'm glad you thought of the gloves.

Mom, don't send any canned food for bivouac. The Army gives us enough food and none of the other boys are getting stuff and I definitely don't want any food sent. Thanks for the dates, prunes and the gum drops. If you get a chance, you can send for more dried fruit and a little candy next week, no special delivery though.

It was a beautiful day today. Gee, the weather is very changeable. It was real Spring today. The work was very easy. We did a lot of work with the carbine, a small gun and the mortar. No walking or any work. Just that all day and I got a sunburn on my face.

I have a date with the girl I met in Columbus tomorrow night. I'm meeting her at one of her dad's stores. We're allowed out on weeknights until 11:30 if we have someone to visit or some business. Since I didn't get out this past weekend, I've decided to go out Tuesday night.

I heard from Alan[64] today. He was sent to camp in Louisiana two days after he returned from his furlough. I haven't heard from Murray since the one letter from Pennsylvania. He's probably on the big trip now. Alan expects to leave shortly.

Everything is hunky-dory. I'm doing well with my work and I'm feeling swell. Knock on wood, I haven't had a cold since I've been at Benning.

Be good kiddies,
Love and Kisses,
Charlie
No food - remember that - Love to Grandma

Tuesday, November 16, 1943

Dear Mom and Dad,

Another day has passed, and all is okey-dokey. It was a pleasant day, and the work was easy and interesting. We spent the entire 8 hours on dry-firing, more preparation for actual firing.

---

[64] Childhood friend, Al Rosman.

I went to town tonight and went out for dinner with that girl I told you about. We had a nice time, and I came back at 11:30.

Got a nice letter from E.
Love and Kisses,
Charlie

Wednesday, November 17, 1943

Dear Mom and Dad,

Received the letter and package you wrote Sunday night. Mother told me about going to the building and Dad asked about the bivouac.

Well, I'm not too keen about your running to 1575 Washington Avenue.[65] Both of you are getting old and you must watch your health and I hate the thought of you working hard in the store and then attending to the building. Don't forget, you can do so much and no more and I'm more concerned about your health than anything else. So, please take good care of yourselves and don't exert yourselves more than necessary. After all, the building isn't worth half as much as both of you are worth to me. And the building is really a goner now anyway. So, use your best judgement.

Now here's a short description of bivouac:

We are considered to be on bivouac when we go to the rifle range for two weeks starting this Saturday. But the real bivouac is during our 11th and 12th weeks. The rifle range bivouac isn't bad. The Army has big tents prepared for us and six fellows live in a tent. Here's the main points: the kitchen crew always follows us, and we get hot meals while on bivouac. We eat out in the field, and we may be on field rations and at times it's the new canned food the Army uses. Well, on Range we do our regular work in addition to firing a rifle a couple of days. There are no lights in the tents, but we're allowed to use candles, though.

Now the other bivouac in the 11th and 12th weeks is the real thing. We live under actual combat conditions and it's just like maneuvers. We live in two-man puptents set up on the ground - and everything is tactical - that is, as if we were in combat. Food is ration, water is ration and in short, we rough it a lot.

---

[64] The building address of the Fletcher's rental apartments.

We spend our two weeks doing problems and reviewing a lot of the work we've learned.

To prepare us for all this, we're having a one-night practice bivouac tomorrow (Thursday) night. We're getting up at 5:30 tomorrow morning, eating at 6, and go on a two-and-a-half mile hike to small range for practice. We stay out all day and in the evening march back to a big field near the barracks, eat in the field and pitch tents for the night. I'll have my longies (underwear) on and the sweaters you sent, plus two blankets and I'll be warm, don't worry.

This may be my last long letter for a while. I won't be able to write more than a postcard while on the Range. We leave for the Range Saturday afternoon, walk 7 miles and pitch tents for the night. We hike another 7 miles Sunday morning until we get to the Range and the big tents.

I'll do okay, so don't worry.

No canned foods, remember. you can send some fruit next week, we get all our mail while at bivouac so there's no rush. Some cookies will also do, if you get around to it. It's not necessary, though. I've already written a letter of thanks to the Bialos.

I'll write soon,
Love and Kisses,
Your soldier boy,
Charlie

Friday, November 19, 1943

Dear Mom and Pop,

We slept under the stars last night and these heavy sweaters come in handy. It didn't seem too cold. I fired a gun for the first time yesterday and did pretty well. We ate can rations last night and it tasted pretty good. I had a good stew and we heated it over a fire. And in another can I had biscuits, candy, coffee and sugar. The coffee is in powdered form. All in all, it's a good meal.

Today's our last day in the barracks for two weeks. We leave for the Range and bivouac tomorrow afternoon. Please send me a batch of postcards real soon. We get our mail on the Range. Heard from E today. She's making me a chocolate cake. Should get it tomorrow night.

It's sunny today.
Love and Kisses,
Charlie

Saturday, November 20, 1943

Dear Parents,

Gee, I celebrated my birthday a day early,[66] but oh what a marvelous day. Finest thing I got was my mother's and father's picture. It was the most wonderful gift possible. I was thrilled when I saw it. Thanks also for the scarf and cookies. Just what I wanted. In addition to your lovely presents, I received a home baked chocolate cake from E. It was swell.

I'm on KP and guess what? Instead of marching 17 miles to the Range I'm riding in the kitchen truck. Isn't that great? Will write very soon. We're busy.

Thanks for everything.

Love,
Charlie

Saturday, November 20, 1943

Dear Mom and Dad,

Just have time for a short letter before I leave for the Range. As I told you in my postcard, I got KP today and we're going out in a truck. The rest of the company left about an hour ago. Now I won't have to sleep out tonight. On the Range you sleep in big tents, and I'll stay in one tonight.

---

[66] Charlie's 20th birthday, November 21.

You can't imagine how thrilled I am with your pictures. Gee, I get excited every time I look at it - it's marvelous. When we get back in the barracks, I'm going to put it up on my shelf. The scarf is very nice and sure it will come in handy, and the cookies were good. Didn't I have a nice birthday?

With all your nice stuff and Eadie's birthday cakes, it sure was a good day, even though a day early. I'll be off KP early tomorrow and I'll have a nice day. No passes while on Range but at least I know the end of bivouac is around the corner.

The past week was very easy. The bivouac Thursday night was a little rough, but not too bad. We pitched tents at 8, got to sleep around 9 and got up at 4:45 AM. It was the first time I slept on the ground, but I slept fairly well.

Another Thanksgiving and another wedding anniversary. I mailed your card early so I wouldn't take it to the Range. You know how much I love you both and I wish you everything you desire. May all the rest of your years be happy and healthy ones.

Love and Kisses,
Charlie

P.S. I'm feeling fine - don't worry.

Take care of yourselves. Have a nice Thanksgiving. We all have a lot to be thankful for. Thanks for the cards and Grandma's $3. Thank her and I'll try to write her soon.

Sunday, November 21, 1943

Dear Folks,

I went out to the Range last night in the truck and we helped set up the kitchen. Got to bed at 10 and had a good night sleep. There are five men in my tent and although there are no lights at all, the candles we have light up the tent pretty well. I bought a lot of candles in town and they're sure coming in handy. We have regular beds (cots) but we use a straw mattress. The floor in the tent is the good old earth, but it was very comfortable.

This morning we had a nice breakfast and the seven KP's rode back to the barracks to help load some trucks. Right now, I'm in my barrack waiting for a truck to take me out to the bivouac area.

We were allowed to take out all our blankets and our comforter and one barrack (duffle) bag full of clothes and our equipment. I have plenty of stuff for the two weeks. I'll call you up when we get back to the barracks in two weeks.

Keep well, will write again soon,
Love,
Charlie

Monday, November 22, 1943

Dear Mom and Dad,

Well, I'm a real Soldier now. I fired a rifle for 8 hours today and shot at least two hundred bullets - called rounds in the Army. I surprised myself and shot pretty well. The rifle kicks back a little but I didn't even get a scratch. Some of the boys have black eyes and swollen lips - that's the worst that can happen, so don't worry. All our shooting today was practice work. We work in the pits tomorrow - that is working the target for the other fellas - and on Wednesday we again get to shoot all day and it's the qualification test - you get expert, sharpshooter, marksman ratings. I'll be content with marksman, that's the lowest classification, but I'll be trying for something better.

We're really roughing it - although this is just how many soldiers live all the time. There's no plumbing at all and we use a field latrine (toilet) and get water from cans and drinking water from lister bags in which the water is purified. When we want to wash, we fill our steel helmets with water and wash from that. We get our food from the field kitchen and eat on the ground out of our mess kits. There are no lights at all and I'm writing under candlelight. We have a few candles in our tent and it's not bad.

This is a brand-new experience for me and I'm getting on to it. You just have to sacrifice a few luxuries - no hot water, light, sinks, etc. - and you'll do all right. It was the first time I fired a big rifle for such a long time and I even liked that - although not for war purposes.

The food is good; here is something funny, while we were eating chow tonight, Retreat sounded[67] and of course, we all had to get up and salute the flag. We laid our mess kits down and saluted. While one of the boys was at attention near me, a dog came up and ate the two pieces of bologna the boy had in his kit. Gee, it was so funny.

Don't worry if you don't hear from me, I'll try my best to write but it's a great strain on the eyes under this candlelight.

Love and Kisses,
Charlie

P.S. The Marshaks sent me a nice scarf for my birthday, isn't that a coincidence. Now I can use the scarf you sent for dress uniform.

Enclosed is an article I wrote for the ASTP paper.

Tuesday, November 23, 1943

Dear Mom and Dad,

Got a good wash job on myself tonight when I got in from the Range at about 5 PM. I got some water in my helmet and washed my hands real well, then I got fresh water and outside of my tent I shaved, washed my ears, neck, etc. and upper body. Then with the soapy water, I scrubbed my feet. Some bath, eh? I brush my teeth every day, so you see I keep pretty clean.

Today I worked in the pit, as I told you I would. It's not hard, just a little boring. They want to get so much firing in during daylight, that the noon day meal is brought out to the field right near the Range. It's cooked back at camp just 10 minutes away and brought to us by trucks. Today we had hot dogs, string beans, succotash, bread and butter, jello and of course, coffee. We also had meat tonight, so you see we're eating pretty well.

---

[67] "Retreat" is the bugle blast at 5 PM, signifying the end of the workday. "Retreat" is traditionally a time to secure the American flag, and pay respect to what it stands for.

I got your letter today. Folks, when you get my $15 next week, please get my diploma and ring. When I sleep at night I wear an undershirt, a long sleeve winter shirt, the big blue sweater and two sleeveless sweaters, so I just can't be cold. I'm warm and comfortable at night and sleep like a log.

[68] צדוק לייב בען שמיל

Dad, is Ma still a changed woman?
Did you have a nice Thanksgiving?
You'll get this letter Friday, I hope.

Thursday, November 25, 1943

Dear Mom and Dad,

Had a very nice Thanksgiving Day. It was an easy day and just listen to the menu for our big meal; we had it at noon out on the Range. Gee, it was great - just like you read about the soldiers getting big meals for Thanksgiving. Stuffing, turkey, corn, peas, dressing, olives, cranberries, mashed potatoes, fruit cocktail, jello, two pieces of pumpkin pie, two oranges, cocoa and cookies. We had paper plates as a treat and all in all it was a grand affair.

This morning it was so cold that we had orders to wear our overcoats. This afternoon around 5 PM when we came back to camp, we were roasting. That's how changeable the weather is. It was the first time I wore the coat, and it sure keeps you warm.

I'm pretty sure we change camps next week. We leave here Saturday night and march to another Range about 3 miles away. It sounds silly to move like that, but that's the way things are done. We have more free time here that we do at the barracks. However, we don't have any facilities to do anything except write a few letters.

The Army is so funny. They decide to hold a Thanksgiving church service and then make everybody go. Your little boy pretended he was in bed and didn't go. There were three of us in the tent and sure enough a lieutenant came in and asked why we didn't go. We each gave a funny reason and he said he didn't see

---

[68] *Tzadok Leib Ben Shmuel* – Tzadok, the son of Shmuel. Shmuel was the Hebrew name for Charlie's father, Sam Fletcher.

why they made us go to church and we should forget the whole thing. He's a very nice guy, comes from West Virginia.

We don't do machine gun work until next week. We had demonstrations and lectures all day and sat in football stands. Remember Thanksgiving in the past with the NYU /Fordham football games, and then Uncle Doc and the rest of the family coming to 1366 for a big dinner and your anniversary? Gee, they were the good old days. But then, we'll have plenty of nice days in the very near future when this mess is over.

Be good children,
The eighth week is practically over.
Love and Kisses,
Charlie

Friday, November 26, 1943

Dear Mom and Pop,

You're probably getting a letter today in addition to this card, so I won't write a line.

We had an exceptionally easy day, and I got a nice burn on my face. If it wasn't so cold at night and in the morning, the weather would be excellent. We're moving out of here tomorrow and going to another Range a few miles down the road.

Thanks for the postcards. I don't need any more so don't bother sending them. I'm glad you're busy. I hope you're both working well together, if you know what I mean. Keep up the good business so we can splurge when I get a furlough. The 8th week is practically over. Doesn't time go fast? Five more weeks and Basic will be a thing of the past.

Feeling fine, have a good week and send my love to Grandma.
Take care of yourself,
Charlie

Saturday, November 27, 1943

Dear Folks,

We're firing at targets in the field today. I knocked down 7 out of 9 targets, which is a pretty good score. Now we're waiting for the other boys to shoot. When we finish here, we're marching to our new encampment.

It was warmer than usual during the night and it was very enjoyable. It's very cloudy today. The food has been exceptionally good on this bivouac. Our noon chow is brought out to the field and it's excellent. Most of the boys are too busy to go to breakfast, so I get all I want. This morning I had eggs, potatoes, coffees and corn flakes. Got a letter from Mems Nelson. She and Ellie are fine. Today ends the 8th week.

The sun is coming out now. I'll probably get some more sunburn.

How's Grandma?

Regards to the family,
Love,
Charlie

Sunday, November 28, 1943

Dear Mom and Dad,

Just received the letter and postcard you wrote on your anniversary day. Yes, I do hope we're all home next year to celebrate the day. The way things are going it looks like we may be home in a year or so for good. I hope it's no longer than that.

We're now in our new "tent city" and we have today for ourselves. We ate breakfast at 8 and since then I cleaned my rifles and just lazed around in my tent. We have regular mattresses this week and it was sure swell sleeping last night. I slept well last week but there's nothing like a mattress.

This is a beautiful camping site. We're in a forest area and there's a clearing for the tents. Last night when we got here, we ate the C-Rations[69] from cans. It was

---

[69] The C-Ration was a prepared and canned wet combat ration. This ration was used when fresh food (A-Ration) or packaged unprepared food (B-Ration) were not available.

good. I suppose I enjoy it because we only eat them occasionally. But if you had to eat the can food regularly, I suppose it would be distasteful.

Mom, you told me to think about what I would do. Well, of course I have done some thinking. The ground crew of the Air Corps would be my best bet because there are plenty of schools, but it is very difficult to get in, especially from a basic training center. The ground crew was open six months ago and now it's crowded as everything else is, and there is only a need for skilled mechanics. I'll ask for the ground crew and hope. Now, outside of the Air Corps there are very few schools, but don't worry, I'll get something. Even if I get into the Infantry, they always need clerks like Artie is or typists - so things will be all right.

I know it's hard for civilians to believe it, but there's no way of planning things in the Army. You don't know what's going on and they do whatever they want with you. Artie is supposed to go to another camp within a month, that may prove to be a rumor and he may stay at Bowie for the duration, nobody knows. If he is changed, I hope his unit's moved up North, you could see E more often.

Enclosed is the latest letter I have from Eadie, the coat sure sounds nice. The little picture you sent me is just what I want. I'll see the big ones when I get a furlough. Don't send them down here.

The work on the Range is very easy. We fire for a while and then we lay around while the other fellas shoot. Yesterday was a real loafer's day. We got into our new camp early and help get it set up.

Aunt Rose sent me a lovely package of cookies and candies; she sure treats me royally.

Dad, I know how tired you must be at night. Don't worry if you don't get to write too often. A postcard will do, and only a one cent stamp is required, not two and three cents like Mom puts on. I expect to receive the dry fruit tomorrow.

Love and Kisses,
Charlie

Monday, November 29, 1943

Dear Grandma,

I hope you're getting along nicely. I was very sorry to hear that you had to go to the hospital. Let's hope you'll be home real soon.

Things are running smoothly down here. I'm in my 9th week of Basic Training. Before we know it, I'll be through. The course is over on January 1st.

It's nice and warm during the day, but it sure gets cold at night and in the morning.

I am feeling swell. Everything is just fine, we're getting swell food.

Love,
Charlie

Monday, November 29, 1943

Dear Mom and Dad,

We had some delicious, canned salmon tonight and it sure reminded me of home. It was good to read in your letter today that last Friday night you had boiled white fish, fish soup, cooked peas and coffee. I'm sure looking forward to having that stuff when I come home on a furlough.

Folks, use your own judgment on the building. Don't put in any money, it's not worth it. That's my opinion.

It rained last night but it stopped by this morning. Today was very cloudy and chilly but it was an easy day. We marched two hours to the Range and had four hours of lecture. Then we had chow in the field, in the afternoon we had some demonstrations and then marched home in combat formations. So, you can see there wasn't much doing. We're wearing full field packs every day this week, but I'm used to them by now and it doesn't bother me a bit. The one that we're wearing now only weighs about 15 lbs. and that's light.

I dropped a card to Grandma tonight.

Nothing more, it's freezing tonight.

Love and Kisses,
Charlie

Tuesday, November 30, 1943

Dear Mom and Dad,

It's pretty late, so just a postcard.

I received your package and thanks loads. It was swell, and I still have plenty left over for the rest of bivouac. I qualified as an expert machine gunner this afternoon, now I can wear a medal. We wore our overcoats this morning and had a good two-and-a-half mile hike. Same distance coming back at night, we still eat out in the field.

It's freezing tonight and I'm getting under my covers.

Love and Kisses,
Charlie

Wednesday, December 1, 1943

Dear Mom and Dad,

Your fruit sure has its effect on me. I've been going to the latrine quite often. The figs and prunes are good laxatives. I really don't need one though, as I've been having regular movements. In fact, I've trained myself to one a day on bivouac, but your dried fruit makes me run a little more often. The best thing is that chocolate. I take some to the field and it sure is tasty. The gumdrops are also delicious, I still got some put away.

Today was another easy day. We loafed in the morning while some fellows finished firing the machine guns. I fired an expert's score yesterday; I can wear two medals now - one for the rifle and one for the machine gun. This afternoon we fired the mortar. It's fired by four men groups and no score is kept. We shoot the rifle a little more on Friday and then we're through with our firing.

We leave for the barracks Saturday evening and march straight back. We should get in by Sunday 2 AM; it's about a 13 mile walk and that's not bad at all. I don't think we stop to bivouac Saturday night, so I don't mind walking all the way. It's better than to stop and pitch tents for the night.

Remember Lenny Weinberg? E, used to go with him? Well, I read in the Times that he married a doctor's daughter. He's an MD now also, I didn't write anything about it to E; she shouldn't be interested.

It's mighty cold at night and in the early morn, but your sweaters are coming in handy. Gee, first call sounds at 6 AM out here and we can't get enough nerve to *schlep*[70] out of our covers until 6:30. No steam heat, you know.

I hope you had a good week. Now you should enjoy your weekend, take a good rest. Got paid yesterday $20.75; get the $15 yet?

Be good my dear kiddies, take care of yourselves. You're all I have.

Love and Kisses,
Charlie

Thursday, December 2, 1943

Dear Folks,

Surprise, we're riding instead of walking to a demonstration today. The place is about 10 miles away and it would have been natural to walk. However, we're being transported by trucks, it's now 6:45 AM and we are free for about half an hour until the trucks arrive.

It's a little cloudy this morning, so it's pretty mild, thank God. It's usually freezing and I didn't have to wear my heavy sweater this morning.

We had a hearty breakfast; oranges, eggs, corn flakes and coffee. You'd be surprised how quickly you become used to this kind of living. In some camps the tents are better than the barracks. However, I'll take the barracks.

It's just about getting light now.

Nothing more,
Love and Kisses,
Charlie

---

[70] Yiddish: haul, carry or drag.

Very easy day. Fired about 40 shots on a rifle. Rode to a few Ranges, no walking today.

Too bad the truck won't be with us forever; we march home Sunday night.[71]

Friday, December 3, 1943

Dear Mom and Dad,

Oh, what an easy day we had.

We walked about two and a half miles out to the Range and fired for about 10 minutes in the morning. Then my squad watched the other three squads in the platoon fire and by that time it was time for chow. We had a very good meal in the field and then we marched back to camp and arrived here at 2 PM. We cleaned up our rifles for an inspection at 3:30 and since then we've been free. I took advantage of the free time by taking a good scrubbing out of my steel helmet. Now I feel nice and clean.

You'll probably receive this letter Monday morning. I'll call up Monday morning at about 10-11, I better make it 9:17 so I can get both of you at home. If for any reason you both can't be home, don't accept the charges. That's all you have to say to the operator, "I won't accept the call" and I'll understand that and call back some other time. Don't forget. If I don't call by 10, don't wait, I may not be able to phone.

We are supposed to leave here Sunday morning at 8:30 AM and then back to the barracks about 3. But those plans may be changed, you can never tell in the Army. Monday was planned as a free day, but I hear we have a one-hour training film between 11:30 and 12:30. So that'll sort of break up the day. However, I expect to go to town in the afternoon.

Well, no more news right now, hope to speak with you real soon.

Love to Grandma-
Love and Kisses,
Charlie

---

[71] Written on the back of the envelope, later that night.

Sunday, December 5, 1943

Dear Mom and Dad,

I'm back in the barracks and it's a marvelous feeling after bivouacking for 2 weeks. One sure does appreciate living in a nice warm place with electricity, a wooden floor, and complete plumbing facilities. You can't imagine how swell it is.

We started the march at 8:30 this morning and hit home at 1:45 PM. It was pretty rough, but I came through like a major. We had a delicious meal in the Mess Hall and that was another treat, after eating on the ground and in the dark.

I just loafed around during the afternoon. I shaved and took a warm shower and of course, that made me feel real fresh. I had a light supper and now I'm all set for a good night's rest with sheets. We didn't have sheets on the bivouac.

The three other companies in the battalion were allowed out this afternoon, but we couldn't get passes. It's just as well, because I rested up a lot and sort of got straightened out for the coming weeks. In your last letter you stated that I was finishing my 8th, it's actually my 9th week. We start the 10th week tomorrow, so when you receive this letter (Wednesday, I suppose) I'll be finishing up week number 10. That sounds pretty good, doesn't it? Just one more month and I'm sure it'll go fast. The cycle officially ends on January 1st.

There was nothing difficult about the Range bivouac. We were roughing it a bit, but aside from that it was okay. I feel more confident in myself and know I can do many things that some other men can't.

I planned to talk to you about the following matter tomorrow morning, but if I don't get around to it, I'll tell you about it now. As you know I'm not sure where I'll go after this. After thinking things over, I have decided to consult a physician (Army) about my undescended testicle. It hasn't bothered me one bit, but I figured that if an operation is required I might as well have it done while I'm in the Army. It'll waste time and also save me some time when I return home. Of course, the doctor may say nothing should or can be done, but in case he tells me that the Army will operate, I want to know what to do. Therefore, I would appreciate it if you called Dr. Elisberg and ask his advice. He's treated me and ask him what he thinks of an operation - or ask him if I shouldn't let any work be done on it. I'll write you as soon as I go see the doctor.

There's no rush on Elisberg - but call him up this week and let me know what he says.

I think Murray Goldblatt is over by now. I haven't heard from him in a long while.

Love and Kisses,
Charlie

Monday, December 6, 1943

Dear Folks,

It was nice speaking with you this morning. I went to Columbus in the afternoon and had a good steak.

I could use a couple of bucks; my glasses broke, and it cost me $3 to repair them.

Love and Kisses,
Charlie

P.S. A big letter tomorrow...

Tuesday, December 7, 1943

Dear Mom and Dad,

I used the typewriter in the orderly room to write some stories for the paper, so I might as well give you a break from my lousy writing and type you a line.

We had a very easy day, and it was nice and cool and cloudy. It rained a little in the morning, but it let up after a while.

Don't count on that business I spoke to you about. I was given a small physical exam yesterday and it didn't amount to much. The doctor said I'd have to talk to someone else about it and I'm not anxious to do so until Basic is over. And even when I do consult a physician, he may say that nothing can be done. So, don't expect anything, I feel really swell, as you can well imagine. I've never been in such a good physical condition in all my life and thank God I've avoided those awful colds I used to get every year.

The phone call was probably expensive, but it was the best time to call. I got you immediately and it was a good hour. At night there's always a three to four hour wait, and I can't waste so much time. You both sure sounded close by - not 1100 miles away. The telephone is a marvelous thing, isn't it?

Mom, don't be too ambitious about the house. I agree with Dad and Aunt Rose that it isn't worth a damn and be careful about investing any money. If the last agent Aunt Rose had for it will continue to run it and give you a certain amount of money, then you should leave it with them. Don't let Dad collect rent or anything like that. Neither of you are strong enough for that task, and I know how hard it is. And don't worry about Colored people moving in. As long as they pay rent, it doesn't matter who lives in the building. My main wish is that you don't invest any of your hard-earned money in the damn place. Keep your dough for yourself - and while I'm on the subject, to save me a bit for my furlough. I really want to have a good time and I won't be coming home with any extra dough.

I have no idea as to when I'll get a furlough. If I'm very lucky I'll be home early in January, but that's very remote and I'm not planning anything. If I do get a furlough, then I'll be pleasantly surprised.

I spoke to the First Sergeant today and he's finding out if there's any chance to transfer to Finance, Transportation or the Quartermaster. If he doesn't find out anything I'm going to see my Captain later on this week. Some boys in my position are going to drive trucks after Basic, but since I can't drive, I'm not in line for a job of that sort. But I'm not worried, everything will be okay.

Love and Kisses,
Charlie

Wednesday, December 8, 1943

Dear Mom and Dad,

Today I got the first break I've had since I'm in the Army and I'm keeping my fingers crossed. You both used to kid me at times about my paperwork, but that's where my break might come from. Don't count on anything, nothing is definite.

Here's the story, I got the afternoon off to go to the classification office. I couldn't find out much so I went over to the paper office - the paper I wrote that article for, and I was merely talking with the editor and I happen to ask, "How are public relations coming along?" He asked me if I was interested in journalism, and I said sure. Before I knew it, he had my name and other information, and he took me in to see the Special Service Officer who is a major. Well, the Major said he didn't have an opening, but he called some officers and put in a good word for me and made an appointment for tomorrow morning. I've already gotten permission to get the morning off and I just hope that this officer needs a man now.

That's the important thing, you must have the luck to be there on the spot. That's what the whole Army is, luck. I'm going to build up my paper experience. I also told them I had radio experience because they plan to start a program and I thought that would help.

So if I'm very lucky, tomorrow I may be doing public relations work after Basic. It sounds too good to be true, but I'll try my best.

Don't worry about me. I seem to be able to take care of myself and if worse comes to worse I think I can go to cooks and bakers school. That's really an easy job, so I'll see what's what.

Once again, I like to tell you to go easy with the building. I'll always take care of both of you and don't want you to put a damn cent into the building. It's definitely not worth it. Please don't try to get it out of the red. The building is a flop and squeeze out everything you can but don't invest or waste any strength on the building.

Have a pleasant weekend.

Love,
Charlie

P.S. Don't expect much, if any, mail the next two weeks, we go out on bivouac again Monday morning.

Thursday, December 9, 1943

Dear Folks,

We had a four-hour march and practice bivouac tonight, so I haven't time for a letter.

Received yours telling me what Dr. Elisberg said. If I see any way to do it, I'll suggest the injections. It really doesn't worry me, I may not be able to have anything at all done. Examination the other day was just for hernia. Had the interview this morning and although nothing is definite, prospects are pretty good. I have to go back after our next bivouac. It's been nice and warm all week, I hope it keeps up this way during bivouac.

Would you believe that at 11 PM it was so warm, that I sweated a little. Sound change over last week's cold nights.

Love and Kisses,
Charlie

Friday, December 10, 1943

שיבביס ביא דינארט[72]

Dear Mom and Pop,

The 10th week is practically over. Only four hours tomorrow morning and the week is ended. 3 more to go and before you can say the "*Shemona Esray*" I'll be through with Basic.

I know I should have waited before telling you about my idea of the operation. It's all so indefinite that I shouldn't have mentioned it at all. The only reason I did so was to find out what Dr. Elisberg thought so that I could give an immediate answer if asked by an Army doctor. Nothing will occur until Basic is over and I go to my next post. Then I'll see a doctor. Mom, you say you think I know more about it than I let you know; well, that could mean a few things. But the most important thing I want to impress upon you is that it doesn't bother me a bit. I do all the walking and running and I'm glad to say I'm fit as a fiddle without bothering with it and I'll be okay. But if the situation presents itself, I'll

---

[72] Incorrect spelling of *שעבס ביי די נאכט* Yiddish: *Shabbas Bi Di Nacht* - Shabbos (The Jewish Day of rest) starts in the evening.

have something done if they'll do it. You both can forget about it until I write that I'm going to see a doctor.

The Army sort of messed up my plans again, but I'm used to that by now. I have a date with a girl I know for Sunday afternoon and evening and that means a few good home cooked meals. But we all have to be in by Sunday noon. You see, we leave for bivouac Monday morning and they probably want us well rested. I just called Irene (that's the kid's name) and asked to see her Saturday night, but she already has a date. So, I'm out of luck. I'll see her in her father's store tomorrow afternoon because she has my glasses which were repaired in town. She may get me a blind date.

I'm on guard tonight for the last time and I was a lucky boy, I got the 7 to 9 shift, so I walked my post and now I'm free for the rest of the night. I sleep with the guards but I can sleep right through until morning.

Nothing more
Have a [73] גיטע וואך
Love and Kisses,
Charlie

Sunday, December 12, 1943

Dear Mom and Pop,

I had a very nice time yesterday. I told you I didn't have a date, but I got one with one of Irene's friends. She's a good-looking girl and we had a pleasant evening. There's no place to go in Columbus but you have to make the best of it.

Well, today is our last day in the barracks for about 13 days - we're supposed to return from bivouac for Christmas. We leave here tomorrow morning at

---

[73] Yiddish: *Gutta Voch* – Wishes for a good week.

8:30, don't worry if you don't hear from me. I doubt whether we'll be able to write, but I'll try to get off some postcards.

Dad, here's another favor I want. I have no idea as to where I'll go from here, but I want my traveling bag - the one the Marshaks gave me. Sending it will be cheap by Railway Express or via mail, you decide. Send it out about December 20th, not much later in case I get a furlough. I'll need it as I have some personal stuff to take when I change to another assignment. Don't forget, please.

It's a little bit chilly today but the sun is shining. One pair of my GI shoes needed heels and I just got them back from repairs. They do a very good job, it'll all be free. Whenever your equipment wears out, you just salvage it and get new stuff. After Basic I'm going to get some new socks, they're in good condition, but I might as well get some new ones.

If you haven't mailed me any money yet, hold it up until December 22nd so I'll get it when we come back. Will be getting mail while on bivouac, so write.

Nothing more,
Lots of Love and Kisses,
Charlie

PS. Enclosed are two articles I wrote for the paper. Put the articles away some place.

Sunday, December 12, 1943

Dear Folks,

I wrote today's letter before your letter reached me. Thanks for the dough. If you send me another $15 next week, I'll be all set January 1st for a furlough or whatever comes up. I'll have $27-$30 and that will take care of me. Thanks for mailing me the package, it will be delivered to me at the bivouac area. I'll probably get it Monday or Tuesday.

We had a good meal today, delicious roast beef. Had a restful day, ate breakfast at 8:30 and went back to bed until 11 then waited around writing letters. Heard from E today, she expects to move shortly. Feeling fine, mail will slow up due to Christmas rush.

You'll be getting another $15 next week, January 1st.

Love and Kisses,
Charlie

Monday, December 13, 1943

Dear Mom and Dad,

Today turned out to be a very easy day - not half as bad as I expected. We left the barracks at 8:30 and arrived at the bivouac area at 9:45, so you see, we didn't have too long a march.

As soon as we got here, we pitched our tents. Then we dug a little ditch around my tent in case of rain. Since this whole thing is tactical, we have to dig prone shelters 2 feet deep and 6 feet long in case of attack by airplanes. That's what you would do if you were really in battle. Incidentally, the boy I'm tenting with is an Italian from Rochester. We gathered all the pine needles we could and put them inside our tent, they make for a real good covering. Over that we put a comforter which we will sleep on and over that we have another comforter and four blankets. Our overcoats were also sent out here so we will manage to be pretty warm.

The kitchen comes out for every meal; we may eat rations a few times, but not too many. They cook the stuff back in the company area and bring it out in a truck. The only real hardship will be the lack of any light at night and early in the morning. We're not allowed to burn any candles, so that's not really a hardship and you get used to that.

We're free the whole day, just have to get our tents set up and I'm all finished. This bivouac is supposed to be real tough, but between you and me, it's not hard at all. It's really an experience and that's the way I look at all of this stuff.

I'm glad you mailed the package. I said not to mail food to the bivouac area, but I now see that it will come in handy. The package is being anxiously awaited and I'll probably get it tonight or tomorrow.

I always seem to be able to get letters off to you. I think I'll find time to write you every day, not sure though.

Nothing more, be good.
Love and Kisses,
Charlie

Tuesday, December 14, 1943

Dear Folks,

Kept pretty busy. Got your package last night and it sure was swell. Also, was glad to hear that you went to the Opera.

Feeling fine.
Love,
Charlie

Wednesday, December 15, 1943

Dear Mom and Dad,

Slept until 11:15 this morning and had a good dinner a little while ago. We went out on a night problem and got in 2:45 this morning. We had a good breakfast then and I got to sleep around 3:15. The work at night isn't difficult at all, it gives us practice in walking around at night. We have a little physical training this afternoon and another night problem. Then we're free all day tomorrow and in the evening, we get ready to go back to the barracks. We'll get in sometime Friday morning.

There's going to be a big Christmas dinner Saturday noon. We have the whole day off, of course, and it promises to be a good feed. If I can get into town Sunday, I'll go over to that girl's house.

What do you hear from E? Where is Artie's new camp? I'm anxious to hear about them. I should think E would come home if Artie is on maneuver. It would be swell if she stayed home with you awhile.

Only 7 more working days and Basic will be over. It went fast, didn't it?

See Dad, I'm glad to hear that Mom is still a gorgeous woman. You sure made a good choice. You know what I say, "I want a gal, just like the gal that married dear old Dad." Did you get a new overcoat, Pop? Be sure that both of you take good care during this flu epidemic. Keep warm and don't go around too much.

Love and Kisses,
Charlie

P.S. Have a pleasant weekend, I hope you go to the movies occasionally.

Thursday, December 16, 1943

Dear Mom and Dad,

I hear you're having some real cold weather. Well, please take good care of yourself. We are having our share of the cold waves. In fact, it actually snowed for a while yesterday afternoon. That's a rare occurrence in Georgia. I've been sleeping very well in my little pup tent. With all the covers we have, we sure keep mighty warm.

The toughest thing is getting up when it's dark. There's no room to move around and it's quite a task. It's all very funny. We are doing a lot of night work, so we get the mornings off. Last night we marched for 2 hours and today we are free until 2 PM. The sun is coming out and it should warm up soon. When you get this card, I'll be my 12th week. We go to the barracks Sunday to clean up and then come back to our tents until Thursday night.

Love,
Charlie

Friday, December 17, 1943

Dear Mom and Pop,

Received your air-mail postcard this morning. It's good to hear that you're busy, you people will be millionaires yet. We had another night problem last night and we're off all day, except for two hours of physical training.

Here's what we did last night:

They want to teach us how to march through the woods at night, so we went for a little hike. You have to walk right behind the man in front of you so you don't get lost. Well, it was the funniest thing you ever did see. No one knew where he was and all we did was follow the man in front. It's quite dark when you walk through dense woods, and at times we had to hold on to the man in front. It may not sound funny, but it was. I was laughing all the way. We got in around 9 PM and I slept until around 8 this morning, so I'm getting plenty of sleep.

We had a nice fire going now and we're all lounging around. You people are having a cold wave and we have our share. The ground is all frosted in the morning. A week from today we'll be back in the barracks and then we'll have just one more week. Yippee! Sunday morning, we march to the barracks and spend the day there. So, actually we only have five more bivouac days. I'll tell you all about it when I see you. The work is really easy, the living is a bit rough but an experience I'll never forget.

I'm feeling grand, I kept my normal weight throughout the training and that is sure a good sign.

I received a nice letter from Aunt Rose today. She asked me what I want for Christmas and I believe I'll tell her a pair of dress gloves. I know she wants to get me something, so might as well be something I could use. She's been very nice to me. It's swell to have an aunt like her. I heard from Mimi but not from El. They're both well and like it in Baltimore.

Nothing more, Love and Kisses,
Charlie,

Have a *Mazeldika*[74] week, when the two of you go out, enjoy yourselves; don't think about E and A. Have a good time. We're both fine. Love to Grandma.

Saturday, December 18, 1943

Dear Folks,

All is well down here. We go in tomorrow morning to wash up and come out in the evening. Thursday night we go back for good.

---

[74] Yiddish: Good luck or good fortune.

Dad, got your nice letter today. I had to laugh when you mentioned the mild weather down here, it's really freezing, and I'll be used to the New York cold when I get home. Will write more tomorrow.

Love,
Charlie

Sunday, December 19, 1943

Dear Mom and Pop,

We were sure a happy bunch of soldiers when we hit the barracks this morning. We're all filthy and it was a great relief to take a shave and have a good shower. I cleaned up real well and got into my OD's. We leave for the bivouac area at 4:15 PM so I'm just hanging around for the few hours.

We had a delicious breakfast and in a little while we'll have a good dinner. It's marvelous to be nice and clean. It's such a wonderful feeling, even though it's just for a few hours.

They collected laundry for the last time this morning and I gave them every-thing I had. I'll have all clean stuff when I leave here. I'm anxious to see that Lieutenant after bivouac, he may have something good for me.

Just heard from Ira Fogelman. He just returned from a 32-day trip to England and is now on a trip to the South Pacific. He sends his best regards to you. It's been mighty cold down here, especially at night and in the morning. There is only a few more days of bivouac. We leave for the barracks Thursday night at 10:30 and are due early Friday morning. We'll have some problems on our way and we should hit here at 6 AM. This morning, we marched home in an hour and a quarter, not a bad hike at all.

Nothing more, don't worry if you don't hear from me; we'll be pretty busy for the next few days.

Take good care of yourself,
Love and Kisses,
Charlie

Sunday, December 19, 1943

Dear Mom and Dad,

Well, I'm back in the woods. We did the 4 miles in 50 minutes. It was more or less a forced march, and we were really traveling. I'm all cleaned up and the four days will be gone before I know it. Yes, the 12th week starts tomorrow. It seems like yesterday that we were saying 12 more weeks to go.

We're all sitting around a nice fire singing old-time favorites.

Love to Grandma.
Love and Kisses,
Charlie

Monday, December 20, 1943

Dear Mom and Dad,

We had a very easy day. But we have a problem tonight which will last until around 3 AM. When we come in, we will have breakfast and be off all Tuesday.

Tonight, our platoon is taking a defensive position on a hill and another platoon will try to get through us. All that means for us is to stay in our foxholes and try to spot the "enemy." We started digging the foxholes this afternoon and mine is half done. So, we'll finish digging tonight and then get in the holes and wait. Sounds silly, but it all goes in the making of a soldier, I guess.

It was a summer day in the afternoon, but it was freezing until noon. That's how funny the weather is.

Nothing more,
Love and Kisses,
Charlie

Tuesday, December 21, 1943

Dear Mom and Dad,

Received your letter, Mom, in which you say that Mimi has a friend in college. Well, at the start of Basic I definitely told you that I wasn't going to college. Mimi's friend was a sophomore when he was drafted. College graduates aren't being sent to college under ASTP unless they majored in Engineering. The program is being drastically reduced, and although I would have been sent to college for languages a year ago, I couldn't get in now. Why you still talk about it, I don't know. When I tell you a thing is definite, it is. I hope you haven't told people that I'm going to go to college. About Artie, even though he's a clerk, he goes on maneuvers. Whenever his battalion does anything, he goes along. I don't know anything about him not being a clerk. As far as I know, he still has his same job. What does Eadie intend to do while he's on maneuvers?

You say, "If I could only help you both." Mom, you can't do a darn thing for either E or me. If you flew all over you would only see us, not help. In fact, I don't see how you could help and I don't see where we need help. Be content that you're busy and that your children are in good health. I know you both love us very much. Everything will be okay, before you know it we'll be home. Just take care of yourselves and be busy and have some fun.

Off all day, another night problem tonight and we only have two hours of physical training tomorrow. We leave here Thursday night.

Love and Kisses,
Charlie

Friday, December 24, 1943

Dear Mom and Dad,

Well, I'm back in the barracks once again and the home stretch is here. This time next week we'll all be finished except for a little parade before the Colonel.

We left the bivouac area at 10:30 last night and took a 15-mile hike back. We landed home at 5 in the morning after eating breakfast in the field. The chow truck met us just outside the company area. This was done to show us for training purposes how troops march to the battle area and eat before going into action.

Yesterday I received a letter from E telling me that she might be able to pass through Columbus on her way to meet Artie. Well, at 5 this morning I tried to call her up but I couldn't get any number at the Bowie White House, so I sent her a telegram saying that I could see her if she came up. I haven't heard from her yet and it may be that I missed her. She may have left Texas before my telegram reached her. At any rate, it would be swell if E could meet me here. This weekend would have been ideal because 3-day passes were available for Friday, Saturday, and Sunday. I'll be around all weekend and perhaps she'll call up from some nearby spots and we'll meet.

Slept until noon today and had a good dinner in the Mess Hall, took a good shave, a 5-day growth, and around 3 I took a pass for Columbus. However, the one bus I waited for was crowded, so I decided not to go since I had to be back here at 7 PM. I'm on KP tonight and tomorrow. You see, all the Jewish boys volunteered for duty on Christmas. That seems to be a universal custom in the Army. It does a lot to promote goodwill. So, I stayed in camp and had a haircut,

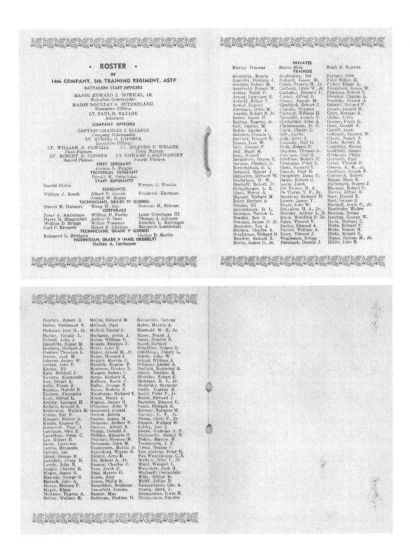

and a good shampoo. I am going to the kitchen in about an hour, it will be very easy since very few fellows are around and there are a lot of fellows on KP.

Sunday I'm going to town for dinner at Irene's house. I spoke to her today and I was invited over. So, I'll have a very restful weekend. We go on a 20-mile march on Monday, so I want to be in good shape. It's the last march of the cycle and won't we be happy. The last week will consist mainly of physical training, but I could do anything in the world knowing that this is the end. Not that I dreaded Basic so much, but knowing that I'll go to a different job, whatever it may be. I will see the officer about the paper job early next week.

We're not having a white Christmas but we're sure having a cold one. Today reminds me so much of New York around Xmas. It's real cold and I wore your lovely scarf and my overcoat.

Nothing more, have a good week and a happy healthy New Year.
Love and Kisses,
Charlie

I'm enclosing the menu for our Christmas dinner, we'll have it tomorrow afternoon.

Saturday, December 25, 1943

Dear Mom and Dad,

Well, here it is Christmas day and it's raining to beat hell. It started to rain during the night and it got real cold and when we got up today, icicles formed on the clotheslines and trees. So, you can see we're having real cold weather. It must be down to about 20 degrees.

My KP today was a laugh. I didn't do a blessed thing last night, and this morning I didn't get up until 11. Then I helped them set the tables for about 2 hours and then at 1 PM I got dressed in my OD's and went with all the boys to the dinner. The officers acted as waiters, a custom in the Army on Christmas Day. The dinner ended at 5 and the new KP's went on then, so I didn't touch a dirty dish or anything. I picked a good day for KP.

The dinner was something you had to see to believe. I sent the menu home, so you know what we had. Every time we finished a bowl of peas or anything that was on the table in bowls, we would give it to an officer, and they would fill it up. I never ate so much turkey in my life. At home I wouldn't ask for more after 2 or 3 helpings and with company you'd be afraid of making a hog of yourself, but today we all ate, ate and ate.

They had an organist playing Christmas carols and it was all very nice. You know the song "I'm Dreaming of a White Christmas;" well, we must have some of that about five times. That's the favorite song right now. It's the first time most of the boys have been away from home for Christmas and they're pretty blue. In fact, Christmas always meant home and merry making to me although we don't observe the religious side of the day. Many were the white Christmases I spent in Wilkes-Barre. Oh, I had such a good time. Let's hope we'll all be celebrating Christmas and the New Year home in 1944.

The President's talk yesterday was pretty encouraging.[75] It's a sure thing that will win the war. The only thing is how long it will take. You know Roosevelt said we'll have five million men overseas by Summer. And now of course the most important thing - Artie. Folks, you just had to expect it. His outfit has been active for 2 years and it had loads of training. They've been ready to go over ever since they came to Texas from California and it's lucky he's been here this long. He's in the office and I wouldn't worry about him a bit. He'll be okay. I'm surprised he didn't tell E he was going over. He had to tell her sooner or later and now I suppose she's all excited trying to get home in a hurry. How's Anna taking it? I imagine she's going nuts. Both of you shouldn't get excited. There are over 3 million men overseas and most of them will return along with Artie. E will get over it soon. She should get a job right away and the days will pass quickly. Don't let her hang around, make her get a good position as soon as Artie leaves.

Just hanging around tonight, will write a few more letters and get to bed early. I know the mail is slow but that's on account of the rush. I'll mail this letter and the one with the menu from town tomorrow. No mail is leaving camp until Monday morning, so you'll probably get a few letters at once. Mom, time and time again I will tell you not to send things special delivery. It doesn't help a bit. If anything, just insure the package. I haven't received the valise yet, so probably get it Monday. I got a marvelous package of candy, cake and figs from Aunt Rose. I held my own with all the other fellas as far as passing out food today. Mary also sent me a very nice box of candy from Barracini. I'll write her a letter of thanks.

---

[75] An excerpt from President Roosevelt's Christmas Radio broadcast address, delivered from his home in Hyde Park, New York. "On this Christmas Eve there are over ten million men in the armed forces of the United States alone. One year ago, 1,700,000 were serving overseas. Today, this figure has been more than doubled to 3,800,000 on duty overseas. By next July 1st, that number overseas will rise to over 5,000,000 men and women.... But — on Christmas Eve this year — I can say to you that at last we may look forward into the future with real, substantial confidence that, however great the cost, 'peace on earth, good will toward men' can be and will be realized and ensured. This year I can say that. Last year I could not do more than express a hope. Today I express — a certainty, though the cost may be high and the time may be long...." (http://opiniojuris.org/2009/12/24/roosevelts-christmas-eve-address-december-24-1943/)

Love and Kisses,
Charlie

P.S. Folks, don't tell anyone what branch of service Artie is in or where he is sailing from. That's a big military secret and you never know who you are telling.[76] It sounds silly, but you may be saving thousands of lives by not telling it to anyone. Be sure not to mention New London.

Sunday, December 26, 1943

Dear Mom and Dad,

Here it is Sunday and I'm in town at the USO. I just had three cups of delicious coffee and now I'm going to spend a couple of hours writing letters before going over to Irene's house.

Nothing much has happened since I wrote you last night. We were all passing around food until midnight and I still have loads left over. I had a good night sleep and came to town on the 11 o'clock bus. Columbus is on Central War Time[77] and therefore is an hour behind Benning and New York Time. Noon in Benning is 11 AM in Columbus.

I took a hot shower last night and feel swell. There's nothing like a few days' rest from the regular routine.

What's new with Eadie? When did she come home?[78] I'll be calling you up one of these mornings at home around 8 or 8:30. The phones are actually busy this time of year. Would you believe that there is a 6-hour wait on all calls to New

---

[76] Both a civilian and military censorship were in effect throughout World War II, and special protocols were applied to incoming and outgoing US mail. Letters were opened and examined, resealed and then given a censor's stamp. This precaution was two-fold: firstly, to avoid the situation of military information ending up in the hands of the enemy if the letters were lost or intercepted; secondly, to maintain the morale of both the military and civilian population by redacting damaging news. (https://americanhistory.si.edu/blog/mail-call-world-war-ii-communication-told-soldiers-diary)

[77] Congress implemented a new law in February 1942, instituting a national daylight-saving time designed to help conserve fuel and "promote national security and defense." Nicknamed "War Time" by the public, the zones were known as Eastern War Time, Pacific War Time, etc.(https://www.defense.gov/News/Feature-Stories/story/Article/1779177/daylight-saving-time-once-known-as-war-time/).

[78] With Artie's pending deployment overseas, Eadie returned from Camp Bowie, Texas to move back in with her parents in their home in New York.

York? I'll wait a while and avoid the rush. It stopped raining last night but is still cloudy.

Tomorrow is the beginning of the end. I'm not so anxious because Basic is over, but I'd like to know where I go from here. I'll keep you posted. On Tuesday I'll see the officer about the public relations job.

Nothing more. All day yesterday we were in the barracks and all we heard over the radio was carols, I probably know them all by heart.

Love and Kisses,
Charlie

Monday December 27, 1943

Dear Mom and Dad,

I received my bag this evening, thanks loads. The stuff enclosed was great. It'll last me for an entire week. Don't send any more food until I ask for some.

I had a marvelous time last night. It's *Hanukkah*[79] now and we lit the little candles and we had a great time at Irene's house. Before dinner we had a few eggnogs with rum, a marvelous drink. Mrs. Witt served the following dinner which reminded me so much of home. Tomato juice, fried chicken, tongue (hot), salad, potatoes, beans, lemon meringue pie and tea. They are so hospitable. Mom, I want you to do me a favor when the next $15 comes. These people have been so nice to me and I'm a complete stranger and there's nothing between me and their daughter. So, I would like you to spend $5 on a little trinket in David's. A little bracelet or pin will do, use your good judgement. Have E write a little note for me saying, "Thanks loads for your swell hospitality, Charlie."

Have David's mail it to:

Miss Irene Witt
2421-19th Avenue
Columbus, Georgia

---

[79] Hebrew: Hannukah, also known as the "Festival of Lights" is a Jewish festival commemorating the recovery of Jerusalem and subsequent rededication of the Second Temple at the beginning of the Maccabean revolt against the Seleucid Empire in the 2nd Century BCE.

Please do it soon, as she's leaving for college shortly. Don't you think I should show my thanks? Do attend to it, please.

Here's another thing which may be of interest. I don't know how your payments on the cemetery plot are coming along, but if you find it too difficult to pay, I found something out. Dad, remember what a blessing Veterans Administration was? Well, as a veteran with discharge papers, you have always been entitled to a beautiful plot for you and your wife in Long Island National Cemetery, a place which is run for veterans only and their wives and it's a marvelous place just like the hospital. One of the boys' dad is buried there and he says they take excellent care. I know that for quite some time your greatest worry has been that you had no plots and all the while you had the cemetery available. Plus $100 contributed by the government for expenses.

I hope you don't need the plot for another hundred years. But if you get stuck and can't pay up on your current plot, remember you have this other place and it's not charity. As a veteran it's your right and privilege to be buried there. It's worth looking into. Now I'll never have to worry about a plot for myself when I get home. It's as good a cemetery as any in New York, now you don't have to worry about you or Mom. See, Dad, you never learned how much was coming to you.

It's getting late, thanks again for the bag; it looks grand. The food was swell.

Love,
Charlie

Tuesday, December 28, 1943

Dear Mom and Dad,

Am in town tonight and waiting for the 10 o'clock bus to take me back to camp. I came in with another boy to buy our Lieutenant and Cadremen (non-commissioned officer who trained us) presents. We got a nice shirt for the officer for $10.50; we bought two of the non-coms Johnnie Walker Black Label at $8.50; one guy we got a cigarette lighter and we bought a pair of gloves for the fifth fellow. I had a nice steak dinner and I'm now set for the last three days of Basic. We're off all Saturday except perhaps for a small parade in the morning.

I saw the officer about my job, and he told me the Major had requested me and if the classifiers haven't already assigned me somewhere else, I'll probably be kept at Benning. It's still not sure and I'm not banking on it. If I get the job, I'll consider myself very lucky. Won't know for another week or so.

Did okay on my test today. Got 80% on a written exam, average about 75. All about the stuff we learned.

Nothing more right now.

E- thanks loads for your Christmas package; all the stuff is swell and it arrived in good shape. Will write you soon.

Love,
Charlie

Wednesday, December 29, 1943

Dear Mom and Dad,

I hope E is home now and everything is okay. She'll be doing some fine baking for you. I just ate some chocolate cake E baked for me and believe me, "she's got a little bit of talent."

I'm sure Art will be okay and Eadie will be sensible about the whole thing. She joins a million other women who have husbands overseas and she will show the real courage of the American Woman. Don't worry Sis, your husband will be home real soon, and he'll be safe and sound.

Got the letters you wrote Christmas Eve. Dad, Basic is all through in two days. All we have on Saturday morning is a short parade at 9:45, so we're really finished Friday. Tomorrow morning, we take a 4-mile forced march and that's the last tough thing we do. We have to do the 4 miles in 50 minutes. I've done it before and it doesn't bother me.

It was quite cold today, but it could be real warm tomorrow. That's the way it is.

Love and Kisses,
Charlie

P.S. Mom, to hell with the house if it gives you too much trouble.

1944

Saturday, January 1, 1944

Dear Mom and Dad, and Eadie, of course (I forgot that you are home),

A very Happy New Year to you all. I hope we can get high together next New Year's. By that time the war should be coming to an end.

I had a very nice time last night. In fact, it was a grand surprise that I could spend New Year's Eve in such a nice way in Columbus. I had a date with Irene and I called for her with my fraternity brother. The boy and myself had a good dinner first in one of the nicest restaurants in town.

We knew about a private formal dance in the Reformed Jewish Club, so we took Irene home (we met her in her store) and she put on an evening gown. When we got to the place, I was all set to pay a few bucks, but we were invited in as guests. Arnie, my fraternity brother, found himself a gal so we were set. There was a buffet table all night - delicious shrimp, celery, cheese sandwiches, etc. I had a glass of champagne on the house, and it was so good. It was a small, nice crowd, all formal and that's something out of the ordinary for New Year's. At 2:30 they served breakfast - American cheese, turkey sandwiches, and coffee. I finally got in at 5 this morning.

We paraded at 9:45 and since then we've been free. We had a good turkey dinner, and I took a few hours' shnooze so now I feel fine.

E, help Mom attend to the bracelets or pin I want her to buy for Irene. Nothing at all serious between us, but the Witt's have been so hospitable, and you know how odd that is in a soldier town.

Pop, have a very nice birthday. I'll let you know where I'm sent by telegram if I'm shipped to another camp. I have no idea as yet.

Are you still getting bond receipts? I could have a War Bond by now.

How's business?
Love and Kisses,
Charlie

Monday, January 3, 1944

Dear Mom, Pop, and E,

We're having a little rain these days, down here in Georgia they call it the "Dog Days." It started raining yesterday afternoon and kept up until this morning. It let up a while ago but it's still really cloudy.

I had a swell time yesterday and it completed a lovely weekend. I met Irene and Arnie (my fraternity brother) at the movie house in Columbus at 3 o'clock; we saw "True to Life." I'm sure you'll like it. Try to see it when it comes to the neighborhood. Franchot Tone, Dick Powell and Mary Martin; no soldiers in the picture and that made it a treat.

After the movie - which, by the way, takes place in New York and Sunnyside in particular, it was good to see the Old Town - we went over to the Witt's house and had a delicious dinner of vegetable soup, veal cutlets, tongue, cauliflower, candy sweets, salad, small baked apples with jelly, ice cream and marble cake. Oh, it was real good. Mrs. Witt is quite a cook. Then we sat around and played a little rummy and Arnie and I left at 10. Do attend to the presents for Irene this week, E. I'd like her to get it soon.

We got up at 7 today, no one has received the shipping orders yet. We're going to have one hour of physical training and one hour of dismounted drill every day until we leave. That's just to keep us a little busy. There really isn't much else to do.

E, thanks a lot for the subscription to the Reader's Digest. I haven't received any copy yet, but it should be coming soon.

Nearly all of the equipment we're turning in has already been collected. We still have our rifles, but they are going to be turned in this afternoon. I hope I never have another one issued to me.

I saw Roosevelt in a newsreel. Hasn't he aged something awful? He looks like a man of 75 in the picture.

Nothing more, be good and write soon. Take good care of yourselves and don't work too hard. Your daughter is home, and she will do a lot for you, I'm sure.

Love and Kisses,
Charlie

Tuesday, January 4, 1944

Dear Folks,

Well, I'm heading for Texas. I leave Benning for Camp Swift[80] tomorrow afternoon (Wed.) so, by the time you get this letter I will probably have arrived in Texas. I'm going to the 102nd Infantry Division.[81] There's nothing to be alarmed about, a division is a mighty big unit and there are many different kinds of jobs I could get. I'm still very optimistic and believe I'll get some kind of position which would be suitable for my education and environment. It takes about 36 hours, so I'll probably get there late Thursday night. I'll write you my address, and whenever you get it, please mail me some dough Air Mail. I'm a little short and may need some money. If you already sent me some money, it will be forwarded to me, so don't worry.

It's too bad that E still isn't down in Texas. I feel badly about that, but that's war and the Army. Only a few truck drivers are left at work in Benning. Another "overeducated" boy in my platoon was sent down to the motor pool. He has a driver's license and will become a truck or Jeep driver.

I do regret one thing, folks, and that is not joining the Navy. I feel sure that I could have done much better in the Navy because it's a rarity when they get a college grad in the enlisted ranks. But we all have to make the best of things and I'll get a good job at the place I'm going, I'll keep you posted.

I'm in town now, I had a good lunch and now I'm doing some writing. Enclosed is a letter I got from Murray. Eadie, don't forget to attend to the gift for Irene. Incidentally, Edith, your friend Bernard Filbrian had a second brother killed in action. He was a paratrooper in Sicily.

Nothing more,
Love and Kisses,
Charlie

P.S. Today's your birthday, Dad. And I'm wishing you everything you desire. Pretty soon all this mess will be over and we'll be home together. Gee, my head is still shaped just like yours.[82]

---

[80] Established in January 1942 on 56,000 acres north of Bastrop, Texas. During peak years of operation, Camp Swift trained over 90,000 US military personnel, and held some 10,000 German prisoners of war. (https://txarchives.org/)

[81] See Chapter 3 Historical Introduction for more background information on the Division.

[82] Seems to be a running family joke at the time.

Wednesday, January 5, 1944

Dear Mom, Dad and Sis,

We left Columbus at 4 o'clock and now we're going through Alabama. We just passed Sylacauga, a very small, typical Alabama city.

Camp Swift is near Austin, or did I tell you that already? That's very near Brownwood, isn't it Eadie?

We're traveling Pullman.[83] 27 fellows are making the trip. No driver is hitching up until we get to Birmingham, which will be at 10 PM. So we just had a box lunch which was delicious. Southern fried chicken, two spread sandwiches, cake and coffee.

Nothing much has happened since I wrote yesterday. Spent an easy morning hanging around the barracks. I suppose this is one of the sad facts of the Army. Going through Basic together and then all going a different way. I didn't mind leaving Benning, but I was sorry to say goodbye to all the fellas I got to know so well in the four months we've been together. You get so, that you called the barracks "home." I was very fortunate to do Basic with such a fine group of boys.

I'm carrying my traveling bag with me. My barracks bags (2) are in the "women's room" on the car. I hope the porter makes our beds early. There isn't much to do and I'd like to get to sleep early. We're due to arrive at Camp Swift at 6 AM Friday. Will probably get there a few hours late.

E will tell you about the terrible living conditions you see as you go through the South. It's unbelievable the way the people live. But that's the way it is.

Take care of yourself,
Love and Kisses,
Charlie

---

[83] In the United States, the term Pullman was used to refer to railroad sleeping cars that were built and operated on most US railroads by the Pullman Company (founded by George Pullman), from 1867 to December 31, 1968.

Thursday, January 6, 1944

Dear Folks, and folks includes Eadie,

Here I am in Louisiana. The Army is sure showing me the southern part of our great country. We hit Birmingham, Alabama at 8 last night and we hitched on to another train. We're staying in the same car all the way. Got to sleep at 9 and slept until 1. Was very comfortable in my upper. I slept alone while the fellows who had the lowers doubled up. I slept right through until 3 AM and then the train got pretty jerky, but I slept fairly well, waking up each hour until 7. It was funny, every time I looked at my watch another hour has passed.

This morning we are in Jackson, Mississippi and then we hit Vicksburg. We went over the Mississippi River next and then we were in Louisiana. The river was pretty big, but if I didn't know it was "Ole' Man River" I wouldn't have noticed it. We've just been through some small towns in Louisiana; the first big town we passed is Monroe and then we hit Shreveport. Right now we're in Holly Ridge, some hick town, eh?

Had a good breakfast in the diner - all on the Army; tomato juice, oatmeal, bacon and eggs, home fries and toast and coffee.

We're very comfortable in our car, the train is pretty crowded with soldiers and some civilians. That's all now.

Love and Kisses,
Charlie

P.S. E, did you send the gifts away yet? Please do so soon.

Thursday, January 6, 1944

Dear Folks,

I'm in Shreveport, Louisiana now and it's very cool outside. The sun is shining but it's not warm by a long shot. We had chicken a la king for lunch with spinach and mashed potatoes, also peas. A very good meal, so much unused land along the way.

Love,
Charlie

Thursday, January 6, 1944

Dear Folks,

We hit Shreveport at 3 PM and we're still here. We missed connections and our car is in the station. We're due to pull out at 11:30. This is the nicest town I've seen since I'm down South. It's very modern and plenty of good hotels and restaurants and business buildings.

Had a good dinner in a restaurant and looked over the shopping center. Now I'm in the USO, a very nice place. Our beds will be ready when we get back to the car. I doubt whether we'll get to Swift before tomorrow evening. All the big lights are on in the city and it reminds me of New York.

Hope you're all feeling well.
Love and Kisses,
Charlie

RETURN IN 5 DAYS TO:

Pvt. C. Fletcher 32999032

Hq. Btry. 102d Div. Arty.

CAMP SWIFT, TEXAS

CAMP SWIFT
JAN 17
10 AM
1944
TEXAS

3 CENTS   3 CENTS

Mr. and Mrs. S. Fletcher
590 West End Avenue
New York City #24
N.Y.

AIR MAIL

Chapter 3:
In The Army Now - Camp Swift, Texas

Chas. Fletcher 32999032

Btry. 102d Div Arty

mp Swift

January 1944 - June 1944

UNITED STATES POSTAGE

1 CENT   1 CENT   1 CENT

UNITED STATES POSTAGE

TEXAS

Mr. & Mrs. Samuel Fletcher
590 West End Ave.
N. Y. C.   24

Air Mail

June 15 - N.Y. 44

RETURN IN 5 DAYS TO:

Pfc Charles L. Fletcher 32999032
Hq. Btry. 102d Div Arty.

CAMP SWIFT, TEXAS

AIR MAIL

Flet 25
44

CAMP SWIFT
FEB 25
10 30 AM
1944
TEXAS

2 CENTS   2 CENTS   2 CENTS

AIR MAIL

Mr. & Mrs. Samuel Fletcher
590 West End Avenue
New York City #24
N.Y.

On January 5, 1944, Charlie was reassigned and on the move from the Induction Center at Camp Benning, Georgia to Camp Swift, Texas. He was placed with the 102nd Infantry Division – also known as The Ozarks – in a clerk position within the Headquarters Battery Division Artillery. Although authorized near the end of WWI, The Ozark Division was not completed by the time the Armistice was signed in 1918. During the inter-war period, the 102nd was transferred to the Army Organized Reserve and assigned to the States of Missouri and Arkansas. The Division only existed on paper from 1921 until it was re-activated on September 15, 1942, under the command of Major General John B. Anderson. The Division was to muster at 15,000 men divided between its various regiments and battalions to form a stand-alone fighting force. The Division included the 405th, 406th, 407th, Infantry Regiments; the 379th, 380th, 927th, 381st, Field Artillery Battalions, and Support Services. These included the 327th Engineer Combat Battalion, 327th Medical Battalion, 102nd Quartermaster Company, Headquarters Company,102nd Infantry Division, and Headquarters Battery, 102nd Infantry Division Artillery.[84]

The name and insignia of the Ozark Division paid homage to the Division's home states of Arkansas and Missouri, the Ozark region. As outlined above,

---

[84] With the 102nd Infantry Division Through Germany, pg. 17-20

the emblem combined a golden O/Z, flanked by an arc on a circular blue background. This was a tribute to the bow and arrow proficient Native Americans who inhabited the area at the time of the French settlement. They dubbed the entire region "*Terre aux arcs -* Bow Country," with the Americanized term "Ozark" soon to follow. The arc in the insignia represented the Native American bow and signified marksmanship, while the gold and blue colors were a traditional nod to the associated qualities of valor and distinction.[85] Although the name of the Division implies a certain geographical allegiance, in fact the men in the Division during World War II came not only from the Ozarks region, but from across the United States. Charlie was a New York City boy through and through, but he was joined by soldiers from 20 US States who sent more than 250 men each to serve with the Ozarks, while states of Pennsylvania, New York, New Jersey, and Texas supplied more than 1,000 men each to the Division rosters.[86]

After the initial period of Division activation from September and December 1942, the Division entered an intense period of training and maneuvers from December 1942 until August 1944. The imperative of this period was to transition its raw recruits from civilians to soldiers, and to create a well-integrated fighting machine.[87] Their training began in Camp Maxey, Texas, and in late November 1943 the Division moved to Camp Swift, Texas. It is here that

---

[85] U.S. Army Center for Military History, https://history.army.mil/documents/eto-ob/102id-eto.htm

[86] With the 102nd Infantry Division Through Germany, pg. 20

[87] Ibid, pg. 22

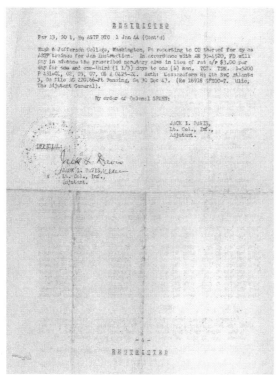

Charlie joined the unit in January 1944, and participated in training while anxiously reading the War Department pamphlet, Preparation for Overseas Movement. Those new orders would reach The Ozarks in June 1944.[88]

---

[88] Ibid, pg. 22-29

Friday, January 7, 1944

Dear Folks,

In another two hours will be around a mile away from Camp. We had another stopover this morning in Fort Worth. We were there for about 3 hours and had breakfast there. It's a very modern town and I visited the City Hall and the public library. The city reminded me of New York, as it is very industrial looking.

We passed Temple, Texas a little while ago and we're on the last leg of our trip. It was raining all day and just let up a little while ago. Slept well last night and I'm feeling fine considering the 50-hour trip.

Texas appears to be a progressive state compared to Georgia and Alabama. The big cities are real modern. Right now we're going through some hick town named Holland and it looks mighty primitive - one General Store, etc.

Eadie will tell you about the prairies. You can ride 4 hours looking at open land.

Will write next from camp.

Love and Kisses,
Charlie

Saturday, January 8, 1944

Dear Folks,

This may be my big break here. I was assigned to the Artillery headquarters.[89] Now I am no longer in the Infantry, thank God. Everyone here seems very nice and I'm sure I'll like it.

I'm going to work for the adjutant,[90] who's a major. My immediate boss is a sergeant. They put my bed right next to his. I'm sleeping in the barracks with all the other office men. Most have stripes,[91] so I may be a Corporal soon. My CO (Commander) is a first looey (Lieutenant) and he talked to me this morn-

---

[89] 102nd Infantry Division, Division Artillery, Headquarters Battery.

[90] An officer who acts as an administrative assistant to a senior officer and assists the commanding officer with unit administration, mostly the management of human resources.

[91] Marking on the sleeve of a uniform to designate enlisted and non-commissioned officer ranks.

BOTTOM ROW: BRITTON; WILLIAMS; SHARP; STAGGS; GUSTAFSON; MERKLEY; KNIGHTS; MOREHEAD; TILLSON; DOBBS; KINNEY; FRUTCHEY; GEORGES; MALONE; CONSTANT; EMMONS; WEAVER
2ND ROW: ANASTASIOU; TUCKER; RHODES; COLEMAN; WRIGHT; ELLMAKER; GRZEBCZYK; DISHNEAU; HENLEY; DUSCHENE; IERACI; HARDISON; THEROUX; LECOMTE; DELPERCIO; PITMAN
3RD ROW: BURTON; PELLANO; CAVENDER; CASSATA; B. TAYLOR; JACOBS; LEACH; WORLEY; WOJTANOWSKI; ZELENSKI; KING; DEFIN; BACHOFNER; LEONARD MILLER; MACGILLIVRAY; TODD
4TH ROW: PIKE; LARSON; WILKIE; FLETCHER; CLARK; WOOD; MOSER; GILBERT; BROYLES; WILSON; FOWLER; PRISCOPO; OLIVER; GOWER; WEHRENBERG
5TH ROW: LYNFORD MILLER; MCNAMARA; CARPENTER; SHANKLE; BRUCE; CLEGG; BURGE; LEVE; O'DONNELL; CHAMBERLAIN; HEEB; MARTEN; MILCHUS; PETERSON; HOPKINS; FISHER;
6TH ROW: J. TAYLOR; BROCKETT; RAY; GUTHRIE; HOLLAND; PUZIN; D'ANTONIO; GRABKE; EULER; RASH; SOLAND; COURSEY; JAMISON; LAWSON; SCHIPPER

ing and assigned me to headquarters. He told me I get a furlough in March or April, so I'll be seeing you soon.

I've got a lot to do so that's all for now, food is delicious.

Love,
Charlie

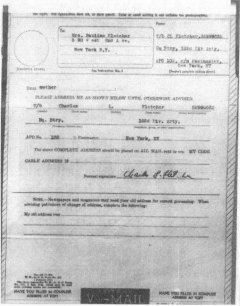

Sunday, January 9, 1944

Dear Mom, Pop, and E,

It was marvelous speaking to you last night. I was feeling very happy at the time and I knew it would make you feel fine to hear my good luck. I'm so thankful that I got a good-shaped head just like Daddy's. That's why I got the job - all the Lieutenant did was look at my head and gave me the job.

Everything is okay, slept until 9 today. I met a fellow I know from school and we went to the Service Club for a while. Had a very good lunch in the Mess Hall. I'm eating out of dishes at last, no more mess kit.

We're right in the center of camp and the two Service Clubs are right nearby. There is a PX[92] about 200 yards away. Austin is only 30 miles away and my friend says the Jewish Welfare Board is very good, so I'm very contented.

I sleep between two fellas I'm going to work with. One of them is private, another is a sergeant. I'm going for chow, I'll be back.

Here I am. Our day room is very comfortable. We have a good radio, nice lounge chairs and some good magazines. There are two excellent libraries in the Service Club, a lot of books we have in the Commerce library.

I'll be looking out for a furlough, my Battery commander, a first looey, told me I get one in March or April. So, I'll be seeing you real soon.

Be good and kiss each other for me.

Hope Artie is still around.

Love and Kisses,
Charlie

PS. Hope you sent me money, by now I'm broke. Also send some airmail stamps, please.

Monday, January 10, 1944

Dear Mom, Dad, and E,

Everything is coming along nicely. I typed up a few letters today and they were very neat, if I must say so myself. I also did a few routine reports and everything tallied. Tomorrow morning, and I think a few mornings every week, I'm going to drill for half an hour with the other men in the Battery. I don't mind that at all, I could use the exercise.

The Battery has a basketball team and I played with them tonight. We won our game and I got one basket. I only played for a little while, the fellows are very nice considering this is the regular Army.

---

[92] Post Exchange, a type of retail store found on United States military bases.

I'm pulling "charge of quarters" in division headquarters. Eadie, will explain what CQ means.[93] My first duty is on January 17th. Maybe I'll get out of KP on account of it. I'm not sure, though. At any rate, KP is a cinch here. I can't say anything about a rating. There's another private who does the same work and he's been here for a long while. However, I won't be disappointed if I don't get a rating. It's pretty late to get ahead in the Army and I was lucky to get the good job I did.

It was cool today with a nice sun. I had a complete physical and I'm getting some GI glasses, and my teeth need a little fixing. I don't think anything can be done about the condition I spoke to you about. It doesn't seem to bother me a bit and it's hard to fake anything. If we do ever go over, I'll be in the rear so I'm not worried.

Feeling fine, take care of yourselves.
Love and Kisses,
Charlie

Tuesday, January 11, 1944

Dear Folks,

It's drizzling a little now. We're probably in for a rainy day tomorrow.

Did quite a bit of typing today and my work looks pretty good. I was sent to eye clinic for my GI glasses, so I missed the entire morning. My civilian glasses are still perfect and now I'll be getting two extra pairs, all for nothing of course.

I went to the movies tonight and saw "Cross of Lorraine," it was good as far as the acting went, but it was the same old stays of Germans capture some French-man and the prison camps, etc. same stuff.

You'll have to understand that very little new happens when you're doing a regular job such as I am doing. Therefore, my letters will be pretty boring. There

---

[93] A tasked duty to guard the front entrance to the barracks. Usually two soldiers, one a non-commissioned officer and the other a junior enlisted service member, sit at a desk to monitor incoming and outgoing traffic into the barracks. Sometimes there were additional duties, such as sweeping the entryway, cleaning the entrance restrooms, and checking the barracks laundry room for laundry left overnight. Other duties may include performing radio checks every few hours with other company barracks and battalion headquarters.

just isn't anything to write about. I do the same work every day and that's all. But I'll try to keep writing daily.

Lights go out in the whole camp at 9. That's very early, so most of the men are going to the day room to read, write and listen to the radio. I just heard Bob Hope. If I get to bed too early, I can't sleep, so I usually hit the hay about 11. That gives me seven and a half hours sleep, plenty for the kind of work I'm doing. I haven't received any of my mail from Benning yet. I wish it got here.

Nothing more, be good and write me the news. Send my love to Grandma.
Love,
Charlie

Wednesday, January 12, 1944

Dear Mom, Pop, and E,

Got the letter you wrote Sunday night. It was postmarked 10:30 Monday morning so that's pretty good time. I thought it would take much longer, even for Air Mail. I really expected some dough. I certainly need some. Please send it right away if you haven't already done so.

They "bust" men very often in a regular outfit like this. "Bust" means to demote a grade. Our First Sergeant was busted to Staff Sergeant and many times in the office I see sergeants and corporals broken to privates. Well, they can't bust me any lower. That's one advantage of being a private.

Dad, remember when I had $35 or so withheld on my salary last summer? Well, I put it in the last book of the little Encyclopedia set we have, I mean the receipts. Send it down to me and I'll try to get it back. I'll file a tax report and submit the receipts and should get the dough back, please send it soon.

It's real nasty today, rainy and cold as heck. It's much colder here than it is in Georgia. Real New York weather. We get as much food as we want. Since we're in headquarters, our Mess Hall gets the pick of the rations. 10 men sit at a table and all the food is served family-style in bowls. As soon as a bowl is empty, a table waiter refills it. I have to watch that I don't eat too much, I'm not kidding.

Tomorrow the whole Battery goes through a close-range combat course. We fire the carbines at targets as they pop-up. I've been through a similar course at

Benning. I'm going out with the morning groups. This morning I drilled for half an hour and must admit that we marched much better at Benning. The day was easy in the office with very little to do. It's practically a gold brick job.

The wind is howling, but we're mighty warm in the barracks. We have an automatic heater and we regulate the heat by the use of a thermometer on the wall just like in a high-class home.

No more news right now.
Love and Kisses,
Charlie

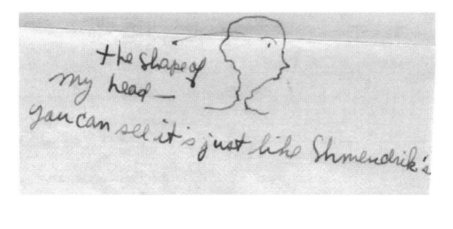

Thursday, January 13, 1944

Dear Mom, Pop, and Sis,

Here I is again. We had a very warm day and I can already see what a delightful summer we will have. We're pretty near the gulf and I understand that is fairly comfortable here. I'll just wait and see.

Another easy day. Did a couple of hours of typing in the afternoon, but nothing else.

Our General just came back from the entire division headquarters, that is the 102nd Infantry Division. He was acting Commander, but the new Commander came in today[94] so now the general of the artillery is back in Artillery HQ.[95] It's funny having a general running around the place. His name is Busbee.[96]

Got the book "Undercover" from the library. That's the book which exposes all the fascists. It's pretty good, but it gets boring and parts.

I'm waiting for the tax receipt, Dad. Please send it soon.

How's the weather folks? I bet you could use some of our sunshine. But for all we know, it could be freezing tomorrow.

The shorthand is a little too difficult to learn by yourself, so I'm giving it up. It'll take me years to pick it up well enough to take dictation.

Say, E, do you get into bed with Mom on Sunday mornings? That's what I'm looking forward to on my furlough. Say, the four of us will all crowd into Ma's bed. How is that? And Daddy will keep yelling that the bed will break and he hasn't the money to buy a new one with. Oh, what a *Shmiel*[97] he is. He's so cute, isn't he, girls? Does he ever sing his Yiddish songs with that fine bass voice of his? He has a lot of talent, my Daddy has. (Incidentally, how's his shape-head coming along?)

I love you all and think of you all the time. Be good children and take good care of yourselves.
Love and Kisses,
Charlie
צודעך לייביש בען שמיל

---

[94] General Frank Keating (February 4, 1895 – April 28, 1973) took over command of the Division from Major General John B. Anderson. General Keating was a career officer in the United States Army since 1915. He led the 102nd Division from January 1944 until February 1946. After commanding the 102nd Division in World War II, he was appointed Governor of the US Zone of Germany and was later Chief US Military Advisor to Korea.

[95] HQ - Headquarters.

[96] General Charles Manly Busbee (1893-1970) was the commander of the 102nd Division Artillery from August 1942 until February 1946. In February 1946 he became the commander of the 102nd Division until its de-activation later that year.

[97] Yiddish adaptation of Samuel Fletcher's Hebrew name, Shmuel.

Friday, January 14, 1944

Dear Comrades,

Don't get alarmed at the time. We have to have someone up all night at head-quarters and three fellows are taking turns. I'm staying up from 12 to 2, so pretty soon I'll retire. I had one and a half hours' shnooze before 12 and I'll sleep from 2 to 6, so it won't be so bad. It doesn't happen very often. It's very cold tonight and they're afraid the gas heaters which are in all the buildings might go haywire, so every building on the reservation has a guard.

Now you don't have to believe me, but it's snowing to beat all hell. Gee, it's so strong. There's at least two inches of snow on the ground and it's still coming. This sure reminds me of home. Everything is so nice and white.

I thought I'd be getting away with KP but the rules have just been changed and all privates in HQ, two others besides myself, will pull KP. It's a snap down here, so I don't mind it.

There's a disadvantage of getting into a division so late. This outfit has been going for 14 months, and of course, all the ratings have been handed out. So, I doubt whether I can get one. No matter how good you are, you can't be pro-moted unless there's an opening under the "tables of organization." And as far as I can learn, there's no openings in HQ's TO. But as long as I'm in the rear, it's worth it going without stripes. Don't you think so, folks?

Saw "What a Woman" tonight. Very good, any picture is good today, in my opinion, if it has nothing GI about it. No soldiers in it, then it's a good picture.

Be good,
Love and Kisses,
Charlie
What's the latest on Artie?

Friday, January 14, 1944

Dear Folks,

Received your letter with the $5, thanks a lot. Snowed all day and just stopped in the early evening. It's white all over and looks very nice.

Work is very easy. The Commanding General of the Division came to our office today. He used to be the Commanding General of Artillery, now he's boss of the whole works. He recognized me as a new man and asked me my name, I told him it was צודעך לייביש.

Went to basketball game tonight. Pretty good, but I'd rather play than watch. Got an OD suit out of the cleaners, they do a poor job as many of the spots are still on the trousers. But you can't help it.

Nothing more, have [98] גיטע וואך
Love,
Charlie

Saturday, January 15, 1944

Dear Mom, Pop, and E,

I'm getting all the letters you wrote to Benning. They're just being sent down to me and I get some every day. I'm glad that E is doing such a good job in housekeeping. She does have a little bit of talent and I'm happy that she helps you the way she does. Although it would be nice if she was still with Art. Perhaps E's premonition that Artie is still in the States is correct. I hope so. But, again, let me tell you that you have to expect it and you should be confident that he's coming back. He's a personnel clerk and those men have to keep doing their same routine job even if their outfit is in combat. So don't worry, Artie will be in the rear echelon and that's the safest place.

Texas is a winter wonderland now with all the snow on the ground. It's melting pretty rapidly and should disappear soon. It warmed up so today, that we're walking around in our shirts. That's how funny the weather is in the South. Snow is such a rarity here that people go nuts. Enclosed is an article from the

---

[98] Yiddish: Good week.

San Antonio paper. With a war going on the headline is about the snow, so you can imagine how rare it is here.

Had another very easy day, got off at 11 in the morning to practice with the basketball team. Went back to work in the afternoon and got through a little after 3:30. There's no such thing as half-day here but we usually finish on Saturday around 3. Weekend passes are very hard to get unless you live in Austin, so I won't be doing much traveling. I'm going to try to get my furlough pushed up but I don't know if I'll have any luck. I'd like to come home next month sometime or else early in March; as it is now, I'm due for a late March or early April furlough.

I doubt whether the Division will go overseas for some while yet. We're sending replacements to other divisions that are ready to leave the country and that weakens us and puts us below normal strength. That means we have to get replacements and train them before we sail. The way it looks now, we'll go on maneuvers in the summer or fall. The Division returned from their first maneuvers late in November. All this is unofficial, and I may be all wet, but that's how it looks. Don't be talking about it much to people because the strength and readiness of divisions is supposed to be restricted information.

I'm doing my first KP here tomorrow. It's too bad it had to come up on a Sunday, but I don't mind. Now I won't have it on a Sunday for a long while. We just got a new man in the barracks. I think I told you he was going to work in headquarters. Well, he's doing some other type of work. The thing I wanted to say is that he has a good radio and now we have music, news, etc. in the barracks all the time. One of the fellows left on furlough tonight to Altoona, Pennsylvania. How I wish I was traveling in that direction.

Thanks for getting that gift for Irene. When I heard that Mom and E picked it out, I knew it had to be good. What marvelous taste those two women have, eh, Dad?

Love and Kisses,
Charlie

Sunday, January 16, 1944

Dear Folks,

KP was a snap today. Had time for a nap during the afternoon and got off for the day at 5:30. That's 6:30 your time. I heard Jack Benny and the Finch Bandwagon and then I went over to the library. Took out "A New World a' Coming." It's about the Negro in the US and it's centered on Harlem, mainly. There's a very interesting chapter about the black Jews. The congregation in Harlem has nearly 5,000 members. There are about 10,000 black Jews in the country and close to 3 million in the world. The author even describes the congregation during the singing of *Kol Nidre*.

We had a very nice day. The sun was out and there was a nice snap in the air. The library facilities are excellent here and I plan to do a lot of reading. I've got some shorthand books out, but it's very hard to learn it without instruction. But I'll keep trying. As yet I haven't been asked to take dictation and I doubt whether they expect me to.

The adjutant in the office comes from Wilkes-Barre. I haven't had a chance to speak with him yet, so I don't know whether he knows the Nelsons. His name is Becker, but I can't tell whether he's Jewish. It would be funny if he knew Mendel.

Sunday is a lazy day in the Army. Everybody sleeps real late and in the true sense of the expression, "it's a day of rest." If I get off early enough next Saturday I may go to Austin with the boys I know from home.

You want to hear something funny? I want to know how all the boys that I did Basic with did in college, and whether they like it, etc. So I typed up a stencil and mimeographed about 20 copies in the office and sent it out to the fellas. Some timesaver, eh? Oh, am I thankful to have the head like Daddy's. Say, Edith, I never looked at your head shape. If it's like the Old Man's, consider yourself very fortunate. It's a great blessing to have a head like *Shmiels*.

Nothing more, will write again soon. I've written every day since I'm here. Ain't I good?

Love and Kisses,
Charlie

Monday, January 17, 1944

Dear Folks and Eadie,

Was kept busy this afternoon with some typing so I feel as if I've earned my pay today.

We saw a training film today, "Know Your Ally, Britain." All about the English people and how similar their ideas are to ours.

Tonight I heard the Division band give a concert. They played marches and college songs, it's a pretty good band. You have radios all over the place, so I keep up with the news and some of the old programs. There's really nothing new, the snow has disappeared and it's getting pretty warm.

Feeling fine, take care of yourself. Send me the tax receipt and E send me a blank (tax). Get it at one of the banks in the neighborhood.

Love,
Charlie

Tuesday, January 18, 1944

Dear Mom, Pop, and *Yentele*,[99]

Every day I say I won't write the folks because there's just nothing to write about, but sure enough, when night comes and I sit down to write a few letters I always end up by writing to you. Incidentally, I haven't heard from you in quite a while. With Eadie home, I should be getting mail a little more often - don't you think? I hope everything is okay and that E got good news from Artie.

Yesterday it was pretty cold and there is some snow on the ground. Today it was a real spring day, so you figure it out. The sun was good and strong and it was just like Georgia.

I received a letter from Irene today and she said, "I want to thank you very very much for the bracelet. It is simply lovely. Whoever selected it has a grand taste. It is one of the nicest gifts I've ever received." So, thanks a lot for sending her

[99] Yiddish: Edith's Yiddish name, Yenta, meaning "aristocratic; noble," or, literally, "nice; well-meaning; good-hearted." The "le" added to the end of the name is a term of endearment.

such a nice gift. I'll probably never see her again, but I felt I owed her and the family something and I'm very glad I did send her something. Other people also appreciate your talents, Mom and E, you two ought to start a buying syndicate. With Daddy's head, you'll go far. Incidentally, E, rub your hand over Dad's head and tell me if it has still got that good shape which indicates genius.

Heard from Al Jacobs today, he is still in South Carolina and recently transferred into Special Services; my racket is probably just as good. I also heard from Irv Fogelman, Joe Nelson and the gal I correspond with from Connecticut College for Women. I had a pretty good day with the mailman. The girl from Connecticut is the one who lives in Brooklyn and the one I took out a few nights before I left to serve my country in this great organization. If I knew then what I know now, I would have told the psychologist that I never went out with girls; explain that one to the folks, E.[100]

One of the boys (I call anybody a boy) in my section is going to the hospital for hernia operation so now there's only the Sergeant and myself. We may get another man, I hope not because this way I'll be kept busy and show them what I can do, or can't do, take your choice.

All the men in our Battery who do survey work went out on a long night problem this evening. That's one good thing about the job, no field work while we're in Camp. We all have to take one 25-mile hike a month, though. Believe it or not, I miss some of the exercise I was so used to doing. I'm living an entirely different kind of life now. I'd prefer the kind I led at Benning, if there wasn't a war going on, but for the duration I will try to stay close to the typewriter; don't go showing this letter around because it's not such a good way to look at the Army.

Nothing more right now. Take it easy and before you know it, it'll be 1950 and all the boys will be home - that's a joke, so don't get scared. Between you and me, if Artie and myself and all the other guys are home by the summer of 1945, I'll be very very happy. What's your guess? I'll be sweating it out in the Army, that means to keep waiting for the day or time until something will happen.

Irv sends his regards. He just returned from Hawaii. I'd like to have his job. He's really not in danger especially since his plane avoids combat zones and he

---

[100] A reference to the policy of the United States military at the time of excluding homosexual persons from the draft or volunteering for military service.

sees the world. I think I'll quit this job, I'll speak to the boss tomorrow and tell him I'm going home.

Love,
Charlie

Wednesday, January 19, 1944

Dear Folks,

Received nice letters from both of you today. Thanks for the buck, if you send me a few more of them it will tide me over until payday.

Dad, everything I tell you is the truth. I'm not trying to make you feel good. I never complained during Basic because there was no sense to you knowing all the stuff we did. Of course, Basic was tough and you and Mom probably knew it. But I'm through with Basic and an altogether different story now. I do hardly any work and the job looks pretty permanent. If I hang around long enough I'll probably get a rating, after a couple of guys die or something.

Tonight, the Battery's basketball team is playing a game and I'm going over to the gym about 8. I'll probably play in the game; the gym is a five-minute walk from the barracks. That makes it so nice, at Benning it was about a mile away and I never did get over to the place.

Enclosed are two blanks and here's a story about them. I'm entitled to a Class B allotment if I can show that I contributed approximately 40% to mother's income. If you have two people sign affidavits, $22 will be taken out of my pay and the government will add $15 making a total of $37 for Mom. I think it's a pretty safe bet because most of the boys are doing it here. At Benning, very few boys applied for it and I didn't want to take a chance. So talk it over and see if you want to get two friends, anybody, and have them sign it. I've done over one in pencil to show how I think some answers should be made. Let Eadie help you. You'll get the regular $15 for February but if you send these papers back soon you'll get $37 for March. Out of the $37 I want you to send me $17, so you'll be keeping $20, a $5 increase over your present allotment. We might as well get the extra $15 from the government and I think you should send the papers back to me signed. There's no checking up, but be sure not to spread the news to a lot of people that you're getting an allotment. Just keep it to yourself.

The reason I asked for $17 for myself is that after the $22 is taken out, I'll be left with $30 and I want to have around $30. So works out better both ways.

Very mild today, almost warm. The sun is very strong. There are two swimming pools on the post, so I'll be going swimming once it gets hot. Mom, I know you'll do everything possible with the building. Nobody has to tell me that, I'll drop Grandma a line tonight, don't worry.

Hi, E. Dad tells me you had no word from Art. Don't worry, kid. No news is the best news possible in his case. Before long, you'll hear

Charlie's graduation photo.

from him and he'll be safe and sound wherever he is. How are the folks getting along? Has Dad explained to you what I mean when I ask him if Mom is still a changed woman? Ask him to tell you about it.

Nothing more,
Love and Kisses,
Charlie

Sunday, January 23, 1944

Dear Folks,

It's 11:15 now and I suppose *Shmiel* is serving Mom breakfast in bed and that E is reading the Times in the breakfast room. Have any bagels this morning? How are Daddy's eggs tasting these days?

I went to Temple Friday night, and I was very disappointed with the services. I enjoyed going at Upton and Benning, but I doubt whether I'll go here very often. It may be due to the lack of a regular chaplain. Swift's Jewish chaplain left some time ago and his replacement isn't due for another month. So, the JWB[101] representative from Austin comes over to run the service and some soldier acts as the rabbi. So it was a pretty poor service and in addition, I didn't care one bit for the class of Jews that attended the service. It was a real *mocky*[102] bunch and when the Christian chaplain was nice enough to deliver the sermon a lot of the men started to read magazines. Well, there are good and bad in every race. It was a pleasure to go to services at Benning because there was such a nice bunch of Jews.

After the service we had some refreshments and even though I didn't like the whole thing I thought that I had better sample the food. I was right, wasn't I? So I had some herring and salami sandwiches and two bottles of Coke and two pieces of homemade cake and some potato chips. That was the only good part of the evening and the stuff was delicious.

I'm glad that you're back at 590, E. I hope you're completely recovered from the sore throat. Take care of yourself. The folks have enough worries as it is. I bet Mom tells you the same thing. I think $5 is enough for the *bar mitzvah*.[103] Some close relatives only gave me $5 at mine and it was sufficient. Have a nice time and don't throw too much candy at him, I doubt whether it'll be Orthodox. I'll drop Jack a line, perhaps I'll be able to meet him.

Now about Artie. I knew he would be okay and now you know he's landed safely. I understand why you should get blue, E, but you'll get used to it. Get a good job and you'll be doing a lot for both of your futures. He'll be coming

---

[101] Jewish Welfare Board.

[102] Yiddish: Term of disapproval, from Hebrew word "*maka* - plague."

[103] The coming-of-age milestone in Judaism, at age 13.

home safe and sound and you'll be ready to take off right where you stopped. Mom and Pop, there's no reason to worry about Art. E is doing all the worrying necessary and save yourself the aggravation. I repeat that he'll be okay and please don't worry.

What's Simmy doing, E? I thought he'd write to me but he's probably been too busy with school. He graduated already, hasn't he? I'm glad that Stelly is happy at school. I'll write her a line up there. She writes a nice little letter.

Say, how about an answer on that war bond receipt. Have you received any yet? I have a $25 bond all paid up for it and I start on my second bond this coming payday. Don't worry if you haven't heard about them, but let me know and I'll check up. It takes a long time to work these things out and I know some fellas who had quite a few bonds but no receipts.

E, in the near future please get my diploma and ring. Have the bookstore send the ring down, please. I'd appreciate it loads. And when you start working, or if there is some money left from my $15, attend to my graduation picture at De Kane. All I want is three big ones and cap and gown. They're only $12.

What's new with the family? How is Grandma and Grandpa? I dropped them both a line recently. Mom, if you haven't mailed out the package yet, put in a lot of cookies from Cake Masters. That's what I like. But if you already mailed it, don't bother to mail me another package for a few weeks. I get enough to eat and you might as well save the packages for maneuvers or something like that. I don't do too much work now and I will never work off the meals. So I don't like to stuff myself.

Well, here's the latest about the weather. It was a real summer day yesterday and it looks like rain today. It's much warmer here than it was in Georgia. Real short-sleeve weather.

No more right now. Will write again tomorrow. Please excuse the little lapse in my correspondence, I took a day off from writing.

Love and Kisses,
Charlie

Sunday, January 23, 1944

Hiya Folks,

Just came back from the movies, I saw "The Fighting Seabees" - it's a good war picture but you wouldn't go for it. Too much noise and excitement. Had a quiet day, wrote a lot of letters and had a very good dinner in the Mess Hall, roast beef, etc.

I could use a couple of bucks. I've got some stuff in the cleaners and I wanted to take it out. It looks like rain and it should come down any minute.

One of the men in the office just became a daddy, a baby girl. I'm just about the youngest guy in the Battery although there are many fellas in their early twenties. Is E getting a $40 or $50 job? With her talent, there's no telling, eh Pop?

Love,
Charlie

Monday, January 24, 1944

Dear Mom, Pop, and Sis,

Well, I did my good deed for the day already. I just finished a V-Mail letter to Artie, and told him all about the place, etc. He'll be surprised to hear from me so soon but that's the least we can do for the boys overseas. That's just about the only personal contact they have with folks back home. How often are you writing him, E? Or should I be able to answer that one myself?

It finally rained, I think I told you it looked like rain yesterday. It held off until today and it's been coming down all day. Tomorrow we go on the monthly 25-mile hike. I hope it stops raining by then. Everybody must take the march and all the officers from the general down will be tagging along. I'm ready for it, I was in excellent condition when I left Benning and I think I'm still in pretty good shape although this soft job is wearing me down.

Today the new general of the division came visiting and I was "elected" to yell "Attention" when he came in. That's no honor, I sit near the door so I was the logical one. Boy, did I come out with a loud, "Tenshut!" They must have heard me miles away. While we were drilling this morning, that Lieutenant called on some of the men to drill the Battery and since I never drilled the boys before, he called on me. And if I must admit it, I was pretty good. This outfit doesn't even compare with the ASTP boys at Benning. We drilled real well there, here they just don't give a damn and with my Basic Training experience I was really able to drill them well. After another ASTP boy who is here and I drilled the Battery, the officer commented on what good men the Battery is getting, etc. A lot of baloney.

I would mail this letter Air-Mail but I haven't any more stamps and my limited capital of $0.25 does not allow me to purchase any. Therefore, excuse the regular mail. And it's also a hint to send a few bucks.

I think I told you I'm reading "Undercover." Well, Mom, remember your old friend William J. Cameron[104] who used to give a short speech during "Old Ford Hour"? Well, he's a fascist through and through and one of the biggest anti-Semites in the country. And you always made Eadie and I listen to him and you made Daddy shut up when you knew he was talking. Hah, hah, hah. You never know who a person is, the author of the book tells all about Ford's[105] anti-Semitic feelings and how Cameron edited his paper and what they wrote about the Jews.

Had an easy day, didn't do one darn thing except type for 5 minutes. Boy will I be a gold brick when I get home. And so will a couple of other million soldiers.

One of the boys in the barracks had a big can of peaches in his footlocker. He stole it from the Mess Hall a few days ago. Well, he opened it up tonight and I shared the can with him. Darn good. I shouldn't say that he stole it, he knows the Mess Sergeant and he gets anything he wants. We got a lot of canned goods, this Mess Sergeant of ours is an old-timer and he seems to know how to get the best of everything. It's an established fact and we have the best Mess in division artillery.

No more right now, write soon, keep well, God bless you all.
Love and Kisses,
Charlie

---

[104] Newspaper editor most well-known for his work at The Dearborn Independent, a Michigan newspaper owned by Henry Ford. Through that publication, he authored a series of anti-Semitic articles known as "The International Jew."

[105] Automobile manufacturer, Henry Ford.

Tuesday, January 25, 1944

Dear Mom, Pop, and E,

Boy, what a hike we had today. 25 miles is a lot of walking, let me tell you. You know how happy I am that I have Daddy's shaped head. Well, if I was lucky enough to have Dad's marvelous feet, I wouldn't mind the hike one bit. (What a joke that is, eh Dad?) In the Infantry we walked very slowly and 25 miles is a snap but we went along rapidly today and I was a little tired at the end. However, I finished the whole march and all I've got to show is a few blisters, and they'll go away in a couple of days. Tomorrow the whole Battery fires the carbine for qualification and I go along. After that I'll probably be cooped up in the office for a few months.

Got a nice sunburn today. It was a cloudy but the sun came out for a while. I got a tax form today and I'll mail it in soon with the receipt of my withholding tax. I hope it doesn't take 2 years for the government to refund the money. I received the receipt today in Eadie's letter.

I'm sorry to hear that Mom has a cold. Please take care of yourself, Mother. You can't afford to get sick these days. I hope Eadie feels better now. Get rid of that sore throat, Sis. If Anna's cold was so bad, you shouldn't have stayed around for so much. Next time, watch out. Now, how is Daddy's health? I know he's a very smart man - he should be with his head - and I'm quite sure he's watching out for himself. Say, Pop, are you taking 5 or 6 vitamin pills a day?

I dropped Jack Nathanson a line and I should hear from him in a few days. Incidentally, I still hear from that friend of yours, Bernard Fillion. He is still at Benning and I just got a letter from him the other day.

I definitely do not like Alan as a name for your first son. The main reason, of course, would be that Alan Jacobs would never get over it and will talk about it for the rest of his life. I'm not kidding. Why is he going to Alan? Is it the nicest name you can think of? I like the girl's name, though. When am I going to become Uncle Charlie? Mom and Pop will make such nice Granny's, don't you think so? I hope the kiddies have heads like our Old Man's. Then they'll be ok. Oi, such a fine head on *Shmiel*.

Hope you have mailed me a couple of bucks by now. I'll be expecting some greenbacks to fall out of one of your letters soon. What are you doing about the application blanks I sent home? It's pretty safe and I wouldn't worry.

Nothing more right now. Everything's fine and I'm feeling swell. Be well and don't any of you get sick. That's an order, even if I'm only a buck private. Write soon. I'll be seeing you in a couple of months. Yippee!

Love and Kisses,
Charlie

Thursday, January 27, 1944

Dear Folks,

This is turning out to be a very busy week. We fired the carbine yesterday morning and I qualified. In the afternoon I was in headquarters. Today the Battery had to go through the infiltration course, but since I had gone through a short while ago at Benning I was excused.

So I had an easy day in the office, tomorrow I'm on KP and Saturday we have a big inspection by the new general. So I'll be busy. Tomorrow we all fire the pistol in the morning, so I'll be away from the kitchen for a while.

E, you told me Artie already has a new job, assistant to the first sergeant. That job is just as good as the one he has. He's still in the office and he'll have in pretty soft if he's with the first sergeant. That's a very important thing in the Army, to be on the right side of the first Sarge. It'll be okay, don't worry. Have you written to him yet? Or more important and I meant to say, have you heard from him yet?

Thanks for your letter, Pop. It was nice to hear from you directly. I'm glad Mom is still a changed woman.

I'm completely recovered from that 25-mile hike, not that I was ill or anything. Just that the muscles which were inactive for such a long while were bit stiff for a day.

Today we heard some boys who have seen action give short talks. They all said that the artillery is way behind the lines and suffer very few casualties, and I'll be further behind if we ever go over.

It's very mild these days, no cold weather at all. Everything's just fine. Received a delicious chocolate fruit cake from Mrs. Witt today. I thought it was very nice of her to send it to me.

That's all now,
Love and Kisses,
Charlie

Saturday, January 29, 1944

Dear Folksies,

I'm already in the office, as you got a very early start this morning. The new general's making inspection this morning and we all got up at 4:45. When a general makes an inspection, they act *mashiga!*[106] I'm telling you, they think God is coming. Every inch of scrubs, every window cleaned, and there's no rest for anyone before inspection. We have a full field layout on our beds and every-thing is just so, toothbrushes all in one direction, etc. Well, I'm all set and now I'll stay here in headquarters until 10 AM when the general's due in the bar-racks. A big deal!

It's raining very hard now. It started during the night, when it rains it really pours here. I got my two pairs of GI glasses yesterday. Now I have three pairs of glasses, boy I'm getting rich. Glasses were also fitted for my gas mask but I haven't received them yet. I'll probably hear from the dentist soon. I know I need some work done and they'll be after me soon. Oh, you don't know how much I hate going to the dentist.

And very glad to hear that you got a letter from Artie. He sure does abide by all the censorship rules. In a few weeks he'll be able to tell you his location - some-where, someplace. I'm glad you're getting used to it, Eadie. You just have to make the best of it. While he's away you can take good care of the folks, because

---

[106] Yiddish: a form of the word *mashugina,* an exclamation to describe something as crazy or bizarre.

after the war you'll be spending all your time with Artie in your own home. Have you got the job yet?

KP was pretty easy yesterday. I got off for a while to go for the eyeglasses in the morning. I had to fire the pistol. KP is just a pain in the neck, nothing hard about it.

Some of the officers are coming in now so I'll close. Will write a bigger letter soon. Let's hear from you. How is Grandma feeling?

Love,
Charlie

Sunday, January 30, 1944

Dear Folks,

Hiya all, here it is another Sunday and the news is so good today that I just hope I'll be spending all my Sundays at home soon. I had such a good time last night that I'll tell you all about it. My friend from NYU called for me about 4:30 yesterday afternoon and we started off for Austin, some 35 miles away. We got a hitch down to the main gate a mile away from the barracks and there was a bus just loading for Austin. We got two seats and off we went, we made the trip in 50 minutes.

Austin is about the cleanest town in the state. It's the capital of Texas and so much nicer than Columbus, that it isn't even funny. We went into a very good restaurant and I got a filet mignon dinner for $1.35 and it was delicious. Then we went over to the Jewish Welfare Board and my friend signed up for a bed. I couldn't stay overnight as I had to be back in Camp. Then walked around town for a while, they have a beautiful Capitol Building. The University of Texas is also located in Austin and it's a beautiful school. I didn't see much of it, but it presents a real college site, nice buildings, large campus, etc.

Well, we went back to the JWB. They have dances every Saturday night and the girls from school attend. One week the Alpha Epsilon Phi sorority attends, the next week the STD girls come and DPHIE the following week and the independent girls come another week. Eadie will explain the name. They're girl sororities at University of Texas and believe me, nearly all of the girls are attractive. They come from all over Texas and they're all very nice.

There are so many pretty young girls in town. There are a few thousand co-eds at school and only a few hundred Navy boys at school, so the girls welcome the soldiers. In all the other towns there aren't enough girls for the fellows, but it was swell last night. At the dance there were more girls than boys. I'm glad that the JWB runs our little clubs. It's a place to meet nice girls and if I ever want to sleep in town, they always have cots available. So if I get a pass every once in a while, it'll be all right.

I must tell you two funny things, pure or coincidence. When I walked into the JWB, I could have sworn that I knew one of the girls from NYU. After a while I approached her and asked her where we met and sure enough it was a girl who sat near me in a Sociology class. Her husband is an Air Cadet at a nearby field. Now the other stories, I have a fraternity brother Lou Beck, who is a navigator cadet, and I knew he was stationed nearby. I didn't write him yet but for some reason I had a premonition that I'd meet him. And sure enough, about midnight when I was going for my bus, I bumped into him. He's getting his commission next week and may stay around here for a while. He used to be a pretty frail guy but now he's built out. He was called to active service last January 31st and he's getting his commission practically a year to the day of entering the service. So are few of the other boys from the fraternity; well, I suppose I'll remain a private.

I'm glad to hear that Eadie is getting cheerful letters from Art. It's nice that he's writing so often. Just write to him often, E, and he'll be satisfied. By the way, you asked me if you could bake anything for me. Well, when you get time after taking care of Grandma you can make some cookies or cupcakes. Tell Mom not to bother with a package. I have all I want to eat and really don't need any extra food. Why are you going to Brooklyn so often? I heard from Stelly and I'll write her today.

I go on guard tonight at 5 AM. We pull guard about once every 20 days, or something like that. We're on until 7 tomorrow morning. You walk for 2 hours and sleep for 4, and then repeat it. Oh me, the life of a soldier. If it wasn't for those little details this job would be a snap.

The inspection was a farce yesterday. We were up at 4:45 as I told you and nobody came around until 2:30 PM and then it wasn't the general but some lieutenant colonel. Well, that's typical Army for you.

Take good care of yourselves, E, don't try to do too much. Take care of your health and stay with the folks. Go out, of course, so don't run around too much and don't run yourself down.

Send my love to everybody. How's Grandpop?
Love and Kisses,
Charlie

Monday, January 31, 1944

Dear Folks,

All's well on the Texan front. Had a nice easy day after walking guard last night. I didn't enjoy that any too much.

E, please attend to this affidavit as soon as possible. If you don't send them back right away I have to wait an extra month. I told the Battery clerks to put me down for the allotment on next month's payroll and don't wish to fail him by not submitting affidavits. Then they'll be a lot of red tape. So please get them signed, by anybody and mail them to me this week, the latest.

Have you received any bond receipts yet? Let me know please, because I want to check up. The bonds are good as gold, but I want to play it safe. Thanks for the $2, it came in handy. If you send me $5 of the $15 you got this month, I'll be okay for the rest of the month, I hope. I don't spend any money needlessly, but everything costs. I must keep my OD's clean for the office and that costs dough. It also costs at least $3 to go to town. And that's doing it mighty cheap.

Saw "A Guy Named Joe" tonight. It's an Air Corps movie and pretty good. Spencer Tracy is a fine actor.

Nothing more now. Will write soon.
Love to all,
Charlie

Tuesday, February 1, 1944

Dear Folks and Sis,

It's 12:50 PM now and I just finished a good dinner. I got back to headquarters a little early so I'm going to get off my letter to you now, if I can.

Nothing new since last night. One of the fellows who works with me is supposed to go to the hospital tomorrow, he's been putting it off for some while now but it seems that they finally caught up with him. If he does go, I'll probably get out of KP and the table waiter will be short-handed at the office. I hate to see the guy go (he's going to get a hernia operation) but it'll be pretty good for me.

It's cool but not cold in the least. We haven't seen the sun for quite a few days but having quite a little rain. It's funny the way I go to the movies here. It's the major entertainment of all Army camps. I haven't been going to the movies a lot the past few years but here I take in a few a week. "Madame Curie" is playing tomorrow night and I'll be sure to see it. The movies cost $0.15 and yesterday I bought a book of 10 tickets for a dollar twenty. Now if I run short of dough, I'll have tickets for the show.

I'm nearly finished with "Undercover" and I'll get another good book out of the library, I might as well do a little reading.

The Battery is taking a 2-hour hike this afternoon, but I'm not going along. Drilled a little this morning and we all had a gas mask drill. Serious.

Mrs. Witt has your phone number and may give you a ring when she hits New York in March. So just send my personal regards.

Nothing more.
Love,
Charlie

Friday, February 4, 1944

Dear Mom, Pop, Grandma and Sis,

Received Eadie's nice letter today. Say, Pop, did you forget how to write? I'd like to hear from you occasionally.

I know how swell it must be to hear from Artie every day. I hope he continues to write daily. With all your mail and Anna's and Eadie's packages, he'll be okay. He'll even get along without them. Don't worry, they take good care of the boys overseas and although he won't get everything he wants to eat, he'll have enough. Perhaps now that he's missing the steaks, etc. he'll appreciate them more when he comes home. I think all the boys will. So, E, you haven't a thing in the world to worry about. He'll be coming home safe and sound.

Don't even count on it, my furlough may start on March 16th, Thursday. It's not definite so I shouldn't have mentioned it, but it's a likely date. Only five more weeks - yippee!

Have you done anything about a job, Sis? I know some girl who just got a clerk's job with the War Production Board in the Empire State Building and is making $36 a week. So with your experience I know you'll get something real good. Keep me posted.

Hello, *Bubba*.[107] I'm so glad to hear that you're out of the hospital. Get well real quick and stay well. I'm going to take you out dancing when the war is over. How's your boyfriend, Sammy? I hope he's getting along okay.

We're just counting the minutes until we go to chow, so I thought I'd knock off a letter to my dear ones. I could use a few more stamps. In fact, I haven't any right now. I haven't received the package yet but it should be coming in this afternoon or tomorrow.

I won't be on KP for a while. I'm pulling Charge of Quarters at Headquarters while my boss -the Sarge - goes on his furlough. Eadie will tell you just what the CQ does. Artie probably had it as his duty at Bowie.

It's real summer here already. The sun is good and strong. How's the weather up home?

Thanks for the tax receipt. It's not important but I'll hang on to it. Answer me about my bond receipts. Have you been getting them?

---

[107] Yiddish: Grandmother.

Nothing more right now. I'll write soon again. Let's hear from you, Mom and Pop. Regards to the family. How are the Bialos? I'll drop them a line soon.

Love,
Charlie
צודער לייביש

Saturday, February 5, 1944

Dear Mom, Pop, Sis, and Grandma,

Another week gone by already. The weeks sure do fly by. I was supposed to be CQ Monday and Tuesday night, but I changed with a boy. I'm taking Saturday and he's going to take the two weekdays. I didn't intend to leave Camp anyway, so it's a pretty good deal for me. I'll be relieved at noon tomorrow (Sunday). Next week I'm definitely going to Austin again - unless something unforeseen pops up.

Today I really did some work and that's because I was by myself. The Sergeant started his furlough yesterday and the other fellow is in the hospital. So I had to do everything myself and I was kept busy. It felt pretty good to be hustling. I hope they don't bring anyone in to help me. I like to be busy, I feel I'm doing something useful.

This evening at 5 PM I played a little basketball with the Battery team. We lost as usual, and only by one point. I got in the office at 6 PM with a quart of milk I took from the Mess Hall. With the milk in one hand and your delicious cookies in the other, I went to town. Yes, your package arrived today and it sure was swell. Everything arrived in good shape and the cookies are nearly gone. They were sure swell - Cake Masters, I bet. I haven't had much of the other stuff. I'll save it for a while. Thanks a lot. Now you don't have to send me a package for a long while.

How are you all feeling? Still hearing a lot from Artie. I wrote a long letter to Jo-Jo and added a little message for Sammy Weisberg and Aunt Rose.

This CQ is a snap. I sit in the office and do whatever I want. There's a good radio and I have a few books to read. I open a cot when I'm ready to go to sleep and I have my sheet and comforter. I'll get a good night's sleep tonight. It's also a good chance to catch up on my letter writing. That's what I plan to do tonight.

What's new by you, *Shmiel*? How's Mama behaving? Is she a changed woman? I'm sure she's not working too hard. Is she closing up by 8 PM every night like a good girl? Say, Pop, does Ma still snore like an *AK*?[108] Remember how she used to snore when I was home and she always said she didn't, and she tries to say you snore. Why, Dad, I never heard you snore in my life. That noise you make when you sleep is just your healthy breath.

Nothing more right now. Right now I suppose Daddy is shopping for the week and is waiting in line in the Farmery. Are they still busy as usual? How are the pushcarts, Mom? Any good bargains lately?

Love and Kisses,
Charlie

Sunday, February 6, 1944

Hello Folks,

Heard from you today and got those affidavits back. Surprised that Edith didn't follow instructions. You had to show 40% dependency at least to get an allotment and I gave you a sample copy. Mr. Charman only showed 10% and probably wouldn't sign the other statement showing 40% because he knows it's not true. Well, leave it until I come home and we'll see what we'll do.

Yes, it's a shame that Clapper is dead. He was one of my favorite columnists and commentators. Enclosed is a letter I received today from Murray Goldblatt. I wonder if he's anywhere near Artie?

Eadie, I hope you're working by now. I can't see any sense in delaying going to work. You should be kept busy so your moods can't get the best of you. I hope you're acting very nice for our parents, they have nothing else but you and me.

It's hot as anything. Today was really a scorcher. I went to the movies this afternoon and saw "Standing Room Only," enjoyed it.

Mom, don't think about sending me another package. I can hardly eat all the stuff. Wait until we go out in the field or something. Not worried about money.

---

[108] Yiddish: *Alte Kaker*, meaning an elderly person, old timer.

However, it costs $43 and change to come home (RETURN TICKET), I'll need $50 on or about March 1 for the trip. I'm buying it in advance so I can reserve a seat on the train coming back from New York. It's almost definite that I'm leaving here the 16th of March. Will arrive in New York on late March 18th. I go from Austin to St. Louis and then straight through to New York. I can use a couple of bucks, not much.

Please try to get along, the three of you. It's about time there was some harmony in the home. E is married and I hope that Mom doesn't force her to practice the piano. That's her business now.

No more right now, be good and take care of yourselves.
Love to all of you,
Charlie

Monday, February 7, 1944

Dear Folks,

Yesterday marked my fifth month in the service. I'm still a rookie compared to some of the fellows in the Division. Most of the men have been in for at least a year. Well, I have a long way to go for that.

Gypsy Rose Lee visited Camp Swift tonight. I passed by the gym and stepped in to see her perform. It was the same old burlesque stuff Dad and I used to see down at Minsky's. Remember when you took me down to the girlie shows, Dad, and we told Mother we went to the aquarium?

Was in the office until 2 PM today and then the whole Battery went out to the combat village. We fired 15 rounds of ammunition at various targets through a make-believe German village.

Getting along very well by myself. I'm a little inexperienced but I think they realize that after a few more days, I'll be as good as the other fellow who has been here for a year. There's nothing like doing the work yourself. The Sergeant showed me a few things at times, but he always did the actual work himself. Now that I'm doing the stuff, I'm catching on to all the little tricks and I'm really learning my job.

Will Grandpa be home in March or do you still think he'll be in Wilkes-Barre? I go through Pennsylvania on my way home and in order to see him and get it over with, it may be worthwhile to stop in W-B for a few hours and then to continue on to New York. Once I'm home I don't want to take a day out to travel down there, I'll have enough travelling to do without that. Let me know what you think.

The entire Division Artillery is going to Camp Bowie for an Army Ground Force test around the 20th of March. We'll stay there for two weeks or so. I don't think that will interfere with my furlough - at least I hope it doesn't. There's always so many rumors concerning the Division. Eadie will tell you how many rumors Artie must have told her about the 4th. Well, the latest is that a cadre[109] is leaving the Division to help form another artillery unit and that definitely means that we'll be over here for another six months. But I find that it's best not to pay any attention to any of the latrine gossip and just wait for the things to happen. So all I know is that we're here now and should be here until May 1. After that, I doubt if anyone knows what will happen.

I had some snapshots taken tonight and you should have one in two weeks. I just took a cheap picture. I'll wait for a good one in uniform when I get home. Well, nothing else. Hello, Sis, I received your letter. Thanks, it's nice to hear from my big *schwester*.[110]

Love,
Charlie

---

[109] In this instance, a cadre is a group of soldiers responsible for the specialized training of new recruits.

[110] German: Sister.

Tuesday, February 8, 1944

Dear Folks,

Received your nice letter today, Mom, and was glad to hear from you. I'm still waiting to hear from the Old Man. I'm sure Grandma is getting along okay.

Say, Eadie, I hope you're not neglecting the piano. You got something worth a million dollars and you shouldn't give it up altogether. You might not want to follow it as a career but since you are an accomplished pianist you shouldn't lose your skill. Wouldn't it be silly to forget all that you know? When Artie comes home you'll be stepping out and I'm sure he'll want to show off your talent. Isn't it worthwhile to practice occasionally so you won't waste everything Mother and Dad gave you? I hope you see what I mean and spend some of your free time at the piano.

Nothing of importance happened today. Getting along okay. Took some letters from the General. He knows I can't take shorthand and he went nice and slow. He's a pretty nice guy. Also did some court-martial orders by myself. The Sergeant will be mighty surprised when he returns. I'll be able to do nearly everything he does.

Read Sunday's Times tonight at the library. It's always nice to read the hometown paper. I received February's Digest, Sis, gee that was nice of you and Artie to send me a subscription.

It's still very warm. The entire Division Artillery is going out in the field Friday night for some practice firing tests. I don't know whether I'm going out, I may stay in the office with the Major - the adjutant. I've forgotten what it is to be a field soldier. But once we go on maneuvers, I'll learn mighty quickly.

Munching on the prunes and figs right now. Still have a lot of the stuff leftover Please don't send another package until I ask for one. I really shouldn't be eating all the stuff.

I took an OD suit out of the cleaner's this evening. They charge 50 cents for a dry-cleaning job, but they don't do such a hot job. I'll let Mr. Israel do some of my clothes when I get home.

Well, there's really nothing more. Mom, I can see in your letters that both you and Dad are working much too hard. Why don't you lay off a little? Just don't try to do every little thing. You're getting old, both of you, and you should ease up a bit. Please.

Love to Grandma,
Love and Kisses,
Charlie

Thursday, February 10, 1944

Hello Folksies,

Took a night off from writing last night. But I'll try to make up for it tonight, although there isn't too much to write about.

Have been kept very busy for the past few days and I'll probably be on the go until the Sergeant comes back from his furlough. The Division Artillery has a firing test on Friday night and Saturday and everybody is going out in the field Friday night. I want to see just what I do in the field, so I don't mind going out tomorrow night. I'll be with the office section and will be doing some typing, it should be a lot of fun. I'd like to see the Artillery in action, I've never seen any of the big guns fired. I type up all the crazy things about them but have never seen them. All my work has been satisfactory and I think the Major likes the way I work - at least I think he does.

Have been leaving the office a few minutes after five recently, and by the time we eat at 6 I already have my daily shave and shower. So after chow, I'm set to do what I please. There is a Beginners Spanish course starting tonight and I'm going to attend to see what it's like. Perhaps I can pick up some Spanish while in the Army. I've intended to do a lot of work, but after a day's work I find it very hard to sit down at a desk again. I'm sitting all day and I like to walk around. I'm really lacking in exercise and at times I worry about it. We may go into combat some day and although I'll still have my present job, living conditions won't be too good and I'll be soft. Oh well, we'll wait until the time comes. Before our next 25-mile hike, I'm going to walk a few miles every night to get into shape. That should make the big one much easier.

I had planned to go away for the weekend but I doubt whether we'll be back until late Saturday from the field, and it would be foolish to take a weekend pass that late. So I think I'll wait until the following weekend and perhaps go to Houston where I have a good friend from my school.

I received a nice letter from Stellie. She tells me she writes almost every day to her big brother overseas. Boy, that guy is probably getting the most mail in his company.

How are you feeling, and especially Grandma? Is she coming along nicely? Nothing more of interest right now. Take it easy and have a good week. The weather is nice, although it showers a little too often.

Love and Kisses,
Charlie

Friday, February 11, 1944

Dear Folks,

I've never written to you under these circumstances, so I'll take a little time to describe what we've done so far tonight and just what it's all about.

We left the office at 6 PM in a 2 ½ ton truck with a trailer attached. Now the entire headquarters staff comes out in one truck, but when we arrive in the field - all wooded, the truck leaves the S-1 and the S-4 section[111] off with the trailer. I'm in the S-1 so I get off and all I need is in the small trailer. Tonight, I'm with the sergeant of the S-4, and the first thing we did was set up our tent. It falls right back from the trailer and is about 10 feet long and 6 feet wide. We brought out a big field desk and set it up on a wooden desk in the tent. It opens up and I put this typewriter on the bottom part. We have a few folding chairs inside another desk. The Major has a big lantern and that gives us all the light we need. Now we're all set up for work although there won't be anything for us to do. We're supposed to dig foxholes outside but we're not going to do it unless they tell us to, and I hope they forget about it because it's a pain in the neck to dig in the pitch dark. I just stuck my head out of the tent and it's very cold and black as anything.

Isn't it funny? For the past three weeks we were running around in our shirt sleeves and then last night we got a cold wave and tonight it's very cold. The winds really blow down here and that's what makes it so uncomfortable. I

---

[111] S-1 section is responsible for administrative support activities, whereas the S-4 section is responsible for supply and logistics.

think we'll sleep in the trailer and it won't be too bad. One thing I like is that you hardly carry anything. We threw our bed rolls in the trailer and you just grab it when you're ready to make a night - a favorite expression of Mother's.

Gee, this chair is very unsteady on the ground and I start tipping over every few seconds. I brought out a couple of oranges and a box of cookies in the field desk, so I'll be able to *nosh*[112] a little tonight. Boy, this is living in the raw - but much better than those bivouacs at Benning. At least I have a chair here. The Major has a big stove, but I doubt whether he'll set it up just for one night.

Tomorrow the Division Artillery is going to put on its demonstration and the entire Division came out tonight. When the Artillery is on the road in march formation, the column stretches for about ten miles. Everybody comes out in some kind of vehicle. The Major just came out and he looks pretty cold. I'm wearing that big heavy blue sweater and my long johns and a field jacket and am pretty warm.

Gee, Dad, I'd love to have you here now. You'd die laughing to see how the whole thing looks. The Division is all laid out now and we probably extend for about five miles in the field. Telephones are rigged up right away and the General has direct control. His tent is just a little distance away.

Saturday, February 12, 1944

Hello again,

The enclosed letter (Friday the 11th) was written last night, but I wasn't able to mail it so I'll send it along with this letter. I had to end it abruptly as the Major came in and we set up the stove I mentioned. It was plenty warm in the tent. The Major shot the breeze with us for a little while and then we went to bed about eleven o'clock. The Sarge and I slept together in the trailer and we had loads of blankets and comforters and were plenty warm. We missed breakfast and slept through until 8:30 this morning. There just wasn't anything for us to do. About ten o'clock the Sarge went back to sleep, and I read "The Battle is the Payoff" a very good book by Capt. Ralph Ingersoll, former editor of PM. We had a very good dinner at noon and then all the officers and a lot of the men went out to see the shooting.

---

[112] Yiddish: Snack

I stayed in the tent with the Sergeant. I was sorry to miss the shooting since I've never seen the guns in action. As soon as everybody left for the observation post, we took down the tent and packed all our stuff. We laid a blanket out on the ground and the sun warmed things up quite a bit, so we laid down and slept. I must have slept for three hours before I came in with the Major in a big command car. So that was all there was in going to the field.

It was silly to take our section, but that's the way the Army wants things done. We got in garrison about 5 and after doing a little work in the office, we were free. I washed up and shaved and then had supper. After chow, I showered and put my stuff away and took off for the movies. I saw Frisco Kid with James Cagney, it's an old picture but I hadn't seen it, so I went. I enjoyed it. Tomorrow, Broadway Rhythm is playing and I'll probably take that in. I'm not going to town this weekend so I might as well go to the movies. I still have plenty of tickets left in the book I bought.

It's pretty cold tonight, I understand February is the cold month of the year in Texas but it really isn't bad. The days are very comfortable, and the barracks are good and warm at night. I got a good sunburn today and I feel swell.

Dad, I haven't had time to look at the tax return yet but I'll do so tomorrow morning and I'll write you an air mail letter about it. However, right now I think it's best to pay the $23. I haven't been able to keep up with the taxes lately, but I know they're hitting most everybody and if you can get away with $23, it sounds pretty good. At any rate, I'll look over the papers and see if I can improve on the tax.

Until I write tomorrow, I remain your ever-loving son, Private in the Army of the United States,

Charlie

Sunday, February 13, 1944

Dear Mumsy, Popsy, and Sissy,

Just thirty-three more days and I should be starting my furlough. I'll start counting the days now. We're going to Camp Bowie for a week or so around the middle of March and I may leave from there. But nothing's definite as yet so I'm not sure of a thing. I just hope my furlough isn't delayed on account of the trip to Bowie.

I heard from my good friend, Al Rosman, who went to school with me,[113] the other day. He's the fellow I met down in Alabama one weekend when I was in Georgia. Well, he was a cadreman at Ft. McClellan until last week. Now he's home on an eight-day furlough and after that he's off to Ft. Meade, a POE.[114] See, you can never figure it out. For a while it was a break for him to be a cadre, but just look how fast things change. A cadre is the soldier who trains new men. Well, I hope he has some good luck when he goes overseas.

The weather is very, very nasty. It's cold and it has rained all day. But we're in garrison now so it really doesn't make any difference. Our barracks are good and warm and I'm always indoors. I went to the 2 PM show today and saw Broadway Rhythm, which proved to be very entertaining. We had a very good roast beef dinner at noon. Mash potatoes, tomatoes, peas and carrots, peach pie, ice cream and coffee. The meals are excellent on Sunday. I slept until 11 today so I didn't have any breakfast. Next weekend I want to go to town because I get a little stale hanging in Camp all the time.

I heard from Irene Witt today. She finally landed up in Newcomb College, the women's college of Tulane University in New Orleans. Also heard from Aunt Rose and she gave me all the dirt about W-B. I hear that my kid cousin Joe is developing into a good poker and crap player.

Dad, I looked over the figures today and won't be able to do anything until I get a blank tax form. I'll be able to pick one up tomorrow and I'll see if I can work anything out. I doubt it though, and you may have to depend on the Rothenberg fellow.

---

[113] Charlie and Al were childhood friends since elementary school; they stayed in touch during WWII and for the remainder of their lives.

[114] This refers to a Port of Embarkation. Devoted to efficiently loading overseas transport, an Army POE was a command structure and interconnected land transportation, supply and troop housing complex.

Went to the Spanish class the other night and I think I'll continue to go. A 2nd Lt. in the WAC's teaches the course and she is a native of Mexico and knows the language. The class meets for one hour on Tuesday and Thursday evenings at 7:30.

Well, nothing more right now. Will write again tomorrow. Hope there's some news. Eadie, I think the folks are right about a job for you. You should have some time for the folks, they really need you. If you make ten dollars less a week, it won't make a bit of difference a few years from now. But the time you give to the folks may help a lot. Think it over.

Kiss Grandma for me,
Charlie

```
Here are some of the more important items and I'm following y
    figures to a certain extent. I've made some changes and just
    compare them with your figures.

Labor        Mary's $30 / $587      =      $2147
Materials- purchases                       2095.45
Rent                                       1200
Electricity- you have no gas in store      175
Social Security Expense                    15
Unemployment Insurance                     40
You counted $40 twice but you really
only pay Workmen's Compensation
Advertising                                162
Window cleaning                            36
Judgement paid in 1943                     473
```

Monday, February 14, 1944

Dear Mom, Pop, and Sis,

All's well and serene on the Texas front. Not a darn thing out of the ordinary occurred today and I haven't much to write about. I was supposed to be CQ Wednesday night, but I took a fellow's place tonight and I'll be through with it for the rest of the week. I'm in headquarters now and a few of the officers are taking some map reading tests and it's pretty quiet.

We're going down to Camp Bowie on March 9th and as far as I know we'll be leaving for our furloughs from there. But as I told you before, nothing's definite so don't bank on anything. Eadie, what's the best way to travel if I come home from Bowie? Is it easier to go through Chicago or is via St. Louis the best route?

Oh yes, after I got in bed last night we had just about the biggest rain storm I can remember. All of a sudden at about 11 PM it came down in bucketfulls, with the lightning and thundering to beat the band. Boy, I got under the covers quick when the lightning started. It was just like those heavy showers we get in New York in the spring. I fell asleep shortly after the downpour started, so I don't know how long it lasted, but while it did it sure came down mighty fast.

Now Dad, I'll take some time out and try to work on the tax return. I just got a return from my friend and I'll use it as a guide. Dad, one thing you neglected to do was mail me a copy of last year's return. I believe I gave it to you before I left, or else it's in my drawers in the little room, in the top drawer. I'm sending the papers back with some suggestions and a list of expenses you should show the tax man. If you want me to work on them some more, I'll be glad to do so if you mail me back last year's return with all the papers. Remember we worked out some depreciation schedule - well, that has to be continued this year and it's a deduction from your tax, so be sure to show it to Mr. Rothenberg. I'll put down figures, etc. on the next page. But before doing so, I'll make some comments. Whenever they ask you for figures, don't give them round figures. Make believe you figured things out exactly so instead of giving labor as $1,400 or whatever it is, give it as $1,426.35 or some odd numbers like that. Also, your purchases on last year's return were $2,150 and this year you say you only bought $1,175 worth of goods. That means a lot as far as reducing income goes, so you might as well say you bought $2,095 worth of material. I'm enclosing a copy of the new tax return and am putting in figures in pencil. The form will be pretty complete except for the Victory Tax, which I know very little about and the depreciation schedule will follow.

Here are some of the more important items, and I'm following your figures to a certain extent. I've made some changes and just compare them with your figures.

Labor- Mary's	$2,147
Materials - purchases	$2,095.45
Rent	$1,200
Electricity- you have no gas in store	$175
Social Security Expense	$15
Unemployment Insurance	$40
Advertising	$162
Window Cleaning	$36
Judgment Paid in 1943	$473
Doctor Expense	$75
Value of Shop	You'll have to figure that out
Fixtures, Value of	$685

On the tax form in c(2) I have as an expense under 5. Materials and supplies $63.75 - that can mean wax for the floors, pins, brooms, lights, machine needles, etc.

I'm sorry that I can't be of much service, but it's hard doing it when I haven't you at my side to talk the thing over with. But if you increase your purchases a bit, I think it'll help some. Dad, I was thinking about your tax return quite some while ago and I figured that if you could get away with $50 or less you'd be lucky, because they're really getting everybody this year. So if you can settle for $30 or so, I think it's a pretty good deal although I know how much $30 means to you. But that's the way it is. If you still want me to work on it, be sure to send last year's return back soon. You still have some time but don't wait until the last minute. Don't forget window cleaner, store cleaner, and figure in the errand boy under labor along with Mary, if you haven't done so already. If you don't want to show materials so high, cut it down to $1,175 as you had it and increase materials and supplies which could mean plush, garter elastic, etc. It works the same way. Good luck on it and let me help if you want me to.

Too bad my furlough isn't coming earlier so that I could help you. How are you feeling, Pop? Write me and tell me the truth. Are you taking any vitamin pills? Have you still got a cold or are you all better? Please take good care of you and Mother. We want to have a few good years together yet. Take care and send my love to Grandma, Pop. I love you and the Old Lady a little. Do you think E, you, Mom and I can get in the big bed one Sunday morning when I'm on furlough? You *schlamozzel*,[115] you will have to make my breakfast on the Sunday I'm home. And the eggs better be scrambled or you'll have to make them over.

Love,
Charlie

Wednesday, February 16, 1944

Hiya all,

Rain, rain, go away, please come back some other day. Golly, it's been awful this week. It drizzles for a while, then stops, and sure enough starts drizzling again. Oh well, February is supposed to be the bad weather month down here and it will soon be over.

Today the Battery fired the carbine on a combat course. However, work piled up in the office and I couldn't get away. So, I'll have to make it up at some future date. It was good to know at the time that they couldn't do it without me. But once the Sergeant returns from furlough, I'll be playing second fiddle again. That's the way it goes, I guess. Did a lot of work today and most of it turned out pretty good - in fact, all of it was okay.

I just saw the picture "In Our Time" with Ida Lupino. It's a very good picture with some fine acting. It's about Poland and the German invasion, etc. Not too much war in it and I think you would like it.

I have made plans to visit a friend of mine, Bob Milles from NYC, in Houston this weekend, but I'm still thinking it over. Houston is 150 miles away and although that isn't too far, transportation is poor and I don't think I'll get off too early this Saturday. So I'm afraid I'll have to break the engagement. The kid made a hotel reservation for the two of us and he made dates, but I doubt whether I can get there before 9 or so and that'll be by hitchhiking, so I guess it's a little silly. If I weren't alone in headquarters now I could probably get permission to leave right after noon chow. Oh well, that's the way it goes.

Nothing else new right now. We are definitely going to Bowie on March 9th and I'm quite sure I'll go along. Furloughs are going to be continued, but they may need me - I really don't know. If I leave while we're at Bowie, we first drive

---

[115] Yiddish: unlucky person.

back to Swift and leave from here. So I still don't know anything for sure. The worst that could happen is my furlough be put off to March 25th or around there, so I'm not really worried.

Love and Kisses,
Charlie

Friday, February 18, 1944

Dear Mom, *Schmiel*, and *Yentela*,

Received your nice letter, Mom, and although I don't recall asking for Jo-Jo's picture it was nice of you to send it along. The only things I've mentioned about pictures in my recent letters is that I had some taken down here and will send them home when I get them.

How did Paul Bialo make out at the draft board? I hear of so many physically unfit fellows that they are taking now, that it's practically unbelievable. I know a few boys who were given physical discharges last August who were recalled recently and are now doing Basic Training in the infantry, just about the toughest branch of the service, so go figure it out. Well, I hope he manages to stay out. If you see him, tell him to drop me a line. I would like to hear from him. Send my best regards to the rest of the family. How are the girls growing up?

Next week over 1,000 recruits from Camp Upton and Ft. Dix are coming to the Division. That's a good sign, as far as I'm concerned. A basic training regiment will have to be started for these new men and that means the entire Division as a whole won't even be ready for overseas as a unit for quite a while. However, there is always the chance of individual replacements going over, but I'm sure that I'll be safe for a while. And I'll even be safe if I go over, so there isn't anything to worry about. I bet I know some of the boys who are coming down here from New York. Oh, the poor devils, Basic Training staring them in the face. I'm glad I'm over with that stuff.

Had an easy day and did accomplish quite a little work. The Sergeant returned from his furlough tonight so I won't be so busy from now on. Incidentally, the General was standing near my desk today and I was going over some accumulated papers. I didn't know he was watching me but went on with my business. I was throwing a lot of stuff away, as there were duplicate copies and things we don't save. Well, the General pipes up, "Fletcher, you're the kind of filer I like - the vertical one." Meaning, up from the basket and down into the wastepaper basket. That man knows his onions and is a very nice chap. The Battery is awarding good conduct medals tomorrow and one man isn't eligible on account of a court martial. Well, the General had me type up a letter of commendation to the fellow because he's been an exemplary soldier since joining the organization. I won't be eligible for one until I've been in a year.

It's raining again, as usual. If I get off early tomorrow I may still try to make Houston. Now that the Sergeant is here, I may be able to take off.

Have a good week and take care of yourselves. Love to my Grandma. I'll think about stopping in W-B first. I think it's the best thing, but I'm not sure yet. Regards to everybody.

P.S. Save the enclosed paper. It's a copy of the orders assigning me to the 102nd division. Maybe I'll show it to my kids someday.

Love and Kisses,
Charlie

Sunday, February 20, 1944 - "Lamar Hotel, Houston, Texas"

Hello Folks,

Well, I finally decided to make this little trip, and boy, was I lucky. I left Camp at 3 and got a ride to Bastrop. As soon as I hit the highway, I caught an MP truck to Smith-Hill, some 30 miles away from Camp, and then I immediately got a hitch with some contractor in a nice Chrysler and sure enough he took me straight to Houston - wasn't I lucky? I hit Houston at 6:30 last night and got into the hotel room at 7- two big beds and a nice room, so it was very worthwhile.

My friend, Bob, was out eating when I came but he left a note. I took my first bath (in a tub) since I got in the Army and at about 8 or so we met the girls in the lobby. Two very nice girls and we went out to eat, and I had a delicious steak. Then we went to a very nice dance hall - I would say it's like a New York night club but there wasn't any entertainment, it's like one of the rooms in a New York hotel. We stayed there to midnight, took the girls home and then retired to our lovely room. I slept like a baby on the big mattress and I didn't get up until 10 today. We went out for bacon and eggs and I took a walk around town.

Houston is a town of about 500,000, and it's still in its infancy. A very prosperous city, oil fields, factories, etc. and all the Jews own the stores on Main Street - Levy's, Battlestein, Sakowitz; some fun, eh, it's too bad we're not near Houston. I'm satisfied with Austin, but it's always better in a big town. You've never seen as many girls in your life. I hear that in peacetime there are three women to every man. Mother, come down and protect me from these women.

We're calling for the girls this afternoon and going to a movie. I am catching a 6:30 bus this evening and I should be in Camp by 1. I don't like hitching at night or else I'd thumb my way.

Nothing else right now.

Love and Kisses,
Charlie

Monday, February 21, 1944

Dear Fletcher Family and Annie,

Well, I'm back at Camp Swift again after a very pleasant weekend. I got into Camp about 12:30 this morning. I hitched halfway back to camp and took a bus the rest of the way. It was getting dark, and as I told you, I don't like to stay on the road when it's dark. We just walked around Houston Sunday afternoon with the girls and visited the library and municipal auditorium. The theaters were just too crowded, and we didn't try to get in. I took a picture in Houston with my friend and I mailed it to you this afternoon. Tell me how you like it. I think it's pretty fair, considering it was taken by one of these camera men in the streets.

Now, a little news you've probably read about, and just to show you that you can never tell what's going to happen, and that whatever does happen is for the best. The ASTP is being discontinued except for some advanced engineering, medical, and dental courses. Well, all the boys I went through Basic with will be leaving college very shortly and will be sent to infantry outfits. In fact, many of them will be sent overseas right away because that's been the policy with ASTP soldiers. Now if I were in ASTP, I'd be leaving college after a few weeks' stay and there's no telling where I'd go. I was lucky enough to get out of the infantry because there were just a few men at the time reporting with me. I think it's going to be mighty tough for the whole mess of boys coming down from school to seek individual assignments. They'll probably be herded right into the infantry en masse. Well, I hope things turn out for the best for all of them. And I feel mighty happy that I wasn't sent back to college. See, God does things for the best.

A little good news, although it doesn't mean much. My Battery commander used to be the General's aide and he's always hanging around headquarters. This morning the General was near my desk, and he said to my BC (Battery commander) "John, Fletcher has done some mighty fine work around here. See if you can give him a little something." Which really doesn't mean much, but at least the General knows I'm around. I'll probably make private first-class on account of the General saying something. Too bad the dummy didn't say to make me a corporal. A little something is mighty little. Perhaps I'll be corporal by 1945. I'll have to give the General a nice rosy apple tomorrow for being so kind.

We had a big Division Artillery parade tonight at Retreat. It's the first time we've had Retreat since I'm here, and it's a new Division ruling that each organization must have one ceremony each month, so we had ours tonight. It was very impressive to see the entire artillery parade on the field. We're 2,000 strong in the Division Artillery, some 14,000 in the whole Division.

The sun finally came out for a while. It was drizzling this morning but the sun came out in the afternoon. But I suppose the nasty weather will return soon.

I saw "The Sullivan's" tonight and it was good. If I didn't think you'd cry too much, I would tell you to see it. The only time it gets sad is near the end, so if you think you can stand a little sobbing, go see the picture.

I got a V-mail letter from Artie Saturday. He said he hasn't heard from me yet. I'm surprised because I wrote him while he was still at the POE and then I wrote him a V-mail letter after he had sailed. Perhaps my mail hasn't caught up to him yet. Edith, didn't you tell him where I was? He wrote to Ft. Benning and had no idea as to what I was doing. I bet you fill your letters with all kinds of mush, and you don't even say anything about the family or anybody else - well if you do, I don't blame you one bit.

I'm glad you're working, Sis, and I hope you continue to find the job pleasant. $42.50 is a nice salary to start off with and perhaps after a few months you might manage to get a raise. What's the highest paying clerical job in the place? It's nice to be doing government work and I just hope it doesn't tire you out too much so that you can't help the folks a little and be pleasant at home. No one I know works too hard at their government jobs and I hope you don't wear yourself to a frazzle.

Mom, don't you worry about coping with the Army cooks. You have them so badly beat, it's not even funny. Your *borscht*[116] tastes better than their steak, and you know how much better I like steak than borscht. I know you'll do wonders with the house but be careful not to work too hard. You know, you're no spring chicken. The figures I sent home to Dad are the figures he should show Rothenberg. He had better work the whole thing out with him.

We're taking a 25-mile hike Thursday and I wonder if I'll make it after sitting on my fanny for a whole month. Well, I'll do it and it won't be too bad.

I received a nice letter from the lieutenant who was my platoon leader at Ft. Benning. I wrote to him a couple of weeks ago and he wrote back a very nice line.

Nothing more right now. Take care of yourself and I'll be seeing you real soon. Better get the $50 ready and mail it to me early in March because I may be leaving here the 16th. Less than a month - yippee!! Don't worry about getting extra help when I'm home. You don't have to fuss a bit, just leave things normal. I'm no guest, but just one of the family and no fancy pantsy business. Don't make too many plans for me to go visiting with you that's out. I'll stay home with you and go out with you, but I don't intend to go traipsing all over New York. Also leave the weekend pretty free, because there's some dating I want to do. Edith, perhaps you can get some show tickets - a new play is supposed to be good, "Polsheka and the Colonel" or something like that. It's a very good comedy. Two tickets will be enough. But if you can't, don't bother - there's plenty of other places to go.

---

[116] A traditional soup made of beetroots.

Please be careful and take good care of yourselves. Don't catch colds and don't work too hard. I hope Grandma is feeling a little better. Will write soon again.

Love and Kisses,
Charlie

Tuesday, February 22, 1944

Dear Folks,

I was very lucky tonight. The Battery went out overnight for night training, but it happens to be my turn on Charge of Quarters, so I'm spending the night in headquarters. I may also get a break Thursday when the Battery goes on the 25-mile hike. I'm on guard Wednesday night and the hike starts at 7 in the morning. So I doubt it very much whether I'll have to make the hike Thursday. Guard usually doesn't get relieved until 7:30 AM, so the boys will have left by the time I get back to the barracks. Well, that'll be okay if it works out that way. Guard isn't too bad, as we only get it about once a month.

It rained again as usual this morning, then stopped for a while until the afternoon when it started to come down real hard. It stopped about 4 and it's still dry but not for long. It'll be a nasty night to spend in the field.

I'm going to do a lot of letter writing tonight and I'm sending a V-mail letter to Artie, Charlie Zwerner, and Murray Goldblatt. Edith, I just finished Ingersoll's "The Battle is the Payoff" and it was real good - just about the best war story I've read. It's true and his descriptions of a battlefield are very vivid. It's easy reading and if you're looking for something good, I suggest that book.

Had an easy day in the office. Nothing much to do when two men are around, but I manage to keep busy. The Sergeant doesn't mind if I do a lot of the work and he just takes it easy.

The kitchen went out in the field with the Battery since there were only about five of us left behind. Well, we had to make our own supper and boy, it was just like playing with the icebox when I came home late on Saturday nights. I had some cornflakes and milk, a lettuce and tomato sandwich and a jam sandwich. I made an extra tomato sandwich and brought it over to headquarters with me. I just ate it and it was good. I still can make those good sandwiches. I had nearly a quart of milk myself in the Mess Hall. If I had my way, I'd always make my own supper.

The boy I met here from NYU is leaving on his furlough Thursday. He's calling on you up one day next week to send my regards. His name is Seymour Rosenberg, so don't be surprised to hear from him. My furlough starts three weeks from Thursday, supposedly. I think I'll be able to make it. But don't count on it - I wouldn't want you to be disappointed if I didn't hit New York when you expected me. But I'll be home in March sometime.

Nothing new, so I'll close now. Probably won't get a chance to write until Thursday night. I could use a couple of dollars, if you haven't sent any money yet.

Love,
Charlie

Thursday, February 24, 1944

Dear Folks,

Well, things turned out pretty well the past few days. I walked guard last night and my post was in the Division Artillery airport, where we keep our ten liaison airplanes - planes that do observe for artillery firing. The 25-mile hike was postponed until Friday, and I was quite sure that I would have to go. However, the Major decided that the Sergeant should go since I made the last one and that makes me feel pretty good. Guard sort of tired me out and I was in no mood for a 25-miler.

Now the real big news. I have received my first promotion in the Army and although it isn't a big one, it's a start. I'm now a private first-class and entitled to all the privileges attached thereto. As if there are any privileges, except a four dollar raise per month. Enclosed you will find the order making me a PFC. A big deal, eh Pop? But you can't be a general overnight. This raise is due to the General speaking up for me the other day to my Battery commander. Remember, I told you about it? Now I'll have to sew - or have sewn- a stripe on most of my clothing. That'll be a pain in the neck. I'd rather not wear the one stripe but they make us.

We're having a big showdown inspection Saturday. It's to check to see whether we have all the equipment that was issued to us. The Army pulls a check like that every once in a while and if you're missing anything you have to sign a statement of charges. I believe I have everything that I got at Upton - or reasonable facsimiles. It's also practice for the inspection they have at the POE - if that day ever arrives.

My furlough is now definite and I'll be leaving Swift for home three weeks from today. It'll be here before you know it. When you send the $50, please try to send it in money order form. I don't want to have so much cash on my person, especially with the trip to Bowie coming up. I'll be sent back to Swift from Bowie on March 15th and will leave that night. So I should hit Wilkes-Barre or New York by Saturday morning. I may try to leave from Bowie, but the plan is to send all men back to Swift first, so there isn't much I can do about that.

Enclosed are two prints of a picture I had taken at the PX. It's a cheap picture but is fairly clear. Please give one to Grandma and keep the other for yourself. I'll take a good picture when I come home.

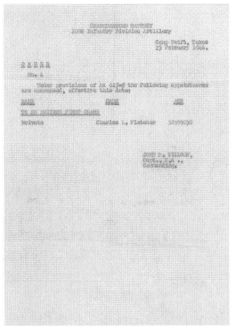

181

Nothing more right now. Your son is a real big shot now, a Private First Class. Wow!

Love and Kisses,
Charlie

Friday, February 25, 1944

Hello again,

Boy, what weather. We got up at 5:30 this morning and what a rainstorm. I never remember having seen it rain so hard. They cancelled the hike on account of the rain. At about 7 it subsided a little, but a little after eight the rain began to come down again for a couple of hours. It broke up a lot of the dirt roads and made them practically impassable. And the payoff - about 2 this afternoon, the sun came out and it started to warm up and we all sweated during the afternoon and now it's 8:30 and plenty hot. Those OD wools keep you pretty warm. I sure wish we could put on our khakis when it gets warm, but once you put them on you have to continue to wear them, so I guess we'll have to wait until March to change into the suntans. I can imagine what kind of summer we're going to have, if this is any indication of the weather.

Everybody is getting ready for the inspection tomorrow. We're having the showdown inspection I told you about. Some of the fellows take it so seriously that they are laying out all of their stuff tonight and sleeping on an empty bunk. But we have plenty of time in the morning to set up and all I did was get all my equipment together so that I'll have it ready to lay out. I also dubbed my shoes. Incidentally, that's a new Army regulation. GI shoes no longer have to shine, but instead must be dubbed once a week. Dubbing is the application of some grease substance that's supposed to soften the leather and preserve the shoe. I like it because I never have to worry about having my shoes shined. The reason we got up so early today was the hike - the usual time is still 6:30.

Had my stripes sewn on one OD shirt so I can wear it to work. I'll have the rest sewn on soon. It only cost 15 cents a set and it's worth it. I doubt whether I could do a very neat job with the one stripe, Dad knows how handy I am with a needle.

It was very slow all day until about 4 and then we got a little work that kept us going to 6. It's just like your business. For a while it's very slow, and then it all comes in at once.

Nothing more. Plan to spend a quiet weekend at camp. Did you send me a couple of bucks? Twenty more days and I'll be choo-chooing up to New York. Won't I be a happy man!

Well, that's all now,
Love and Kisses,
Your First Class Private,
Charlie

Saturday, February 26, 1944

Dear Folks,

I received your letter today with the three bucks and stamps. Thanks loads. Now I have most of my clothes in the tailor for the stripe to be sewn on. Next week I'm taking my civilian shoes into the repair shop for soles so that the hoofs are okay for my trip home. I'm getting most of my stuff cleaned so I'll look dapper on my furlough - as if you can look dapper in GI's.

The inspection turned out to be nothing, as usual. I was picked as a recorder and went along with the inspecting officer to go over the checklist as we examined the men's equipment. We got to my stuff last and he didn't even bother looking at it. However, all of my clothes are in good condition and serviceable.

It was very slow in the HQ today and I didn't do a darn thing. I left about 3 o'clock and went over to the barracks. We had a beer party scheduled for this evening and it started at 4. I understand the Battery has one every couple of months. They have it in place of the regular supper, and believe you me, it was mighty good. All the beer you want; I only had two bottles in addition to two cokes and all the fried chicken you could eat plus, cheese, chips, salami, and potato salad. I concentrated on the chicken and had three big helpings. They had over a 100 pounds of chicken, so you can imagine how much each man had. I really had my full. About 5:30 I laid a mattress on the upstairs porch - a little extension- and took a sun bath for a while. It was hot all day and the sun was very strong.

It's 7:30 now and I'm going to write a few letters. Then I'm going to see "Rationing" with Wallace Berry. I'm not going to town this weekend, but I think I'll go to Austin next Saturday. My friend is home on furlough now. Has he given you a ring yet? I read last Sunday's Times in the library a few days ago and I noticed that some good friend of mine got engaged. I used to date the girl and I went to school with the boy. He's a private in the Army. But everybody is either getting married or engaged. Richard Bernstein and Eleanor Feigenblatt.

Eadie, your job sounds fine and I'm glad you like it. Keep up the good work and I'm sure you'll get along okay. How's it coming so far? Is it very tough or have you caught on to it already? They're taking out enough, but as you say it's all savings, so it's okay. Too bad about Lazar and Lipps. I read about Morty in the Times a couple of weeks ago. Well, that's the way it is. I dropped Jack N. a card but he's probably very busy now getting settled in his new job. The trip home sounds good the way you describe it. I think we'll have to leave from Swift even though we'll be in Brownwood. Real snafu.[117] I better go through St. Louis because that's the way all the boys go from here. Was surprised to hear that Irwin Keit became a daddy. Time does fly. I expect to hear that Al Jonas's wife gave birth before long. That's just a hunch though, and nothing definite. Al is 4F[118] and is living in Brooklyn with his Mrs., an NYU girl. Keit is also married to a NYU grad. Send me a copy of the latest alumni bulletin and I'll bring it home with me, if you're saving them.

Well, kid nothing more.
Have a nice week, you'll get the letter Wednesday, so it'll be happy *mit'voch*.[119]

Love to *Bubba*,
Charlie,

---

[117] SNAFU – "Situation Normal, All Fouled Up"

[118] 4F - Registrant not qualified for military service.

[119] Yiddish: Middle of the week.

Sunday, February 27, 1944

Dear Folks,

Received Mother's nice letter with the two dollars enclosed. Thanks a lot. Now I have both the $3 and the $2, I'm buying little things that I need. After-shave lotion, toothpaste, blades, soap, etc.

I saw "Rationing" with Wallace Berry last night and I'm sure you will like it. It's funny and very entertaining and no war connection at all, so try to see it. Tonight I'm going to see "The Bridge of San Luis Rey."

Went to sleep around 11:30 and got up at 7:45 for breakfast. Went back to bed right after breakfast and slept until 11. Then I showered and by that time dinner was ready.

I think I told you the Division received some replacements this past week. Well, a friend from NYU came down and I went over to see him this afternoon for a little while. You may remember the boy. His name is Alan Marcher and he worked for me on the paper - he used to bring stories over to the house on Sunday mornings.

When you send me the money, use the postal money order. That's the easiest to have cashed. Don't worry about me being careful with it, it's only for my trip home and nothing else.

I'm leaving for Bowie on the 9th so if it's possible, mail the dough around the 2nd or 3rd of March. Be sure to mail it by the 9th if you have to wait awhile. Send it to the regular address at Swift. All the mail will be sent by truck to Bowie every day - it's only 180 miles or so.

How's E doing at her job? Say Dad, she has a little bit of talent, eh?

It's a nice day, a cool breeze making it very comfortable. Well, that's just about all. Take care of yourselves. Will see you very shortly. Love to Grandma.

Love and Kisses,
Charlie

Monday, February 28, 1944

Dear Folks,

Not a blessed thing happened today which would be of any interest and there is very, very little to write about. It was a cool day but the sun was shining strongly.

About 4 in the afternoon, we all went out with the Battery for some marching drill - for parades, etc. We have a night motor march tomorrow night, but I don't know whether I'll have to go on it. It won't be much. Ride out a couple of miles in a truck, perhaps dig foxholes, and then come back in the trucks. These night marches are mainly taken to give the drivers experiences in night driving.

Was going to see Ginger Rogers in "Tender Comrade" but I decided not to go. It's probably a real tear-jerker with a lot of sentimental scenes about a wife and her soldier husband. I'm not exactly in the mood for that kind of picture. So instead, I read some articles from the Reader's Digest and then went over to the library for a while where I read Saturday's Times and took out a book. Now it's 8:25 PM and I'm in Headquarters pecking on the typewriter.

It was very slow today. I didn't do a darn thing except compile the daily strength report and type a little paragraph on a court martial. I took a real GI haircut this afternoon. The new General of the Division has been stressing close haircuts, but that doesn't bother me. I took mine on Monday so that if I go to town on Saturday I'll have some hair by then. Boy, you'd die if you saw me now. I have coarse clippers all around except for the very top of my head.

Time does travel. Just two weeks from Thursday and I'll be on my way home. Please mail out the dough soon. Say, is Riley still with Grandpa? I've been wondering about that but no one ever mentioned anything about it. I'm glad Carrie comes around now. Don't keep her on my account, though, I don't need her one bit. But if you need a little help, she's a good girl to have around.

I heard from your friend, Bernard Fillion, Edith. I didn't think he'd keep up our correspondence after I left Benning, but sure enough I still hear from him. Personally, I don't see any sense in it, except to exchange views with a totally strange serviceman, but as long as he writes, I'll answer.

How's the weather in New York? It'll be a little different to wear an overcoat when I'm in New York. I've been going around in shirtsleeves for such a long while now. I gave my shoes in to be soled today- that's the civilian shoes I'll wear home. They sure needed soles.

Well, my dear parents, sister, and grandmother, there isn't anything else I can write about. Take good care of yourselves. I won't be able to write tomorrow night if we go out in the field. Take it easy, I'll be seeing you soon.

Love and Kisses,
Charlie

Wednesday, March 1, 1944

Dear Folks,

Went out on the night problem last night and the only after-effect is the lack of sleep. We had a blackout motor march for about 10 miles and then we took positions in the area. We were supposed to dig foxholes but there were a few foxholes already dug, so I didn't do any digging. We had to walk guard and do some crazy patrol work, and I only got about an hour's sleep. We climbed in the trucks for the homeward march at about 4 AM this morning and we got into the barracks at 5:15. I'm in Charge of Quarters today so I'm back in headquarters from an early chow. The Battery is having the afternoon off, but I think I'll have to stick around to 5 and then I have to spend the night here because I'm CQ.

It's easy to see why the men in the Battery are jealous of all the boys who work in headquarters. We're near the General, have office jobs, and the other men think it's a racket. Whenever we miss anything, they all put up a howl, etc. But today when they're all getting off and the headquarters boys are working, they don't say a word. But that's human nature, I guess. You know, I haven't done KP for almost a month now, and I'm just keeping my fingers crossed. However, the First Sarge will catch up with me sooner or later. But it's been pretty nice without any kitchen work.

It was cold for two days but it's warmed up considerably today and the sun is good and strong. It's a nice day for a sunburn but I'll have to stay in house. Boy, I'm going to open my cot early tonight and get a good night's sleep.

Nothing of any importance going on, so there's very little to write about. There's the usual rumor making the rounds about a cadre going out to start some new Field Artillery group late this month, but it's strictly of the latrine variety.

Have you mailed my dough down yet? Please do it right away if you haven't done so already. I'll still get it here at Swift. Don't forget to keep addressing all my mail to Swift while I'm at Bowie. We'll get all our mail every day.

Say, Sis, did you receive the copy of the Ozark song I sent you? It was just written a couple of weeks ago, and it's a pretty hackneyed tune. But I thought you'd like to keep it on file for later years. How's the job coming along? Did Stellie get over that sore throat okay? The Marshaks, you included, seem to be very susceptible to sore throats. Glad you're hearing regularly from Artie. I wouldn't worry about the bombings too much.[120] You know that everybody is taking a chance over there so it would be foolish to say he's absolutely safe. However, as long as he obeys the sirens and goes to the shelters, and I'm sure all American soldiers have to follow the regulations covering bombings, he'll be okay. And it would be a coincidence if a bombing occurred just when Artie is in London. So don't fret. He's just as safe there as you are when you cross 42nd Street. Take your pick.

Two weeks from tomorrow I'll be on my way. Hot dog. Take good care of yourselves and send my love to Grandma. Don't work too hard and don't worry, everything will be okay.

Love,
Charlie

Thursday, March 2, 1944

Dear Folks,

Another day in my military career has come to an end. That's the way I consider each day. Every day brings me closer to the day I'll get out of this khaki uniform and that's the day I'm waiting for - as if we aren't all waiting for that day. Well, it'll come someday. The news is so encouraging now that you can't

---

[120] At this point, Artie is stationed with the 4th Armored Division in England, undergoing training in preparation for the invasion of Normandy, France.

help but think that it may be over before we expect it to be. Oh, what a happy day that'll be, heh?

Well, I told you yesterday that the First Sergeant will catch up with me sooner or later. He didn't waste any time because I'm on KP tomorrow. It's nothing real bad but as I told you before, it's a pain in the neck. It's just one of the things you have to put up with in the Army. That's the reason I'd like to make corporal. Then you don't have to do KP. That's a Corporal in headquarters. However, all the other T-5 do KP in the Battery. We have so few privates that the T-5 has the same rank as corporal, but it's a technician's rating have to do KP.

Went to a USO Camp show tonight. It was pretty good. The USO sponsors these small show groups and they tour all the Army and Navy stations in the US. Nothing pretentious, but it's entertaining for the boys. Tonight there was an acrobatic dancer, a juggling act, a comedy act, a female vocalist and a trumpeter. So it's a regular variety show that goes over big with the boys.

Had a very easy day, as usual. There wasn't a darn thing to do and I just loafed away my time. Went to bed at 8 o'clock on Wednesday night, so I made up for the lack of sleep I had the previous night on the problem. Slept like a baby right through to 6:30.

All applications to the Air Corps have been stopped. I heard from my friends at the Citadel - fellows I did Basic with - and now that the ASTP was discontinued they were all applying for the Air Corps. They'll be a sorry lot when they find out about the new ruling. The rule indicates a few things. Either the Army Ground Forces were losing all the good men to the Air Corps, the Air Corps have all the men they think they'll need, or the AC is just stopping taking in new men for a while in order to call up all the men they have on reserve. Nobody really knows the reason for stopping the applications but that's how it seems to me.

Putting in for a pass this weekend. Would like to go to Austin on Saturday night and get over to the JWB. I haven't been there for a mighty long time. Say, did my friend call you up yet? The boy who is in my Division and who's home on furlough now?

We're leaving for Bowie at 6 o'clock next Thursday morning. It should take us about 5 hours to get there. It normally doesn't take that long but we're going in regular motor formation, and we'll only travel 30 or so miles an hour. We'll be stretched out for about ten miles on the road; that's some expansion, isn't it?

Well, there's nothing more right now. It's hard to find interesting things, so little happens here. It's just the same old baloney day in and day out.

Be good and take care of yourselves.
Love,
Charlie

Saturday, March 4, 1944

Hello Folks,

This past week has been pretty busy, so that's why I haven't written every day. We had another problem last night and we got in around 11. I helped the driver of our truck wash it up and I got to bed around midnight. Today I was table-waiter, so that kept me on the run. Table-waiters help set up the tables before meals and then clean up the dining room after chow. It just requires about an hour's time at each meal – half an hour before and after. I had to be on hand at tonight's meal so I didn't bother trying for a pass. I'm getting my furlough soon so I'm not too anxious to go to town. I may go to Austin tomorrow afternoon, but I'm not sure. I took one of the sergeant's CQ tonight. He has his wife down and this is the last weekend he will see her before we go to Bowie, so I told him that I'd do his CQ. I'll catch up on my correspondence and get a good night's sleep. There isn't any work attached to Charge of Quarters.

Well, eleven more days and I'll be on the choo-choo train. I leave here Wednesday night, March 15. Boy, I can hardly wait. I don't think it will delayed, Mother, and don't worry about Mary not being around. I'll still see you enough. Hey Dad, are you happy I'm coming home? Maybe I can deliver some packages for you, eh? I wish I were coming home to stay, but maybe it won't be too long now that we'll all be coming home for good. Gosh, I often think that Artie and I want to come home more than any of the other boys. But don't worry, that's one thing all the boys are hoping for, the day that they can all call it quits and come home.

Boy, Eadie, six letters in one day from the man you love. That's doing all right, isn't it? That sure was a good meal you had with the Marshak's at Lundy's.

How are Art's folks taking him being away? I heard from Stellie yesterday and now I owe her a letter.

What's new in New York? Glad to hear that you got a little merchandise from my friend, George. When the heck are they going to draft that guy? They sure are taking in some physically unfit men. I saw some of the new recruits in our infantry regiments and I doubt whether some of them could walk a mile, no less 25. The men are either 18 or 38 and I pity the older men because infantry Basic Training was never meant for anyone over 30.

Well, there really isn't anything new. "See Here, Private Hargrove" is playing here tomorrow and Monday, and I'll probably see it. I read the book and it was very humorous. They could make a good picture out of it and it's bound to be very funny.

Take good care of yourselves. Send my money if you haven't already done so. I can't hold up my furlough just because I haven't the dough. Mail it to Swift and I'll receive it at Bowie.

I'll be seeing you soon.

Love and Kisses, kiss Grandma for me. Tell her I dropped her Sammy a line Thursday night.
Charlie

Sunday, March 5, 1944

Dear Folks,

Received the $25 money order this morning. Thanks very much. I'll hold on to it until I'm ready to leave and then I'll cash it in. Send the rest of the dough as soon as you get it. In fact, I don't have to purchase a round trip ticket so if you just send another $15 or $20, it will be okay. I think I'll stop off in Wilkes-Barre for a couple of hours and then go on to New York. I can hardly wait. Ten more days, that's all, and I'll be on my way. Yippee.

Had a pleasant day. Slept until 10. We have a regular cot and mattress which we set up in the office when we're Charge of Quarters. We had a splendid dinner consisting of broiled chicken, peas, mashed potatoes, lettuce, ice cream, and fruit salad. The Sunday meals we have here are hard to beat. It's an accepted fact that Headquarters Battery, Division, Artillery, has just about the best chow in the division. In fact, the men still talk about the excellent food they had on maneuvers.

We received some special orders here this morning. Six hundred infantry men are leaving tomorrow for Ft. Meade, and from there it's overseas. That weakens the Division a great deal, 600 doughboys are quite a lot to take out of one division and it will be a long time before the men are replaced.

After lunch today I went to Austin. I had a pass for one day, so I thought I'd go to town. Nothing much was doing at the JWB because the University of Texas is in between semesters and most of the students are home. I went over to the campus and gave the place a real look over. It's a very fine school with plenty of land and many buildings. I watched some people play tennis and when I'm home I'm going to get some tennis shoes so I can play when I go to town. I met a house mother near the courts, and we chatted for an hour or so about the school, etc. I practically know her life history by now.

It seemed funny to be on a college campus. You still see a few fellows in sports clothes and a couple of roadsters motoring by with boys and girls. Those things seem to me so far away, that it's hard to see other people doing the things that I used to do not so long ago. There are plenty of Navy boys on campus and they seem to be having one heck of a good time. Unlike the Army, the Navy is continuing its college program. You know, I have some friends who left school before I did and landed good jobs in the Merchant Marine[121] out at Sheepshead Bay and are still stationed there. I wonder whether I would have been better off to have left school a little earlier and tried to get out there. But there's always that chance that they might have sent me out to sea after a while, and that wouldn't have been any picnic. So perhaps I'm just as well off here. But the ratings those boys are getting, wow! Most of them are petty officers now. Don't you worry, before the next war I'll get into something that'll keep me close to home. Or it would be better if I'd be a little too old for the next war. I know Mother is probably saying there will never be another war and I hope she's right.

---

[121] The Merchant Marine is comprised of both civilian and government-owned cargo and transport ships. In times of war, the Merchant Marine serves as an auxiliary and can be commissioned to deliver troops and supplies for the military.

I'm going to the late show tonight and seeing "Private Hargrove." So, I will have spent a very nice Sunday. Nothing more right now, take good care of yourselves and write soon. Don't stop writing just because I'm coming home. Send my love to Grandma, and I'll be seeing you soon.

Love,
Charlie

Monday, March 6, 1944

Dear Mom, Pop, and Sis,

Not a darn thing new on the Texas front. Received your letter today, Dad, and if I recall correctly you paid something like $2.65 tax on that return last year. The return isn't due until April 15, so I'll hold on to the papers until I come home and we'll try to fix them up.

I'm celebrating an anniversary today. Yes, six months ago I entered this fine organization and I've been married for half a year today. I hope I get a divorce real soon. This is the one thing I don't want to be married to, and don't you worry, I won't. Six months after this mess is over, I'll be on my way home, àéï à âàèò ùòä.[122]

Played basketball tonight with the Battery team and we lost, as usual. Seems that every time I play with the team, they lose. Had a pretty slow day in the office but I usually manage to find something to keep me busy or make me look busy. Most of the people in headquarters are busy with the Bowie trip and the way they fuss about a little thing like that makes me laugh. They'll probably go crazy when our turn comes to go overseas. Say, Edith, have you seen that confusion yet in your office? To be truthful, I've never seen a government or Army office run efficiently. There are always too many people employed and work that could be done by five capable employees is performed by fifty.

I saw "See Here, Private Hargrove" last night and it was very good. Be sure to see the picture and Grandma will like it also. It's very funny and strange enough, most of it is truth. There is quite a lot about the Field Artillery because Hargrove did his Basic Training at Ft. Bragg, North Carolina which is a Field Artillery Replacement Training Center. I sure did have some good belly laughs.

---

[122] Yiddish: In a good hour.

Poor Hargrove is always on KP and scrubbing garbage cans. You'll enjoy the show, so try to see it.

We all go through a gas chamber tomorrow afternoon. We were supposed to go through this afternoon but according to the best Army traditions, a slip was made somewhere and it was postponed until tomorrow. I went through a tear gas chamber at Benning and it wasn't bad. I hear they'll use chlorine tomorrow but there's nothing to worry about. Everybody in the Division has to go through it and nothing ever happens. It only takes a few minutes.

I'm going to retire early and get all the rest I can before our trek to Bowie. As I told you, we're leaving here at 6 on Thursday morn, and we'll probably get up around 4. We're eating breakfast off the mess truck as all the equipment will be loaded Wednesday night. We're due to arrive at Bowie a little after 1 PM. We're setting up a permanent tent camp and it's not going to be tactical, so it won't be too tough. Anyway, I'll only be there for a week so I don't care.

Nothing more right now. Take good care of yourselves and will see you very shortly. Love and kisses. My love to Grandmother, how is she getting along? Will be kissing you in person real soon.

Love,
Charlie

Tuesday, March 7, 1944

Dear Folks,

I just found out that I can go on furlough Saturday night. I imagine that you already have received and complied with the telegram I'll send you in a few minutes, as soon as I can get away from the office.

I hope you didn't mail the money because I don't know whether I'll get it by Saturday. Everybody is going to Bowie Thursday and I'm going to see if I can get away before Saturday night, but don't count on it.

Here's how I got the furlough for Sunday. A cook was originally scheduled to go on the 12th of March but he has to stay here while the Division Artillery is at Bowie so there was an open date. I asked the Major if it was all right and he said okay. Then my battalion commander gave his permission so it's all set. I prefer it this way because it will give me one entire weekend in New York.

I've been corresponding with a certain girl from Brooklyn who I met at Wakonda this past summer. She attends Connecticut College for Women and is a very nice girl. I plan to see her a couple of nights on the weekend of the 18th so don't make any plans for Friday or Saturday night. She's going to come in for the weekend from school.

Nothing more. If you don't tell Aunt Rose, I'll be able to surprise Grandpa. They don't expect me until the 19th. I'll see you around Tuesday. Too late to have all my stuff cleaned, so I'll have to wait until I come home.

See you soon, love,
Charlie

Wednesday, March 8, 1944

Hiya Folks,

It's still pretty early and I received last night's CQ so I'm in the office right now. I'll try to knock off a letter before the officers start coming in.

Didn't do anything much last night. There was a double feature playing but I knew the pictures would be crummy. When the boys got back from the show they all complained about the terrible movies. They were just a waste of time.

Edith, I wrote to my friend Jerry Evans, who is now sports editor of the Commerce Bulletin. I told him to get us some tickets for the basketball games on the nights of the 16th and the 20th. The Invitation tourney starts on the former date and the NCAA tournament starts on the latter day. So, I hope he can get us some tickets. See, I'm always thinking of my sweet sister. You will be the one who'll go to the games with me. Jerry lives at 2914 Jerome Avenue, if you want to get in touch with him and find out whether he got the tickets. I want to see the games and I hope he got some ducats. Too bad NYU isn't playing in one of the tourneys, but I suppose the team wasn't strong enough.

If I make good connections, leaving here Saturday night should bring me into Harrisburg, PA late Monday night and then I should be in W-B sometime

195

Tuesday morning. If you haven't said anything to Grandpa yet, I'll surprise him. I told him I'd see him sometime in March or April.

Oh, do me a favor. If Mrs. Gersh is still operating her salon, make some appointments for me in the morning. Maybe I can get to see her three times, I still think she did a lot for my skin.

That's all now, love,
Charlie

Thursday, March 9, 1944

Dear Folks,

By the time you receive this letter I will be somewhere in Virginia or a point further North. I thought it might be possible to get out of here earlier that Saturday night, but the Corporal who is in charge is afraid to let me go ahead of schedule. I can't blame him, though. There's always the slight chance of someone finding out and then he'd be in serious trouble. I'm getting out early Saturday afternoon, but there isn't a train to St. Louis until 9:30 at night so I'll have to wait for that train. There are only two trains for St. Louis, one in the morning and one at night. Too bad there isn't an afternoon train. I would have gotten a head start, but as it is, I've had a good break. It rained all day today and the poor fellows have to sleep outdoors. It's bad enough when it rains during a bivouac, but when it rains when you're setting up the area it makes it very uncomfortable and difficult. So it's a break in not having to go on the trip.

I'm really loafing the few days I'll be here. I was supposed to do KP today but I just stayed in headquarters and acted as Charge of Quarters. The Lieutenant who stayed behind needs me to help him on little things that come up, so I'll be in the office until I leave. The Division Artillery is getting about 1,200 men for Basic Training and the infantry is getting over 2,000 of the ASTP men, so you see the Division is building up.

No one knows what's really going to happen. It'll take quite a while for us to train the new men. The Division is going to send out some men in the lower IQ classifications to make room for the ASTP men. It's all mixed up but as it stands now the Division will net a gain of about 2,000 men, bringing us up to strength.

Went to Bastrop today to get the telegraphic money order cashed. Thanks loads, I can sure depend on my folks. I got the telegram Wednesday evening. It was the first time I've ever been in Bastrop and I hope it's the last time I'll ever go there. Oh, what a horrible place. It only has a population of 2,000 and it's a very small, undeveloped town. I doubt whether there are any fully paved streets. It's a good thing we're near Austin.

My friend who was in New York on furlough just returned and he dropped in to see me - I'm in the office now and I'm going to sleep here tonight. He lost the phone number and that's why he didn't call you up. He said the minutes just fly in New York, but I can imagine how fast time goes when you're home on furlough. Here's how I figure the trip. I'll be in St. Louis Sunday night and if I'm lucky I might catch a train for New York right away - that's about midnight and that'll bring me into Harrisburg around midnight the next night Monday. Then it'll be a matter of hours before I get to Wilkes–Barre. If I don't make connections in St. Louis, I'll have to wait until the following morning and take the early train bringing me into Harrisburg around Tuesday morning.

I'll definitely be in New York Tuesday night and I'll probably come in on the Martz bus which leaves Wilkes-Barre about 7 PM. Don't plan to meet me. I can find my way home by myself. I'm quite sure my furlough calls for thirteen days plus a day of grace, so I'm due back in Camp by midnight of the 25th. In order to get back in time, I'll leave the Penn Station 6:15 on the 23rd on the Jeffersonian, an express to St. Lou. So, I'll have about 8 days at home.

Furloughs are supposed to provide seven days at home and that's all most of the men are getting. They cut it to seven days last fall. I'm lucky to get a furlough right after six months. Some poor fellows haven't been home in over a year. I'm sure I'll have a nice time and it will be great to see you all. I wonder whether you're anxious to see me?

It's too bad that furloughs aren't for a couple of months instead of a couple of days. Then it would be something, eh? Well folks, that's about all I have to say right now. It's raining now and I feel lucky to be indoors in a nice warm building. I'll be kissing you tomorrow night (you should get this letter Monday night) and sleeping on my good old couch in the living room. That'll be heaven. Mom, whatever you make will taste good, even *borscht*. Maybe some good Pauline Fletcher tomato soup and perhaps some liver *mit* onions? And I'll look forward to the Swiss cheese when I come home from a date. I definitely am not coming home for a rest. I want to get good and worn out from running around and having a good time. I'll recuperate when I get back to Camp.

Sis, what's the latest poop from Arthur? Well, you'll be able to tell me all about it soon. Dad, save some packages for me to deliver, and maybe I can sweep out the workroom every night while I'm home. Or do you want me to help put away the stock? What stock, am I kidding? I can see Mrs. Gersh Wednesday morning if you can get me an appointment, and also Friday morning. Have to look nice for all the *sheine madeles*,[123] and especially for my sweetheart, Pauline. Say, Mom, you had better reserve room for me to crawl into bed with you Sunday morning. No cutting in from Sam or *Yentela*, either. Hello, *Bubba sheine*,[124] I'll see you before you can recite the *Haftorah*.[125]

Love and Kisses,
Charlie

Charlie during furlough with Mom, Dad, and Edith outside their home.

---

[123] Yiddish: Beautiful girls.

[124] Yiddish: Beautiful Grandmother.

[125] Hebrew: The *Haftorah* is a series of short selections from the book of Prophets, read in synagogue following the recitation of the Torah portion on the Sabbath and Jewish festivals. Charlie is using the term as an analogy to describe the short time remaining before he arrives back home.

Saturday, March 25, 1944[126]

Dear Folks,

I was very surprised when I saw Mom's letter waiting for me. You mailed it Thursday night and it got here this afternoon. Quick service, eh?

The trip wasn't bad at all. The Jeffersonian is an excellent train but it pulled into St. Louis three hours late. However, I was still in time for the 6 PM train to Austin and I got a very good seat. I reached Taylor, Texas at 3 this afternoon and I got off there. Taylor is nearer to Camp than Austin is and I took the bus to Camp. I got in in time for supper. Then I fixed up, showered etc. and went to see "Heavenly Body." The duck was good and came in handy; I saved a piece for Friday lunch.

Just want you to know I arrived safely. Thanks for a marvelous time and E, you were certainly very generous and kind. Send me the Kufflers address.

Keep well, love to Grandma, and will write a long letter soon.

Love,
Charlie

Sunday, March 26, 1944

Dear Folks,

I mailed the letter dated Saturday last night but I only put six cents of stamps on the envelope. I had forgotten that air mail now costs eight cents. Therefore, the letter was returned to me this morning and now you'll get a bigger letter, although it will be a little late.

More about the trip. As I said, the Jeffersonian is a very modern train. There is an observation car in the rear and that's where I spent most of my time. The seats were very comfortable and I met some nice people including a lieutenant, a sergeant, a co-ed from the U of Missouri and a refugee from France. We had a grand time together. I was due to arrive in St. Louis about 1 but we didn't get in until 4. It would have been nice to spend a couple of hours in the town and

---

[126] The time lapse in letters was due to Charlie's furlough, plus significant travel time home and back.

look it over but since my train left at 6, I only had time to drop over to the USO and walk around the city near the railroad station. St. Louis is supposed to be a very nice place but I really couldn't say because I didn't see too much of it. I got a very comfortable seat on the train going to Texas. The seats went way back and I really had a good night's sleep. I was none the worse for the trip when I got back to Camp.

It's quite warm now. It's a little cloudy today but you can see that we're in for a hot spring. The movie I saw last night "Heavenly Body" starred William Powell, an old favorite of mine, and Hedy LaMarr. There is one scene that struck me very funny. A crowd of men is drinking vodka at Powell's home and they start a Russian show out of the sky. One fellow starts throwing knives from his mouth, another does the real Russian dance and it was much like the floor show we saw at the Casino Russe that I got a big kick out of it.

Everything is just about the same at Camp. I saw the Sergeant last night and he brought me up to date on the happenings. The boys passed the test at Bowie but didn't do as well as expected. That made the General sort of mad for a while, but he's back to normal now. The General asked for me the other day. The Sarge told him that I was on furlough, it took him a long time to find out that I was gone. You know this fellow who is in the hospital, well he's been gone for seven weeks now and the General still hasn't asked for him. Boy, what a memory.

Slept until 8:30 today. May go into town for a little while later on. I have a lot of mail to catch up on. Heard from Artie and he says he misses his chum, Eadie. Edith, I should have done this when I was home, but it all slipped my mind and I didn't want to bother. There's no real hurry, but here's what I want you to mail me. First, try to find my baseball glove, I may be able to use it a little. Then, in Daddy's drawers, somewhere, there are some athletic shirts - white crew shirts with the quarter sleeves. One is a New York University shirt and there are one or two others. Send them down, please. If you can't find any, have Mom buy me one for about a dollar in Davega - large size.[127] I intend to play some tennis at the University of Texas and that's all I need because I have my bathing trunks. I have a pair of sneakers in the closet and if you look hard enough, you'll find them. One pair is the low whites which I want, and the other pair is the

---

[127] Davega Stores was an appliance, sporting goods, and apparel store founded by I. Davega in 1879 at 3rd Avenue and 34th Street, New York, New York.

high basketball. Send me the low whites if you can find them. Or if you want to send both, do so. Just get the stuff together and Daddy will make a package. No rush, but soon. Don't send it special delivery, Pop.

I'm in very good spirits, Mom, so don't worry. Dad, I read the letter you sent. I think I did get a break. Many boys are worse off, including college men.

Love,
Charlie

Monday, March 27, 1944

Hello again,

Received your letter with the 3 cent stamps, thanks loads and I also appreciate you writing so often. Next time, send me two cent stamps. I have enough threes, but I'll need the twos to get 8 cents worth on the envelope.

I can see something right down my alley opening up. The artillery just appointed some 2nd Lieutenant Special Service officer. Well, I didn't waste any time. I grabbed him this morning and told him I was very interested in special services and that I could print out a newspaper. He was impressed with the newspaper idea and told me to start working on it. However, he is going to special service school for a month, and we won't start until he returns. But it's something to look forward to. I told him I've done publicity work, etc. and I'm quite sure I'll be his right-hand man.

When the General sees the paper he'll be impressed, because he likes stuff like that. Incidentally, the old man welcomed me back today and said that he missed me. He's got some lime, eh?

Oh, good news. We're taking the last 25-mile hike tomorrow and I'm not going. After the 1st of April, we're taking ten-mile hikes once a week and ten miles isn't anything. I'm already back in the groove and accustomed to the old Army life. Everything's fine. Just take care of yourselves and don't worry. Love to everyone at home.

Hiya, sis. Poppa, she's got a little bit of talent, eh?
Love,
Charlie

Tuesday, March 28, 1944

Dear Mom, Pop, and Sis,

Was kept pretty busy today. The Sergeant went on the 25-mile hike and I was alone. It's a coincidence, but whenever we're alone it's always busy. Have the two of us in the office and there's not a darn thing to do. Well, it was good to be alone because I did some orders for the adjutant and also typed a lot of papers for the S-3, the department that's in charge of training.

We start our last phase of training next week and it ends May 6th. Then we're supposed to be ready for anything, but as I told you before there's no way of telling what'll be. One thing, though, and I want to impress this upon you. There's a very strong possibility that we'll go overseas at some future date and I don't want you to be surprised when the time comes. Everybody got so upset when Artie left because it was so unexpected. I want you to be prepared and that's why I'm telling you that we should be overseas by the end of the summer. If we don't go over it will be a pleasant surprise for both you and me.

There's nothing to worry about. Field Artillery is a pretty safe place to be. In fact, we have the lowest casualty rate of any ground force unit. And the type of work I do will keep me in the safest position. So, if we do take a ride, it won't amount to a thing.

It was pretty warm today, but we had a heavy shower this afternoon and now it's cooling off very rapidly, in fact it looks like a real cold night. I'm on Charge of Quarters tonight and will try to catch up on my correspondence. I fell way behind on account of my furlough. I'm going to write V-mail letters to Artie and Murray tonight.

I'm on guard tomorrow night. We all get that about once a month. Besides losing some sleep, there's nothing hard about it. I'm confident for some reason that I'll become corporal before long. I don't know why I expect it, but I think my work has been good and that the General thinks a lot of me.

The General has a subscription to the Christian Science Monitor, a newspaper, and he leaves it in the office very night. I always read it and find it to be a very good paper. It's quite authoritative and has a very good reputation. It's published in Boston.

It's real spring down here. The grass is very green and most of the trees are very much in bloom. Oh, in yesterday's letter I forgot to tell you what I did Sunday. I went to Austin and met the boys I know from New York. We went to the AEPHI house, a sorority, and they have a beautiful place. We stayed there for a while and chatted with the gals. Then we went over to a lieutenant's home. It seems that one of my friends met the fellow at the JWB recently. Well, the officer is a NY boy and married a very religious girl from NY. They keep a kosher house and did we have fun kidding them. They served us herring, salami and eggs, and cream cheese sandwiches. Don't worry, the wife saw that we didn't mix the dishes. She's trained him so that the Lieutenant wore a *yarmulke*[128] when we ate; they were very hospitable people. The name is Silverglick.

Well, that's all for now. Take care of yourselves and don't worry.
Love,
Charlie

Thursday, March 30, 1944

Dear Folks,

Nothing much new. Was very lucky on guard last night. All the Officers of the Day[129] come into our office during the day to fill out the guard uniform blanks.[130] Well, the OD yesterday is a fellow I've had some contact with and I mentioned that I was on guard. So at guard mount, he appointed me orderly. The orderly stays in the guard house all the time and doesn't walk guard. So I had a full night's sleep and didn't do a damn thing. That was sure a lucky break. There is always an orderly selected and this is the first time I made it. A big deal!

I think I was a little too optimistic about the paper and the special service business. It seems that the higher-ranking officers in our headquarters aren't too interested in special services. In addition, the lieutenant who is in charge isn't a very forceful or confident man, and doesn't speak up for what he wants or

---

[128] *Yarmulke* in Yiddish, *Kippa* in Hebrew is a brimless cap, usually made of cloth, traditionally worn by Jewish males to fulfill the customary head covering requirement.

[129] The Officer of the Day is designated on a rotational basis, generally for 24-48 hours. This Officer attends to administrative tasks and incidents that require attention regardless of the time of day, in addition to other normal duties.

[130] List of guard duties.

thinks correct. So, I don't know how far we'll go. At any rate, I put out a little bulletin for him. I have enclosed a copy. The Major saw it tonight and told me not to run the thing off for distribution. He said he wanted to "straighten Lt. Schieble out." Maybe the Major wants to read everything before we print it or something like that. Anyway, he wasn't too well pleased with the whole idea and I think he's one of the guys who doesn't want to get entangled with a paper. But I'll let you know how things come out. In civilian life if they wanted a paper, I could have put one out already, but this is the Army and they dibble and dabble. The war will probably be over by the time they decide to have a paper.

Good news tonight about our Navy making some attacks in the Pacific.[131] It would be nice to end this damn thing very soon. Got two letters from you today. Thanks. Don't bank on my becoming a corporal, Dad. I hope to, but there aren't any openings at the present time and it'll be a matter of time.

We might have a short night problem tomorrow night and will probably come in about midnight. We're supposed to go out at night at least once a week. If I was in the Division a longer while, I might have been able to get in the Special Service office. There was an opening about three months ago. When we get into combat they take care of the graves, etc. so I don't think I'd like that too much. Let well enough alone. I'm lucky as it is to be in most of the time.

---

[131] On this date, the United States Navy commenced "Operation Desecrate One," part of the preparations for the Allied invasion of western New Guinea. In this attack, aircraft carriers launched against Japanese bases on and around Palau, with 36 Japanese ships sunk or damaged in the aftermath.

[132] Yiddish: synagogue, traditional Jewish place of worship.

Wrote to Artie and sent him your regards. I told him how much you miss him, Eadie. Why don't you write, kid? Not too busy for writing to Artie, are you?

Well, that's all right now. Take care of yourselves and sleep tight at night.
Love and Kisses,
Charlie

Friday, March 31, 1944

Dear Mom, Pop, and Sis,

It's 10:30 now and I should get to bed but since I love you all so dearly, I'll drop you a line before I retire. Now isn't that nice of me, I ask you?

I went to "*shul*"[132] tonight. The Jewish chaplain arrived at Camp Swift recently and I've never heard him speak, so I decided to go over to the chapel tonight and see what's cooking. The service was pretty nice and the rabbi, chaplain here, is a fellow from Philadelphia who impresses me as being a second-class rabbi but not too bad. We went to a Mess Hall after the service and had salami sandwiches and herring. The herring was so good that I had about five pieces. Gosh, Dad, you don't believe that, I bet. Incidentally, I met Wilby's son here. Wilby is the guy who owns that restaurant between 89th and 90th in Broadway, right next to the candy store. Which reminds me that the candy store man told me you owe about $3.50. Give him a couple of bucks. Wilby's boy just came into one of our infantry regiments, he was in the ASTP at University of Maryland.

There are big doings in Austin Friday night for the *Seder*,[133] etc. I don't know whether I'll try to get off. I just got back from furlough and to go off again for a couple of days isn't too good. I don't like them to see that I can get away from headquarters whenever I want, because then they might feel they could grab me anytime they feel like it. So I'll think it over.

The Battery went out on a night problem tonight and is due back at midnight. The Major told the Master Sergeant - the guy who is in charge of all the enlisted men in the HQ - that he didn't want his Sergeant or me to go out in the field. He said we work hard enough here and do extra work at night and that he saw

---

[133] Hebrew: the Seder is a celebratory meal that marks the beginning of the Jewish holiday of Passover, commemorating the Exodus of the Israelites from slavery in Egypt.

no reason for us riding around on top of a truck. Boy, it made me feel good when I heard that, but I don't know how long that will last.

I may go to Austin tomorrow night. Some sorority is having a party at the JWB and it may be pretty good. Nothing much new so I can't really go on writing about nothing. I'm glad Dad is behaving himself.

Have a good week and take care of yourselves.
Love,
Charlie

Monday, April 3, 1944

Dear Folks,

Excuse the slight delay, but I took a vacation from letter writing over the past weekend. I received both Eadie's and Mom and Pop's letters. Thanks. I wrote to the Bialos as soon as I came back to Camp thanking them for everything, E. See, I remembered that you told me I am a little forgetful about things like that, so I didn't slip up this time.

I had a very nice weekend. A Jewish Sorority Sigma Delta Tau were the hostesses at the JWB Saturday night. All the girls came in formal gowns, and it was a lovely affair. I met a very nice girl from Corpus Christie, Texas and I took her out Sunday afternoon. We went to the movies and then went in for a soda. That's just about all there is to do in town. Her Old Man is in the coat and suit business and owns a couple of big retail stores. It's nice to be out with someone who has a similar background and is an intelligent person.

I bought myself a little shaving kit tonight for $2.40. It's a little leather case to hold your toilet articles. When I go to town for the weekend I need a little kit for my stuff and this is just right. I also need it to put my stuff in when it's in the footlocker. The kit I brought down the PX fills the bill. If you send me a couple of bucks I'll be okay for the rest of the month. I expect the refund of my tax return shortly and then I'll be okay. Thanks for the stamps. They all come in handy.

If you're home April 12th, Fred Warringin's orchestra is dedicating his broadcast on that night to the 102nd Division, so tune in if you're around a radio.

Everyone in the Division is required to attend a three-day mine school and I'm going the first three days of this week. I went out today, go tomorrow and all day Wednesday until midnight. We don't do a darn thing but listen to lectures and watch demonstrations in mine fields. It was nice and sunny and I got a good burn. It was strange being out in the field again. My Sergeant is staying in while I'm out and he'll be going on Thursday, Friday, and Saturday, so it will be impossible for me to go to Austin for the Seder. It's just as well because I wasn't too keen on asking for a three-day pass anyway.

Edith, don't worry about Artie and forget those crazy ideas about going to London. The folks need you now and it's crazy even to think of going over. If you did get the chance, and that would be practically impossible, you might never be able to see Art anyway. So, just pray that we all come home soon, and let well enough alone. Be thankful he's in the office, because I can see that it's the safest place to be.

Some boys I did Basic with went to the University of Maryland and they're now in our infantry. I went over to see them tonight and had a good bull session with them. Boy, they're pretty downhearted, but you can't help that.

I've been invited over to that couple from NY-Thelt I told you about, who married a religious girl. I met her in town Saturday and she told me to come over for some *matzohs*[134] next week, so don't send me any.

Enclosed you will find a picture I took last Sunday at a Sorority house at the University. It was a real summer day and you can see how I'm squinting.

Take care of yourselves.
Love and Kisses,
Charlie

Tuesday, April 4, 1944

Dear Mom, Pop, and Sis,

Boy, is my face sunburned. We were all out again today and although I tried to stay out of the sun, I got quite a burn. I brought a jar of Noxzema[135] and I will apply it freely tonight when I go to bed. Tomorrow is the last day of this mine school. We don't do a darn thing and it gets very boring just sitting around. We keep going tomorrow until midnight.

Have been busy last night and tonight with work for the Special Service Office. I hope somebody knows the amount of work I'm doing for him - but they usually find out who's doing the work, so I'm not worried.

Listening to Bob Hope now, he certainly is good. Glad you bought tickets to the Opera, E. I'm sure you will enjoy it. See that Daddy doesn't come out singing.

Dad, about the tax. Marvin Hirsch is friendly, and I suggest that you call him. It's not a big item at all and will only be a few dollars if anything. I left you a copy of the income tax return I turned in, and you may have to refer to it. Just call up Marvin and tell him what return it is and he'll give you the necessary information.

Take good care of yourselves. Don't worry, Mom, I'm back in stride and I'm doing good work. How did Grandma make out with the apartment? It seems as if she was "held holding the bag." Well, perhaps she'll get a tenant soon.

Love and Kisses,
Charlie

---

[134] Traditional unleavened bread, eaten during the holiday of Passover.

[135] Moisturizing face cream.

Thursday, April 6, 1944

Dear Folks,

It's certainly been swell hearing from you so regularly since returning from furlough. I hope you keep up the fine work. I'm trying to keep up my good record of writing daily but sometimes it's impossible, as you can well realize. But don't worry, I'll keep my letters coming. The reason I didn't write last night was because we were out at the mine school until 11 PM. It was a busy day since we were on the go from seven in the morning.

Tonight it's my turn at Charge of Quarters again. We pull CQ about once every eight days. This job with the Special Service Officer is becoming a pain in the neck but I don't mind it. He doesn't know too much about the stuff and I tell him what to do. I've been kept busy a number of evenings with his work but as Mom keeps telling me, make myself indispensable in the office and that's what I'm trying to do.

I'm very happy to hear that you're paying back some of the old debts you incurred. I think that's one of your most important obligations at the present time. Has Edith talked to Aunt Rose about her proposition yet? Aunt Rose suggested that in all seriousness and I think you should go through with it. You borrowed the money in good faith and by all means it should be paid back. Edith can help now because many of the debts were made for her and I know she's willing to do her share, so try your best to take care of them.

Dad, for the little business you have, I think that Marvin Hirsch would be more than willing to help you out with those little items. This estimated income tax isn't much and he can tell you what to do in less than ten minutes. As far as any of my friends at school go, I wouldn't want them to be so familiar with your affairs. So give Marvin a ring and I'm sure he'll help you out. Incidentally, you still have the copy of the tax return I sent in for you, don't you? Hold on to it, it's important.

I was sorry to hear that *Tibby* is as good as gone. She looked like a ghost when I saw her up the store and I was shocked momentarily. It's a shame that Charlie is so far away but in a way it's good that he doesn't have to see how his mother is passing away. How is *Motle*? How's *Yetta* taking all this *sooras*?[136]

---

[136] Yiddish: Troubles

The days are very warm now but the evenings and mornings are still cool. Something like Georgia weather except that it's been a little drier here. Can you imagine, we haven't had rain for about a week. I wondered what's wrong. I read about the cold wave you people have been having. Keep warm and don't take any chances. It's crazy weather when it gets so cold in April.

Well, there's really nothing more right now. Love to all and be good kiddies. How you doing Sister, dear? Isn't that lovely, E? Regards to your in-laws.

Love,
Charlie

Friday, April 7, 1944

Friday Night and Happy Passover! May the war Passover quickly!

Dear Folks and Edith,

I hope you had a nice *Seder* tonight. Did Daddy *daven*[137] well, mother? I suppose Eadie said the four *kashis*.[138] Well, it'll be my turn to say them next year. Furloughs are starting over again and if we're still in the country, I'm going to try to come home for *Rosh Hashanah* and *Yom Kippur* next September. You must wait four and a half months before you get another furlough, so it'll be okay then. That's planning a little in advance but it's nice to think of home around New Year's time.

Was alone yesterday and today in the office. As I told you, I went to Mine School first and the Sergeant had to go out for the next three days. I've been doing okay and all's well. I put out another bulletin today and you'll find it enclosed. If you look at the bottom of the center column you'll see my name there. Enclosed is another picture I took in Austin. I have a few more being developed now and I'll send them home as I get them. Please save them so I'll have proof that I was in the Army. Perhaps my kids and grandchildren won't believe me.

If I get a pass tomorrow, I may go to Austin for the weekend. I still have cash left from payday and it's good to get away for a few hours. I sure wish the pool

---

[137] Yiddish: Pray

[138] The Four Questions, a section of the Passover Seder where the youngest member of the household asks four traditional questions regarding the special customs of the evening.

opens soon at Camp. We have a very nice one and we sure could use it during the day. It's plenty warm now although the evenings are still cool.

Yes, Eadie, I also wish you were here with Art now. It would be good for you two and it would be swell for me to have a sister and brother-in-law so nearby. Thanks for your long letter, Sis, and I do understand how busy you are. It's very nice of you to plan to show the folks a good time. I sure wish I were home so I could help you. We both owe them so much. I think we are both in-debted to Mother and Dad. Let's do all we can for them.

Went to the early movie tonight and saw "You Can't Ration Love." It was light but entertaining. It was about a college campus

Shoeshine in the park

which was hard hit by the draft and the girls were left with very few men. So the gals decided to ration each man on campus and each girl was allowed a certain amount of ration points with which to spend on the dates she went on. You'd all enjoy it.

Nothing more right now. I'm depending on you for a lot of my mail because I find it difficult to correspond with a lot of other people, so keep your

Out with friends

211

mail coming. Regards to Grandma. Hope everything is okay.

Love,
Charlie

Sunday, April 9, 1944

Hello Mom, Pop, and Sis,

It's 10:45 AM now and I'm in Austin. I came here last night and there's a little story attached to my getting here, so let me tell it to you.

I give my clothes that have to be dry-cleaned to one of the boys who lives in Smithville, a town about 20 miles from Camp. The fellow is usually reliable but he forgot to bring back my blouse and clean suit Saturday morning. So I went to Smithville yesterday evening with him and put on the clean clothes and left the suit I was wearing then. They have a big dance in Smithville on Saturday nights but it's a small town and not too attractive. So I figured that if I could hitch to Austin - I was now 50 miles away - I would, and if not I would spend the evening in Smithville. Well, even before I hit the highway some man stopped for me and took me straight to Austin. There wasn't much doing at the JWB so I decided to go over to the university.

There was a play on, given by the Drama Club, and I saw the last act. The Medical Battalion of our Division was the guest and there was a big formal dance afterwards. So I just went along and no one bothered asking where you were from.

There was a good band there from Camp and some good sandwiches, etc. I met a nice Jewish girl who I've seen before at the JWB and I took her home. She is from Pensacola, Florida. The girls at school must be in by 1:00, so there is no place to go if you want to stay out late.

I slept at the JWB last night and had a good breakfast at the Austin hotel. I may go back to Camp early today, but if there's anything doing, I'll hang around.

Well, that's all now.
Love,
Charlie

Monday, April 10, 1944

Hello Again,

This is *Zudek Leibish* writing to *Pessa*, *Shmiel* and *Yentela*.[139] Nothing new has happened since yesterday. It was very warm today, two weeks from today we're going into our khaki uniform. I can't see why they're waiting so long, we could certainly use them now. But that's the Army.

The General came back from a five day pass today. He spent a "lazy five days" in Paris, Texas - that's where his wife and kids live. It was a pretty slow day in the office today. Did a little typing for a colonel late in the afternoon, but aside from that there wasn't anything much doing.

We're having the general inspection office from Division down at the Battery tomorrow and they are going to inspect us. Another big deal! The barracks were scrubbed this evening and windows washed, a big house cleaning.

Edith, it was very nice of you to buy opera tickets for the folks. You're a real nice daughter with a little bit of talent. I forgot the opera you went to; what was it and how was it? Did they sing as well as *Pessa* can, *Shmiel*?

Boy, this letter is like pulling teeth from a baby. Hardly a thing to tell you about. Let's see!

I'll call it quits, really nothing else.

Love and keep well,
Charles

Tuesday, April 11, 1944

Dear Mom, Pop, and Sis,

I was pretty lucky today. The Sergeant and I were the only ones to stay in head-quarters during the inspection today and tonight we stayed in although the

---

[139] The Yiddish names for Pauline, Samuel, and Edith.

Battery went out on a night problem. They left at 6 this evening and won't be back until 10 tomorrow morning. Boy, I'll be unaccustomed to the field when I have to go out again.

The General had a meeting with the battalion commander today and he said he thinks all personnel in the Division will be frozen. That means we're here to stay in the 102nd and he thinks we'll move out of here by the beginning of June. He didn't say where we're moving - just said moving. It may be to another camp or to a POE. If it's the latter, I hope it's Ft. Dix. It would be nice to spend the last couple of months in the US near New York.[140] A lot of Divisions have used Ft. Dix as a ready camp before going overseas. However, the General said that none of this stuff was official, but it's the latest information he could get. So for all we know, we could still be here next fall. A general sometimes knows less than a private because all these things are worked out in Washington and sometimes even a general doesn't hear about a thing until it happens.

It was pretty hot again today but it isn't bad in the office. It manages to stay cool indoors. Took a nice shower this evening and plan to see the second showing of the movie tonight. "Meet the People" with Dick Powell is playing and it's supposed to be pretty good. We have a big division parade Friday afternoon. It's a motorized review and all the vehicles we have in the division will be used. All I have to do is ride along in one of the trucks. Some fun, eh? The parade is in honor of Governor Stevenson of Texas.

The swimming pool at Camp is scheduled to open soon. I'll sure make use of it. I'm not going to bother too much with this Special Service stuff. The Lt. Colonel who is in charge of training makes sarcastic remarks about it and he's not too pleasant a fellow. So to avoid any trouble with him, I'm not going to do anything unless the Special Service Officer gives it to me. The Special Service Officer is going away to school for a month and unless the Major tells me to keep up with it, I'm not going to worry about it.

Everything is swell. Feeling fine - although a little soft - not too much exercise, but once the pool opens I'll get enough of it. Nothing more right now. Will close until tomorrow.

Love,
Charlie

---

[140] Ft. Dix is located 16 miles (25.9 km) south of Trenton, New Jersey, some 75 miles (120 km) from Charlie's home in New York City.

Wednesday, April 12, 1944

Dear Folks,

I'm Charge of Quarters tonight and am in headquarters. I was supposed to be on Friday night but I switched with the Sergeant. The first four grades - sergeants and up- are having a dance tonight and he wanted to get off, so I changed with him. I read "A Tree Grows in Brooklyn" for a couple of hours and now at 8:30 I'm starting to write. I'm still way behind with my correspondence and I'm trying to catch up gradually.

The Special Service Officer bought me the stuff I wanted today. They didn't have everything in stock though, and I didn't get shorts and two pairs of woolen socks. However, I got my shoes - only $3.31 and you couldn't buy them for $7 on the outside- four pairs of cotton socks - and four undershirts. Pop, if you need a pair of low brown shoes, tell me what size you take and send me $3 and I'll try to get you a pair. The shoe is very good and you'll enjoy wearing it. Be sure to tell me the length and the width if you want a pair.

Edith, if you haven't sent out the stuff I wanted, there are a few changes I want you to make. Don't bother sending the baseball glove, it'll just be extra baggage if we move. Just send down one pair of sneakers, if you can find them, and some crew shirts if you have them. Don't buy sneakers if you can't find them in the house. I probably won't get a chance to play tennis anyway. The Battery has a lot of baseball gloves in the supply room and if I play I can always borrow one from them.

The Battery had an organized athletic period this afternoon and I got out for a while. I took my shirt off and got a little sun on my back. I haven't played ball since camp last summer. Furloughs are starting off again on the 15th. I hope we're in the country long enough for me to get another one. I won't be eligible for one till the latter part of August. I wonder just where we'll be by then.

The Major is going to Atlanta, Georgia tomorrow for a week's course in maintenance. A captain from one of the battalions is coming in to take his place and he's a nice fellow.

E, have you read "A Tree Grows in Brooklyn" yet? You'll enjoy it, I'm sure, and if you get the chance read a little of it to Mother, although it would be better if Mother read it herself.

Shmendrik,[141] how's Riverside Drive these spring nights? Remember when I used to sit near the river with you and then we'd go to the drug store for a drink? I hope you're taking *Pessa* down to the Drive for some fresh air.

How's the wonderful piece of property coming along? Is it worth a half a million yet? What a good piece of land it is, eh Daddy? How's Grandma and is there anything new on her apartment? How's *Zadie*[142] getting along? Give them all my love. Did Irene's husband go into the Army or is he still at home?

Nothing new right now, my chickadee. Take good care of yourself and write soon.

Love,
Charlie

Thursday, April 13, 1944

Dear Folks,

Zudik Leibish is now a non-commissioned officer. Yes, I finally made corporal and actually I'm a technician fifth grade, the same rank as Artie. It came as a complete surprise to me. Although I did expect it someday, I didn't think it would come the way it did and so fast. The General usually gives the ratings out to the headquarters staff and he may have authorized mine, but here's how it happened.

My Battery commander came into headquarters today at about 1 and asked for the tables of organization - the book with all the jobs in a unit and the ratings. I showed him where it was and after looking at it, he told the sergeant in my section, "Make him a T/5, clerk, headquarters." He just pointed at me and the Sergeant said who, and the Captain again said him, pointing at me. So right then and there I made Corporal. I typed up the Special Order myself and I have enclosed a copy. Tomorrow in celebration of my promotion I'm on table-waiter so you see that it doesn't mean much in my Battery. I get a $12 raise and that's about the best thing of the whole works. I won't have to walk guard anymore, but I'll be Corporal of the Guard. That's easy, as all you do is post the privates and then return to the guardhouse. I only pull that about once every 70 days,

---

[141] Yiddish: A foolish person.
[142] Yiddish: Grandfather.

so that isn't bad. Then there's the table-waiter once every two weeks. That's not bad as long as it doesn't come on the weekends. The other T/5s in the Battery pull KP, but since I'm in headquarters I don't pull that. So in all it's a pretty good break. A lot of the fellows in the Battery have been in over a year and a half and they're still privates. I consider myself lucky to get the corporal stripes since I entered the Army at a very late stage.

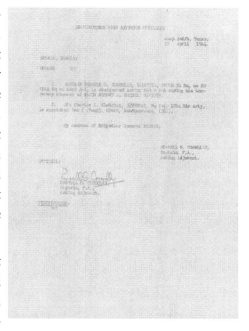

I think I'll go to the late show tonight and see "Uncertain Glory" with Errol Flynn. How's everything going in New York? I signed this month's payroll as a PFC[143] so I won't be getting the extra money until June. However, then I'll get all of the extra money due me for the rest of April. Well, the main thing is that I promoted myself and that's what makes me feel good.

Nothing more right now. I'll write again real soon. The big parade is tomorrow, and I don't know whether I'll be in it. It doesn't mean anything anyway. Take good care of yourself, darlings, and write soon. Thanks for the letter, Dad, and where you get some of your crazy ideas I don't know - especially about spending money. There aren't any bad women in Texas good enough for me. At least some of the New York women are nice.

Love and Kisses,
Corporal Fletcher

Saturday, April 15, 1944

Hi Folks,

Excuse the lack of letter yesterday, but I took a night off for a very special reason.

---

[143] Private First Class.

Just about 5 o'clock on Friday evening we were all called out for a Battery formation. We were just finishing chow (early that day) and the Battery Commander told us that General Keating, the Division Commander, declared Saturday a holiday and we were off until Monday morning. The boys did very well in the parade Friday, so the General probably wanted to reward them.

Well, you can imagine how happy everyone was. Many of the boys took off last night for San Antonio, Houston and other towns; I've given up on the travelling business, though. It's just not worth the time and discomfort to travel to the nearby towns and then find them overcrowded. Austin is just as good as the other cities, so I'll stick to it. Well, last night I saw my friends from Benning and I took them over to my barracks and showed them around.

This morning I slept until 7:30, can you imagine - a full Saturday off in the Army (I still can't believe it) and then I got dressed and ate breakfast. Two other fellows and I, some of the boys from NYU, left for Austin around 9:30; we were planning to go swimming. Well, it was impossible to get into town. The buses were running on regular schedule, and they could hardly take care of ¼ of the men, and there weren't any extra cars, so we had to take a taxi and it cost $2 a piece. But it was worth it since we got into town at 10:30 and rode in style.

As soon as we got in, I called up a rooming house and got a room for the three of us and then we went over there to leave our bag. It's a nice big room, two single beds and one double, but in order to keep it for ourselves we paid for the extra bed. So, instead of the regular $1 man charge, we're paying $1.33 a piece.

Then we took the bus out to the city swimming pool called Barton Springs and it's swell. I can see that I'll be spending my Sundays there from now on. It's a big freshwater pool with two big hills on both sides. It's all grass and that's where you lay down and get the sunburn. It's free for soldiers and only 12 cents for civilians, so you can see it's not run for a profit. I did a lot of swimming and got a nice burn. It was a real hot day so it was a relief to get away from the city.

The girl I planned to take out tonight had a date. The JWB was too crowded so there wasn't much doing tonight. It's now 11:10 PM and I'm in the student building on the campus. Our room is nearby. I guess we'll hit the hay soon. If there was a little more to do here on Saturday night, it would be a pretty good deal.

Since we had 2 days off this weekend, it cost me quite a little dough; so if you can send me a few bucks, it would help out. Once I start getting Corporals pay (June 1st) I'll be okay. It's an extra $12.

Well, that's all now. If I don't write tomorrow, don't worry.

Take it easy, love,
Charlie

Sunday, April 16, 1944

Dear Folks, including Edith, of course,

It's 7:45 now and I'm back in Camp. It was a very pleasant weekend and I enjoyed myself immensely. The General ought to give us the weekend off every week. It's really something to be able to sleep late two days in one week. The boys still can't get over it.

I got to sleep a little after midnight Saturday night and slept until 11 this morning. Then we went for breakfast. It was a perfect day for swimming, but we were afraid that our burns wouldn't stand any more sun, so just to play it safe we didn't go to the Springs. Instead, we went over to the sorority house at school and had a nice time. The girls are going to have a formal open house the first Sunday in May, and that should be good. Things are strictly informal when we go over on Sundays but once a month all the girls attend and they serve refreshments, etc.

It was sure swell sleeping in a full-sized bed for a change. The house was very quiet, and I slept like a log. Had a good steak dinner in town before we took the bus for Camp. It was a tenderloin steak on a $1.35 dinner, and it was swell. So, you can see that I had a nice time for the two days. Edward G. Robinson is playing in "Tampico" tonight and I think I'll go to the second show to end a perfect weekend. If you can spare a five-spot[144] I could use it until the end of the month. It would have been a shame not to go all-out on this weekend because it'll probably be the last day off we'll ever get. Right, Pop? I can just see my Old Man smiling now as he's reading this letter.

Say, Pop, how do you like the idea of your son being a corporal? Perhaps in another two years I'll be a sergeant. Right now there's no chance of it because

---

[144] $5 bill.

there's no opening. But if I learn shorthand and something happens to the Sergeant, I'll be next in line. Boy, just by looking at this typing you can see that I haven't typed for two days. Well, folks that's all right now. Send my regards to everyone and write soon. I haven't heard from you for about three days.

How's everything, Sis? Are you still contented with your job?[145] You might as well be. How are the letters coming from Artie? Have you told him that I'm now a T/5? See he doesn't outrank me now. Does he say anything about his outfit - or does he abide by the rules? See any of your old cronies around, E? How about writing me a letter with all the dirt. I know you're very busy but when you get a chance, drop me a line.

I took quite a few pictures over the weekend, and I'll send you prints as soon as I have them developed. It's going to cost me a buck or so to have my stripes sewn on, so send a couple of bucks, Mom. Once I get my regular pay, I'll be okay. Take good care of yourselves. That's the only thing I worry about - Mom and Pop's health.

Love and Kisses,
Charlie

Tuesday, April 18, 1944

Dear Folks,

All's well on the Texas battlefront. Last night I finished reading "A Tree Grows in Brooklyn" and it took me to 11 o'clock to complete it, so I didn't get around to any letter writing. I've been a very good boy with my letters lately, so I'm sure you'll excuse me for the one-night lapse.

It was a little cool today, but summer is definitely here. We go into khakis on 24 April – Monday - and God knows how I'm going to manage with three pairs of khakis. I'll be sweating so that I'll have to change very often. I might be able to buy an extra pair of suntans. It'll sure be worth it if I can.

I didn't get to the movies Sunday night. Instead, I went to the open-air dance they have here every Sunday night. It was pretty nice, and I danced a lot. I wasn't cut in on too much, just luck though. Usually, those dances are like rat

---

[145] During this period, Edith worked as a secretary and typist in a government job. Though not explicitly stated, it appears that she was employed by the Department of the Navy.

races. Dance with a girl and they hit you on the back and then you hit someone else on the back and that's the way it goes.

"Tampico" with Edward G. Robinson played in another theater tonight and I just saw it. It was good and I enjoy his acting a lot. Edith, Robinson reminds me of my brother-in-law, Arthur Irving Marshak. What do you say? They both have the same stature and complexion, although I grant you that Artie may be slightly better looking. What do the folks think about that? Bob Hope will be going on in a few minutes and I'm going to listen to him. He sure keeps up the standards of his broadcast week after week. I received a letter from Stellie recently. I'll have to answer her soon. Gee, I owe so many letters, I don't know when I'll be able to catch up.

I think I told you that Major Becker went away to school for a week or so. A captain is taking over the job while he's away and is doing a good job, he's a very nice fellow. I'm still doing the same work that I did as a private. The fellow who used to work here and then went to the hospital for a hernia operation returned to the Battery yesterday. He's not going to work in headquarters anymore. The Battery Commander has an extra sergeant in the Battery, and I understand that he's going to send him over to us, but I doubt whether Major Becker will let him stay because we really don't need any more help in our section, especially a sergeant. But now that I got my rating I'm not worried, because he can't get my job.

The General hasn't been himself since the Division went to Bowie. As I told you the boys didn't do too well there, and he's been a little grouchy ever since. He used to speak to all the boys but now he's very quiet. He'll probably get over it soon enough. He continually speaks about us going overseas and he's probably praying that we do. But as yet we've had no indications of any immediate movement. Furloughs have started over already. Boy, if it was sure that we'd be here permanently, I'd be getting home every five months or so. That's not bad, eh? As it is, I think I may get home again before we go overseas. If I get home by September, it'll be twice in one year. I think that's mighty lucky.

Nothing more, write soon,
Love and Kisses,
Charlie

Wednesday, April 19, 1944

Hello Folks,

It was another hot day today and good and muggy. I hope the weather is better back home.

I've enclosed some negatives, Edith, and would like you to have two sets of prints made. Keep one set for yourself and send the other set to me. Please do it right away and return the negatives as soon as possible, as there are some other fellows waiting to have prints made. Try to mail me the one set and the negatives by next Wednesday. Don't lose the negatives, please. The pictures are pretty good. The new ones are the ones we took at Barton Springs last Sunday.

I'm going to the first show tonight to see "Follow the Boys" then I'm coming back and taking CQ for one of our tech sergeants. He's giving me a buck and it's worth it because all I do is sleep here. Then again, he's one of the married men and this is his last chance to get home until Saturday night. The Battery is going out tomorrow at about 2 PM and won't be back until midnight Friday. I'm quite sure that I won't have to go. I only hope so. But I doubt whether they'd take me away for two days. I need some work on my teeth and I'm going to start going to the dentist this week.

E, I understand that Al Campenis is in the Navy. I got a letter from Len Bates the other day. He's a Sergeant in some quartermaster baking outfit and just passed his Warrant Officer Exam and is waiting for an appointment. It's very difficult to read his writing but I think he mentioned that there's a chance for him entering OCS.[146] A smart colored boy sure climbs the ladder fast.

Dad, I got your letter today and was glad to hear you had a nice Sunday while the girls were away. Did you bring any strange women up to the house? Now don't get jealous, Mother. How did you gals enjoy the trip to Wilkes-Barre? Everybody there in the best of health? I received the letter you wrote from W-B, Mom, and I do agree that the best thing God could do was to give Grandma a nice quick end, but what can you do?

Dad, about the clothes. The shoes feel swell on me, but they're plain top - no perforations. They cost $3.32 and if you send me the dough and your size I

---

[146] Officer Candidate School.

Swimming with friends at Barton Springs.

think I can get you a pair. Send me the size, around 44, isn't it? I believe the shirts are about $.25 a pair. The shorts are either all white or khaki, but they're good material. If you're interested, send me the dough. The socks are $.16 a pair and cotton khaki, but they wear very well. I probably can get some officer to buy the stuff for me, and then I can send the stuff home.

I've worked up a sweat just typing this letter to you. Don't pity me. The boys in battle now are having it much hotter than I am, so thank God I'm still in this country and doing pretty well. I haven't been out in the field for so long that I've practically forgotten what it's like.

That's all. Take care of yourselves and get these negatives made up in a hurry. Please be careful and don't work too hard. It'll be getting hot soon and you're not so young anymore.

Love,
Charlie

Friday, April 21, 1944

Dear Mom, *Shmendrick*, and *Yentela*,

Well, they fooled me and sent me out to the field last night. Everyone from Headquarters went and they brought us back at seven this morning. The Battery is staying until midnight tonight but we came back in order to work in the office today. Some of the boys went back this afternoon but my Sergeant and I didn't have to go. And, boy what a night it was.

We didn't have to work too hard but it started to rain about three in the morning and no one had bothered to put up tents. It was very nice out when we went to bed around 10:30 and rain was the furthest thing in our minds. But sure enough, I was laying on my shelter half with one blanket over me, that's all we needed since it was extremely warm, and then the rains came. At first, I folded the blanket and crept under it and I stayed that way for about twenty minutes and didn't get wet a bit. After a while I put my hand out of the blanket to see how I was getting along and sure enough there was about a ¼ inch of water on my shelter half, none on me as I had the blanket folded around my body. Well, I could have stayed in that position but I thought that the water might get through the blanket at any time so I went over to our truck and went into the front seat and the rest of the night I slept behind the wheel. Everybody got caught. I didn't get wet very much and it was an experience - sleeping under the stars and then rain in bucketfulls. I wonder if I'll ever use an umbrella again. Last night we just threw ourselves on the ground and went to sleep - no leaves or grass - just solid earth.

Before we went to bed we had to dig in the command post. There were about six of us working on it, so none of us overworked. Around 9 PM the Battery Commander called me to the side and told me to make believe that I was hit by fragments from an artillery shell. So I went back to the fellows and after a minute or so yelled that I was hit and wounded. Then I just acted like a casualty and the medics were called and carried me to the aid station on a stretcher. Some fun, eh? Till they got me on that stretcher, it seemed like ages. It was all very funny as the boys tried to comfort me as if I were really hurt. I kept yelling for the chaplain, just fooling around of course, and the boys gave me first aid. What a big deal.

Well, there wasn't much doing in the office today. I did type up some stuff, but not a lot. Major Becker will be back early next week. I've been getting along fine with the captain who is taking his place. The General just phoned here and wanted to speak to the Junior Duty Officer who is always in headquarters. It seems that the Division Commander General Keating didn't receive an invitation to a dance held by the Division Artillery tomorrow night. Now that's just tragic for regular Army men and Busbee (my General) wanted the matter traced. Well, just to show you how we can do things - a radio car is set up at the Battery and they have contact with the Battery which is a good ten miles out on the woods. Now, I just had a radio message sent to the Sergeant who delivered the invites and he already radioed back that he gave the invitation to some sergeant. in the General's office.

Things travel fast around here. I'm just hanging out around the office writing some letters. I'm CQ tomorrow and that means in HQ until Sunday noon. Then I'm taking off for Austin and Barton Springs.

Take it easy. It's real hot down here. Thanks for the letter, E. No sense writing a special letter to you, as you get all the news in the letters to the folks. But I'll write a special one to you soon.

Love and Kisses,
Charlie

Saturday, April 22, 1944

Hello Folks,

Here it is Saturday night and I'm Charge of Quarters. It's a heck of a night to be in CQ, but you have to take it as it comes. We work on a roster so we all get the same number of Saturdays and Sundays. I won't be on again on a Saturday for another seven weeks. Next week I'm on Sunday, then Monday and it goes around that way. I plan to do a lot of writing tonight and catch up with my correspondence.

We had a very slow day and the General left at 1:30, so we didn't do a thing after that time. The Battery gave us a sergeant today and he's going to work in our section. The Battery Commander grabbed him when he came down about two months ago, but then saw he had no use for him. We have only one buck sergeant's rating in the whole Battery, and that's in the survey section. This fellow doesn't know the first thing about survey and he's taking away the rating of some fellow in the survey section. It's not his fault; just the fault of the BC for taking him when he knew he had no need for a clerk who held a sergeant's rating. But that's the way they do things. He's now holding the private's job - the one I held - and they'll probably do something with him real soon.

I got a little touch of poison ivy from that one night I slept in the field. It's not bothering me, but I hope it doesn't spread. It's on the top part of my hand and not too bad. This weather is terrible. It's continually hot and muggy in addition, but I'll get used to it. Just ask Edith about Texas weather. I know I'll have to buy an extra set or two of suntans.

I'm going to Austin tomorrow afternoon as soon after noon as possible. I was planning to go swimming with this girl from Corpus Christie, but her sorority is having an open house for servicemen. So, I think I'll go for a little swim myself if it's nice out and then go over to her sorority house - which is a beauty. Next Monday, Tuesday, and Wednesday the Division is going to present the "Ozark Caper" a musical revue written by the men of the 102nd. It's a regular show like they put on in high school or college. Just how good it is, I don't know, but I hear it's pretty good. Incidentally, 25 University of Texas girls are going to attend Tuesday night and one of them will be elected the Sweetheart of the 102nd Division.

Well, I'm running short of news right now. I hope you have a good week. How long do my letters take by air mail? I'm curious and please tell me in your next letter. I'm not doing a darn thing but I'm sweating anyway. Oi, Dad, do I *schvitz*.[147] Say hello to Ellie and Mimi when you write to them, Eadie. Joe Brand is a very nice chap and would make a good husband. Is he still an ensign or was he promoted to Lieutenant?

Well, kid, take it easy. Some Sunday you ought to have the Old Man take you to the stadium and see the Yankees play. My father is a great baseball expert and will tell you all the rules and players.

Still wasting time here at Swift. We could be here until August and that doesn't worry me one bit. Love and kisses to the three swell *shmendricks*.

Love,
Charlie

Monday, April 24, 1944

Dear Folks,

Well, we're all dressed up in khaki today and it's really a pretty sight - or it might be that it's a different sight. But anyway, it looks nice to see all the boys wear the suntans with the light caps. My cap is too small, and I'll have to buy some new ones. It's the cap that I received at Upton last September - doesn't that seem a long time ago? The pants are a little snug which shows that I grew some - in the hips, just like my Old Lady.

The Division show started tonight, and I have tickets for tomorrow night's performance. Tonight I attended to a little housekeeping. I sewed my chevrons on my fatigues and my class X field jacket. Class X clothing is clothing that is no longer salvageable, and it's given out as extra. I wear the X field jacket when we go in the field - as yet I haven't worn it.

I was in the dentist's chair for three hours this morning and now my teeth are supposed to be in perfect condition. He filled six cavities and it didn't hurt too much. He was a very fine dentist from Missouri and did a real good job. One tooth was in doubt - whether it could be saved or not - but he took his time and said he thinks it'll be okay with a filling; I hope so because I would hate to lose

---

[147] Yiddish: Sweat

another. You know, I have two out now. I sent that package out this morning with some office supplies and you should get it by Friday or Saturday.

What's new with the Bialo boy? From the reports in the newspapers, I don't think they're taking any more limited-service men. If so, Paul is very lucky, because I know a few limited-service men who were just inducted a month or so ago. I wonder if Alfred and Martin Nelson will be able to stay home now. If so, they just made it by the skin of their teeth.

Last night I saw Mickey Rooney in "Andy Hardy has Blonde Trouble" and it was entertaining. Those Andy Hardy pictures get a little boring because they are all along the same pattern. This time Andy is at college and gets into one mess after another. You will all enjoy it, so see it when it comes to the Loews 83rd.

Major Becker came back today around 2 PM and took the rest of the afternoon off. He'll be in tomorrow morning for duty. He's the funniest guy. Very quiet and never says a word - when he walked in, no hello or anything. We haven't much work pending and it looks like a slow week coming up. That doesn't bother me though. The poison oak is pretty bad but of course it's not dangerous so there's nothing to worry about. It's just very irritating and I could itch it all day but I know that's the worst thing for it.

It wasn't as warm as I thought it would be today. Perhaps it'll stay cool for another few days. Took a haircut this afternoon and also got an injection for the poison oak. They give them in a series of five and it's supposed to help a lot.

Well, that's about all I have to write at the present. Take good care of yourselves. How's my piece of property? Isn't it marvelous to be a landowner, Dad? We're lucky to have such a fine piece of land.

Well, until my next letter.
Love and Kisses,
Charlie

Tuesday, April 25, 1944

Dear Folks,

Just came back from the Division show and it was very good. Drawing its talent only from the enlisted men of the 102nd, the show was entertaining and had plenty of good talent. I think I'll see it again tomorrow night.

My poison oak is a little better. I had another shot for it this morning.

When I first came here I was told that the General really gets hot when he's mad about something. Well, he's never been mad until today, and did he blow his top. He was peeved at some second lieutenant at Division HQ for telling our surgeon - a major - when to report to some school in San Antonio. Well, he shook the rooftop yelling over the phone and I saw why the boys warned me about his temper. But he never bothers us, so it's okay.

Still pretty cool but it should turn warm very soon.

One of the men in the Battery went AWOL[148] just before I came here. He was captured and now is back in Camp. He was sentenced to 6 months in the stockade[149] at hard labor. Well, it's a riot. He's with the Battery all day for training and they can't put him on any details, so he lives the life; hard labor, that's baloney.

Well, nothing more right now. Take care of yourselves. Tell me when you get those stationery supplies. Send those pictures and negatives soon, Eadie.

Love and Kisses,
Charlie

Wednesday, April 26, 1944

Hello Folks,

I'm in the phone building now waiting to place a call to Austin, so instead of wasting time, I'll drop you a line. I'm calling the girl I'm taking out Saturday night to make arrangements.

---

[148] Absent Without Leave, i.e. leaving the Army base without permission.

[149] Military prison.

Had a nice day without too much work. I hope you didn't see the story about a couple of boys getting killed at Swift. There was an accidental explosion of a mine in one of our infantry regiments. Was there any story about it in the New York papers?

Dad, I hate to disappoint you, but I don't think I can buy that stuff as I planned. They're getting strict about officers buying stuff for enlisted men and I don't want to impose on any of the officers. So try to get the things in New York; use some of my $15.

It was a little warmer today but still pretty comfortable. Edith, don't get too lonesome, you have to play the part of a heroine. Of course, it's tough having Artie away, but millions of wives are in your plight, so stay strong for a couple of more months.

All non-coms[150] had to attend a first aid class for an hour this afternoon. Nothing else new. Take it easy and write soon. Eadie Cantor is on the radio now. Incidentally, the girl wasn't home; I called person to person, so it didn't cost anything.

Love and Kisses,
Charlie

Sunday, April 30, 1944

Dear Folks,

Another week is drawing to a close and this coming week will mark my eighth month in the service. Oh, the one year mark isn't too far away.

I had a grand time last night. We didn't go to the school dance as I had planned, but instead we went to the nicest dancing spot in Austin. The school dance was formal and since I made the date late in the week, my date couldn't get her gown ready in time. Three sorority sisters of hers had a reservation for a table of eight at this night club (if you want to call it that) so we were the fourth couple. We had one drink (it was the first drink this girl ever had), it was a cheap evening but enjoyable. All the college girls have to be in at 12:45 AM, so you can't stay out too late.

---

[150] Non-Commissioned Officers.

I came back to Camp in a new bus and I slept all the way. It must have been a little past two when I hit the barracks. It took me close to an hour to get on a bus, there must have been hundreds of men in line. Went on CQ at noon and have been writing letters most of the time. I think I'll go to bed early and get a good night's sleep. Listening to the Fitch Bandwagon now. Xavier Cugat is the guest band. I saw him at the Paramount when I was on furlough.

It's still pretty cool and I think we'll have some rain tonight. It's very cloudy. Heard from Al Roseman, he's in Italy with the Infantry - poor boy! Haven't heard from Charlie Zwerner in a long while, I hope he is okay.

Nothing more right now. Thanks for the dollar and the pictures. Be good and take care of yourselves.

What's new, Sis? Did you get an afternoon off on account of Knox's death?[151] Too bad he died; he was a pretty good man. Are you still journeying out to Brooklyn every week? How are all the Marshaks?

Write and let me know.
Love,
Charlie

Monday, May 1, 1944

Dear Folks,

It's after 10 PM, but I'll drop you a quick line before I retire. Ain't that thoughtful of me? Thanks for your letter, E. I'm always glad to hear from you, sometimes I think you forget about your baby brother - but now you've got a husband and who am I to compete?

It's been a nasty, muggy day. It started to rain last night and it really came down. It's been showering on and off today and right now it's very windy and it looks like another rainy night. I pity the poor boys who have to walk guard when it rains like that. I'll never have to do it again and that's one consolation.

---

[151] Frank Knox, Secretary of the Navy, passed away at the age of 70 after a brief series of heart attacks.

Went to see "Pin-Up Girl" tonight and it was very light and entertaining. Nothing much as far as a movie but it has a few good laughs and some good songs. There's one scene near the end of the picture when Betty Grable gives close order drill and the manual of arms to a group of girls, and I certainly got a kick out of that. That's the basic drill all soldiers get, marching and carrying the rifle in different positions.

Was slow this morning but this afternoon reminded me of old times, as I was kept busy straight through the day. Gee, I like it so much better when it's busy. That sergeant who came over here doesn't do so much. He doesn't make any extra special attempt to learn the things we do, so Wojy[152] (that's the old Sarge who's been here) and myself don't bother with him. I don't think he'll last with us very long, but you can't really tell what will happen.

E, I wrote to your old friend Fillion today. I've owed him a letter for months and I wasn't going to bother writing, but I thought I would. Have you heard from him lately? He expected to be overseas by now. How come Alan got such a long leave? Seven days plus traveling time is supposed to be the limit. Perhaps he has a drag with someone but even that shouldn't help with a furlough. Or maybe he went over the hill, that kid is apt to do almost anything. So he's having trouble with Karyl, that's real tough, why doesn't he see the chaplain? Well, you're nicer looking than the chaplain and I don't blame him for crying on your shoulders.

One of the boys in the barracks went AWOL. He was due back for reveille this morning and he failed to show up. He went AWOL once before and this time he'll probably get a long sentence. That's the difference between men with good characters and common sense and the dummies. Smart men don't like the Army any more than anyone else, but they know you can't escape anything by going AWOL and you have to come back sooner or later. That's just about the furthest thing from my mind. It's my duty to be here now and I'll stay till they send me home. We have one boy serving a six-month sentence now, I think I told you about that.

---

[152] Wojtanowski.

[153] Yiddish: Tzadok Leib (Charlie) the son of Sam and Pauline, and the brother of Edith "the Complainer"

Well, that's all right now. Send the other two negatives back, please. Thanks loads for the others.

All my love, take care of yourselves and the best of everything.
Zudik Leibish ben Shmendrick, Pessa and *da bredder* of *Yentela Qvetch*.[153]
Charlie

Tuesday, May 2, 1944

Dear Mom, Pop, and Sis,

Had a fairly quiet day and outside of fixing up some files, I didn't have much to do.

The Battery went out to the field, but we stayed in and had a meeting of the headquarters section. The Master Sergeant just went over things with us, we made some suggestions and that's about all we did.

It's 10:30 now and I'm at the Service Club. It's no use going to bed early tonight because the boys will be in early and they'll wake us all up.

I think we're all going out Friday night. That'll be the usual procedure from now on, at least one night out in the field. That's not bad.

Mom, the best thing I can think of for Mother's Day is a phonecall, if you want something else let me know. I'll have to call real early or else I'll never get you. In fact, perhaps Saturday around midnight - that's the 13th. You can expect a call either then or 6 or 7 Sunday morning. Try to be home then, the three of you. That'll be the 14th of May, okay?

Did you get that package of stationery supplies yet?

Got a nice new pair of trousers today in place of some extra-large pair I got back from the laundry. They're a perfect fit except for the length, a trifle too long. I take 31; I thought I'd ask for 32, and I got a 33. Real service, eh?

Well, nothing more. Take care of yourselves.
Love to all,
Charlie

Wednesday, May 3, 1944

Dear Mom, Pop, and Sis,

All's well as usual, and there isn't much new down these parts. Had another slow day and at 5 PM I went swimming for an hour or so. It was a lot of fun and it's excellent exercise. There's a pool 200 yards away from the barracks and if I can manage, I'm going to take a dip every afternoon around 5 and then get back in time to shower and eat chow. That should be pretty good, just like Wakonda, eh? I wouldn't mind going back there this summer. Perhaps I can arrange it with the General to take two months off this summer. Sound like a good idea?

It was nice and cool again today. Perhaps this will be a fluke summer and it'll stay cool all the time. Good chance of that in Texas, eh Eadie?

I swear there isn't a thing to write about. We just heard Eddie Cantor broadcast from Mitchel Field, L.I.[154] Boy, I know some boys stationed there. It wouldn't be bad to be out there, would it? I'm glad you're getting an abundance of mail from Artie. He must be taking it nice and easy if he can write so often. I bet he's safe and sound and I know you're not worrying about him because there isn't a thing to worry about. What kind of work is he doing at the present time? Still with the First Sergeant?

I think there's a dance going on tonight but I have some mail to catch up with, so I think I'll skip the dance. They're not much good anyway because it's usually very crowded.

Listen folks, I'm not even going to mail this letter Air Mail. It's not even worth a free envelope, but I haven't anything else to write about. Will try to send you a little better letter tomorrow.

Regards to all - love,
Charlie

---

[154] Mitchel Air Force Base, also known as Mitchel Field, was a United States Air Force base located on the Hempstead Plains of Long Island, New York.

Thursday, May 4, 1944

Dear Folks,

Another day - another $2.20 - that's my daily wage, pretty good, eh? Just think, in thirty years I'll be getting $90 a month instead of $66. I know my allotment comes in handy to you, but I want to start saving some dough for a possible furlough and if I don't get that I want to get a three-day pass and that calls for some dough; so perhaps after this payday, I'll cancel the 15 bucks, and if I do have extra money I can send it home. As soon as I know that we're going over-seas I'm going to increase my bond allotment - that's the best saving there is - and send you the rest of the money. I won't be needing much money overseas. Expenses aren't as low as you might expect. You have to have at least two sets of suntans cleaned each week and now with the hot weather approaching, I'll have to buy another batch of towels and socks. So, we'll see how it comes along.

For the allotment you get on June 1, I would really like you to do one special thing, and this is the best time to do it especially since the money will be available. I took pictures in my cap and gown and graduation time last year and I do want those pictures before it gets too late to get them. Edith, please take care of it with the check. I want three; they have the order from a long time ago, the name is DeKane Photographers and they're located on 57th Street. I think their number is some place in the little phone book near the telephone. At any rate, you can find their number in the Manhattan phone book. They have the proof I approved and just tell them "Charles Fletcher of the School of Commerce, pictures for the 1943 Violet." We're not using the same studio for the pictures anymore but I'm quite sure they keep copies of old pictures. So don't fail me. I know that if I don't do it now, I'll never get around to it, so please take care of it at the end of the month. I think my checks hit you right around the 1st, so by June 15th you should have the pictures.

We had a USO Camp show here tonight and it was pretty good. Today is the second anniversary of Camp Swift and they had a little celebration. It was Open House today for the public but it was raining on and off all day and not many civilians came out to the post. This is one of the newest camps in the country and it's the seventh largest in the country. Benning is about ten times the size of Swift, but I like this camp much better, I'm right in the midst of everything and that makes it very convenient.

Did a little work today, but not too much. We've been kind of slow for a couple of weeks now, but it's apt to pick up at any time. We've had lemon pie two nights in a row and believe you me, it's been delicious. The Mess Hall probably had a lot of lemon extract that they had to get rid of. Someone in the kitchen knows how to bake pies because they've sure been good. It was too nasty for a swim today, and this cool weather looks pretty permanent for another couple of days.

Thanks for your letter today, Pop, I like to hear from you in your own letters once in a while. Incidentally, how's that marvelous piece of property I own? Still earning a mint?

Love and Kisses,
Charlie

Friday, May 5, 1944

Dear Folks,

Thanks for the two pictures. I think they came out very good and the large prints helped a lot. Too bad I didn't have any corporal stripes then. I'll have to take some new pictures so I can show my kids that I had stripes. As if my kids will worry about that. Just think of all the dads that will never have stripes.

It was very slow this afternoon. The Battery went out in the field around 2 and my Sergeant and myself were left in headquarters. Around 4 the officers went out to play volleyball and at 4:15 I took off for the swimming pool. I got a nice swim in and I had a big pool all for myself. I went to the camp pool this afternoon and it's a honey. I left at 5 and had supper in the Mess Hall. Then I cleaned my gun and at seven we went to the movies.

"Between Two Worlds" was playing and I was very disappointed. John Garfield, my old counselor, is in the movie and once again they gave him a poor part. He hasn't had much luck as far as roles go. I suppose you have to be in a special mood for the picture and I just wasn't. It had some good parts, but for the most part, it was slow moving and dull. Some good pictures are coming here next week. "And the Angels Sing" is one of them, and it should be entertaining. This new picture "Adventures of Mark Twain" should be very good and I'm looking forward to seeing it.

It's warmed up a little bit but it's still very comfortable. Tomorrow I plan to go to town. There's a dance at the JWB in the evening and I'm going to attend. Sunday afternoon one of the sororities is having an open house, so it should be a pretty enjoyable weekend.

I certainly enjoy your letters, Mom. You have such grand plans and expectations. I hope I don't disappoint you. Glad to see that you're getting around to the different shows. I would like to see "Othello" when I come home again - whenever that may be. We're all expecting the invasion any day. In Dallas and Ft. Worth, Texas, all the church bells and the factory whistles are going to sound when the invasion starts. Have they planned anything like that in New York? Our General thinks we'll beat Germany by the end of the year. I hope he's right, but his guess is as good as the next guy's. He also thinks that if the invasion is successful, we won't get over in time, but if we're stopped he believes we'll see some action in Europe. But I think that once the invasion comes it'll be the beginning of the end, at least I fervently hope so.

Tomorrow is my eighth anniversary. Yes, eight months ago tomorrow I was inducted into this great organization. Gee, the months fly by. Pretty soon I'll be a veteran of one year. Sometimes I shudder when I think that my childhood is behind me. Not that I'm afraid of my future, but just the thought that I'll never be 18 again and have all the fun that goes with that age. I used to read about people growing up and hating to lose their young teens but now I'm experiencing it. This world is so funny. You're born, spend a few fast years on the earth, and then you're gone. Some quick game, eh. I suppose you might as well do as much as possible while you're around.

Have a nice week and love to all, I love the three of you.
Love,
Charlie

Sunday, May 7, 1944

Dear Folks,

Another Sunday in Austin and it should be a nice day. It's 11:30 and in a little while I'm going swimming at Barton Springs with two friends from Camp.

Then we're going over to a sorority house for open house, so it should be an enjoyable afternoon.

Last night I stayed at the JWB for a while, but it was a little dull, so I went to a dance sponsored by the Business and Professional Women of Austin. There were more girls from the University of Texas than business and professional women, so it was very nice. I slept at the JWB last night and here I am.

Could have left Camp around 1 PM yesterday, but Major Becker was at a meeting and I didn't want to leave until he came back - I was the only clerk there. So, of course, when he came back he said I could have left, but it's always best to play it safe. As it was, I got a ride to town. I never can get a ride back to Camp, though, so I always have to buy a round trip ticket for 80 cents, it's 60 cents one way.

It's a little warmer but still a long way off from the warmest. Nothing else new right now. Take it easy and please take good care of yourselves. E, how's everything by you? How are the Marshaks? Send them my best regards.

Love to all,
Charlie
P.S. How were the bagels this morning?

Tuesday, May 9, 1944

Dear Folks,

I didn't get to write last night but this letter will get off in the morning mail, so it's the same thing. We had a real big rainstorm during the night. It's mighty funny about the storms at night. All the big ones with thundering and lightning come at night. We do have rain during the day but it's never as heavy as the storms we have at night. I had to get up during the night and close the windows. I remember when Mom or Pop used to do that for me.

Last night I went to see "And the Angels Sing." A pretty good picture with Fred McMurry getting into all sorts of pickles. At one time he's engaged to two sisters. Part of the picture takes place in Glenby Falls, New York, meaning Glenn Falls, and the other part of the picture is in good old Brooklyn - but overemphasized, of course. All you see is sharpies, and people saying goil and stuff like that. Gives a bad impression of Brooklyn - especially when there are such nice people living there - Bedford Avenue, for instance.

The Battery is digging in permanent installations for our problems and headquarters had to help out. So we took turns and I went out during the afternoon. Nothing much to do but dig, dig, and dig. I'll never want to dig for my living, and I assure you that I won't. It's no fun, but it was good exercise yesterday and I didn't mind it. It's 7:20 now. I got over to headquarters at 7 to relieve the old CQ. I'm CQ today and I get it again once more this week. I think I'll take it again tomorrow so I'm through with it. One of the boys is on furlough now so we get it a little more often.

I had a very nice time Sunday afternoon at that open house. There were plenty of girls there and we had punch and cookies. There was a lot of dancing and we also sat on the lawn in front of the house to shoot the bull. I met an old friend from NYU. He came down to our infantry from ASTP. I'm always meeting people I know from NYU. I saw that girl I know from Corpus Christie, we're going swimming next Sunday afternoon. I won't go to town Saturday night, but I'll go in right after dinner on Sunday. We're double dating with that fellow I met.

Thanks for the postcard about football, E. I hope it works out although I'm a trifle skeptical. It'll be swell if it does, but to be honest, it doesn't mean too much during these times. Perhaps in peace time I'll get all whooped up again. But I am glad that we'll have a football team, it's a good start for the post-war years.

Just think, a few hours ago it was raining cats and dogs, and now 7:25 the sun is shining strongly, and it looks like a sunny day ahead of us. That's the Texas weather - very changeable. Rain one minute, sun the next.

Well, I better start dusting up. Take care of yourselves. The answer is yes, Mother. Hasn't E taken up Aunt Rose on her bargain? Take it easy and don't work too hard. It'll be getting real warm in New York soon and then you better lay off a bit. I wish I was home to help out, but this is the way it is.

Did you ever get my package? Please tell me if you did. Nothing more, will write soon again.

Love,
Charlie

Wednesday, May 10, 1944

Dear Mom,

This is the first Mother's Day I've been away from home and I sure hope it's the last. It's true that every day should be Mother's Day, but the special day set aside for Mothers gives us a good opportunity to think of all the wonderful things Mother stands for.

To personalize this,[155] where would I be if it wasn't for Ma? All my life it was Ma this, and Ma that, and I assure you that I am ever grateful for all you have done for me. Mothers are the backbone of every American family, and you were sure a swell Mom for the Fletcher family. Oh, I could become very senti-mental and reminisce about the way you saw that Edith and I got all the better things out of life, but all I'll say is that I have been aware of all you have done and only hope that someday I can repay you a little. Though I'll never be able to fully repay you.

My wish at the present time is that God grant you strength to earn your own living until I get out of the Army, and then I want Him to let you live for a long while so you and Daddy can sit back and take it easy in your old age and I can try to give you some of the luxuries you always gave me.

It's silly to say I love you very much. Who wouldn't love such a marvelous Mother? May God bless you - always.

Love,
Charlie

Wednesday, May 10, 1944

Dear Folks,

It's still the same old story and there isn't much to write about. Eddie Cantor is on the air now and he's broadcasting from Ft. Monmouth, New Jersey. Oh, that's pretty close to 590 W.E.

---

[155] This letter was written on a formatted Mother's Day card provided by Camp Swift for the use of their servicemen.

The warm weather is here although it's really not too bad. There's usually a pleasant breeze at night. This evening the Division Artillery had a retreat parade but I was on CQ. While the parade was going on I took a dip in the nearby pool and that refreshed me. I've been tied up here in headquarters for two days now and I'll be glad when tomorrow comes. There's some talk that all T/5s[156] will pull KP, so I may not be doing CQ anymore. However, that's just rumor at the present time. All the T/5s in the Battery except four do KP, so I guess they'll catch up to us soon. I thought I'd get away with that but it doesn't look as if I will.

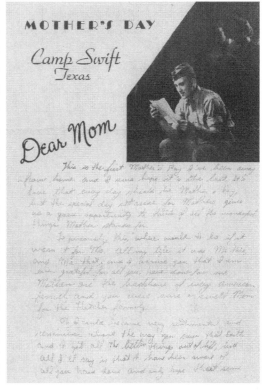

There was very little to do this morning, but this afternoon all the sergeants had to go to a first-aid class, so while I was alone I had some work to do. It's been very slow in HQ for the past few weeks. If this was a civilian place of business only one man would be kept, but the Army keeps three men. Well, I'm not kicking.

The Major and I got into a little conversation today about Wilkes-Barre. I told you he's from there. He's living in Scranton now, but he says Wilkes-Barre is much nicer. Once you start that fellow talking, he never stops; but it's only on rare occasions that he talks. He told me all about the floods in W-B, etc. I think he must have been in the engineering game before entering the Army. He's an old National Guard man.

---

[156] Military rank, Technician 5th Grade. The rank of Technician 5th Grade was added by War Department on January 8, 1942. Those who held the rank were often addressed as corporal. Technicians possessed specialized skills that were rewarded with a higher pay but had no command authority.

Edith, you remember Jerry Hershman who came over to see me during my furlough. He was ASTP at Penn and was being shipped out. Well, the folks know him also - the boy who has the very short mother living on 89th Street. Well, he was sent to the 95th Division at Indiantown Gap, PA and from there he was sent to Camp Pickett, VA. He winded up in an engineer outfit and after a few days was assigned as a personnel clerk. He's learning the ropes now and in a few months, he'll get his corporal stripes. Isn't that a nice break for the kid? Heard from Al Rosman, he's in Italy now.

I have a picture of the whole Battery but I'll hold on to it until I get the Division yearbook. Then I'll send them both home together. E, did you ever get that package of supplies I sent you? RSVP. Well, I'll be speaking to you in a couple of days. I'm looking forward to the call.

We're going out in the field Friday night until midnight. It shouldn't be too bad. I'm used to that by now. Yes, I'm getting to be an old veteran, heaven forbid. The captain who is on duty here tonight has been in 40 months on his present hitch. Can you imagine that? He's been in the National Guard and the Army over 20 years. Ouch! Well, some people consider it their profession. It's not a bad racket at that, that is if you are a West Pointer or a regular officer. But not for this guy.

Nothing more right now. Love to Grandma, don't tell her anything about a furlough because I may not get another one. I've been writing a lot to *Zadie* recently.

Love,
Charlie

Thursday, May 11, 1944

Dear Mom, Pop, and Sis,

All's well deep in the heart of Texas. Went on a "picnic" for lunch today. The Battery was out in the field and the kitchen was also out. So all of the boys who stayed in had to ride out with their mess kits in a truck and eat out in the field. It was just like a picnic. We had roast beef, potatoes, peas and carrots, bread, tapioca pudding and tea. Then we rode back into Camp and back to work. Some fun, eh? And there's supposed to be a gas shortage.

Went to the movies tonight and saw "Once Upon a Time" with Cary Grant. Quite fantastic but pretty good. It's all about a nine-year old boy's imagination and a caterpillar. It's whacky at times but I think you'll enjoy it.

I wasn't going to write tonight because there really isn't a darn thing to write about. If I skip a day now and then, don't be disappointed. When there's nothing to say there's nothing to say and you can't do anything about it.

I'll be out in the field tomorrow night with the Battery so I probably won't get a chance to write. Well, I'll speak to you Saturday night so I'll tell you all the news then. It was a little busier than usual today and I hope it keeps up. There just happened to be a lot of little things to do and that keeps you busy. One of the officers just handed me some report that he wants done tonight, it's close to 10. I get caught like that once in a while when I hang around here at night. I should know when to duck out, but I don't mind doing it.

I'm reading a book now called "Suds in Your Eye" and it's pretty amusing. I got it from the library and the Colonel bought it for two bucks in town. That's democracy – the corporal reading the same books as the colonel. Take off the bars and stripes and you have a man, right? I read Yank, the Army weekly, today and you should hear how the boys who come back from overseas are complaining. They say they're not getting any consideration and they're very disappointed. I would think that the Army takes better care of veterans, but probably they're only interested in the disabled ones.

It was pretty warm again today. We're having a rifle and shoe inspection tomorrow morning at 7:30. We're getting up at 6:15. It's a wonder they're not waking us up at 5:30. I cleaned my stuff tonight and shouldn't have any trouble. The carbines we have are very easy to clean. Nothing like the big rifles we had at Benning.

One thing. The days sure fly. Here it is Thursday night, another week is nearly over. I've been a corporal almost a month now. *Tempus fugit.*[157] Well, I'll close now. Take it easy and have a good week.

Love to Grandma. How's her hearing?
Love and Kisses,
Charlie

---

[157] Latin: Time flies.

Sunday, May 14, 1944

Dear Folks,

I heard your lovely voices less than fifteen minutes ago. You all sounded well and it was nice speaking with you. I hope the overtime didn't come too much. But since I had you on the phone I wanted to speak to Eadie - I am surprised that she didn't get up in the first place to talk to her darling brother. Now, if I were a certain Arthur Marshak, she'd be the first up and she wouldn't get off the phone. However, I'm just her brother and shouldn't expect such consideration.

Did you ever think that I'd be writing letters at such an early hour on Sunday morning? Well, in order to get the call through, I got up at 6 o'clock. Last night at 10:30 there was a three-hour delay to New York., and believe it or not, I had to wait 30 minutes this morning. The telephone company is doing a pretty fair business.

Breakfast in a few minutes and since I'm up, I might as well eat. No use going back to bed now. Stayed in Camp last night and took CQ for one of the married men, and I napped all night. I'm going to Austin right after dinner. I have a swimming date with the girl from Pensacola. It's going to be a good hot day, as the sun is strong already. It's a beautiful morning.

Nothing else new right now. Take it easy and have a nice week. Received your letters with a buck, Mom. Thanks.

Incidentally, I meant to ask you if you received my package? What must I do to get an answer? Edith, don't forget about my pictures from DeKane when you get my allotment. Don't worry about Art, he should be home before too long - give him another six months, okay?

Love to Grandma and the family. How are the Youngs taking Paul's departure? Did he leave from New York or from the coast?

Love and Kisses,
Charlie
P.S. How were the bagels, Pop?

Monday, May 15, 1944

Hello Folksies,

I was out of the office all day and it sure was a change. We had a field inspection in the morning. We pitched tents and laid out our junk - underwear, toilet articles, etc. In the afternoon we took all our sectional equipment out for display. What a farce it all was. Our own Battery commander and a Lieutenant Colonel from our headquarters made the inspection and all they did was look. The kitchen takes out all its stoves and my equipment are two typewriters, two field desks, and a mimeograph machine[158] - some fun, eh?

Tomorrow will be an easy day in the office and tomorrow night we all go on a ten-mile hike. That shouldn't be too bad as it'll be fairly cool and it will only take three hours or so. If I don't write tomorrow you'll know I didn't get a chance before going out.

One of the Division Artillery officers - a captain- a Jew from West 81st Street, just got orders to go overseas to the Far East. He applied for some administrative work in the Far East a couple of weeks ago and now they're sending him overseas. The dumb guy didn't know when he's well off. He had a winner here and now he's going overseas.

It's pretty hot and the sun was strong today, but it didn't bother me.

Nothing more right now. Take it easy and don't work too hard! Dad, I hope you and the Old Lady are getting along okay. Thanks for the two bucks, Mom. E, how about those addresses from the fraternity?

Love and Kisses,
Charlie

Wednesday, May 17, 1944

Dear Folks,

How are you all doing these May days? Just think, in a few days it'll be June. Gosh, how time does fly. I just hope we hold out long enough so that I can

---

[158] Sometimes called a stencil duplicator, the mimeograph is a low-cost duplicating machine that works by forcing ink through a stencil onto paper.

squeeze in another furlough. Most of the boys in headquarters are going home on furlough now and if I'm lucky, I'll be able to get one around the second week of August. Oh well, I can dream, can't I?

The reason that Alan was home so long, E, is that he had a fifteen-day furlough. The Air Corps is more lenient than the Ground Forces. We aren't supposed to be home for more than seven days and we can't go home within four and one-half months of the last furlough. At Alan's station you either get ten days every four months or fifteen days every six months. That's a pretty good set-up. I received a letter from him the other day. I'll have to answer him tonight. I heard from Murray recently. Mom, do me a favor and call up Mrs. Goldblatt occasionally. Her number is in the phone book near the telephone. Artie still owes me a letter.

I got your letter today, E, thanks a lot. I'm glad that the stuff in the package came in handy. Hope you have (or had) a very nice time in Baltimore. How is Elly? Did you get to see Mimi? You may see this letter Saturday morning before leaving, so if you do, be sure to send my regards to the girls and tell them to drop me a line if they're not too busy.

We went on the hike last night and it was a real tough one. However, it didn't bother me too much and it was about time I got some good exercise. Many of the fellows rode in the truck for a while but I walked the whole distance. I was a little tired at the end, but I've done worse at Benning.

We have a number of fans in headquarters, and it really keeps the place cool. I'm on CQ tonight and I have two of the fans going and I'm very comfortable. Tomorrow morning the Battery is going to fire the pistol and I'm going along. I'll be in headquarters in the afternoon while the Sergeant goes out. We've been a little busier than usual the past few days.

In Monday's letter did I tell you that I had a nice time on Sunday in Austin? I went swimming with the girl from Florida and afterwards we went to a small country fair and went on the ferris wheel and whip. My stomach was pretty shaky after that. I remember when I could go on that stuff all day at Rye Beach. I suppose Mom and Pop remember that also. What days we used to have there, eh E?

We'll be out again Friday night, the whole Division Artillery is going out on a problem. We'll be in early Saturday morning and probably have the afternoon off. I don't think I'll go to town this weekend.

Nothing more right now. Take it easy and don't work too hard. How are you feeling, folks?

Please rest whenever you can during the hot weather. So make a few dollars less, Mom? Don't make Dad *shlep* himself up to the building. It's not worth it as far as I'm concerned.

Regards to all.
Love,
Charlie

Thursday, May 18, 1944

Dear Folks,

Hello again from the plains of Texas. Received a very nice letter from my brother-in-law today. It came in two parts. I got Part 2 in the morning mail and Part 1 came in the afternoon mail. Isn't that just like the Army. He says everything is well and is glad that Eadie is taking the folks out. He's right when he says that our families at home worry more about us than we do. I'll write him a nice long letter this weekend.

I received your letter today, Mom. Thanks for the buck. The few extra dollars you sent me sure came in handy this month because I was a little short after a few big weekends in Austin. Now I've got a couple of bucks in my pocket to last me to payday. I don't think I'll go to town until next payday. I am still waiting for the refund from the Tax Department. If I don't hear from them soon, I'll write and ask why I haven't been refunded the money. I filled in the return way before March 15th and should have heard from them by now.

Before I forget, you mentioned that you have a vault in the bank and you want to know where my big war bond is. Well, it's in the big desk in the living room with the books and it's probably in the last book of that small encyclopedia set we have. That's where it should be, and if it's not, look in Wells' big book. Don't worry if you can't find it. It's somewhere and I'll be able to locate it when I come home. But if Daddy looks around a little, he'll find it. He always finds things. Dad, can you find me a pair of socks for tomorrow morning?

The news is sure encouraging and I'm hoping for the best. I hope Eisenhower is right in his prediction that the war will be over in 1944. Oh, that would make things grand. I'm so anxious to return to civilian life where a man is a man. Perhaps the whole thing will come to an end once the invasion takes place. That's the big question of the day. When will it occur? I wonder if anyone knows the exact date? Gosh, it may even start before you receive this letter. I hope so.

This morning I went out on the pistol range. I'm lousy with the pistol and hardly hit a thing. However, that's the least of my worries. It doesn't bother me one bit. Got back around noon and spent the afternoon in headquarters. There was a little to do, not much though. I'm on table-waiter tomorrow. I still pull CQ so it's no KP yet.

Tonight I saw a great picture. It was the first fine one we've had since "Madame Curie." It is "Gaslight" with Charles Boyer and Ingrid Bergman. The acting of both is superb and there's a lot of psychology attached to it. It's worthwhile seeing it when it gets up to the neighborhood.

Write me about your trip to Baltimore, E. Take it easy, folks, and may God bless you all. I want to be with you so much now that I've been away. Maybe it'll be real soon.

Love and kisses — Have a good week and don't worry. Be careful and watch your health.

Love,
Charlie

Friday, May 19, 1944

Dear Folks,

I was a very lucky boy tonight. I was sure that I was going to go out tonight for the Division Artillery problem, but this afternoon I found my name on the list of men not going out. My Sergeant and myself are the only ones staying in from headquarters and that's because Major Becker isn't going out tonight for the problem. Goody, and here's why. We're having the heaviest rain of the year now and the streets are all flooded. Oh, what a terrible night to be out. The boys are probably cursing us out. But it was just luck. I never expected to be left behind. If it were nice out I wouldn't mind going out, but with this lousy weather I sure appreciate being left behind.

I spent the evening reading Yank and Life. I find that I can't accomplish too much in the evenings. It takes a long while to read a magazine, if you want to read it through, and by the time you write a couple of letters the evening is over. I'm reading an American History book now just to bring back some of the things I should know about our country. I'm also reading Gideon Planish by Sinclair Lewis. I'm reading more now than I read while at college.

It was raining on and off all day and really came down this evening. You should see the streets, just like the floods Wilkes-Barre used to get. The engineers will be plenty busy fixing up the streets next week. Spent an easy day in the office. Was a little busy in the morning but there wasn't much doing in the afternoon.

Am in headquarters now with Major Becker and the Sergeant. We're all reading and writing letters and pretty soon I'll go to sleep. There really is very little to write about. Here's something that may be of interest. We have one fellow in the Battery who is a medic, and everyone thought he's a little nuts. Well, last Sunday he stole some drugs from the dispensary and mixed them with Coca-Cola and went a little batty. He started to go wild and start fights with the men and they finally took him to the stockade. He's still in confinement and he's been examined and found to be a little teched.[159] He has the mental age of an eight-year-old and I think he's going to be discharged under Section-8[160] - the lucky boy - at least for the discharge. It wouldn't surprise me if a number of boys have put on such acts just for the sake of a discharge. This one particular guy is too dumb for that, he's just crazy.

Still get some very nice letters from Dean Schiffer from NYU. He was the Dean I was so chummy with at school. He always tells me how much they miss me, etc. A good line of bull—what a salesman he is. Don't worry about what I'll do, Mom, after the war. If I don't go into business, it'll be something else. There are a lot of things I can attempt, so don't worry now. Before you start a busi-

---

[159] Slightly crazy.

[160] A category of discharge from the United States military, used for a service member judged mentally unfit for service.

ness, you have to have some capital - especially something like the furniture business, and I have no capital and knowledge of the business. But I'll pick up something and do okay. I'm still young and there's plenty I can do. In order to be a success, you don't have to be your own boss, you know. I shouldn't have any trouble. First, let me get out of the Army and then I'll decide. Meanwhile I'll think the various things over.

Heard from Stellie today. She'll make some guy a good wife. She's getting an excellent course at her college.

Keep well and take it easy, love to Grandma and regards to the family and friends.

Love,
Charlie

Sunday, May 21, 1944

Dear Folks,

Saved this letter for last this weekend. Took a day off yesterday from letter writing but knocked off a few today. Spent a quiet weekend as a guest of Camp Swift. Yesterday after work I took a shower and after chow had some bunk fatigue (a *shnooze*). I slept until 8:30 and then went to the movies with a buddy. We found the movie house all sold out, so we went back to the Battery area and played some ping-pong in the dayroom.

This morning I slept until ten o'clock and then I went to the pool. I got some sun but didn't do much swimming, as a Red Cross instruction class was going on. Just managed to take a dip. Had a nice dinner consisting of chicken, string-beans, lima beans, and ice cream. Then read Gideon Planish by Sinclair Lewis for a while and then took some more bunk fatigue until 3. Then I started writing some letters until evening chow at 4:30. That's all we do around here and that's eat. At 6:30 I went up to the theatre. I saw an excellent picture, "Dr. Wassell" with Gary Cooper. It's about this Navy doctor who served so gallantly at Java and brought back ten sailors who were all seriously wounded. Of course, Copper is great, and it's a very good production - in technicolor produced and directed by Cecil DeMille.

Didn't do much yesterday. We had a very easy day, especially in the morning when everyone was out on the problem I told you about. They started to come in at 11 and the firing was very good. The General was in an excellent mood and that means he was well satisfied.

It was very warm today. There are three fans going now in headquarters and that helps somewhat. Edith, I heard from your friend Bernard Fillion. He's somewhere overseas but he's so GI he didn't even mention it in his letter, which was censored. That's funny because most of the boys can say where they are although they can't give the exact location. He was pretty sure that his group was going over a couple of months ago, and sure enough they finally did.

I wonder what will become of us. I'm not impatient, but this is just like a good book. You want to know what happens at the end of the book, and I want to know what will happen to us in a few months from now. Well, time will tell. Personally, I think we need maneuvers again, but that's my opinion; as I told you before, I don't know what to expect. We'll be here another month for sure, so that's a consolation. The darn invasion should take place by then. I suppose the bookies back home are betting on the day it will take place.

Nothing more right now. How's the wonderful piece of property we own? How are the grandfolks? Don't worry, I write to them. Say, Pop, how is your family; Aunt Ray, Dora and Fanny and *Moisha*?[161] Say hello for me, will you? I hope you still call or see them occasionally.

Well, take care of yourselves, how are you feeling these days? Tell me the truth. Hello, Sis, keep your chin up. You'll be seeing your honey real soon.

Love and Kisses,
Charlie

Monday, May 22, 1944

Dear Folks,

Received your letter today and thanks for the dollar. I've saved enough money now to go to town this Sunday - if it's nice out, I plan to go swimming in Austin with one of the girls from the university.

---

[161] Yiddish: Moses.

I'm glad to hear that you're busy. I understand the help situation, it's the same all over and you have to make the best of it. If you can't turn out all your orders, you just can't and that's all there is to it. You people work as hard as you can and there's a limit to every person's labor. So don't kill yourself. I know that you would be doing better business with more labor but this just happens to be a bad time to try to get more help. How's the rubber situation? Send my regards to George. I think he's more valuable to us at Grandmother's than in the Army, do you agree?

Saw a fair movie tonight, "Address Unknown" with Paul Lucas. It's about Germany when Hitler gets his start, and how an American art dealer goes to Germany to buy some paintings and gets into the Nazi party and he betrays his Jewish partner back in San Francisco. The same old stuff but pretty good. The best thing of the night was a cartoon with Sinatra and Crosby - as roosters - sing to make the hens lay eggs for war productions. Very clever.

We had the pool this morning and it was raining, but that didn't make any difference. The Battery went swimming and the headquarters bunch just dropped over for a minute to show them that we could swim one lap. I did that very easily and then I wiped myself off and came back to the office. I assure you that if it was a hot sunny day we wouldn't have had the pool, but since it was so nasty and wet we went swimming. Typical Army, my dears.

Had a very easy day as usual. I really don't do a darn thing during the days. The Special Service Officer returned from school but I'm not going to bother with him unless Major Becker tells me to. So far, the Major has discouraged me from helping out, so since it's not my job, I'm not going to fool around unless told to.

Tomorrow night the Battery goes out in the field, and I think I'll go along. We're having a medical test - malaria control, mosquito nets, etc. It'll be a hell of a lot of baloney, that's all. For all I know I might not have to go out, but I'm not counting on it. As soon as I get paid, Dad, I'm going to send you some undershirts and socks. They're selling the stuff in the PX's now at quartermaster prices so I don't have to ask anybody to buy the stuff, I can buy it myself.

Well, that's all about the news I have right now. I wish I had more to write about but there just isn't anything of interest. If I don't write tomorrow, I'll be out in the field. But I'll write very soon. I think you've been getting mail very regularly. I wonder if any other son writes home so often. Is Paul overseas yet? Send my regards to the Youngs.

Love and Kisses,
Charlie

Wednesday, May 24, 1944

Dear Folks,

Gee, that night problem yesterday was a snap. We got in at 9 PM and we didn't do a thing while we were out. It was a medical test more or less, and once we were supposed to make believe we were gassed and the medical officer was going to ask us what we would do under different circumstances. Well, I ran so far away when we got off the truck that no one ever saw me. And at the next stop, when the Doc asked what we'd do for certain wounds, etc., I also was way out of sight. So the whole thing consisted of riding in a truck for a couple of minutes, and laying out in the grass for an hour or so.

Two German prisoners escaped from Camp Swift on Monday night, and as yet they have not been accosted. The newspaper said they were wearing their prisoner of war clothes (blue fatigues with PW printed in orange) and that they couldn't speak English. However, I believe that they must have stolen GI clothes somewhere - Laundry or someplace like that - and just walked out the gate. It would be quite difficult to walk out the camp with a PW uniform. There have been numerous escapes down here and I think we're treating them too darn good. Our guards are very polite, and I suppose that once the Germans are in their own area at camp, the guards relax a bit. They'll probably tighten down, somewhat. Hardly a week passes without some prisoners escaping.

Edith, I just read the May 14th Times - Sunday. Remember Jerry Tarlow of the basketball team? Well, he married a kid, Alice Cilento, who was a freshman with me at NYU and was going out with Warren Dickstein – well, they just had their second child. Oh, my back! Then in the engagement and marriage column many names looked very familiar and I'm sure I know some of the people mentioned.

Started shorthand lessons tonight at the Post Moral Office. Some PFC is the teacher and he seems to know his stuff pretty well. For one lesson I think I did pretty well because I can read a paragraph already. Put on a clean shirt tonight - just got it back from the cleaners recently - and boy, I would like to know what they did to it. The cuffs are so tight that I hardly can button them and the entire shirt seems snug. I bet they sent them to the laundry instead of the cleaners. I'm buying another suntan set as soon as we get paid. I think I told you that we can buy them in the PX.

Very slow again today. In the afternoon, the Battery threw live grenades, and I went out with the first group and then came right back to relieve the Sergeant. It was nothing at all. All you do is pull the pin out of the grenade, keep holding the spring and then heave it and duck. They make quite a noise. That sort of killed the afternoon. One of our battalions is leaving for Ft. Still, Oklahoma tomorrow morning for a period of two months. They're going to be attached to the replacement school there for instructional purposes and it's my guess that since the Commanding General of the Army Ground Forces picked one of our battalions, it means that we're not slated for anything much during the next two months. Okay by me. The entire battalion is leaving and there's quite a lot of work attached to it.

That's all for now,
Love,
Charlie

Friday, May 26, 1944

Hello all the Lovely People,

Wie geht es ihnen?[162] Everything is as usual down here. We worked last night, so I didn't get a chance to write. We had an ordinance inspection - all tools and equipment of the different sections in the Battery. That was this morning and last night all the men in the Battery had to help get things ready. I helped out in the garage and besides getting my hands full of grease, there wasn't anything to the job. We were all in bed at eleven after scrubbing the barracks. We only scrub about once every two weeks - sometimes three- that's pretty good because a lot

---

[162] German: How are you?

of batteries scrub barracks twice a week. We all mop under our beds in the morning, so it's not bad. It's funny when you think of it but practically every soldier in the United States does the same thing at 6:30 or whatever time he arises. That song "GI Jive" has a lot of truth to it. You get up and get dressed. Then you stand reveille and then you get back to make your bed, sweep, mop, and tidy up. That's second nature by now. Boy, what a bunch of housekeepers we'll all be after the war. Can you imagine scrubbing floors just by throwing a pail full of water with some soap suds on the floor and then scrubbing with a broom. New method, eh?

It was a slow day and unfortunately, I had to be CQ today. On account of the night work last night, the Battery got the afternoon off. The same thing happened last week and it will also happen next Saturday. But my turn will come soon for some afternoons off, I hope. Our First Sergeant just came back from furlough tonight. Our Battery commander left on his a few days ago. A very nice 1st Lt. is taking over for the ten days. I just keep on hoping that I get another furlough and the way I look at it, I think I will. We're definitely going to be here until the middle of July, and they can't move us to a staging area so fast - I hope. Don't bank on it, but you can give it a thought.

Thanks for the propaganda from Washington. I'm glad you did a stop there. It would have been foolish not to see the Capital since you were so nearby. I'm planning to visit that place some day in the future.

It's pretty hot, but I'm managing okay. Will spend a quiet weekend in Camp. Want to go swimming, as I haven't been in all week. Perhaps tomorrow afternoon. I'm not going to bother with the paper. I can see that Major Becker doesn't approve of it and no one seems enthused about one, so why should I stick my neck out now that I've got a rating, right?

Received the Serviceman's Bulletin from Commerce[163] - remember me putting it out last year, Mom? To be truthful, it didn't match up to mine. However, I may be prejudiced. I think my idea was original and this year's is a direct steal - but it's still good. My picture is in it. I'll see if I can have one sent to you.

---

[163] A special Soldier's Edition of New York University School of Commerce school newspaper.

Incidentally, did you receive the pictures I sent? I shouldn't have bought both, but they came out at different times. I took the small one three months ago. They're only a buck apiece, though.

Well, that's all for now. Have a nice week and take good care of yourselves. Ever think of me going into the corset business with Mom as a designer and Dad as a cutter?

Love,
Charlie

Saturday, May 27, 1944

Dear Folks,

Everything is just fine except that I'm on CQ today and that ruins the weekend. However that's nothing to gripe about. Well, I could have died today when I heard that Eisenhower announced that his forces had landed in France. That was about 3:45 (4:45 your time) and I was in the barracks changing my clothes. Then I went to the PX to get a few things and when I came back it was around 4:15 and I turned on the radio in headquarters and heard the commentator announce that the news bulletin about the Allies landing in France had been rescinded. Can you imagine what a letdown that was? Boy, for a minute I thought the real invasion had come and then I find it's just a mistake - so they say. That's some mistake for a news telegraph operator to make. I bet he's looking for a new job already. Well, perhaps one of these days it'll be the real thing.

It's been a busy week for a change. In addition to the paper, I was kept busy with work for Major Becker. I think I told you that one of our battalions is at Ft. Still, Oklahoma for two months. Well, there's a lot of work to be done in connection with that and we're always sending telegrams, etc., to Ft. Still and it's got us on the run.

I told you that the enlisted men played the officers in volleyball. Well, from now on we're playing every afternoon. There's going to be four teams playing each afternoon and the enlisted men from HQ are going to be on one team. There'll be two other teams of officers and one of enlisted men and we'll play around so that we all play each other. The General likes the idea of us getting out, so every afternoon at 4 we'll stop work for the day and play ball. Not bad, eh?

The paper is coming along okay. I'm expecting to have it out Thursday, June 8. The General is going to be away on leave then, darn it, but I'll see what the other officers have to say. I know the General will like it. But enlisted men never get the credit in the Army. It's always the officer who is the big shot. Now in my case, the officer I work with can hardly spell his own name and the General will probably congratulate him and forget about me. That's okay, because sooner or later he'll find out that I did all the work.

Instead of going out to the field last night, I stayed in and worked on the paper. The Battery got in very early, so I didn't get away with anything. I was kept busy all night. There really is nothing new right now. I'll let you know about my plans for next weekend in my next letter. I intend to see some boy from New York who was a counselor with me at Wakonda. I'll tell you about it tomorrow.

Love,
Charlie

Sunday, May 28, 1944

Dear Folks,

Received Mom's and Pop's letter this noon and it was nice to receive such a long letter. Yes, the news from Italy is very encouraging and I think we'll clean up there.[164] I still think, though, that we'll have to go through with the invasion. It wouldn't surprise me now if the invasion was held up a couple of months and then started when people least expected it and stopped talking about it. But that's mere guessing. Our General thought we were doing wonderfully in Italy and says that if we have sufficient reserves, we should accomplish our mission there.

Listen to this story. I had a sore throat yesterday and it rained very hard in the evening, so I took a hot shower and got into bed around 8 o'clock and read. About nine o'clock one of the boys returned from furlough and he had a real good bottle of schnaps. Well, he offered me a drink and knowing that it would do my throat a world of good, I took a swallow - two or three - and then I got under the blankets and went to sleep. This morning my throat was all better -

---

[164] Referring to the Canadian Corps offensive which had just taken the town of Ceprano, Italy.

see an old-fashioned remedy still works okay. I'll stay out of the water for a few days so I'll be all cured, it wasn't really that bad.

Got up at 7:30 for breakfast and went back to bed and read the Digest for a while and then *shnoozed* until 11. We had a delicious dinner that would have cost at least $2.00 in town. All the fried chicken we wanted, mashed potatoes, peas, salad, jello, chocolate cake, ice cream, and coffee. Not bad, for Army chow, eh? I'd match our Mess Hall against any, including officer's, in the division. We really have no complaint about our food. For breakfast I had shredded wheat, fried eggs, milk and toast and an orange. In the Army you always eat the hot stuff first, so it doesn't get cold.

Listening to John Charles Thomas now. For some reason I can't get the Philharmonic - are they through with their broadcasts for the season? It's not too warm today. The rain must have cooled things off. Boy, did it rain last night. We didn't close the front doors and when the wind started to blow, once it carried the rain right through the screen door and it flooded the floor. Then one of the boys went out to close the doors. The rain here reminds me of the good rainstorms at camp. I still remember my camp season last year and if you think I didn't enjoy that, you're mistaken. I really had a marvelous time with those kids. And it was a good vacation for me.

Going to see "Three Men in White" with Lionel Barrymore this evening, it's supposed to be pretty good. I didn't bother seeing "Hitler's Children," probably a lot of junk.

Yesterday afternoon the Battery went out to a mine demonstration, which was a lot of baloney about German mines. When we got back we had organized athletics for the rest of the afternoon and I played two good games of volleyball. Then I went back to headquarters and helped finished up the week's work. There wasn't much doing.

I hope you're all getting along okay. For three adults living together, you should be getting along harmoniously. I hope there aren't those old-fashioned arguments going on. Edith, you're a grown woman now, and nearer a mother than being a daughter so you should be very loving toward Mom and Pop. Give in to the folks because they're all we have and soon you will be in your own home with Arthur. So, for a few months yet, go out of your way to satisfy the folks. That's the least you can do. Tell me how the folks are feeling in your next letter.

Is Pop taking some vitamin pills? Oh, he's such a good-looking man. It's surprising that we have a Dad with such a head and such a beautiful mother.

They caught the two German prisoners that escaped and listen to this. Those damn Nazis pulled a sit-down strike the other day and we had to send out some of our soldiers from the Artillery to police their area and see that no trouble started. I never found out what they were striking about, but I assure you they had no grievance. We treat the damn prisoners too good and I doubt whether any of them had it so good in Germany. I would have shot a couple if I were in charge, and they pulled a strike. Can you imagine their nerve? Could you imagine what Hitler would do if some of our kids went on strike in a German prison camp? We Americans are too soft, that's all.

Well, that's about all I have right now. We're taking another ten-mile hike Tuesday night. I really like them, as the miles isn't anything and it's good exercise. It was those 25 milers I didn't like and I only had to take one of them.

I finished Gideon Planish by Sinclair Lewis. It was pretty good and although he was very sarcastic about New York, he was right about many things. One, that even with a substantial income of $8,000 in New York you could still be considered poor. Isn't that the truth if you wanted to live in real style in New York? That's why I think that if I do my work in New York, I will live in the suburbs or some place in Jersey where you can have your own home and live nicely on a moderate income. People making $60 a week and live in a small town live much better than people making $125 and living in New York. Isn't that the truth?

Have a nice week and let's hope we continue to mop up in Italy. Kiss each other for me, and for my sake, get along with one another. Mom, don't try to do too much. If the house brings in $25 as it is, leave it alone. That's good money to throw away, as you say, Mom.

All my love to everyone. Did Martin Nelson ever go to the Army, or did he get away with it when they changed the rule about men over 30? He's lucky if he did. Take it easy and be good and careful. Dad, please don't surprise me with a baby brother. We have enough to worry about as it is. Could you imagine me washing diapers after the war?

Love and Kisses,
Charlie

Friday, June 2, 1944

Dear Folks,

You'll have to excuse me this week for the skimpy letter writing, but for the first time in a long while I've been very busy.

The General decided that we had to have a paper immediately, so I was put to work on it. It wouldn't be bad if that's all I had to do, but I still work for Major Becker and that makes it pretty rough. It won't last long this way because I already told the Special Service Officer that I couldn't possibly do the two jobs well, and that I prefer working for Major Becker. The paper is just a big headache, and I won't get a thing out of it. I can take it easy with Becker and there is no worry or any rush, so why stick my neck out. I'll put out the first issues and then try to get rid of it. I think I'll speak to Major Becker about it.

I went to Austin on Wednesday afternoon to make arrangements with the printer and I'm supposed to go to Austin on Tuesday and Wednesday of next week to put out the paper. That'll be okay, but I know the officers won't like the idea of me being in town so much. So, all in all, I think it best that I stop working on the paper.

Went swimming Wednesday morning and it was fun. Had no trouble with the ten-mile hike Tuesday night. It was easy. I had to miss my shorthand lesson on account of going to town and that's something else I don't like.

E, thanks for your letter and I promise a personal letter this weekend.

I'll sign off now, will write soon again. Take it easy, thank you for the buck, Mom.

Love and Kisses,
Charlie

Sunday, June 4, 1944

Hello again Folks,

Another weekend nearly over. As fast as the weeks go by, the weekends go quicker. It seems like Monday morning has come around so fast. Now if the end of the war would come as rapidly and we can all come home, things would be fine.

I saw "The Eve of St. Mark" tonight and it was pretty good except it was a war picture and it reminded me of how much I do want to be home and be doing other things. But as a movie, it was pretty good. Is the play still on Broadway? I hear that was pretty good.

Had a peaceful day. Slept to 7:45 and then got washed. I told you I was on CQ. Then I walked over to the Service Club for a couple of fried eggs and toast and milk. Then I came back to headquarters with the Sunday paper and spent the rest of the morning reading the news and writing some letters. I wrote to Grandpa and Grandma today. I heard from Miss Riley today and she said that Grandpa was his usual self, but the warm weather is getting him down somewhat. Well, at his age that's to be expected. Let's just hope that he's not too uncomfortable this summer.

After dinner today I took a *shnooze* until 2:30 and then went swimming to 4:15. I had a cheese sandwich and some potato salad for supper in the Mess Hall and then I cleaned up a bit and shaved and then it was time for the show. Dad, I've been looking for stuff for you and all I could get was three undershirts size 40. Now if I know my Dad, you take much more than a size 40. However, if you can use the shirts I'll send them along with ten handkerchiefs I bought for you. I'm going to town this week and I'll get you something nice for Father's Day. I know the best thing you would want is a visit from me but that'll have to wait a while. I'm still hoping for another furlough and it still is a toss-up, no way of telling.

I'm going to try to get a pass this weekend from Friday noon until Monday morning. The Battery is off Friday afternoon and a friend of mine who is stationed nearby is coming to visit me Friday evening and Saturday, so if I can get a pass I'll have a swell time. Tommy Dorsey and his band are playing at the University on Friday night. He's giving both a concert and a dance. I've thought it over and it'll be silly to attend both, so I think I'll take a girl to the dance only. It'll cost $3.50 and that's enough for one night. It would be another $2.50 for the concert and I don't think Dorsey is worth that much after seeing him so many times in New York. For these hicks who never see a big orchestra I suppose it's alright, but not for me.

I have a little material for the paper, and it might come out okay. I'll send you a copy and tell me what you think of it. By the way, have you received those two pictures of the Battery that I sent you?

Well, that's all for now. I'm about even with my correspondence to you and I think I've made up for that little lapse. Be well and take care of yourselves and don't argue with one another. We have bigger things to argue about than the things you quibble about at home. How's the building?

Love and Kisses,
Charlie

Monday, June 5, 1944

Dear Folks,

For the first time in months, I have some big news and here it is. Oh boy! We're moving east by July 1st. Yes, we have to be out of Camp Swift, and today we were told that we're leaving by rail - which means a long trip, and we're making a permanent change of station. All that means is that we're going to another camp to carry on our training and it's no alert so don't get worried. Of course, we're on our way but as it stands now, we definitely are not going over until October. And that's good news as far as I'm concerned.

The General broke it to us this morning by coming out of his office and yelling, "We're changing stations." We're having a practice movement 19th June, so we'll be leaving here between 19-30 June, probably the last week of the month. I, along with everyone else, was getting restless in the camp and we're all tired of Texas - the Division has been in this state close to two years.

Now, of course, everyone is guessing where we'll go to. Well, since it's a train movement we're sure to go over 500 miles but from the way the General spoke I'm inclined to think it's going to be in the good old East. I have three places in mind, and anyone would be good. Ft. Dix, New Jersey (I'm going to say my prayers every night for that), Camp Pickett, Virginia, or Ft. Devens, Massachusetts. Of course, it's just guessing and for another month no one will know, but any one of the three would suit me. Then I'd have a chance to come home on weekends or else you could come up to spend Sunday with me. Now for time. We're due to stay in our next camp at least 2 ½ months, so it's very improbable that we'll be set for sailing before October, so don't worry. Things will definitely be anti-climactic after October and we shouldn't have much to be afraid of then. I hope we travel a long way and don't stop in the south, North Carolina or South Carolina for instance. Well, time will tell.

One thing you have to remember. Don't say too much to people around town. All we're allowed to say is that we're shipping East by July 1st. But in the Army things change so rapidly that we might be here for the duration, that's because conditions change so quickly. But right now, that's the story and Mom, if you think your prayers will help, please pray for Ft. Dix; that would be heaven provided the pass situation is okay. But only time will tell. Don't worry. I'll surely get my furlough in August, and I'll be so close to home that it'll be marvelous not having to travel so far and spending all that money on car fare. Swift is okay and Austin is not bad, but just for the chance of being close to home, I'd like to leave. Of course, we might end up in some hole in the Carolinas, but that's the chance.

Going to Austin early tomorrow morning to start work on the paper. I hope it comes out okay. I think it will. At present we plan to have two issues here and then wait until we reach our next camp to start again. Well, I hope everything comes out okay.

Love and kisses. Don't worry, I think it's best to tell you all but if you worry, I'm going to stop. Eadie, tell me if they worry. Love and kisses. Hope to be within 250 miles of you in three weeks. Oh, yippee, and hot dogs.

Love and Kisses,
Charlie

Wednesday, June 7, 1944

Dear Folks,

Well, it's come! Isn't it terrific news! I just hope everything is going okay with all the boys taking part in the invasion.[165]

I'm just as busy as you can imagine with the paper. Reminds me of the good old "Commerce Bulletin" days. I was in town all day yesterday and I'm back again today. We're going to press in a little while and it should be ready tomorrow. I'm printing out 8 pages, I'll mail you a copy tomorrow.

I really haven't had a chance to breathe this week. Friday night I'm going to Tommy Dorsey's dance, and I hope to get Saturday off, I don't know yet.

Well, I'm going to the press room now, so I have to close. Will write a long letter soon.

Don't worry, all will be okay.
Love,
Charlie

Wednesday, June 7, 1944 - Later That Day

Dear Folks,

Well, it's about time I got a big letter off to my folks. You should have received by now my letter from the print shop that I wrote this afternoon. Boy, it was a busy day, and as it was, I didn't entirely complete the job. The engravers disappointed us on a cut of the General and I didn't get the page proofs. So I have to go in early tomorrow with a jeep and finish up and wait for the papers to be printed. I was afraid to tell Major Becker that I had to go in again but if they want the job done, it takes at least two full days. The reason it was a little slower today was that it was the first issue, and everything had to be set up and I wasn't used to the printers and they weren't used to the paper. I'm sure that it'll be much easier next week.

Tomorrow when I go to town I'm sending home my furlough bag by railway express. I could take it with me on the trip North, but it may get damaged in the freight car or lost and I don't want to take the chance. I hope I'm near enough to home that I can get it on a weekend when I come home to see you. Boy, my next furlough will be swell. I'll be close to home, and no travelling. Oh, I hope all of our prayers come true - Pennsylvania, Virginia, New York, New Jersey, Massachusetts; I'm not asking for much am I?

Well, the invasion is sure going along okay. I'm sure the casualties will be much less than expected. Edith, how are you taking it? Please don't worry about

---

[165] D-Day, June 6, 1944. This refers to the Allied invasion of Normandy and the largest amphibious invasion in history with nearly 5,000 landing and assault craft, 289 escort vessels, and 277 minesweepers. Some 160,000 Allied troops crossed the English Channel on D-Day, with an additional 24,000 airborne troops landing in occupied France.

Artie, I'm sure he's okay. We clerks always manage to stay away from the real stuff. I have a bit of news about someone we know. I was going to wait before I told you, but it happened quite a while ago and you may know about it already. Herb Hoffenberg of TAO[166] was bumped off recently. I don't know what he was in or where, but I know they got him.

I just looked over the stuff that came in the past few days and nearly all the plans have been made for the movement, although there's no rumor as to where. There will be an advanced party leaving around the 16th of June but I think only the Division Headquarters sends out and not the Division Artillery. If we do, Major Becker will probably go and there's a chance that I'd go along with him but that's not definite. Now that I know we're moving I'm all excited, but it'll come soon enough. We'll probably be out of here by the 29th. I hope they don't go and change their minds. You see, all these orders come from Washington and the General doesn't even know what the new order tomorrow could be.

It's pretty hot now. I was going to ask Major Becker for the day off Saturday, but now after being away most of the week I'm a little hesitant. I'll be back in Camp tomorrow at noon and I'll be in headquarters a few hours. However, I'm on guard tomorrow night and I'll have to leave here early to prepare for guard. So that cuts another day. I'm corporal of the guard for the first time tomorrow; this is the first time I have guard since my promotion. It's close to two months, that's not too bad.

I wonder whether this paper will influence the General into giving me a sergeant's rating, there isn't one open, but he might find a way if he wants to. Excuse the typing, I'm tired.

All my love,
Charlie

---

[166] Jewish fraternity.

Thursday, June 8, 1944

Dear Folks,

Well, the paper is out and I think it looks pretty good for a first issue. I've mailed you one under a separate cover. Tell me how you like it.

Dad, I sent home my bag today, collect. Now don't get too excited, it's only 70 odd cents and in addition, I sent you a few things for Father's Day so I know you won't mind paying a small fee. I got you a nice sport shirt and a couple of pairs of under shorts and those handkerchiefs and undershirts I bought at Camp. The other stuff was bought in town in a good store - I even bought you the better quality sport shirt so you see how much I think of you. Put the bag away and I hope to pick it up in less than a month. I don't know why I'm expecting to be so close to home. Don't be disappointed if I'm not so near. We have no idea of where we're going and I'm only hoping for the best. Don't bank on anything - that way you'll avoid disappointment.

Went to town with another fellow who rode the jeep. We should have been done and on our way back to Camp by noon but there was a delay with the General's picture, and we had to stay until 4, so it was another day in Camp. We took in a show in the afternoon - saw "Yellow Canary," a British picture with Anna Nagle and Richard Greene. Pretty good.

Tomorrow night I'm going to town and have a date for the Dorsey dance. I've asked the First Sergeant to find out whether I can have Saturday off but as yet I haven't received an answer. Tonight when I got back to Camp at 5, I distributed the papers and then got ready for the field. We had an easy problem. We went out in trucks and then groups of three and four men were left off at various points with a map. We had to find out where we were and then we had to find some point they gave us. My group didn't have any trouble and after walking a mile and a half we found the coordinates and there were a few men there already. We weren't late, so it was okay. Some guys were very late and missed the trucks going back to Camp and they had to walk a few miles. We rode back in the trucks.

Tomorrow I'll devote a full day to Major Becker's work. I still want him to know I'm in his section because there's no way of telling how the paper thing will continue. The Major didn't say anything about it yet but he's not the kind to praise or criticize, so I don't think I'll get much comment from him. However, a few officers have already told me it's very good and most of the men received it favorably.

I'm already preparing for the next issue. I'll go to town Tuesday and Wednesday and have it all done by Wednesday night. It was a little hard for the first time because I didn't know exactly how they worked, etc. But now I'm on their system and it'll be a snap next time. Incidentally for a town the size of Austin, this print shop is excellent. They're fairly expensive but they do a very clean job and the plant would rank with many of New York's best. They have their own printing equipment and it's the newest and best stuff.

Well, it's close to eleven and I'm a little tired. Be well and have a good week.
Love and Kisses,
Charlie

Saturday, June 10, 1944

Dear Folks,

Boy, I write to you at the craziest hours. I'm supposed to be CQ today but the Sergeant is taking my place but I've relieved the old CQ for breakfast. I went to the dance last night and as I expected it was very crowded with a bunch of hicks who never saw a big orchestra before. Dorsey was good though and I enjoyed myself. I got a couple of hours sleep in the hotel and then I came to Camp. I've already had breakfast and am waiting for the day to come to a close so I can go back to town.

My friend from Camp Hood is coming down this evening and we have dates for tonight. I haven't heard from him lately but he said that if he didn't write, everything was alright so I'm just keeping my fingers crossed. I got him a blind date - I've never seen the girl. I have a date with a nice Jewish girl. Met her once and really don't know much about her except that she's a freshman at the university and comes from some part of Texas. I'll write you about it tomorrow.

When I was in town last night, one thing impressed me. All the retail stores closed at 5 PM; I wish it was that way back home. There's no reason to stay open until all hours. Mom, now that the hot weather is here I'm sure you're closing up at a sensible hour- 7 o'clock or 7:30. You can do just so much in a day and if you stay open very late both of you get so tired that you really accomplish nothing. It's better to do all your work between 9 and 7. For my sake Mom, see if you arrange that. I'd die if you're staying open all hours like you used to. There's not very much doing at night and at your age it's very advisable to close early and get a little rest. I know there's a lot to do, but two people can only do so much.

Eadie, what kind of place is Pine Camp?[167] I don't think Artie liked it so much, did he? I'm not positive that we're going there but it's one of the camps being mentioned and it could be. Tell me what you know about it. We are planning to move out during the week of the 19th. If you don't hear from me for a few days then you'll know we're moving. I wish we were over with the movement. I don't relish the idea of travelling in a troop train such a long distance. The new camp is supposed to be 2400 miles away so it's most likely Massachusetts or upstate New York, time will tell.

Way behind on my correspondence and if I don't catch up soon I won't have a friend in the world. Will try to do a lot of it next week. I have a meeting of all the reporters from the batteries today at three o'clock, I'll try to tell them what I want. Have you received the paper yet? Did you ever receive the pictures? E, did you ever order the pictures from DeKane? Please get around to it if you haven't already done so.

Well, take care of yourself and try to close early and rest up a little. E, you should see that the folks come home by 8, the latest. Have a good week and hope to see you real soon.

Love and Kisses,
Charlie

Sunday, June 11, 1944- Hotel Austin

Dear Folks,

I'm in my underwear now in a room in this hotel. I had a very pleasant weekend and after I take a little *shnooze*, I'll be on my way back to Camp.

---

[167] Military base founded in 1908 and located in Jefferson County, on the northern border of New York. The name of the Camp was changed to Ft. Drum in 1974.

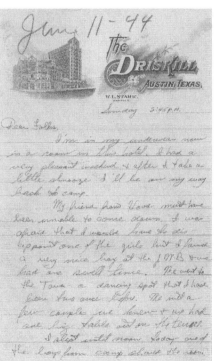

My friend from Hood must have been unable to come down. I was afraid that I would have to disappoint one of the girls, but I found a very nice boy at the JWB and we had a swell time. We went to the Tower, a dancing spot that I had been to once before. We met a few couples we knew, and we had one big table out on the terrace.

I slept until noon today, one of the boys from Camp shared the room. Then we had a big dinner and went for a walk. I intended to go swimming, but it rained and now is very cloudy, so I think I'll go back to Camp shortly and see the movies there.

Nothing new about our movement, probably be around the 21st.

Love and Kisses,
Charlie,

P.S. Thanks for your letter, Pop.

Tuesday, June 13, 1944

Dear Folks,

I'm on the 14th floor of the Hotel Austin, overlooking the city of Austin. I came to town to work on the paper again and I'm staying here overnight, expenses paid by the Army. I'm not going to do a thing but try to catch up with some mail. Boy, I'm very behind.

Had a pretty good day at the printers, got all my stuff laid out and I'm ready to put together the pages tomorrow morning.

I left the printers around 5 this afternoon and went out to Barton Springs; the water was muddy so I didn't do much swimming, but I did get some sun.

No news about our movement. The truth is that no one knows where we're going as yet. We should start moving out next week.

It's mighty hot these days, had a delicious cantaloupe at dinner tonight. It was really good. Also had vegetable soup, chopped sirloin, potatoes, lemon meringue pie, and milk. I have a nice simple room, this hotel is very modern.

Love and Kisses,
Charlie

Wednesday, June 14, 1944

Folks,

I had a marvelous day as far as the Army goes. I slept in a big bed until 8 and then I had scrambled eggs, which tasted like scrambled eggs. I also had corn-flakes, toast and milk.

I got to the printshop a little after 9 and we were ready to put the paper together by 10. By noon we were finished and all I had to do after a delicious lunch was to read page proofs. I was through with the entire thing by 1:30, and I had the rest of the afternoon for myself.

I went back to the hotel, showered and then checked out. Then I went out to Deep Eddy's swimming pool and stayed there till past 6.

Now it's 7:10 and I'm just waiting for the 8:30 bus back to Camp. I'll be able to write a few letters before then. So that was today. The paper looks pretty good, I think they'll like it again. The General should be back tomorrow and I want to hear what he has to say about it.

Dad, your Father's Day card is back at Camp, but I'll mail it as soon as I get back. If you don't get it in time, excuse me. Also, forgive me for getting such a plain card. The assortment down here is very limited.

Well, it's back to the Army tomorrow. We have a ten-mile hike Friday night, they're pretty good exercise.

Nothing more right now. So long - have a pleasant weekend, please take it easy and close early; you're not spring chickens any longer.

Love,
Charlie

Thursday, June 15, 1944

Folks,

Spent a day in Camp today; after being away with civilians for two days, it's a little strange to come back to the Army routine.

Caught up on some of my filing and did some typing. The paper came in this afternoon, and it looked all right. The General hasn't mentioned anything about it. We're not coming out of Swift anymore, and before the paper is published at our new camp I'm going to try to get rid of the job. I've thought it over and I think it's best if I stick to my job with Major Becker, we will see what happens.

The latest information has us moving the 25th or 26th of June for our new station, which is still unknown. I think our General knows and he may spill the beans soon. If you can spare $2 or $3, send it down so I'll have some spending money for the trip. I think it'll take us four days and four nights, ouch! You can imagine how fast the troop train goes, the trip regularly wouldn't take more than 50 hours or so.

Nothing exciting going on. Some of the Battery went out in the field tonight for a Division Artillery problem. The rest of us are getting up at 4 AM; all the boys are going out then for the problem, but my Sergeant and myself are staying in.

Well, that's all.
Love and Kisses,
Charlie
[168] אי"ן גוטע וואך

Saturday, June 17, 1944

Well, folks here it is,

I have very good news. I will be within 100 miles or so from home and you can expect to see me a little more frequently in the future - I hope. Now I'm going to tell you where we're going but don't say a word, as a few boys have already gotten in trouble for telling their families that we're moving. We'll be in Ft. Dix, New Jersey on or about the 29th of June and just wait for the first weekend I can hop into town. Now don't worry about it being POE. It is our staging area before we go to a POE and the average stay at a staging area is three months, so if I'm lucky at all I'll be in Dix until the start of October or the middle of September. From there we should go to a POE, but that's indefinite.

If the pass situation is at all comparable to what it is here, I'll be able to come in most of the weekends. But I have no idea if they'll be lenient or rough with their passes. The paper should come out for a while and although I still want to drop it, I plan to hold on to it for a while so when I come to town to work on it, you can come and see me. Trenton is the nearest town to camp and that's a stone throw from New York. Boy, this is the first good break I've had. I just hope they don't rush us through Dix but let us take our time.

So, I'll be in God's country about two weeks from today. I'll call you as soon as we're allowed to, but don't get excited. We don't know the exact date of our departure but it's somewhere around the 25th and the trip will take three days and three nights.

---

[168] Yiddish: *Ien Gutta Voch*, Have a good week.

I'm on guard today but with the news of Dix, I don't give a darn. All is well, don't worry about me. By the time we get overseas most of the rough stuff will be over. The earliest we could go over is in September, and that's a long way off.

Well, I'll close now, folksies - hope this news makes you feel as good as it does me. I'll be seeing you real soon.

Love,
Charlie

Monday, June 19, 1944

Dear Folks,

Boy, today was the days of days. It soared around the 100 degree mark all day and now at 9 PM it's still hot as blazes. I can just imagine how it is here in the midst of summer. A day like today makes me feel doubly happy that we're leaving here in a week. I think our train is pulling out next Monday at noon, but it's not definite. The advanced party is leaving tomorrow and how I wish I were on that train, but it just wasn't my luck. My Sergeant isn't going either. They're taking that surplus sergeant I told you about a while ago. Here's an important thing I want you to remember - don't address any mail to me at Dix until you receive notification of the change of address. No one is to write to Dix until all the changes of address go out from Swift. Even when we're at Dix we'll have to use the Swift address for a few days. So around next week you can stop writing for a while and then I'll speak to you over the phone and tell you what's what.

Dix is definitely not a staging area of POE for us, so don't worry, Mom. When Artie went East, he knew he was going overseas, I know that I'm just going to Dix just as a permanent change of station. We should be in Dix around the 30th of June, so you can expect a phone call from me sometimes around that date. I think I'll be able to get home on one of the weekends soon after our arrival there. At least I hope so. For one thing, I know it won't be as hot there as it is here; boy the sweat is just pouring off me.

I'll be glad when the trip is over. Even though we're supposed to have some kind of Pullmans, I doubt whether the trip will be very comfortable. In fact, I know it won't be, but I'd travel freight just to get to Dix.

Where's Paul Young? You told me Mollie heard from him. I also wonder about Charlie Zwerner. I haven't heard from him for quite a while and I just hope he's okay. How's Yetta and her family getting along? Incidentally, you might as well stop writing when you receive this letter, because I'll be gone when you write. Just wait until I call you.

We haven't had too much to do lately. The day or two days before we leave we're going to leave the barracks and live out in the field. Just a crazy idea. We'll probably scrub the barracks and they're afraid we will get them dirty. I'm going to see whether I can manage to stay in headquarters.

Well, that's all for now. You'll hear from me soon - don't worry for a few days. We won't be able to mail letters while we're traveling.

Love and Kisses,
Charlie

Wednesday, June 21, 1944

Hello Folks,

Nothing new, Major Becker left with the advanced party yesterday morning. A Lieutenant Colonel in our office is taking his place. We've been kept pretty busy, but all the work is getting out all night. My Battery is leaving here Sunday at 8 PM, so we should be at Dix by Wednesday night. The troop trains go much slower than passenger trains.

Last night I went to the swimming pool and got a good burn. I'm pretty brown already. Tonight I'm going to see "The Mask of Dimitrios" which should be a pretty good mystery - Peter Lorre is in it.

Still nice and hot now, the 10th Division is moving into Swift, their advanced party is already here. It's a ski mountain division. They've been in Colorado for ten months, God knows what they will do here.

We're ready to go, practically everything is packed. The General isn't leaving here until Tuesday, he has to go to Ft. Still to attend a conference and he will be back at Swift to catch the last train to Dix.

Well, that's all for now. Take it easy and be good.
Regards to all,
Love,
Charlie

Thursday, June 22, 1944

Dear Folks,

Nothing new so I'll hold up on the letter tonight.[169] I had planned to see "The Mask of Dimitrios" last night, but they were sold out by the time I got there. So instead I went to see it tonight, it was fairly good.

Hot as hell again. Pretty slow in HQ, as most of our work is done. I may leave here a little later than I expected.

Love to all,
E, I'm sure I thanked you for that big box of candy you sent me a long time ago, finished the last hard candy today.
Charlie

Saturday, June 24, 1944

Dear Mom, Pop, and Sis,

It really doesn't seem like Saturday today, we had a full day and no passes were issued so it's just like a weekday and tomorrow will hardly be a normal Sunday. We're getting up at the regular time and at 7:45, I go with the loading detail to help load the train.

Today was a real goldbricking day. We cleaned headquarters early in the morning and for the rest of the day we didn't have a thing to do. I read some magazine and in the afternoon I went swimming.

I saw the picture "This Is the Army" tonight. I saw it in the New York station two nights before entering the Army, it's a fairly entertaining picture.

---

[169] This note was sent on a postcard.

The Battery is leaving tomorrow night, but I'll have to hang around for an extra day. This time Monday I'll be choo-chooing home. Don't forget, I can't mail letters on the train, so don't worry. Also - very important, don't write to Dix under any circumstance until you receive a change of address.

Love and Kisses,
Charlie

Sunday, June 25, 1944

Dear Folks,

Well, this is my last letter to you from Camp Swift. Tomorrow night this time I'll be choo-chooing North. As usual there was a last-minute change. Only ten men were supposed to wait until tomorrow, but now there are 30 of us going tomorrow and not at 4 PM as planned, but at noon. So you can imagine how many other changes were made during the two weeks of planning for this trip.

Today wasn't bad. Helped load a freight car - all our stuff took up one entire car. Worked fairly hard in the morning but there was very little to do in the afternoon. Came back to the barracks and showered and cleaned up. Had a delicious dinner this noon in a different Mess Hall - ours was closed. I must have had close to a half a chicken, potatoes, corn and ice cream.

It sure is hot today and the boys from the new division aren't going to like it one bit. They've been up in Colorado for a year and it's nice and cool up there and they're not accustomed to the heat. You should see them sweating already. Now that I'm getting ready for a trip, I'm reminded that just a year ago this time I was leaving for Camp Wakonda. Some difference in a year, eh?

I'm staying in headquarters tonight. I don't mind because the other fellows have to get up at 5 o'clock for breakfast, but here I can sleep as late as I want. We'll probably leave for the train a little after ten, so I have plenty of time to do anything I have to do tomorrow morning.

Pardon the letter, this typewriter is the only one we have left and it's sure lousy. Skips every other *lette r*. There's an example of it. I'd write more, but there's simply nothing more to say. You won't hear from me for a few days now, so don't worry. I'll call you up as soon as possible after reaching Dix. Perhaps Thursday night. Keep well and take good care of yourself in this hot weather.

Love and Kisses,
Charlie

Tuesday, June 27, 1944

Dear Folks,

Just left New Orleans, we had a stop there for about 2 hours. We got off the train and just walked around the RR neighborhood. We only had ½ hour off the train so we couldn't do much. The ride has been okay so far, but we have two more days and I think it'll be pretty tiresome by then. We're traveling Pullman and it's not bad. Can't mail this until we get to Dix, so it'll be delayed.

Love,
Charlie

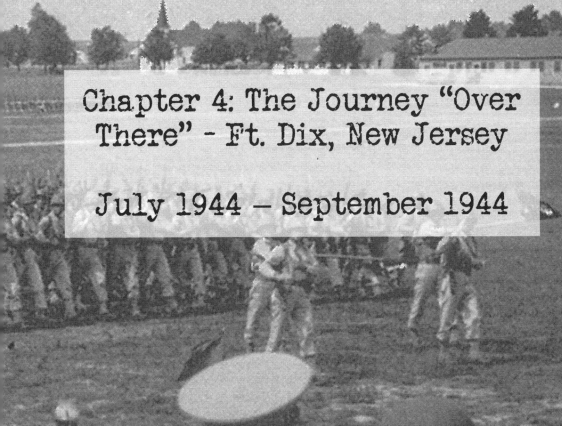

Chapter 4: The Journey "Over There" - Ft. Dix, New Jersey

July 1944 – September 1944

On July 1, 1944 - less than one month after D-Day and the Allied landing in Normandy - the 102nd Division arrived at Ft. Dix, New Jersey on what everyone believed would be its last stop before departure to combat in the European Theater. This movement toward a port of embarkation provided an extra push in training and the perfection of the Division's military capabilities. On July 17, the Division was inspected by Under Secretary of War Robert P. Patterson, accompanied by Lt. General Ben Lear, then Commander of Army Ground Forces.[170] Between August 15-18 the "inspection to end all inspections" took place, during which a War Department Inspector General Team examined the Division thoroughly to ascertain military readiness. After finding everything to be in order, the Team gave the necessary clearance for the Division to move forward to their port of embarkation.[171]

Beginning on September 3, 1944, over 15,000 men of the 102nd Division made the three-hour train journey from Ft. Dix to the Camp Kilmer Staging Area.[172] This move was completed on September 6, when the last trainload of

---

[170] With the 102nd Infantry Division Through Germany, pg. 30-31

[171] Ibid, pg. 31

[172] Located two miles north of New Brunswick, New Jersey. Camp Kilmer became the largest processing center for troops heading overseas and returning from World War II, processing over 2.5 million soldiers. (National Archives & Records Administration Northeast Region, https://www.archives.gov/files/nyc/public/camp-kilmer.pdf)

Showdown Inspection at Ft. Dix.
(With the 102nd Infantry Division Through Germany, pg. 31)

soldiers arrived and *"on whistle signal, formed in a double rank three paces from the coach facing away from the train, executed a right face, picked up luggage and marched smartly off towards their new quarters in the elaborately multi-colored buildings of The New York Port of Embarkation."*[173] All understood the magnitude of the task at hand, and for some brave young men, it would be their last time upon American shores.

On September 12, 1944, just two years after the activation of the 102nd Division and one year from Charlie's induction into the Army, the six ships carrying the men of the Ozark Division took their place in the forty-six vessel convoy for the twelve-day journey on open sea to France.[174] Aboard the *USAT Santa Paula*, Charlie lodged with the other enlisted men in bunks stacked four to six high. The voyage was mostly uneventful, except for a submarine alert mid-ocean which sent *"everyone rushing topside to watch sleek destroyers and escorts race through the convoy to drop depth-charges."*[175]

---

[173] With the 102nd Infantry Division Through Germany, pg. 33

[174] The six ships: *John Ericson, Marine Wolf, Santa Paula, Sea Tiger, Bienville, and the Marina.*

[175] With the 102nd Infantry Division Through Germany, pg. 36

Disembarking at Ft. Dix.
(With the 102nd Infantry Division Through Germany, pg. 30)

On September 22, 1944, the six ships anchored in Weymouth Harbor, England. The very next day, Charlie and the rest of the Division disembarked in the bombed-out harbor of Cherbourg, France.[176]

---

[176] Ibid.

Tuesday, July 4, 1944

Hello People,

All is well here at Dix. Got back okay and had a good night's sleep. Stayed in the office all day yesterday and didn't do a hell of a lot.

We're supposed to get an extra day off this week on account of the 4th, don't know what day yet. Would like to go to the shore, so I don't know if I'll come to New York. Probably be there Sunday. It's nice and cool here, haven't sweated once since we got here. We're still unpacking and cleaning up.

No more for now, will see you soon.
Love,
Charlie

Monday, July 10, 1944

Dear Folks,

Hello. Gee, I haven't seen you for such a long while, huh?[177]

I hope the funeral went off okay. I hope that we don't have any more funerals in the family for a long while.

I took in a show last night with Mary and took a midnight train back. Saw "Two Girls and a Sailor" and Sammy Kaye's band on the stage, pretty good.

Dad, as soon as my suntan suit is washed, send it out - regular mail - not special. Also, if the little stuff I left on the floor is done, send it along. I left the new shirt in the closet - it doesn't need a washing; just let the maid or Eadie press it so I can slip it on next time I'm home.

It sure is nice to get home so often, and I do appreciate it. I doubt whether I'll come in this weekend, but I'll give you a buzz if I don't. If I can get away real early Sunday morning, I may come in.

Was pretty busy today, I think I got rid of the paper - at least I hope I did. Nothing more, I'll be seeing you.

Love and Kisses,
Charlie

---

[177] During this time period, Charlie was home almost every weekend. There was therefore a drop in his daily correspondence of letters being sent home.

Tuesday, July 18, 1944

Dear Folks,

All's going on as usual. Pretty busy in HQ catching up on our filling, etc. Had a very nice time Sunday night. I went to the German-American; Eadie knows about that place.

It was real cool this morning and I sure did need those 2 blankets during the night, some difference from Texas.

Here's some good news - especially for Dad. I have quite a few expenses this week - haircut, 2 suits dry cleaned, some pressing etc. - so I can use a couple of bucks for carfare home this weekend. Don't worry, in a few months I'll be sending home practically half my pay each month, so you can take out then what you're giving me now. After all, I'm not going to be here long, so I might as well have a good time. Next month I won't spend so much in the beginning of the month.

If you care to, tell the Bialos that I'll be in Sunday. Perhaps we'll go there for dinner or Morris will take us out. It's up to you. I hope you're home this weekend.

Eadie, keep trying to get some film. I've been unsuccessful so far.

See you Saturday, I hope.
Love,
Charlie

Monday, July 24, 1944

Dear Folks,

I spent a pleasant weekend in Wilkes-Barre. However, I sure did miss coming home. For the few weekends we have left, I'll settle for home and my Mom, Pop, and Sis. No further developments, but it looks like the home stretch is now. Don't say anything to anyone about me expecting to go over. It's all secret material, please remember that. It's very important.

Grandpop looked well as usual, but you can't tell anything by looks. I spent some time with *Zadie* and in the afternoon we all went to the lake. Everyone is fine and they send their regards.

I'll need carfare to come home this weekend, so send me $3. It cost me around $4 to go to Wilkes-Barre. I'll see you Saturday night, make some plans for Sunday if you want to - Bialo or anything you'd like.

See you soon,
Charlie

Monday, August 6, 1944

Dear Folks and Sis,

Once again, I had a wonderful weekend at home. I'm sorry I rushed so on Sunday, next weekend I'll give you more time. I've made no arrangements for Saturday night, so the evening is ours. We can go to a movie or the Goldman Concert. On Sunday perhaps I had better go to see the Marshaks, although I don't really see why. At any rate, E, tell Anna that you and I will come out to the beach on Sunday. Don't go Friday night, E, wait for me and we'll go together. I meant to call them last night, but I was having such a swell time that it skipped my mind.

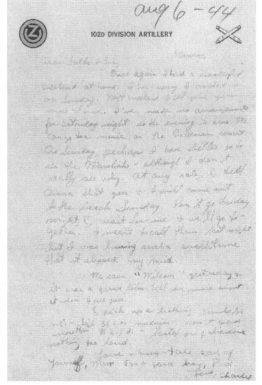

We saw "Wilson" yesterday and it was a grand film, tell you more about it when I see you.

E, pick 2 bathing trunks for me - size 36 or medium - don't spend more than $2.50.

Love and Kisses,
Charlie

Tuesday, September 12, 1944

The Santa Paula, Charlie's transport ship to Europe.

Dear Mom, Pop, and Sis,

Well, the baby of the family is now a sailor. Yes, I'm on the boat now and the trip is going to be really swell.[178] I hit a perfect set-up. If you recall, I told you that I was going to be a clerk on the ship. I got to the boat a little early with three other fellows and we have a room for six fellows and our own bathroom, tub, sink, etc. We work in the Adjutant's office on the ship, and everything is just so.

I'm most satisfied with our fine living conditions aboard the ship. Most of the boys are pretty crowded but it's not half as bad as I expected. Our room is nice and cool and I had a marvelous night's sleep last night. Slept until 7:30 this morning and feel well rested. Four of us are working in the office and we're taking shifts so it won't be difficult at all. I worked this morning and in a little while I'm taking off for a rest period. We were kept busy this morning typing schedules, etc.

Your cookies are coming in handy, I have quite a few left on the boat. I ate the fruit before coming to the ship, that was also appreciated. We forgot my watch, so please mail it to me when you mail me a package. Don't rush on the packages, wait until I see where we go or what we do.

Please take good care of yourselves, I'm not worried one bit, so don't you start fretting. I'm safe as anyone can be. Also don't work too hard with the darn business, and Mom as soon as possible you should start taking colored tenants into the building, I see no reason for not turning the house into a colored one.

That's all for now.
Love to the family and hello to Grandma,
Charlie

---

[178] Though Charlie wrote daily while on the journey overseas, the letters were only mailed back home once he reached his final port of destination in France.

Wednesday, September 13, 1944 - Somewhere On the Ocean

Hello Folks,

This letter is being written on our second day at sea, but God knows how long it will be until you get it. I plan to mail all my letters as soon as we land so you get some mail. However, in the future, remember that no news is good news. At times it might be impossible to write, so don't worry.

My first day at sea was pretty good except for a little spell in the afternoon. I got over that quickly and today I'm feeling just fine. At times, I even forget that I'm on a boat.

Have been doing loads of sleeping. After the first day in the office there wasn't much doing except a bit of typing, so most of my time has been my own. I have some good magazines so I've been reading and sleeping and nothing much else. I should be well rested by the time we get to the other side.

We have no idea as to where we are. The boat takes you and that's all there is to it. The sea has been very calm and it's a beautiful sight. The sun came out this afternoon and helped cheer things up. We had a little rain this morning but it didn't last for any length of time.

There isn't much we can write, the food isn't too bad, there's a library aboard ship and I'm doing a little reading. Really have no more right now. Will write another letter real soon. Too bad I can't mail this as I finish it, but I'll have to wait until we hit our destination. Take it easy and say hello to Grandma and tell her all's well.

A very happy New Year, this may be late but I have no idea where I'd be at the time. Next year, I hope we'll all be home for a happier holiday. E, what do you hear from Artie?

Love and Kisses,
Charlie

Tuesday, September 19, 1944- Somewhere On Water

Hello Folks and my sweet Sister,

Well, here is your sailor boy once again. If they keep me on the ocean much longer, I might as well join the Noivy.[179] Feeling fine, the only thing that is worrying me is that you are probably worried stiff. Well, please don't, for my sake. I'm in great shape and there isn't anything to worry about. E, I'm leaving it up to you to see that the folks don't fret.

What's the latest word from Artie? He must be well into Germany by now. How are his letters and what does he say? I hope he left those foxholes for me as I asked him. Gee, there's no sense in the two of us digging foxholes.

The news has sure been encouraging. We've been kept informed enroute by daily news releases. Too bad the Yankees bogged down, Eadie, perhaps you could have taken in a World Series game. At the present time, it does look like Detroit.

The football season is here at last. How I would like to see NYU play at the Heights. You know we're playing Lafayette there very shortly and there are some other good games at the Heights. If you can spare the time, E, why don't you go to a few, but if the folks need you Saturday afternoon you should help them out. Don't forget you're the only one home now and you should do everything in your power to help the folks. Pretty soon Artie will come home and then you'll be on your own, but for the duration help them out.

Did you have a nice holiday season? We had services on the ship and I attended. The first time in years that I didn't hear the *Shofar*[180] blow. Pop, did you knock your heart much at Temple? Where did you go - the Center on 86th Street? I'm not sure whether we'll have services for *Yom Kippur* on the boat. There's been no announcement yet.

It's been a bit chilly the past few days, but the sun usually comes out in the afternoon and it's not too bad. Have been sleeping a lot aboard. Usually miss breakfast and sleep to 8 or 9 o'clock. As I told you I'm sleeping with five other boys and no one bothers us. They have movies every night, but I read instead.

---

[179] New York-accented pronunciation of Navy.

[180] Hebrew: A *shofar* is made of a ram's horn, blown in synagogue services on *Rosh Hashanah* and at the end of *Yom Kippur*.

There are no seats and it's crowded as all heck so I stay down in our compartment.

There's nothing more that I can report at the present time. Keep well and please don't worry. I'll keep the mail coming as steady as possible, don't worry, but at times it will be out of my hands, so be patient. You saw how long you had to wait at times for Artie's letters. Well, I may be in the same boat, no news is the best news.

Send my best to Grandma and tell her I'll write as soon as I get a chance. I got another GI haircut today. I may not have too much hair but it sure grows in fast. I left the top on but had a close trim around the sides and back, a real bowl haircut.

Well, I'll sign off for now. Take care of yourselves and have a very happy New Year.

Love,
Charlie

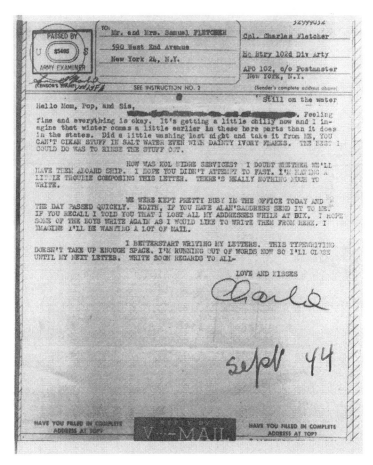

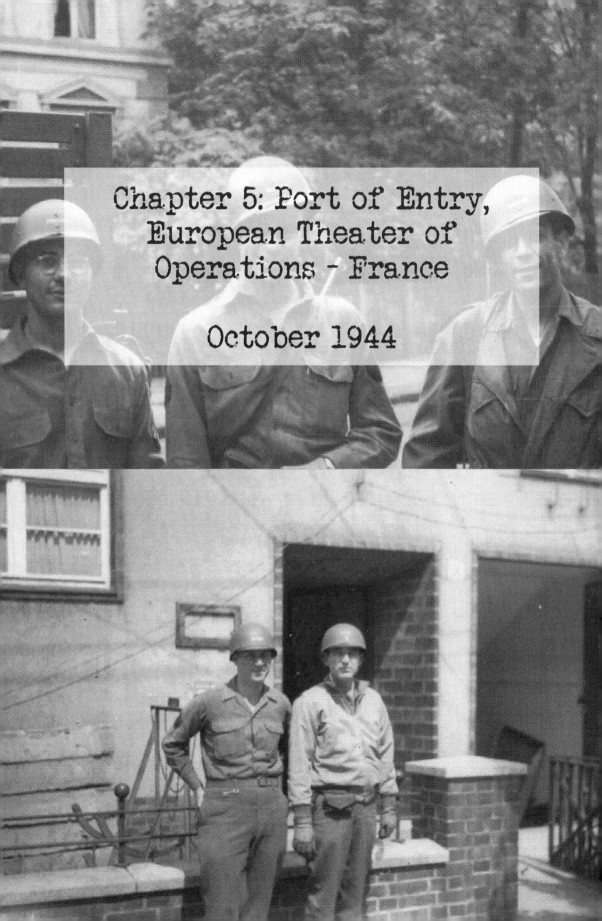

Chapter 5: Port of Entry,
European Theater of
Operations – France

October 1944

Following the 102nd Division's arrival in Cherbourg, France on September 23, 1944, there began a short period of initial training in the countryside near Valognes, France. This was in preparation for the Division's eventual departure to the frontlines some 400 hundred miles to the East, on the border between the Netherlands and Germany. During this time, the Division in general and Charlie in particular, took part in one of the greatest logistical operations of World War II – also known as The Red Ball Express.[181]

On July 25, 1944, the Allied forces finally broke out of their beachhead in Normandy and moved to meet the German forces in central France. During this offensive, code-named Operation Cobra, components of the US Third Army under General George S. Patton Jr. often covered more than 80 miles a week. This lightning-fast advance forced the German Army to retreat across France, but also caused serious supply problems for the Allies.[182]

To tackle this issue, on August 21, 1944, the American commanders created a Red Ball[183] truck-route convoy system with more than 6,000 trucks, tasked

---

[181] With the 102nd Infantry Division Through Germany, pg. 36-37

[182] The National World War II Museum, https://www.nationalww2museum.org/war/articles/red-ball-express

[183] Named after the red dots, commonly used to indicate priority express trains in the United States.

with taking supplies on the 54-hour round-trip route, from Cherbourg Harbor to the forward supply depots in Chartres.[184] Red Ball Express drivers often worked in two-man teams and drove on one-way roads reserved exclusively for their convoys at speeds surpassing 60 miles per hour. Military policemen guarding the junctions guaranteed that the trucks need not stop for anything on their route towards the forward supply depots.

To re-enforce this supply effort, on October 5, 1944, the 102nd Division was directed to form fifteen additional provisional truck companies to function as part of the Red Ball Express, which was then occupied with moving supplies from the beaches of Normandy to the hard-pressed front-line units. At any given time during the operation, an average of 900 vehicles were on the road, delivering approximately 12,000 tons of supplies per day, for 82 consecutive days. By the time the Red Ball Express was discontinued at the end of November 1944, its drivers - 75% of whom were African American servicemen - had transported more than 412,000 tons of fuel, ammunition, and equipment to 28 different divisions. From the Battalion Headquarters, Charlie assisted with the logistical planning of the 102nd Division's personnel and supplies within the Red Ball Express. He was one tiny cog in a massive wheel, one man within an Army that was steamrolling forward to victory.

---

[184] The National World War II Museum, https://www.nationalww2museum.org/war/articles/red-ball-express

Tuesday, September 26, 1944- Somewhere In France

Dear Mom, Pop, and E,

Well, look where I am! Everything is okay and am feeling dandy, I can't write too much at the present time. It's been pretty cool the past few days; it rained this morning but we're having a sunny afternoon. In a little while, 2 PM, a USO troupe show is going to entertain us. There was a movie on last night, but it was a cold rainy evening so I didn't go.

Tonight, there are going to be *Yom Kippur* services in an area near ours. There will also be services tomorrow morning. One of our Captains, another fellow, and myself will go. There aren't any rabbis in the vicinity, but we'll be able to have some kind of service.

Now it's evening, the USO show was very good. There was one excellent vocalist from the ice show "It Happened on Ice" and it was very fine for a USO troupe. They're usually lousy.

Very lovely scenery, just as I pictured France, natives seem nice, and they still wear their berets. Too bad I didn't take up some French. It's difficult to get something over to a Frenchmen in English, even with motions.

Nothing more now, will write again tomorrow.
Love,
Charlie

Thursday, September 28, 1944

Dear Mom, Pop, and Sis,

Just a quick line before it gets too dark. We had a fairly nice day, during the afternoon it was real sunny but it's cooling off now and I guess we're in for another cold night. The nights have been cold straight along.

We had a little work to do in headquarters today, so I was occupied most of the day. I had to sew on our insignias today and you should see me with that needle. It's too bad we had to take them off for so short a time, but it was just one of those things. I'll be a good seamstress after the war.

Eadie, I saw a copy of Stars and Stripes today and there was a story about the 4th Armored. The Division was complimented by a Corps Commander for its excellent showing in the drive towards Germany. General Wood received the message, maybe your husband will be a big hero, eh?

Many of the boys have gone out of our little area and looked over the nearby village, consisting of perhaps one bar. However, I haven't bothered yet. I'm not too crazy about cognac and there really isn't anything to see. A lot of kids around always bothering you for candy and cigarettes, they certainly learn those words fast. My French is still very limited, but I imagine I'll pick up a few phrases every now and then. The most I can say to a Frenchmen is *"Bon Jour, Monsieur"*[187] and that's that.

Found some straw today and put it in our tent, now it'll feel like a Nelson mattress. Nothing like the comforts of home. I've seen a few Red Cross canteens pass by with American girls as drivers. We expect a visit from them one of these days. Don't start thinking, E, your hubby is a long way from France. Haven't heard much news since arriving here. I thought they would give us the latest news regularly but it's pretty difficult keeping up with it.

Have been eating C-rations, but tomorrow we're starting regular chow. I saw some oranges being hauled in tonight and they look good. I keep very clean here, take a shave and wash up every morning and in the afternoon, I usually get a chance for a little sponge bath. We're due for showers Saturday, I believe. There is a traveling shower company in the field.

I'll close now, I have to take some reports up to Division, about CEN-SORED1[188] away. Incidentally, we're having a beautiful sunset. It's dark now and it's a good thing I know where the keys are, or I'd never finish.

Will write again tomorrow, thanks loads for the card, Sis - it was the first letter I received overseas. Don't worry all is well.

Love and Kisses,
Charlie

---

[187] French: Hello, Sir.

[188] The distance and the location of the headquarters have been censored and excised from the letter.

Friday, September 29, 1944

Dear Folks and Sis,

Another day and not much to write about. A Red Cross unit visited us this morning and we had doughnuts and coffee. Had six doughnuts and they were nearly as good as Mayflower's, the coffee also hit the spot as it was a cool morning with rain falling intermittently. We just had another short drizzle a few minutes ago but it has stopped now.

I can now tell you a little about the place where we are living. We're located in a huge pasture surrounded by hedgerows and the hedgerows separate one field from the other. Some of the boys are living in orchards, most of the land is farmland and at one time or another probably yielded rich crops. The soil in the entire vicinity appears to be good for farming.

We have pup tents set up and I'm living with the Sergeant I work with. We put up two tents together so actually we are four in a double tent. It's not too bad considering the fact that you're sleeping on the ground. I manage to keep warm during the night and the hardest thing of all is to get up in the morning. You feel like staying under the blankets.

This morning we had our first meal from the kitchen; despite the fact that the potatoes lacked salt, it was a good breakfast. A piece of bacon, bread and coffee completed the bill of fare. For dinner we had some chopped meat, mashed potatoes, cabbage, beans, canned peas, bread and coffee. So you can see that we're getting enough to eat. We've always eaten well out in the field, and I imagine we'll continue to do so until conditions prohibit it.

E, when you send out a package enclose my big blue sweater, I think I put it in one of my drawers. It will come in mighty handy during the winter and I can wear it when I go to sleep. If it weighs too much, go easy on the rest of the stuff, but send it along. Incidentally, up to October 15 you won't need any letter of requests to send stuff overseas, so if you want to send Artie some extra things, you can do so. Please send me the news about Artie, I'm writing to him but it may be some time before I hear back from him. Also, if I get any mail at home, please send it along.

We're getting the Stars and Stripes daily now, it keeps us well informed. I'll mail a copy home soon. We are going to set our showers tomorrow; I can use one as the steel helmet offers a limited bath only.

Nothing more right now, keep well and let's get some mail. Say hello to Grandma, I'll drop her a line. A couple of booklets of 6 cent Air Mail stamps will come in handy. Also in a package, enclose some powder and some after-shave balm.

How are you doing, Pop? Could use one of your Sunday breakfasts. How about coming over and serving me one in my pup tent? I bet you couldn't even crawl into one, Dad. How's the real estate, Mom? Do anything about colored tenants?

Love and Kisses,
Charlie

Saturday, September 30, 1944

Dear Folks, (Sis is always included in that heading)

For once, we're having a sunny day. It's 5:30 PM and aside from a sprinkling shower early in the day, the weather has been swell.

We were scheduled to take showers this afternoon. Shortly after dinner about 25 of us left in a truck. Our Battery had a good break and found a big building with plenty of showers. It's on some Air Corps base and no one else in the Division knows about it (at least we don't think anyone does). Well, as luck would have it, when we got to the place we learned that the water pumps were broken and we couldn't take showers. That was a slight disappointment because we were all looking forward to them. However, we settled for a good scrub out of the steel helmet when we returned to the area. Perhaps we'll get a chance again soon. There is a towing shower company in the field and we'll have our turn at cold showers at any rate.

The food continues to be good. This morning we had an excellent breakfast of wheatcakes, canned pork, canned grapefruit, coffee and an orange. The other two meals were also good. (I took time out of the letter to eat supper, which consisted of some corn beef hash, potatoes, peas, pudding and coffee). Tomorrow is Sunday and after we fix up our tents, clean our guns, etc. we're off for the day. All towns nearby are off limits, so we'll just hang around and write letters and wash some clothes.

Major Becker had a nice stove and aluminum pot issued to him today and it certainly will come in handy when we start moving. Now that I'm thinking of it, you might pick up the little package of condensed soup if it's not too much of a bother to carry, but those small things would be good.

That's all for now, will write again tomorrow.

Love and Kisses,
Charlie

Monday, October 2, 1944

Dear Folks and Sis,

Sorry I didn't write yesterday but I was kept busy washing clothes and in the evening I went on guard, so I didn't get a chance. Still in the same place and nothing new to report. I'm in our big command tent now and we have a big Philco radio going and we're listing to the special BBC broadcasts for the AEF.[189] There are programs on all day and the reception is very good. We just heard the War and Home news. It's the first news broadcast about the US that I've heard since arriving in France, and it seemed a little strange.

I received your letter of September 17, Mom. Thanks a lot. I'll be expecting mail pretty regularly from the family now. I'm glad to hear that you were busy, but I hope you haven't been working too hard. How's business now, a fall boom? I wish I could be home to help you, but the Army has priority now. Let's hope it won't be long, the news is just fair from what I've heard.

Played a few games of volleyball this evening. There are plenty of sports right after supper. We have a good football, complete baseball equipment and a few volleyballs.

---

[189] Allied Expeditionary Forces.

Today I washed a set of fatigues and here's how I did them: I boiled a big can of water and threw in a hunk of wash soap and just kept pumping with a big stick. The washing machine has nothing on me, does it?

I think we're in for a very cold night. It's very pleasant during the day. Well, well, Amos and Andy are just going on the air, they sure try to bring us all the programs.

Nothing more for now. Keep well and write soon.
Love,
Charlie

Wednesday, October 4, 1944

Dear Mom, Pop, and E,

Another day and of course more rain with it, it rains at the worst possible times. If you want to shave and have all the necessary equipment outside, it'll start to come down and as soon as you put the stuff back in the tent it'll stop raining and it goes on like that indefinitely.

Hit the jackpot with mail today. Received six letters and it was a grand feeling. Three were from you, Mom, and thanks a lot for the dough. I really don't need it now, but I'll hold on to it. Perhaps I'll have a chance to do a little traveling or buy some good souvenirs at some future time. Thanks for the cards, Sis. Next time I'd like to see a few words from you. I know you're busy writing to Artie but try to write to me occasionally. Tell me how the folks are, etc.

Heard a good broadcast this morning, it's called "Mail Call" and it's a transcription especially for the service. This one had Lionel Barrymore, Eddy Canton, and Joan Davis and the program was dedicated to the boys from Pennsylvania.

I don't think Air-Mail helps much, Mom's 3 cent letters beat yours here, Sis. Chow time now, so I'll quit.

Love,
Charlie

Thursday, October 5, 1944

Hello Everyone,

Yes, rain again, but today it was very persistent, and we had loads of it up to 1 PM. It came down it bucketfulls while we were eating dinner.

We just put up a small tent for our own section and it's pretty good this way. Only a few of us work in it along with the Major, and we're away from the CP where everyone hangs out.

Heard the first World Series game on the radio last night. Reception wasn't too good, but we managed to keep up with the game. I'm rooting for the Browns since they are the underdogs. They sure did alright last night (meaning yesterday afternoon), remember there is a five-hour difference in time.

The PX is over here this afternoon and tomorrow. I haven't got a particular crave for candy and I just need a few toilet articles. Some of the boys just die for some sweet stuff, but I can take it or leave it. Anyway, in our weekly rations we get a number of chocolate bars and they do the trick.

I still have ten packages of Dentyne Gum, so I'm well supplied. In one of your packages I'd like to have some sour balls and if you can get salted peanuts, I'd appreciate them. You can use that as a request, can't you? I hate to ask for things, but I know I have to request things in order for you to send me packages.

Today was another good day for me with the mailman. Two letters from Mom, one from Dad, and two from friends. However, I consider any letter written by Mom, Pop, or Sis, as a letter from the three of you and I read them in that way. I know you all are very busy so if one of you writes, that'll be swell.

Payday should be coming around soon, and if I'm correct I'll receive around 15.00 Francs - around $30. If I accumulate too much dough, I'll send a money order home or I'll purchase a traveler's check and hold on to it.

That's all for now. Keep well and take care of yourselves, don't worry about the house, I'm not even counting on it. Take it easy and don't work too hard.

Love,
Charlie

Saturday, October 7, 1944

Dear Folks,

Thanks for all your mail, I've been receiving it regularly and it's greatly appreciated. Eadie, thanks for the booklet about veterans benefits; I'll read it carefully when I get some extra time.

Another rainy spell during the past two nights, and God knows how the pup tents managed to stay up. It was real windy last night and the tent was shaking. Even if it fell down I wouldn't get up to fix it, it would be just as easy to sleep with the canvas right on top as it would be to get up and fix the tent.

I have a little good news, but I can't tell you much about it at the present time. All I can say is that I'm on a different job temporarily and I think it's a break. As soon as things are definite, I'll write you as much as I can about it. However, I'm telling you that it's a good thing, so don't worry. I hope that I can say more about it shortly.

Took a good shower yesterday afternoon and although the water wasn't warm, I managed to get good and clean. One of the boys is giving haircuts in our big tent and I'm next in line.

Feeling fine, eating well and all in all everything is ok. Keep busy but don't work too hard, love to Grandma.

Love and Kisses,
Charlie

Sunday, October 8, 1944

Dear Mom, Dad, and Sis,

It's 1:15 here now so it's a bet that you people are still sleeping, since it's only 8:15 in New York, lucky you! We had an extra hour of sleep today and got up at 7:30. It was the first nice morning we've had in a long while and the day up to now has been perfect. Sunny most of the time and not too cold.

Spent the day on "personal maintenance," cleaned up, took mud off a pair of shoes and oiled them, washed a pair of fatigues and some hankies and underwear. The stuff I washed last Monday got its first chance to dry today, so you can imagine how the weather has been. I hope that I'm luckier with the things I washed today.

Nothing definite yet on that assignment I told you about in yesterday's letter. If it works out, okay, otherwise it'll be a case of nothing gained, nothing lost. It doesn't make too much of a difference either way.

It's the same routine regularly, folks, so there's nothing much to write about. By now you should know that I'm in no danger whatsoever.

Had a good dinner today and am just lounging around now. My skin has improved quite a bit since I've been in the field. The fresh air and the sun we do get helps a lot.

That's all for now, folks. If you don't hear from me for a day or two, don't worry, I may be a little busy if that thing works out. Regards to the Marshaks, will write them soon.

Love to all,
Charlie

Wednesday, October 11, 1944

Dear Folks and Sis,

Excuse me for missing a couple of days, but I told you that I might be busy and I have been. Whenever you don't hear from me for a few days, don't start to worry. I might be moving, very busy, or any number of things and just unable to write.

Well, I've seen France - at least a good part of it. Had an all-day trip Monday and I must have covered over 200 miles. That assignment I told you about worked out. It's just temporary and may end at any time. I'm working with a trucking group headquarters, it's actually a truck express delivering supplies in this theater of operations. It's called the "Red Ball."

We have a headquarters set up in a nice chateau - a summer home of some wealthy Frenchman, is what it really is.[190] Some officers live on the second floor

---

[190] Due to censorship, Charlie does not mention his location explicitly in his letters. However, from letters sent after the end of hostilities and censorship, it's clear that during this period Charlie was located in Montfort-l'Amaury, France some 205 miles inland from Cherbourg harbor. The chateau to which Charlie refers is the Chateau de Groussay. The Chateau was built in 1815 by the Duchesse de Charest, the governess of the children of Louis XVI and Marie Antoinette.

and six men have rooms on the top floor. I was pretty fortunate to get a room. There are two men in a room, and believe me, it's really something to be in a bed after living in the field. I have a nice, soft mattress and it's the nuts. There is a large bureau in the room and I put all my stuff in the drawers, just like home except that none of Pop's things find their way into the drawers. There is a sink on the floor with cold water, but we can heat it up. Our offices are on the ground floor, so we have everything in one building.

There are cooks with us and we eat out in the courtyard; the food is good and there is plenty of it. So just by my brief description you can see how good things are now. I hope this deal lasts for a long while. Between you, the censor, and me, this is the perfect way to be in the Army.

We're located in a small town and I visited there last night. The center of town is only a matter of a few blocks, nothing to see at night but it looks like a lively place. Everything shuts down at around 6, but I'm going to try to visit the place one afternoon for a few hours. Plenty of stores and quite a bit of merchandise. There's a photo store that develops films, and I'll try to take a few shots with a boy's camera. They can't take any in the store because the owner does not have the proper film for his cameras. I had some champagne and it tastes the same as the stuff in the States. A cocktail size glass costs 40 cents, also had some cognac - nothing to rave about. No, I'm not drinking much, just sampling the stuff.

Boy, I can write pages about this place, etc. But I'll save some things for future letters. However, I can now tell you that I've been in Cherbourg, St. Lo, Argentan, Valognes, Montebourg, Falaise, Caen, Bayeux, Carentan, and some others at one time or another. I'll describe some of them to you in future letters. Some great battles took place in most of those places. Have not been to Paris but hope to get the opportunity soon. Just want to get a look at the place, may not get back here again until I'm 60 and retired (I hope).[191]

Received my first V-Mail from Eadie, also heard from Mom. I can tell you how you received that letter from before we sailed. I got on the boat one day early and we were allowed to mail them. More next time.

We really don't get to visit these cities, just pass through, but we see a lot.
Love and Kisses,
Charlie

---

[191] Charles did indeed visit France later on in life, traveling there with his wife Peeps, in the summer of 1969.

Thursday, October 12, 1944

Dear Folks and Sis,

I'll put today's letter on V-Mail, hope you read it. If it beats my letter of 11 October, you'll be a little behind in my adventures. Living very nicely now, won't last too long though. I'm on that temporary assignment I told you about and full details are in yesterday's letter.

Bought some perfume and powder today and will try to send it home for Christmas. Not exceptional stuff, but it's the only thing they had. Have been kept busy here and this afternoon was the first time we caught up with our work. I took a walk to town and saw a real French Catholic funeral, very interesting to watch. The hearse was a carriage drawn by a beat-up horse.

But back to more pleasant things. It was market day, and you should see the activity, something like Hester Street.

Love and Kisses, good luck and take care of yourselves.
Charlie

Friday, October 13, 1944

Dear Mom, Pop, and Sis,

A very nice day, that's one thing we miss here - the daily rain we had in the other area, it's pretty cool but not uncomfortable.

Received two letters from you today, one from Mom postmarked September 28th and one from Dad, dated 30th September. I'm positive that by now you know where I am. Is my mail coming through okay? Which is the fastest method: V-Mail, air mail, or the regular free mail?

We had a French phone installed in the house the other day, and the darn thing is no good at all. It rings every five minutes and when you do answer it you hear people jabbering in French. In the three days we've had it I think we had one official call from Headquarters and the phone must have rung at least one hundred times.

I needed some powder for after-shaving so I bought some in the place where I bought your perfume. It's pretty good stuff, made in Paris. Probably the same stuff as Mennen's but a little different scent.

A little more about my trip. You remember reading about the great battle at St. Lo,[192] and you've probably seen some good pictures of the place, but when you actually see the city then you fully realize what it's like. I approached the city on a steep hill and you could take in the whole place at once. All you could see in the town was downed buildings, and piles and piles of rocks from the busted roads and houses. I don't think I saw one building intact. Most of the men are busy digging up the ruins but it'll take years until the city will be restored to normal, the people seem to be taking it in stride.

In some of the cities business is as usual, although there are piles of debris around their stores, the merchants are selling the little goods they do have. Why, I even passed a window which displayed brassieres and corsets, not of the Pauline Fletcher standard though.

More tomorrow, please take good care of yourselves and don't work too hard. Be sure not to worry, everything is fine and dandy, couldn't be better. Eating cereal every morning. Well, so long for now.

Love to all,
Charlie

Saturday, October 14, 1944 – Letter Number 4

Dear Folks,

I will start numbering my letters so you can tell if you're missing any. No. 1 is the one dated 11 October, No. 2 is the V-Mail written on the 12th, No. 3 was written yesterday and here's No. 4. I hope that I can remember the numbers.

It's 9 PM now and I'm on Charge of Quarters. Nothing to do but sit downstairs near a warm fire and read or write letters. Which reminds me - E, a gift from the family that I would appreciate immensely is a subscription to the

---

[192] The Battle of Saint-Lô was one of the three conflicts in the Battle of the Hedgerows, between July 7-19, 1944. A strategic crossroads, the Americans targeted the city after D-Day, dropping heavy bombardment resulting in severe damages to the enemy. (U.S Army Center of Military History, history.army.mil/html/books/100/100-13/CMH_Pub_100-13.pdf)

overseas edition of Time Magazine. The print is very small, and they get the entire regular edition minus the ads into a handy size envelope. So please do that soon, we have very little to read besides the Star and Stripes.

I'm sure you would like to hear about my experience last night. I was in a photo store around 7:30 purchasing some pictures of the town I'm living in. They were taken on the day of liberation; I'll send them home in the near future so you can save them for me. Well, one of the little (I should say small) men in the store left and returned in a very short while with his son who is studying English and who speaks it fairly well.

We chatted for a while and he told me about the Germans when they occupied this town, etc. Finally, he invited me (his father told him to do so in French) to their home. His father is a pork butcher and the family lived in the back of the store. The boy is 16, a younger sister is 9, and the mother and father. The mother asked me to stay for dinner and when they assured me that I wasn't depriving them, I accepted the invitation.[193]

First we had pretty good soup with bread soaked in. Then, and this will kill you, we had the head of a pig filled with cheese, at least that's what I was told. It looked like the fancy pork displayed in butchers' windows at home. We had soda water, salad, and an apple - in addition to the French bread, which I like a lot. It wasn't bad at all and it indeed was a novelty to sit down to dinner with a French family. The old man explained something to me just by motions and it shows how similar all people are. We were sitting in the living room and he pointed to a big easy chair, and said that in the winter (making a bur-bur noise) he likes to sit in the chair with his pipe and slippers and listen to the radio. Now what man doesn't want to do that? It was an enjoyable evening.

Bought you two ties today, Dad, so you won't feel cheated when the girls get their perfume. They're cheap, but at least you can tell people that your son bought them for you in France.

Love and Kisses, be well and may God bless all of you.
Charlie

---

[193] This was the beginning of Charles's relationship with the Desbrosse family. Madame and Monsieur Desbrosse, their son George (age 16) and daughter Paulette (age 9). During his trip back to Europe on the summer of 1969, Charles spent a few days with George Desbrosse who continued to operate the family business.

Desbrosse extended family.

Monday, October 16, 1944 – Letter Number 5

Dear Folks,

Skipped writing yesterday. Worked all day so I thought I'd take a vacation from letter writing, just to make it feel something like Sunday.

I went over to my friend's home - the butcher I told you about - last night. I did not intend to stay for dinner, but they insisted. I hate to have the people think that the only reason I visit them is to eat and I had the son impress that fact upon his parents. Next time I go to their home, I definitely won't eat. The meal was good; some soup and a nice piece of boiled ham - the exact stuff you get on a "ham on rye" at home. The treat of the evening was a delicious peach pie bought at the bakers, and of course, we had an apple and some good wine. Wasn't that a good Sunday meal?

Enclosed is a picture of the French family. The tall fellow on the right is a cousin. On the left is Monsieur Desbrosse, then Madame Desbrosse and next is George, the son, who speaks English. In the front is the 9-year-old daughter.

Mother, none of your letters, anyone's for that matter, are censored, so if you have any personal things to write about just put them in without hesitation.

George Desbrosse

Writing this letter in our office in the chateau. A nice fire is going and we're all very comfortable. Had a big mail day. Received no less than nine letters, and most of them were from you and Eadie. Thanks loads for writing so regularly, you don't imagine how much it does for my morale.

Incidentally, do you recall me telling you that we had a doctor in the Artillery who knows Charlie Nelson and Golby and graduated from Madison with Artie? Well, he's with the HQ on temporary assignment. He went to school at Yale with Sonny Werblin, a pretty decent chap. Good to know someone from home.

Nothing new, did you ever get the two cable grams I sent? I'm glad you have been getting some mail. How long are my letters taking to get to New York? Today I received a letter from you postmarked on the 5th of October, that's eleven days - pretty good.

Well, my friends, I'll sign off now. Best of luck, Mom, I'm doing the same kind of work I've always done. Don't worry, everything is hunky-dory. Before you know it, you'll be a real estate tycoon, Mom.

Good night, Love and Kisses,
Charlie

Wednesday, October 18, 1944 - Letter Number 6

Dear Folks and Sis,

I mailed a package to you today and I hope it gets there in one piece. I'm afraid my perfume isn't much good, but I expect to have some bought for me in Paris very shortly. E, I sent everything in one package and if you think the stuff isn't too cheap, I want some to go to Shirley Marcus, 333 West End Avenue (Father is Davis I think - there's two Marcuses in the house). And then I want Karyl Steiner, 325 West 86th to have some. However, remember that if the stuff is very common in New York and it would look ridiculous as a present, even though it was bought in France, don't send them any.

Now there are seven small bottles of perfume and two larger ones. One of the large ones is Gardenia - that should be for Karyl, since she's light. The other is Rose Reine and I think it would be good for Shirley. You and mother can keep the other five bottles and also the powder. E, use your judgment and if you think the bottles aren't good, don't send them. Some Sunday afternoon you can walk over to the houses and give a small package to the doorman and enclose a short note, okay? Thanks a lot. It's nice to have a big sister at home who is able to do those little things for her brother. There are two ties enclosed and they were merely bought as a gift for you, Pop. I imagine Woolworth's sell a better tie for two bits but that's all I could get in this town. I'll buy you something better for your birthday if I'm near any town. If I can buy some Chanel or Goudoin or whatever the heck it is, I'll send it home. It costs about five bucks a bottle here, and that's reasonable compared to the price you pay for it in the States.

Eadie, enclosed is an article from the Stars and Stripes that might prove interesting. You were right about Artie all along. You probably knew anyway. And what happened to NYU Saturday, Temple 25:NYU 0, oh my back. At least it's better than 39-0, we're improving every week. By the end of November we should be losing 3-0, eh?

Went to the barber in town for a haircut this afternoon and he did a pretty good job. They don't have the real barber chairs, but instead a comfortable wooden chair with a back. I asked for a little tonic and the barber threw a whole 2-oz. bottle on my hair, boy do I smell pretty tonight. The cost was 28 francs - $.56 to be exact. I'll be a regular Frenchman soon.

There's nothing much doing with the women, I should say girls. Most of them have to be home by seven o'clock and more importantly hardly any speak English, so we haven't any common meeting ground. Some are pretty, all are prettier than the girls were near my last station here. Met a pretty one this morning while buying wrapping paper in town. She was twenty-years old today and has been living here for four years, left Paris when the war broke out. We asked her if she would like to go for a "promenade" (French walk) some evening and she quickly replied "no." These French parents aren't as dumb as some people think.

Must be leaving soon, it's 6:30 PM now and I have a dinner engagement at my friend's house at seven. Boy, what a social life I'm leading, too bad they don't have an 18-year-old daughter. I dropped over there last night for a few minutes and the boy was taking a bicycle ride out to a farm about two miles away. So I borrowed the old man's bike and went along for the ride, and what a ride it was. It was the first time I was on a bike in a long while and this kid is in good shape. So he pooped me out by the time we went one mile. However, I made the trip okay. The kid picked up a rabbit which was all skinned, and it looked pretty good. Perhaps they are serving it tonight, that will be a treat. By the time I get home, I think I will have eaten everything in the book.

Everybody rides a bike over here. I imagine it always was an important means of transportation and since the war it is all the more important. Very few motor cars are going, although many people have their cars stored in their garage. Why, this butcher has a real fine car and uses it a little on Mondays - Monday here is comparable to Sunday at home, don't ask me why. But now the streets are always crowded with bikes and I understand that in Paris you can get run over by them, there are so many.

Well, I better get going, don't want to be a bad guest. Should have some snapshots for you soon, I hope.

Take care of yourselves, and in one of your letters tell me if you ever received the two cablegrams I sent. Did you all register for the election? Don't forget to go to the polls.

Regards to the Youngs, Grandma, and everybody else.
Love and Kisses,
Charlie

Thursday, October 19, 1944

Dear Folks,

Was on CQ tonight and spent a quiet evening in the house. It's close to 11 now and I'm ready to hit the hay.

Took some pictures today and I hope I'll have them by next week so I can mail them to you.

Haven't had any mail for a few days, but I imagine it'll come in bunches. Had a nice meal last night at my friend's house. Soup, roast beef, ham, fried egg and apple sauce. Some mix up, eh? The fried egg was a treat as eggs (fresh) are very scarce. We eat the dehydrated ones and they are not too bad.

That's all for now.
Love,
Charlie

Friday, October 20, 1944 - Letter Number 6, I Think[194]

Dear Folks and Sis,

Nothing new to report today from the Western Front. Heard the good news about the attack on the Philippines this afternoon.[195] I hope they keep going after the Japs so once the European war is ended it won't take too long to complete the whole job. We're off to a good start, I think.

We're having a good shower now, but it's not hurting anyone here. It sure is different when it rains in the field. You can't stop cursing the rain, but here you just stay inside the house. Oh, if this could only last, wouldn't that be paradise? This is one part of my Army career that I'll always remember. Imagine going to town every night while in France, even though the town is very small and there's not much to do. Which reminds me, I'm due for a meal again at the butcher's.

A few of the boys we are with have been to Paris and now it looks like I may get a chance to see the place. Even if it's just a few hours, I would sure like to go. At least I'll be able to tell my kids that I've visited Paris. I hear that it's a beautiful

---

[194] In fact, this is Letter 8. From here on, Charles stops numbering his letters.

[195] The liberation of the Philippines began with water landings on the eastern Philippine Island of Leyte on October 20, 1944. On that day, General Douglas MacArthur made a public speech from a portable radio set: "This is the Voice of Freedom, General MacArthur speaking. People of the Philippines: I have returned." The campaign delivered an Allied victory and the complete retaking of the Philippines by August 15, 1945. However, the price was high: 13,982 Allied troops killed in action and 48,541 wounded in action. (https://www.nationalww2museum.org/)

city - and that's besides the girls. But talking about girls, everyone who has been to Paris can't stop talking about the beautiful women. They must have something, and perhaps I'll be able to tell you what after I've been there. Pardon the typing, trying to get this done before supper.

Think I'll go back to the barber shop for a shampoo one of these days. I think I can stand one, my hair is growing back after a real short haircut. From now on, I'll only have it trimmed around the sides and the back. No more pompadours for me.

The mail situation isn't very good right now, hardly any mail has reached us for the past few days. But when it does come, it arrives in batches. E, do you hear from Alan Jacobs at all? I wonder if he's overseas yet? What a field soldier he would make!

It's getting a little chilly out. It's been very mild until now in the vicinity I'm now in, but I think winter is creeping up on us. We were issued extra blankets and they'll sure come in handy when we go out again. Was issued an extra pair of GI winter underwear. I'm wearing the top part these days but I really don't need the bottoms yet. Don't worry Mom, when it gets cold I'll put them on.

Really very little to relate. The work is routine here and things couldn't be better. Feeling well and very comfortable, this is really a furlough and it's sure appreciated. That mattress feels softer every night.

Well, take good care of yourselves and don't worry, you're foolish if you do. Eisenhower isn't having it any better than I right now. Send my regards to all, hope you receive good news from Artie. Sis, keep me posted please.

Love and Kisses,
Charlie

Sunday, October 22, 1944

Dear Folks and Sis,

Another week gone by and I'm still enjoying the luxuries of this chateau. Here's hoping that it lasts another week.

Enjoyed a pleasant Sunday - still have the night to go, as it's only 6:30. Got up at 7:30 and worked in the morning and for an hour after dinner. Then I was off and I went to my launderers with some clothes. Did I tell you that for the last wash, which included an OD suit, all I paid was a package of cigarettes and a candy bar?

There's a big hill in the center of town and it's a couple of hundred feet high. It's called the Promenade something or other,[196] and from the top you get a commanding view of the countryside. It was a very foggy day, but I understand that on a clear day you can see the Eiffel Tower in Paris. This town we're in is a very old one. Some of the buildings I've seen date as far back as 1259. That's pretty ancient, eh?

Last night I went to the cinema, it's not the movies here. It was some crazy French picture, of course, and I understand practically nothing. There was a nightclub scene just as you see in the American movies with a dancer entertaining. Well, these French don't pull their punches, and the dancer was shown half naked, that is, no bra. And a well-known French motion picture outfit, no cheap company.

I'm headed over to my butcher friend now. No more to write about right now. Keep well, and don't worry one bit.

Love and Kisses,
Charlie

Monday, October 23, 1944

Dear Mom, Pop, and Sis,

Was kept very busy today and I was pecking the typewriter for a few hours straight. Also took some dictation from the Colonel, and it came out pretty well, surprisingly enough.

Took my blankets to the tailor today and told him to make a bed roll for me. I gave him three blankets and he'll do a good job. He made one for one of the other boys and it came out very well. I have a fourth blanket also and I'll keep that as a spare. A three blanket roll should be sufficient, though.

---

[196] Promenade a Montfort.

The only mail I'm getting lately is Eadie's V-Mail, but no one is receiving much mail so I'll be patient. I realize that you're very busy and that you write as often as time permits.

I certainly had a feast at the butcher's home last night. We started off with soup and followed that with some salami. Then I had a real treat. I ate rabbit meat for the first time and it was certainly delicious. I enjoyed it immensely and I'm surprised that more people don't eat it. It might be cheap food, but it is good and I could find nothing wrong with it. Then we had pear sauce, prepared the exact same way you make applesauce and that too was very good. I don't recall you ever making pear sauce. And as the surprise, they had prepared pistachio ice cream by themselves, and although it didn't come anywhere near our ice cream at home, I appreciated it because they meant to please me and that's the only reason they made the stuff. Of course, the French bread was on the table and a bottle of white wine. All French people must have loads of liquor because it seems that at every meal they consume almost a bottle.

I was shown the upstairs of their house. You see, they live in the back of the store and they have their living room and kitchen down stairs. Then on the top of the store they have the bedrooms and three of the four were exquisite. They were furnished very well, and it was real modern. The madam's bedroom was the nicest of them all and although she's just a butcher's wife, she has a good place to sleep at night.

Still hope to get to Paris. I may be able to get in for a little while this week. Some of the boys have been able to stay overnight and although I'd like that, I'd settle for a day trip. I hate to be within such a close distance to the place and not be able to see it.

I received your V-Mail of 8 October today, Sis, and was surprised to hear of the warm weather you're having. The beach and bathing suits were almost enough not to notice that NYU lost its third straight. At least we scored 13 points, that helped some. How is the attendance at the Home games? Tell Mom that I have a good dictionary and that she shouldn't bother. I'm sorry that I didn't bring along one of my military ones. I thought I'd save the set until after the war, but I could use one now. If I can't get one in town I'd like to have one sent to me. I'll let you know in a few days, but get it ready, please. Also I would like some Vitalis or other hair tonic. Something good to rub in my scalp. I don't need a hairdressing here, as you realize.

Well, there's nothing more right now. Send my regards to all. Karyl Steiner wrote me that Howie Kane is in Maryland. Poor boy, so far from home. Dad, don't be jealous about Gersh's son. You'd do the same thing if I were the one to get out. Best of health and don't worry.

Love and Kisses,
Charlie

Wednesday, October 25, 1944

Dear Folks,

I received a great thrill yesterday afternoon as the small truck I was riding in turned down Champs Elysees in Paris,[197] the third largest and most beautiful city in the world.

A little while after lunch yesterday afternoon I had the opportunity to ride to Paris with our doctor, who had to draw supplies. I rode in the back of a small ¾ ton truck and was very comfortable all the way. It was a pleasant trip and as you near Paris you can see all the signs of a big city.

Views of Paris, 1944

---

[197] The Avenue des Champs-Élysées is a 1.9 kilometers (1.2 miles) long and 70 meters (230 ft) wide avenue, running between the Place de la Concorde in the east and the Place Charles de Gaulle in the west. The Avenue is also the location of the Arc de Triomphe. The Arc de Triomphe, a historical Paris landmark commissioned in 1806, honors those who fought and died for France in the French Revolutionary and Napoleonic Wars. The names of all French victories and generals are inscribed on its inner and outer surfaces..

The streets become very broad, people are dressed well, and there are big apartment houses.

Remember that my visit was a necessarily short one. After driving through the streets of Paris, I got off the truck and had about an hour and a half to walk around. Well, you know what it's like to have only 1 ½ hours in New York; you just can't do very much.

I'll write you all about it later, the mail is going out now and I want to send this off.

Love,
Charlie

Thursday, October 26, 1944

Dear Folks and E,

I got to Paris again yesterday afternoon around 5 to spend the night, and it turned out to be a thrilling few hours. Dad has been telling me that it would be wonderful if I could see Artie, and that's just what happened. Yes, don't faint, I met Artie at the American Red Cross Hotel in Paris at about 6:45 PM and we had a grand time together.

After parking our jeep, the sergeant who I was with and myself went to the Red Cross for supper. The line was very long so we settled for doughnuts and coffee. I was looking at everybody's insignia, hoping to find the 4th Armored, and on my way out I met one boy with the insignia. I asked him if he knew Artie Marshak and he nearly died because he came in with Artie. He was in the chow-line and told me to wait and he'd take me to Artie's room. Well, just at that moment Artie came down the staircase and you should have seen him smile when he spied me. We got into line in front of his friend and had dinner together and then we went walking, had a few drinks, and ended up in some nightclub where we had a grand time. Gee, what a thrill.

I'm very busy now and I can't write any more at present. You may not hear from me for a few days, so don't worry. This temporary duty is coming to a close shortly.

Enclosed find two pictures. The house in the background of one of the pictures is the place I've been living in for a few weeks. Some class, eh? I look a little tiff in the picture by the jeep.

Paris is wonderful, can say I've seen the town except I had no time to go into the buildings, etc. More about all this as soon as I get more time.

Love and Kisses,
Charlie

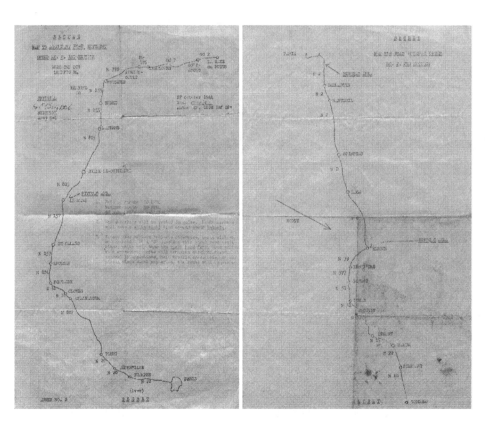

102nd Division Road Map, leaving France and moving into Holland.

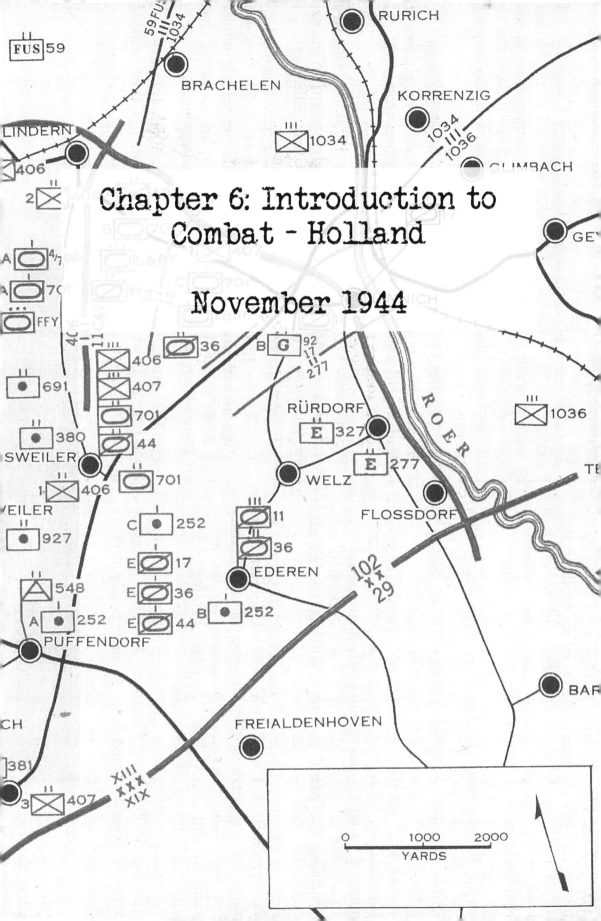

Chapter 6: Introduction to Combat - Holland

November 1944

By the beginning of November 1944, the Allies had successfully pushed the German army back from France, as well as portions of Holland and Belgium. At several points, the Allied frontline even penetrated Germany itself. The deep winter would prove the decisive turning point, and accordingly, Allied commanders were anticipating a full-scale attack through and beyond the Siegfried Line to the Roer River. This would be an essential crossing point for the Allied push into the German heartland.[198] The general plan of operational at-

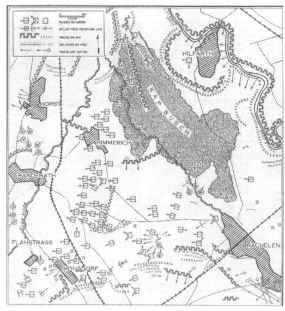

Sketch of a section of the Siegfried Line, between the Wurm and Roer Rivers." (With the 102nd Infantry Division Through Germany, pg. 52)

---

[198] With the 102nd Infantry Division Through Germany, pg. 39

tack was announced by the American 12th Army Group, in which the 102nd Division, as part of Ninth Army 8th Corps, was poised to advance against the formidable German defense works along a 40 kilometer (app. 24 mile) stretch of the Siegfried Line[199] abutting the towns of Geilenkirchen, Laubach, and Aachen along the border of the Netherlands and Germany.

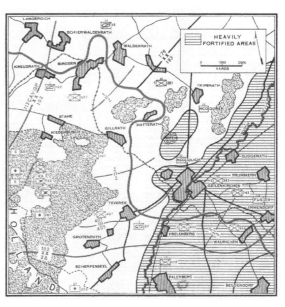

102nd Division positions as of November 4th, 1944. The Headquarters Battery of the Division Artillery is represented by the square with the circle in the center, with two x's above." (With the 102nd Infantry Division Through Germany, pg. 54)

On November 4, 1944, the 102nd Division Artillery was hunkered in position in the dense Hohenbusch Forest, just west of the North Rhine town of Teveren. The next day began the Division's attack on Geilenkirchen, and within twenty-four hours, the Division's Artillery batteries had expended a total of 635 rounds, executed nine close support missions, 81 interdictory missions, and 14 miscellaneous missions.[200] Though censored from his letters, it appears that Charlie and the Headquarters Battery of the 102nd Division Artillery were located in the nearby town of Heerlen, Holland during this onslaught. The location measured a distance of some 11 kilometers (app. 6 miles) to the rear of the forward Artillery positions in the Hohenbusch Forest, and only 14 kilometers (app. 8 miles) from the frontline itself.

---

[199] Known in German as Westwall, The Siegfried Line was a German defensive-line formed during the 1930's, facing the French Maginot Line. It extended more than 630 km (390 mi); from Kleve in Holland on the border with the Netherlands, along the western border of the old German Empire, to the town of Weil am Rhein on the border to Switzerland – and contained more than 18,000 bunkers, tunnels and tank traps. (U.S. Army Center of Military History, https://history.army.mil/html/books/007/7-7-1/CMH_Pub_7-7-1.pdf)

[200] With the 102nd Infantry Division Through Germany, pg. 47

The month of November was one of intense combat for the Division forces. Among other locations, the Division first took the towns of Immendorf, Floverich and Loverich to the south of Geilenkirchen. Additional elements of the Division took the towns of Gereonsweiler, Beeck, and Apweiler. Finally, as the month of November drew to a close, the towns of Linnich, Flossdorf, and Rudorf fell to the men of the 102nd Division as part of the Ninth Army's push towards the Roer River.

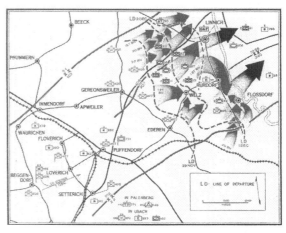

The 102nd attack towards the banks of the Roer River." (With the 102nd Infantry Division Through Germany, pg. 76)

The intensity of the fighting up to this time may be measured to a certain extent by the Division's ammunition expenditure. Despite the fact that certain types of ammunition - notably artillery - were strictly rationed, the Division expended nearly 24,000 rounds of 105 mm ammunition, 8,184 rounds of 60 mm mortar ammunition and 1,712,550 rounds of small-arms ammunition aggregating a total of 1007.5 tons.[201] Additionally, the recorded number of the casualties for the month of November speak to the magnitude of the encounter with the enemy. In just one month, the Division recorded 205 soldiers killed in action, 1,056 wounded, 208 missing and captured, as well as an additional 675 non-battle inflicted casualties.[202] By November's end, the 102nd was no longer a group of fresh-faced replacements; they were seasoned soldiers who had learned the cost of war.

---

[201] Ibid, pg. 66

[202] Ibid, pg. 275

Thursday, November 2, 1944

Dear Mom, Pop, and Sis,

Things do happen quickly in the Army, don't they? Well, I've already written you letter Number 1 from Holland, so if you get this first you can expect the other one soon. I know that some letters written days after another get to their destination first.

That temporary assignment I was on ended for all of us and we rejoined the Battery. We left our old place and have seen quite a bit of Europe. I had the opportunity to go through Belgium and believe me, that country is beautiful and now I know why Morris and the Bialo family rave about it. Of course, I saw one part of it, but every town I did see was beautiful and I think I can say that the ride through Belgium was one of the nicest that I've ever taken. The scenery is lovely and the thing that impressed me the most was the modern housing and the lack of slums of any nature. Everyone seems to live in a nice house. Two towns that I saw in Belgium were Tongeren and Namur. Morris will probably get a kick out of that. The people all appeared friendly and very well-dressed. I was really surprised because things in France were not at all comparable to conditions in the US while the people, dress, and homes in Belgium were very similar to the things we know in the States. Holland is also very beautiful and though I've just seen a limited portion of it, I believe it's like the US in many respects.

Before I forget, Paris is the one city that I want to visit again. It's just about the only place in France, outside of Versailles, that appealed to me at all. I imagine it's the history and background about the buildings in Paris that makes it so interesting, but it sure has something. There are just so many things to see there and to do that it reminds me of New York - just about the only city that comes near our hometown.

I received Mom and Pop's letter written October 8th today. Dad, I just as well write the regular letters instead of these V-Mails, but many times I don't have my stationary on hand or envelopes and these blanks are very convenient. I realize that this is very difficult to read and I'll try my best to write most of my letters to you on regular paper. Remember though that if I ever have a moment to write that it's easy to grab this paper and jot down a few words. And another thing Dad, even though Mom writes the news, I'd like to hear it from you also. Why don't you write me without looking at Mom's letters?

Mom, the news about those 50's to Mollie sounds swell. It would be nice if you could continue to clean up little things like that.[203] Don't deny yourself though of any necessities. If it's there, take care of it, otherwise wait for another week. It's lucky that the Bisoyer boy got a furlough from Africa, but he's been over for a long while and it was just a break. Look how long I was in the States and then near home before coming over.

Everything is swell. I'm living indoors right now and am able to keep nice and clean. There isn't a thing to report about. Really enjoying this travelling around. At times I may not be able to write for a few days, so please do me a favor and don't worry.

I received a nice letter from Artie written before he went to Paris. Say Dad, in your letters you asked me to see Artie if possible, Well, I did it alright, didn't I? Best of luck. I hope that you're all feeling fine and are in good health.

Regards to all. Keep smiling, Eadie, Artie is fine and dandy.
Love and Kisses,
Charlie

Friday, November 3, 1944

Dear Mom, Pop, and Sis,

I have time for a short note, so here it goes.

Was able to see a little of the Dutch town I'm in[204] and it reminds me so much of a small American town. The people don't have any luxuries now, they claim that the Germans took away everything. However, as we've always read or heard, they are extremely clean and neat - unlike the French who were quite filthy. All of the homes have lace curtains.

---

[203] Charlie's parents had a few significant business loans from family members and friends, which they were in the process of repaying.

[204] Heerlen, Holland.

Bought some delicious pies, cherry and apple, this morning in a nearby bakery, and also some tarts. Gee, they were good. Enclosed is a souvenir that E or Mom might like to wear. Have some fine postcards and I'll send them when I can. Also was able to pick up a pocketknife- I've wanted one since I've been in Europe.

Charlie and his section

How long do my letters take to get to you? I've received some from you in ten days and others in 3 ½ weeks. Just luck, never stay up late to write. I hope everything is okay and that you are all feeling well.

Had a couple of beers tonight in a café, just like home - modern, etc.

All my love to you, be well and may God bless you all.
Love and Kisses,
Charlie

Monday, November 6, 1944

Dear Mom, Dad, and Sis,

Once again I had to miss a couple of days of letter writing, but you'll have to get used to the delays because it's well much impossible to write daily.

On Guard

Things are running pretty smoothly now, but there isn't much that I can tell you outside of the fact that I'm feeling fine and that everything is in good shape. I've made another short

Officer Staff of the Headquarters Battery

Liberation of Montfort

trip and Holland is quite the place. We always read about the cleanliness of the Dutch and now I know that it's true.

On Saturday morning I was riding through a few villages and everywhere you looked you saw women scrubbing the porches, windowsills, and to top it off - the sidewalks in front of their houses. I understand that these people even clean the streets in front of their homes. That's going some, eh? All the kids are cleaned to the ears - you can notice that just by looking at them. This is so different from France where the kids looked so dirty.

Living conditions are excellent. I'm under shelter and have three good meals a day. A soldier couldn't ask for much more over here. We've been on the go and very busy - I've even forgotten the days of the week. Now we're really out of contact with the States and things in general. None of the boys has a radio and the Stars and Stripes comes only occasionally. Have had no mail for a number of days but it should start catching up.

Enclosed are the pictures of the town of Montfort in France where I had such a pleasant stay and met that French family I wrote you about - the butcher. The pictures were taken during the celebration of the liberation of the town by the Americans.

Eadie, please save all of the junk I'm sending home. I'd like to have some souvenirs of this experience, so hold on to some of this stuff. Don't take it all for yourself - take some of it.

Nothing more right now. Regards to all and take good care of yourself.

Love and Kisses,
Charlie

Wednesday, November 8, 1944

Dear Folks,

All's well on the Western Front, and I hear that Roosevelt did okay at home, so everything is honky-dory. We have no official results on the election, but rumor has it that Frankie is leading in 33 states. Now let's hope he gets this darn thing over with so we can all come home.

The weather is nice. It's a bit chilly but not bad at all and it rains very little. However, I'm living indoors so it doesn't bother me either way. There's very little to write at the present time. I have very little contact with the civilians, and I can't relate anything about night life or things like that. Haven't had that since the good old Montfort days. Here it's work, eat, and sleep.

Chow is excellent and there is not a thing to worry about. Just because my letters are brief doesn't mean that things aren't going well. It's just the simple fact that there is nothing new and really nothing to write about.

I'll try to send you a cablegram for your anniversary, but if it doesn't get there let me wish you a very happy anniversary and a reunion with your son at the 1945 anniversary. My mother and father are the most precious possessions I have, and I want you to know that I realize that. May God grant you both long life, good health, and heaps of happiness.

Love and Kisses,
Charlie

Thursday, November 9, 1944

Dear Mom, Dad, Eadie,

My morale improved 100% today all because of six letters; three from home, one from Murray Goldblatt, and two from other friends. Boy, that makes me feel real swell.

Your letters were as late as October 29th and that's just about as fast as I've been getting them. I still have a lot of your mail coming and I imagine it will start catching up with me now. Dad, the packages still haven't arrived but one of these days, I'll get them all at once and I'll be able to feed a regiment. Thanks for your letter, Pop, and I know that your prayers are with me, but believe me, there isn't too much to worry about. I'm in a good spot - and that's a lot to be thankful for.

We have the Colonel's radio going again and it's good to hear American broadcasts again. Most of the stuff is on records, they record the program originating in the States and they re-broadcast them on the special American Expeditionary Force program. Then there are special news broadcasts and concerts from England. All in all, we have a variety of programs which are very interesting.

It snowed some today and it's getting a little cooler. However, I repeat that I'm well protected and am very comfortable. If it's like this all the time, I'll be very grateful.

I hope you went ahead and got rubber from the man in Philly. That should help. Glad that the house is holding its own. If you have to start shelling out dough, you better get rid of it because it's not worth it.

Eadie, your husband is okay. Don't worry, we'll both come home safe and sound. May God bless you all, I'm always thinking of the three of you. Please take care of yourselves and don't worry or work too hard.

Love and Kisses,
Charlie

Saturday, November 11, 1944

Dear Folks,

I had a shower today for the first time in ages and it was sure good. A big coal mine[205] fairly near where I'm staying welcomes soldiers to its showers. It was a very interesting experience visiting a Dutch coal mine and let me tell you, this one has it over any that I've ever seen in the vicinity of Wilkes-Barre. [206]

The thing that impressed me most was the shower room consisting of about 400 individual showers and hot water too. Every miner has to take a shower before leaving the mines. Everything about the place looks so much cleaner than our American mines. The entrance is like an entrance to a country club.

We have the radio going now and there's some swell music on. It's hard to believe that it's Saturday night and that Times Square is going full blast right now. I sure hope this thing gets over with soon. You know, I celebrated my fourteenth month anniversary on the 6th.

Feeling fine and am very comfortable. Always seem to get lucky breaks when it comes to living conditions. My new job is coming along nicely. Of course, it was swell working for Major Becker, but the people are very nice in the S-3 section.[207]

Enclosed are some pictures of Paris. Please save them for me so I'll have some souvenirs of the place. That's all for now.

Love and Kisses,
Charlie

---

[205] Likely referring to one of the three mines owned by the Oranje Nassau Mijnen Company, established in 1893 by Friedrich Honigmann located in and around the town of Heerlen.

[206] Wilkes-Barre, located in Northeastern Pennsylvania, was a major coal producing town up until the late 1900's.

[207] The S-3 Section is responsible for training and combat operational planning.

Monday, November 13, 1944

Dear Folks and Sis,

Received three nice letters from my sweet sister. Isn't she a darling? She has a bit of talent, eh Pop? I also got one letter from Mom and Pop. Thanks a lot. E, you have the right idea about mail. It sure is a shot in the arm. Just keep the letters coming and I'm sorry for saying that you, meaning Sis, weren't writing often enough. I still haven't seen any of the packages you sent out but I'm sure they'll catch up soon, and then won't I have a good time digging in?

Am in a school building once again and it sure is nice. This is where we're getting the steam heat I told you about in yesterday's letter. I've really gone back to school in Holland. The American soldiers are a real friend to the Dutch youngsters. Every time troops billet in a schoolhouse, the kids get a vacation. These schools are very much like ours - good brick buildings and the rooms are full of pictures, spelling aids, etc. E, a good place to do your practice teaching. In one of the rooms we're in there appears on the blackboard the following, probably written by a teacher:

WE THANK OUR LIBERATORS. WE PRAY FOR YOU, THAT YOU HAVE GOOD LUCK AND A GOOD COMING HOME.

These people are very appreciative and now they can't do enough for us. It seems that the Americans have made a big hit over here, and I imagine we do all over. This school is for girls and the little toilets are out in the school yard. Oh, what fun using a toilet meant for a sweet seven-year-old. And Dad, you know who I take after in the hips.

Pop, I got a kick out of hearing about the haircut. Why, those women in the house just don't appreciate your head. When I notice your shaped head I can always tell when you have a haircut because it stands out so prominently. I'm still glad that I have your shaped head. Mom and Sis will realize it someday. The next time they don't notice a haircut, refuse to make Sunday breakfast, that will show them. Don't forget, we have a date for a Sunday breakfast the first Sunday I'm home after the war. Won't that be a nice day. We'll sleep until about 10 or 11 and then make each other's breakfast. Mom will probably make you cut[208] in the afternoon, but we'll have some time together in the evening.

---

[208] Working in the shop.

Mom will no doubt have you cutting on my wedding day. Boy, Mom must be burning up by now.

The mail situation is very bad and it just can't be helped, so the Army says, but I'm inclined to agree. There's just too much air mail at the New York APO[209] and the bulk of it has to be sent across on a ship. Sooner or later it catches up though. E, you might write some of your letters on V-mail forms so I'll get some of the news a little quicker. Today's letters were all dated 17th October and that's practically a month. And about a week ago I re-

---

[209] APO: Army Post Office.

ceived mail as late as 31st October from Mom, so you see there's no way of telling. If the mail is in a lucky sack it might be thrown on a plane, otherwise it goes by ship. I'm trying my best to write everyday and if I must say so, I think I've done pretty well thus far. Hope I can keep it up.

Sorry to hear that Grandpa left Aunt Rose. That was the best place for him but I realize that she couldn't keep him forever. Send him my love. How is Grandma? I'll write her a line soon.

Mailed out some Christmas cards today.

Love and Kisses,
Charlie

Tuesday, November 14, 1944

Dear Mom, Dad, and Sis,

Fifteen big letters today - ain't I the lucky soldier! Believe it or not, I received Mom and Dad's New Year card, postmarked September 7th, today. That just shows you how crazy the mail situation is, and E, now you should be convinced that even if you don't hear from Artie for weeks at a time, everything is okay. In today's batch from you, some of the letters were dated the 19, 26 October, and the latest was November 3rd, thanks loads.

Went out to a bar tonight for a few beers and had a grand time talking German with the proprietor, his daughter and son. The funniest thing happened, and it reminded me so much of the States. All civilians are supposed to be out of the cafes at 8 PM and off the streets at 9. Well, the door to the place was closed and a little after 9 the bell rang and the two civilians in the place ran like hell for hiding places. Two cops came in, looked around, and left. The civilians were friends of the owner and weren't really doing any harm. The owner lives in the back of his store, as do most store owners in Europe.

My friend from Montfort mailed me some of the pictures we took there. More and yet to come. Enclosed are the negatives of most of them. I'm holding on to some of the prints. Have a couple of the prints made and please mail me a few of the good ones. One with the kids looks good. The woman is just for the sake of the picture, just asked her to pose for me. The boy with the gun is my friend.

Love and Kisses,
Charlie

Wednesday, November 15, 1944

Dear Mom, Pop, and Sis,

Had a nice day. Am really taking it easy these days and having a good time. Sleep until 7:30, have a good breakfast, wash up and then go to work. We're not rushed at all so we have plenty of time to take care of personal things.

I got my laundry back today and it turned out grand. I have ten handkerchiefs, about a dozen pairs of socks, two Turkish towels, leggings, and a load of underwear. It was a pretty big load and now I'm set for another stretch. I had that other pair of trousers washed by a GI laundry company and this lady is pressing them for me.

Now I have a pleasant job for my sweet sister, Edith. Enclosed find one money order for ten bucks. It is for one purpose and one purpose only. That's a good time for Mom, Dad, and you. I detail you to buy tickets to a show or opera, if the season is in, and it's my present to the folks for their anniversary. Be sure to do it soon, as I want the folks to feel as if it's a real anniversary treat. Go out and have a pleasant evening and be sure Pop goes along. Don't leave him home cutting (I'm only kidding). I want you to forget about the war and just enjoy whatever you're seeing. If you buy $2.20 seats you'll still have enough to eat out - if you add a little, Sis. So let's give Mom and Dad a nice treat. It's from Eadie and I, folks, and next year we'll go out together and Artie will be along too.

Eating very well and I think that I might be putting on a little weight. Had 3 pieces of chocolate cake at supper tonight.

The people in the part of Holland I'm in seem to be pretty hard-up for food. At each meal there are about a dozen kids at the gate with pots - waiting for the leftovers. I'm surprised the people let the kids do it, but I imagine they can really use it.

Well, I'll sign off now. Take good care of yourselves and have a nice time when you go out.
Love and Kisses,
Charlie

P.S. All letters addressed to Mr. and Mrs. Fletcher are also meant for Mrs. E. Marshak, just don't take the room on the envelope.

Thursday, November 16, 1944

Hi Mom and Pop,

E got her own letter today, so I'll leave her out. Just for experiment's sake, I'm going to send this free instead of Air Mail. E's letter is going Air Mail. Tell me which one arrives first and we'll see if it's worthwhile using Air Mail stamps.

Caught up with a little writing during my stay in this schoolhouse. Just dropped Ann and Walter[210] a line with a note Artie and I wrote when we met in Paris. You see, I was behind in my correspondence. You get first licks every night and in my odd time I drop my friends a note. I try my best to write daily, and I hope you get the letters okay.

Mom, I sure hope you can get away for the vacation you plan. If anyone in the world deserves a rest, it's you and please do your best to get it. Of course, I'd be thrilled if Dad could also get away for a few days. It would be just marvelous, and it would be great news for me. Promise me that you'll try.

No, I don't need any money and in fact I'll be saving most of my pay (around $30 after the deductions) or sending it home. I might be able to visit some big city some time or other so I may hold on to the money or I might want to buy something. But I don't need any extra from home, thanks a lot.

You also asked about food in a letter dated early in October. By now, I think I've convinced you that the food is grand, and we get plenty of it. I'm afraid I'll never go hungry and as for getting thin; well, my behind looks as big as always.

Wrote to the Grannies this afternoon and sent them a picture of myself, I think they'll get a kick out of it.

That's all for now.
Love and Kisses,
Charlie

---

[210] Ann and Walter Marshak.

Friday, November 17, 1944

Dear Mom, Pop, and Sis,

Gee, the days fly by. Here it is near the end of another week. The news sounds pretty good but there's still plenty to go until we reach Berlin, and that's what we want to do.

Everything is in first-class shape. Took another hot shower at the coal mine today and it was swell. Put on clean underwear right after the shower and that makes you feel real good.

Visited the bar I told you about tonight. The boy, about 18, told me how the German SS troops were the real backbone of the German army. He said that many of the ordinary army soldiers were ready to surrender many times, but it was the SS men who made them continue the fight. He told me about the first American tanks to come into town and you should have seen his face light up. The Germans just ran the hell out of here, he said. They didn't offer any resistance.

Most of the food that the people are getting comes from America. I was glad to hear it from this kid because you can see how much they need it and appreciate it. Americans have no idea of the tragedies of war - even the hardships suffered by civilians in these countries.

It's not necessary to send that French family anything, Mom. It was a nice thought, though. That's all for tonight. Keep well and take good care of yourselves. Don't worry! All's well.

Love and Kisses,
Charlie

Saturday, November 18, 1944

Dear Mom, Dad, and E,

Saw a picture tonight, so it was something like a Saturday night - although I had no date and didn't get an ice cream soda after the movie. "Secret Command" was the film, with Pat O' Brian, Chester Morris and Carole Landis. Not bad.

Nothing much happened today. Received a letter from Mom and Dad dated November 6th and a V-Mail from Sis written on the Sunday she stayed in with her cold. I expect to take the afternoon off tomorrow and visit a nearby town - a little larger than the one I'm living in right now.

No, Dad, I'm not being diplomatic when I tell you that I'm feeling well. It's really the truth, I assure you. You'd be surprised to see how comfortable I am now and how well I have been. Steam heat, cold running water in the schoolhouse - couldn't ask for much more.

Did I tell you that I had my bed well repaired by the tailor here? It's much better now. He sewed it real tight, and the blankets don't crease up now. Boy, it's a wonderful thing to have and it'll sure come in handy.

Did you do your shopping tonight? I bet Pop had to go to the grocers as late as 10 PM. How's the cake master, yum- yum.

That's all for now.
Regards,
Love and Kisses,
Charlie

Sunday, November 19, 1944

Dear Mom, Dad, and E,

Had a very pleasant day and it was a little like Sunday at home, although I was around 5,000 miles from the place I'd like to be.

I worked this morning, but right after dinner I went out on pass with another boy to a nearby town. The population is around 15,000, so it's a fairly large place.

We hit it on a bad day as everything is closed on Sundays, just like the States. We walked around the place and it was very similar to a small American city. There was a large line at the movie, Mickey Rooney in "Edison the Boy" was playing. They probably have Dutch subtitles - like the good old silent days. We noticed a theater where a USO show was going to go on at 3 PM, so we planned to go there.

We had a little time before the show so we looked around. There was a very large department store, about four stories high, and all the windows were out from some shelling. As I was walking back to the show I bumped into a boy who I did Basic Training with. He comes from White Plains and is a very nice kid. He's been over since March and has been on the continent since D-Day. After comparing my Army career with those of the other men who did Basic with me, I think I made out okay.

He came along to the show with my friend and me. The USO shows are never too good, but just a couple of American girls and a joke or two make the show a success. I'd like to know where the big-time entertainers perform? Artie has never seen any of them on the front and neither have many other boys I've spoken to. I imagine they hit the rear echelons on the rest areas, but as far as being on the front - well I don't think very many have (and I can't blame them).

Some of the boys have received packages, but none of mine have come in yet. One of these days I'll get a whole sack full. But I do get enough to eat so I really don't need them. I haven't made any requests lately and you may need one, so I'll suggest a can of sardines, some salted peanuts (if you can get them), some after-shave lotion, and a fruit cake (bought in a store). Those fruit cakes seem to come over in good shape. Don't bother about the soap if you haven't sent some yet, I have plenty of it now.

That's all for now. Best of luck, take it easy and don't work too hard.
Love and Kisses,
Charlie

Monday, November 20, 1944

Dear Mom, Pop, and Sis,

I'm feeling exceptionally fine tonight and this marvelous mood is entirely due to the six letters I received today from the three best people in the world. Can you guess who I mean?

All of your letters contained good news and especially one item in Eadie's letter of November 5th. In it she told me that Mother has decided to go to Florida for a few weeks in February. Folks, if that is the truth and Mom does go, I'll be the happiest man in the US Army. Really, E, make her go and don't listen to any objections. Mom, for my sake, do it without any hesitation. It'll be a great thing and if anyone in the world deserves a vacation, it's you. Not only will you help with the dough, Sis, but I'm sending home some money as soon as I get a money order and as soon as I get paid I'll send some more. Eadie, I want you to save this and when Mom is ready to go you'll have a tidy sum. I have no use for the money whatsoever, and it will be a marvelous investment for me to have Mom rest a while. Please do it, you'll have the dough from Eadie and I.

And Pop, I'm not forgetting about you. Either before or after Mom goes away you should get a couple of days in to rest as well. You need rest and quiet, Dad, so it doesn't matter where you go as long as you get good food and a lot of re-laxation. As soon as I get some dough together for Mom, I'll save some for you and I'll send $30 to Eadie who will hold on to it until you go away. Even if you only can get away for a week, Pop, please be sure to go. It'll mean a great deal to me if both of you have a vacation. Promise me to do your utmost to take off. My only regret is that you can't go away together, but in a few years I'll attend to that. May God only grant you good health!

The other letter that was a great thrill was Mom's of October 27th. That's the one where Mom told me how she took care of David Weisbrod, Mr. Lebanon and Molly Zwerner. Gee, that made me feel grand. You're a wonderful Mom and you too, Pop, for cleaning those things up. Who said we wouldn't do it someday? E, I know you're helping out a lot and it's just grand of you. Gee, you're all great. A soldier couldn't wish for a better family back home.

Mom, you mentioned in your November 3rd letter that your writing is more or less limited because you don't know enough about ball games, etc. Listen, I'm satisfied just to see yours or Dad's writing, and your letters are the best I ever get. Don't worry about your material, you just keep me posted on the fam-ily news and other little things. I love every letter I get from home and forget about how interesting they are, just keep them coming. Be careful about the address, Mom. You slip up on it sometimes and that delays the mail. It's 102 Div. Arty. And not 102 Arty. Div. and never leave out the APO 102!

Dad, you mention in your letter of October 26th the grand weekends we had when I was at Ft. Dix. Yes, they were great days and it's too bad it wasn't for the duration, but you couldn't expect that. Once again, I assure you and Mom that I'm warm and have not been cold yet. Pop, dictate a Jewish letter[211] to E, and

---

[211] A letter written in Yiddish.

send it to me for the grandfolks. I read Eadie's Jewish better than yours so let her write it. Mom, you keep out - Dad's doing the dictating. Pop, remember the fun we used to have when Mom would butt in when you dictated letters to me?

Took a haircut in town today. Nothing more, all my love and may God bless you all.

Love and Kisses,
Charlie

P.S. Sorry you're not going to the Army Navy Game[212] Sis.

Tuesday, November 21, 1944

Dear Mom, Dad, and Sis

Had a very nice birthday considering where I am. I received my first package from the States and it was from Aunt Rose. She sent two cans of tuna fish, a can of sardines, Nestles chocolate, almonds, candy, and some bouillon soup. So we had a party and tonight there were tuna fish sandwiches making the rounds and it sure was good. I only opened one can, so we have some leftovers, I'll carry the sardines for a while. Never know when it'll come in handy.

This afternoon we had a movie and I took time off to see it. It was "The Unlimited," an old picture but fairly good. I think I saw it a long time ago, but I'm not sure. Not a bad birthday, eh? Enclosed is fifteen bucks, E, towards Mom's trip to Florida. I wrote all about it in yesterday's letter so if you get this first, wait a while until the November 20th letter arrives.

Took a hot shower this morning and as usual, it was swell. Got a new field jacket and had the tailor sew on the stripes and the insignia. I have plenty of clothes, in fact a little too much.

That's all for now, folks. All's well. Keep smiling, news is good.
All my love,
Charlie

---

[212] The Army–Navy Game is an American college football rivalry game between the Army Black Knights of the United States Military Academy (USMA) at West Point, New York, and the Navy Midshipmen of the United States Naval Academy (USNA) at Annapolis, Maryland. The game has been held annually since 1930.

Wednesday, November 22, 1944

Dear Mom, Dad, and Sis,

Celebrated Thanksgiving a day early, and for turkey that was shipped for 5,000 miles it wasn't bad at all. In fact, it was darn good. Just finished the dinner, I had three helpings of turkey, cranberry sauce (more like a juice), potatoes, corn, celery, bread and coffee. The Army sure did its best to get the food over and as far as we are concerned, it did a good job. I hope that all the boys got as fine a meal as we did. Incidentally, most of our food is canned, as you know, but a surprisingly large quantity of meat is shipped in frozen form and then defrosted when ready to use.

Remember all the swell Thanksgiving dinners we had in the past? They're sure fond memories of home and the family. I hope next year we'll all be eating a Pauline Fletcher Thanksgiving dinner at home. Dad and I will gladly do the dishes (what a lie!). Can you still cook, Mom, or is Pop doing all the cooking? Mom never could cook well, could she, Dad?

At 7:30 this evening we're having a movie "Meet the People" with Dick Powell. I'm sure I saw it a long time ago, but I'll see it again. Not a bad day, eh? That's all for now, how are you, E? Keep smiling and keep that chin stiff. Everything will be okay.

Love and Kisses,
Charlie

P.S. We've been told that most of our Air-Mail letters will go by ship so don't be surprised if my letters take close to a month to get home. V-Mail always goes by plane, but I know you don't like it. You keep sending me the regular letters Air-Mail. Every once in a while they hit a plane and I get them in 10-14 days.

Thursday, November 23, 1944

Dear Mom, Dad, and Sis,

Don't get excited over this letter, everything is okay and I'm feeling fine. I've written to you daily, but this V-Mail letter may beat the Air Mails. I always write Air Mail, but I can't get to my stamps right now.

Had a very good dinner a few minutes ago. We had roast beef and I had about five good pieces with halves of peaches for dessert. Pretty good for Germany, eh? Just remember that everything is honky-dorey.

It's Thanksgiving today and I hope you enjoyed a nice restful day. Who cooked the turkey, Mom or E? Did the stuffing turn out okay?

That's all for now, will write an Air Mail letter tonight or tomorrow morning.

Love and Kisses,
Charlie

Thursday, November 23, 1944

Dear Mom, Pop, and E,

I wrote you a V-Mail early today and now I'm following it up with this Air Mail letter.

Well, I'm in the Fatherland now[213] and it sure looks like hell. I thought parts of France were in ruin, but this has it all beat. It serves the Germans right and I have no sympathy for them, whatsoever. They asked for it and we're sure giving it to them. The towns are simply in ruin and there's no two ways about it.

The people don't look like the "super-race" they're cracked up to be. I wonder what they think about as the "decadent Americans" come through their towns?

You can realize why my letters will be much less informative now. There isn't much I can tell you,[214] but the main thing I know you're interested in is me and I can assure you that I'm just fine and very comfortable. It's quite warm - thought it would be much colder living outdoors.

Love,
Charlie

---

[213] Charlie's current location with the Headquarters Battery of the Division Artillery is in the town of Beggendorf, Germany.

[214] This is due to the strict military censorship enforced at the time.

Saturday, November 25, 1944

Dear Mom, Dad, and E,

Everything is fine in the Fatherland, but there is very little to write about. Don't expect daily letters - it's practically impossible - but I'll say hello as often as possible. Also don't expect too much news, we're not allowed to say much.

Today's your anniversary, folks, and I do hope you enjoyed a pleasant day. I know you had the store open but perhaps you did a little celebrating in the evening and you'll have a day of rest tomorrow (Sunday).

What have you heard about Charlie Zwerner? I haven't heard from him in at least 6 months. Do the Young's tell you anything about Paul? Send them my regards.

Eating hot meals and am very comfortable. It's all business now and we don't bother with the civilians or anything like that.

Be well and take good care of yourselves.
Love and Kisses,
Charlie

Sunday, November 26, 1944

Dear Mom, Dad, and Sis,

Hardly any news, it was Sunday today. There is so little difference in the days, one is just like another.

Am feeling swell and the only thing that is troubling me is that I haven't much to write about. I know you look forward to my letters and I hate to have them boring and dull but there's nothing that I can do about it.

Very muddy where I am but there isn't too much rain. It's gradually getting cold and before long we'll have real winter. I'm ready for it, have enough warm clothing and the cold shouldn't bother me at all.

Living very comfortably and my food is good - hot meals all the time.

I think I've decided what to do immediately after my discharge (whenever it may be). If conditions at home permit I would like to go back to school for at least six months. That would be the best way to return to civilian life and it would give me an opportunity to brush up on some accounting, and think seriously about the business I should enter etc. The Government will bear all expenses so I don't have to worry about that. We won't make any definitive plans but we'll wait and see how things are.

Just received the mail and I received 2 packages and a few letters. I got the sweater, scarf, and watch. Thanks loads. The watch is in good shape, it's the first package I received from home and it was mailed October 10. The others will probably follow. The other package was from Mr. and Mrs. Kane and it was a Macy's Xmas box and real swell. I'll write them a letter of thanks. A nice card would be nice for Howie, E. It's LT Howard Kane, Base Weather Station, Phillips Field, Aberdeen Proving Ground, Maryland. Sign Mom and Dad's name.

Got Mom's letter of the 11th and it was the first word I got acknowledging my meeting with Artie.

That's all for now.
Love,
Charlie

Monday, November 27, 1944

Dear Mom, Pop, and Sis,

Well, the packages must be starting to arrive in the Theater of Operations. I received one today and it's the first I got in the line of food, etc. This one had a Nestles Chocolate bar (I could sell it for $5 but I wouldn't), a marvelous big fruit cake which is in excellent condition, Nestles hot chocolate (oh boy), a can of sardines, and peanuts (reminded me of a baseball game). Gee, I can't thank you enough. For a few moments as I look over the contents of the packages, I feel as if I'm right in my own home because I know that all the good things come straight from my own folks, and it's the kind of stuff I always got at home. Many, many thanks. I know the packages are from all of you, but I also know that Eadie does most of the packing and mailing, so special thanks to you, Sis. Artie must feel like a million bucks when he gets these packages from his own wife. I bet you wrapped the cake, E. Wax paper galore, and it was E's work. She's got a little bit of talent, eh, Dad?

I received your stamps and I thank you for them. Just send one every now and then, I have a fairly large supply now.

Heard from Murray yesterday. He's still in Belgium and is getting along okay. Going to have some of the hot chocolate and cake right now. We have two stoves going and I can even shave with hot water. Pretty good deal, I say. Everything is fine, don't worry.

Love and Kisses,
Charlie

Tuesday, November 28, 1944

Dear Mom, Dad, and Sis,

Boy, that fruit cake was superb and I really appreciate it and enjoyed it. As a request for a future package, I'll ask for another one. That's just a request in case you need one. A package a week is plenty. I'll have plenty when all of them catch up to me.

Received a nice letter from Mimi Nelson today, and also a recent one from Dad, dated November 16th. I hope you got your new clothes by now, Pop. Of course, Mom wants you to buy the best. Didn't she always prefer the best? I can just picture you all dressed to kill, Dad. How are the women dressed this year?

Did you enjoy "Since You Went Away"? I saw it at the Capitol Theater on my last pass from Ft. Dix, it was very good. Took a good hot shower this morning, never expected to get one but the chance came and I grabbed it.

Nothing much going on and there's little I can tell you anyway. All is well and I'm okay. Putting on my long underwear tonight. I had it on once before but it warmed up a lot so I took them off. This time I think they'll stay on.

Sending our laundry to a Quartermaster Laundry CO tomorrow, hope I get everything back.

That's all now. Keep well and may God bless you all.

Love and Kisses,

Charlie

Wednesday, November 29, 1944

Dear Folks,

Everything continues to be the same. I'm feeling well and am very comfortable. Couldn't ask for anything better.

Bought a pair of combat boots today and they'll come in handy. They have an extra piece of leather attached at the top and there are two buckles. This eliminates the need of leggings, I also got 3 pairs of woolen socks and a bath towel.

Am kept pretty busy, but I managed to get a good night's sleep. I'm practically always in bed by 11:30 or midnight and I get up at 7:15. Breakfast is either eggs or pancakes and cereal. I sure love my cereal now, we get oatmeal, or cream of wheat.

Gee, it's hard to fill up this page, there's so little to write about these days.

What are you doing these days, Sis? Still working hard? Haven't heard from you in ages. Will probably get a batch of letters at one time. How's your old man (meaning Artie)? See any good movies lately? The basketball season will begin soon. I took Pop to a few games and he liked them. Why don't you try both Mom and Pop on a few this year? It may be fun for all of you.

That's all for now. Take care of yourselves and don't work too hard, best of luck and may God bless you.

Love and Kisses,

Charlie

Thursday, November 30, 1944

Dear Folks,

All is well on the Western Front. Catching on okay to my new job and I like it a lot.

CENSORED CENSORED CENSORED

The weather is still mild considering the real cold I expected. Can still go out in my OD shirt (with a sweater GI), woolen and cotton undershirt on. Wore my new boots today and they are very comfortable, a good investment – cost about $7. Going to save the blue sweater until I really need it.

We ate evening chow at 4:30 so by the time 9-10 o'clock comes around, I get a little hungry at times. Tonight, I opened the sardines E sent in a package and they were sure good. Send another can along in a future package, please.

No mail for the second day in a row, hope it'll come in soon. Sleeping indoors and there's a small fire going so I'm really comfortable. Some life, eh?

Nothing more right now. Keep well and regards to all.
Love and Kisses,
Charlie

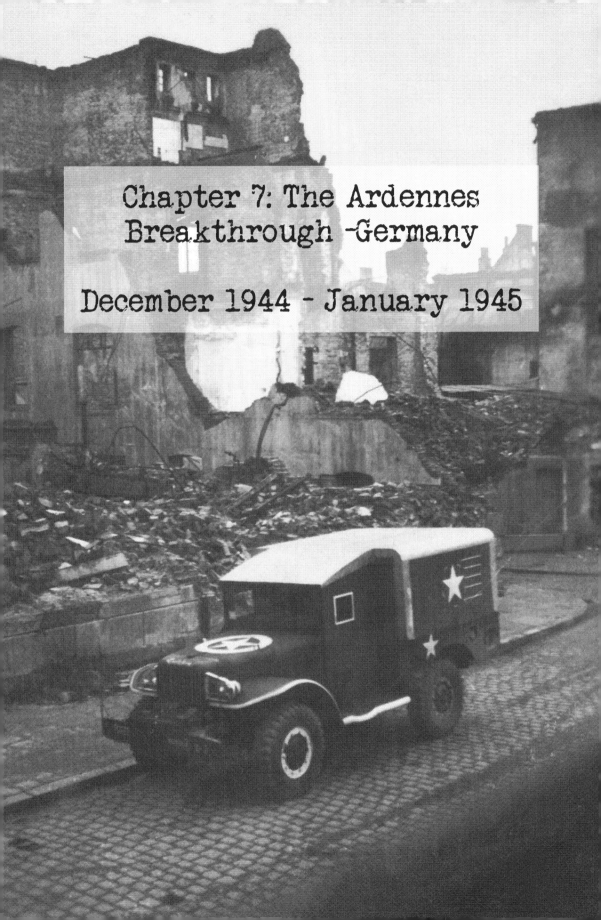

Chapter 7: The Ardennes Breakthrough -Germany

December 1944 - January 1945

The first two weeks of December 1944 found the 102nd Division re-grouping after its advance and consolidating its defensive positions before the final offensive planned to cross the Roer River. To that end, river patrols and scout parties were formed to gather intelligence of the enemy positions on the opposite bank. These Division plans were put on the backburner when German Field Marshal Gerd von Rundstedt led an attack on December 16, 1944, against the Malmedy-Bastogne sector through the Ardennes Forest, some fifty miles south the 102nd Division's location.[215] This military action, later known as The Battle of the Bulge, lasted from December 16, 1944 - January 25, 1944. It was the largest and most costly single battle fought by the United States in World War II.

In response to the German counterattack, the entire Ninth Army, as well as most of the First Army, was transferred to Field Marshal Sir Bernard L. Montgomery's 21st Army Group, which led to a new area of operations and orders for the Division. The 102nd was now tasked with holding a defensive-front some 20,000 yards long (app. 11 miles) in a semi-circle formation to stop the German enemy advance to the critical towns of Suggerath-Geilenkirchen and Linden-Pufferndorf. During this time, the Germans launched a series of patrols against the lines of the 102nd Division, though never managed to claim

---

[215] With the 102nd Infantry Division Through Germany, pg. 93

any tactical victory.[216] On New Year's Day 1945 the Luftwaffe opened with a flourish, bringing FW 190's, ME-109's, and JU-88's out in force, blitzing roads and bombing rear areas. All along the Western Front, the Luftwaffe launched a combined total of more than 900 planes. The 102nd Division's sector was strafed by at least twenty low-flying planes, which hovered at treetop height.[217]

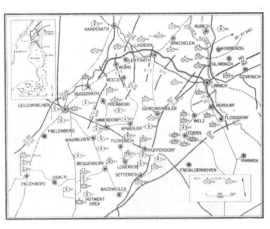

102nd Division's defensive line during the Battle of the Bulge." " (With the 102nd Infantry Division Through Germany, pg. 96")

The 102nd Division continued its defensive posture through the end of January 1945, until the decisive Allied victory in The Battle of the Bulge. At this point, the Division reverted to its original mission of crossing the Roer River and began its attacks on German forces on January 26, in the vicinity of Brachelen and Randerath.[218]

During this time period, Charlie and the Headquarters Battery were located in the town of Beggendorf, some 10 kilometers (approximately 6 miles) from

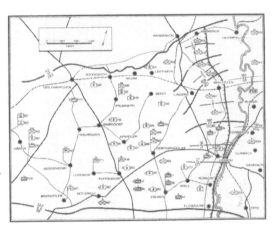

The Division's offensive push towards Brachelen and Randerath."" (With the 102nd Infantry Division Through Germany, pg. 113)

the forward-most positions of the Division. Entrenched in the relative safety of his headquarters paperwork, Charlie maintained gratitude and prayed for the safety of his comrades fighting in an epic battle just a stone's throw away.

---

[216] Ibid, pg. 96-99

[217] Ibid, pg. 95-97

[218] Ibid, pg. 109-110

Friday, December 1, 1944

Dear Mom, Pop, and Sis,

Received some nice letters from you today, thanks a lot. E, I got your V-Mail letter in which you request full information about Artie. I hope I gave you enough in a later letter. Did you receive it? Thanks for the news clippings, I always like to see newsprint from the States. Incidentally, did you ever subscribe to the overseas edition of Time Magazine for me?

I also got two other letters from home. Two V-Mails, one from Mom and one from E dated October 30, that's a pretty good while for the letters to arrive. Did you ever get the negatives I sent you? That lamb stew Eadie made sure tastes good, yum-yum. Thanks for Alan's address, that's sure a lucky break. Enjoyed John David's letter to service men.

Everything is fine and dandy. Take care of yourselves and don't worry, I'm okay.
Love and Kisses,
Charlie

Saturday, December 2, 1944

Dear Mom, Dad, and Sis,

I know that a few days ago I told you that I wouldn't be able to write every day but you see, I have been writing daily and I hope you're getting all my letters. I hope I can always write so often.

Had a pleasant evening. Heard the Army-Navy game and won a dollar on the Cadets. A very good game to listen to, I could picture myself attending the game. I haven't seen a college game for such a long while.

After the game, I opened the can of sardines Aunt Rose sent in her package, they were sure good. I just washed up and brushed my teeth and am ready for bed. Oh yes, there's a piano in one of the buildings and I played a little tonight. All those songs I managed to pick up on the keys by ear. Nice fire going, it's very warm. I'm very comfortable and everything is coming along nicely. Contented and I know I'm going to get home okay.

Love and Kisses,
Charlie

Sunday, December 3, 1944

Dear Mom, Dad, and Sis,

Received a letter from Mom and one from Pop today. They were both written on Sunday night, November 19th, exactly two weeks ago.

I'm glad that you received the first package I sent home. I hope you received the real good perfume. I mailed it about 10 days after the first package. Say, was that perfume and good, girls? Dad says that Eadie is thrilled with the perfume - is that the truth? Thanks for wearing one of the ties, Dad. I thought you might not like them, I'm happy that you're using them. Perhaps not many boys would do it, Pop, but remember, not many Dads would do all you've done.

By now the National City Bank should have received an allotment. $33 is sent to the bank every month and two months' pay has accrued, so I should have $66. Check again, please. It may take a while for it to come through. Meanwhile, I'll check with our clerk and write a note to the bank. I'm getting a $20 money order and it's for Mom's vacation to Florida. I would send more but as I told you, I bought some clothes and shoes this month. I should have the money order in a day or two.

Mom, don't feel badly about not writing too often. I know you write as much as possible, I'm glad you're kept busy. How is business? From Mom and Dad's letters I gather that it's pretty good.

Are the Grandfolks okay? Did Grandma go to Florida yet? How's the Old Man doing? Send them my love and let me know their addresses.

It's miserable outside tonight. Raining, windy and cold. You can imagine how thankful I am to be having it so good. I thank God for his kindness every night. Here I am, dry and comfortable, things could be so much worse. I have a dry, warm place to sleep, hot water to shower and wash, and good hot food.

This morning I had scrambled eggs, pancakes, cereal (oatmeal) and coffee. For dinner, chicken (plenty of it), peas and potatoes, fruit salad and coffee. For supper it was chili con carne, potatoes, carrots and canned pineapple. Are you poor civilians eating as good?

That's all, hope you have a very pleasant holiday. Be good, take care of yourselves. When are you leaving for Miami Beach, Mom?

Love and Kisses,
Charlie

Monday, December 4, 1944

Dear Mom, Dad, and Sis,

Nothing new to report on the Western Front. Enclosed is a $20 money order for the expressed purposes of going to Mother's trip to Florida. E, hold on to this and when Mom is ready to leave; you can put it towards the car fare or some other expense.

No mail for anyone today. I'll write a couple of letters to some friends tonight. I haven't been doing too much writing lately. It's hard to keep up a good correspondence with people in the States because it takes so long for us to exchange letters.

Reading a little now. Read a book called "The World We Want to Live In" and it was a summary of the 1941 meeting of the National Conference of Christians and Jews. It all pointed to a better world after the war, and it was interesting reading. I try to keep my mind active by reading.

Every week we get 5 packs of cigarettes, a stick of chewing gum and a little candy free of charge. Occasionally we receive tooth powder, I like paste so much better. Please send a tube of Kolynos[219] in your next package. We usually get some when we have a post exchange, but I haven't seen any around lately.

I see that NYU won its first basketball game. Perhaps we'll have a decent basketball team.

That's all for now, take care of yourselves and the best of luck.

Love and Kisses,
Charlie

Tuesday, December 5, 1944

Dear Mom, Pop, and Eadie,

Went for a shower today at the same place, and it was good. While there I met some boys from Bernard Fillion's outfit and I was told that he was only a few blocks away. I started to walk to his place, but I changed my mind as I didn't want to hold up our vehicle. The vehicle left us off at the showers and then

---

[219] Brand of toothpaste.

went to some other place and was to return around 4. As it was, it didn't come back until 4:30 and I could have made it. Perhaps I'll get there again and I'll try to say hello to him. If you still correspond with him E, tell him why I couldn't get over to see him.

Not one bit of news, going to have some work done on my gums tomorrow. Our dentist is right with us. Did I tell you that I received a nice letter from Mimi Nelson? I wrote to her last night. Is everyone busy with X-Mas as usual? I wonder where I'll be next X-Mas? Sure, hope it's at home.

Got a nice fire going and it's real warm in here. No mail today - again. I get my share, though, when it does come in, so I'm not itching.

That's all for now, sorry I have no news for you. Regards to the family. Tell me if you received all of my money orders, have sent three already. One for $10, one for $15 and one for $20.

Love and Kisses,
Charlie

Wednesday, December 6, 1944

Dear Folks,

Received two old letters from you today. One was from Mom dated October 26th and one from E, dated October 25th. That's a pretty long while to take for them to get here. I imagine delivery will be faster when the Xmas rush is over.

Heard from Artie today. He wrote on November 27th and said that he was on the move and doing okay. He seems to be in good spirits. He told me that he hadn't heard from the home front in almost two weeks. That's the mail situation, but he realizes that all your letters will eventually catch up to him.

I suppose by now you have seen some articles about the 102nd Division in the newspapers. I can't tell you as much as you will probably read back home. It sounds funny but it's true.

I'm not doing much at present, having it pretty easy. Spend the evenings reading or writing and keep good and warm. I shave every other morning now and that seems to be enough. Wash up in the morning and evening and with an occasional shower thrown in, you can see that I keep clean.

How are you doing, Pop? Cutting a lot? Get your new suit yet? Mom, I know you're going along with your plans for Florida. I'm counting on you to go. Keep smiling, Sis.

Love and Kisses,
Charlie

Thursday, December 7, 1944

Dear Mom, Dad, and Sis,

Received some real recent letters from you today. One from Mom and one from Dad written on Sunday, the 26th of November and one from Mom written on my birthday. Thanks for sending Nate Kelne's letter along. It was a New Year's card; I dropped him a line this evening.

Did you receive the second package I sent - one good bottle of perfume? A number of little bottles, I think. I'm glad you got the perfume from Artie, Sis. Pop, it's a good idea to help the women use the stuff. You'll smell so sweet! Just like you smell after a visit to the barber. Have you been getting the "works" recently?

Mom, I was indeed surprised that you finished the whole deal with Dave Weisbrod. I'm sure proud of you and Pop, you are sure cleaning those things up. Won't I be happy if you're able to do some more by the end of the year? How do you stand with the Zwerners? Youngs? I'm not worrying about it, just curious.

Thanks for all the birthday greetings and the compliments. Boy, I should be conceited by now, but I'm not. I still have to prove myself after this mess is over.

I'm glad my cable gram reached you on a Sunday morning when you were all at home. Were you cutting yet, Dad? I intended to send you New Year greetings but we can't send cablegrams on account of the rush. Perhaps I'll send one after X-Mas, so don't mind if it's a little tardy.

I checked up on my allotment and I have that October and November $33 coming to me - not November and December as I told you before. We get paid at the end of the month, so I was just paid for November a couple of days ago. It takes some time for the thing to go through. When we got over here the allotment form had to be sent back to the States and there it had to be processed, so don't worry if the bank doesn't get a check for a while.

All your packages still have to catch up, just received one with the food - I told you about that and one with the sweater, don't need it yet, still in moderate weather. Please send some strong brown shoelaces for high shoes.

All's well, no need to worry, living nicely. Take care of yourselves, don't worry please.

Love and Kisses,
Charlie

Friday, December 8, 1944

Hello again,

Your *Kosher*[220] reporter, Charles Fletcher, reports again from the Western Front. He's with the Ninth US Army, somewhere in Germany. So now you know just how I stand.

Nothing new. I received a letter from Paul Bialo yesterday. He told me his folks sent me a X-mas package. It'll catch up to me one of these days. I answered him last night via V-mail. Incidentally, how do the V-mails I write reproduce? I know you don't like them, but I'd like to know how they look. I'm writing a V-mail to E tonight and I bet she gets her letter first. Some of your air mail comes over by plane but I think all our mail, except V, is going by ship.

Shirley Marcus told me she received the perfume I sent her in very good shape. She said that she liked it very much, I hope that you got your good perfume okay.

---

[220] Hebrew: *Kosher*, or *Kashrut*, a set of dietary laws dealing with the foods that Jews are permitted to eat and how those foods must be prepared according to Jewish law. Figuratively speaking, it is used as a term to imply something which is up to standard.

It's a little colder today, heating some water now for a good shave and wash before retiring.

That's all for now.
Love and Kisses,
Charlie

Saturday, December 9, 1944

Mom, Dad, and Sis,

Received two nice letters from you today. E's V-mail was dated the 27th of November and Mom's Air Mail was as late as November 28th. That's swell service, isn't it?

By now you should have had the negatives printed. How did the pictures come out? Please send me a few so I can send them to some friends. I expected to have a few more pictures, but as yet my friend in Montfort hasn't sent them to me. I hope he doesn't let me down, as the shots were pretty good.

My gift for your anniversary wasn't anything like I would really want to give you. However, under the circumstances, it's the best I could do. Perhaps in a few years I'll be able to do much more. I hope I can. Did you enjoy yourselves - or haven't you been able to go out yet?

Mom, Carrie[221] should be your biggest worry, eh?

Received a very nice V-mail from Anna today. She told me how excited she was when Artie's letter, which told of our meeting, arrived. "It made me feel good to read. Both Walter and I have come to love our daughter -in-law very much indeed and my only hope is that Arthur will return to Eadie in good health and that they will live out their years in peace and happiness together." That's also my hope, Eadie.

Am on duty till 3 AM tonight. I don't pull this night shift but I'm doing a favor for the boy who works the night hours. I'll get up for breakfast in the morning, but I'll go back to sleep until dinner time. It's very pleasant working now,

---

[221] A woman who worked in the Fletcher household.

all you do is keep a fire going, write letters, read, and fix up a few signs for the following day.

It was a raw day with quite a little snow, but I'm still indoors and very comfortable, thank God. Munching on some cookies now and drinking grapefruit juice.

Feeling fine and everything is okay. Don't do any worrying, I assure you that I'm safe and sound.

Regards to all.
Love and Kisses,
Charlie

Sunday, December 10, 1944

Mom, Dad, and *Yenta*,

Received Mom's letter of November 30th. Glad to know that some of my mail is reaching you in 10 days. You said that you had my letter of November 20th.

Murray told me about his day in town - I think it was Namur. I'm glad that business is good and I hope it continues. It's about time that things are a little better. It'll be nice to clean up with the Youngs. Gee, you're all doing such a grand job at home.

I think I forgot to tell you in yesterday's letter that we had a movie. We saw "Double Indemnity" with Fred Mac Murray, and Barbra Stanwyck. Now, don't tell me I told you about it. I saw the picture before, but since it was a good story and some fine acting, I didn't mind seeing it again. And don't think we only have movies on Saturday night. I just saw "Take It Big" or something like that. It's with Jack Haley and a host of others, including Ozzie Nelson and Orchestra. It's a musical and although it was a little slap-stickie, it was quite entertaining. One of the actors sang "Figero" and it was good. Which reminds me, I hope you enjoy the opera. Shirley Marcus told me she heard "La Boehme" recently. If I'm not mistaken, I heard Lily Paris in that a few years ago.

Received a package from June and Charlie today. It contained a jar of olives - filled with some red stuff and darn good, a can of anchovies, pimento cheese, crackers and a package of prunes. Nice of them to send me it, I'll write a letter of thanks shortly.

It continues to stay cold. Saw a lot of planes today and it's sure good to see ours up there. Don't worry - I wonder if all my telling you not to worry helps any? Everything is fine and I'm in good shape. No more for now, keep well and may God bless you all.

Love and Kisses,
Charlie

Monday, December 11, 1944 – Letter to Dad

Dear Dad,

You're due for a birthday on January 4th, and more than anything else in the world, I'd like to be able to celebrate it with you at home. However, that will be impossible, and we'll just have to settle for this letter. I pray that for the 1946 birthday I'll be right at home, with you, Pop.

There's not much I can say that's special for your birthday. I always tell you how much I think of you and how appreciative I am of all of the things that you, along with Mother, have done for me. But I'll repeat it again for the sake of custom.

Remember that I'm always thinking of you and praying for you and Mom to have a long life with lots of happiness. In closing, I'll say what I would if I were home: "Happy Birthday, Pop."

Love and Kisses,
Charlie

Monday, December 11, 1944

Dear Folks,

Here I am again. You should be plenty satisfied with the mail situation. Since I was in Holland you've had a letter from me every day. I hope they're coming through okay.

Received a package from Karyl Steiner today. She sent some jelly, biscuits, tuna fish, candy and gum. Very nice of her, wasn't it?

Took a shower this morning in the same old place again and sent regards to Bernard Fillion. I can't manage to get to see him. So I feel good and clean this evening. Very quiet here and nothing much doing. Am still in the same place and things are the same. I'm comfortable and everything is swell.

One of the boys got a hold of an October issue of the "Reader's Digest" and I'm looking it over. Will read mine real well when it arrives. E, how about mailing me the special servicemen editions of some of the newspapers at home; I'm quite sure a few of the papers put out something like that? Did you ever subscribe to Time Magazine for me? If you haven't done so yet, the address is Time, 330 East 22 St. Chicago, Illinois. The price is $3.50 for the year. I'd appreciate that.

It wasn't too cold today; it was pretty clear. Having a little treatment every day for my gums - just rinsing the mouth with an astringent - chromic acid.

Nothing much new to report, take it easy and don't let the newspapers scare you. Everything is fine, regards to the family.

Love and Kisses,
Charlie

P.S. How's the job, E? A lot of ensigns still coming in? Say hello to Mary, what do you hear from your old friends?

Tuesday, December 12, 1944

Dear Folks,

Received Mom's letter written December 5th and postmarked 7:30 AM December 6th, today. That's just six days and the fastest mail has ever come. It sure makes you feel as if you're right at home - the letter is so up to date.

As I told you in a previous letter, the $33 is deducted from my pay automatically before I get it. It's just a question of time until the bank receives the checks. Now about the $15, I did not send it home to go into the bank. I sent it for Mother's trip to Florida and if it isn't used for that purpose I'll be greatly disappointed. I think that $33 is plenty to save every month for the time being.

Just because I'm in Germany doesn't mean it's time to get scared and worry. And E, try to tell Mom and Dad that the worst thing to do is worry. I'm perfectly okay and I think very safe; as safe as anyone can be in Germany.

Saw a marvelous picture this evening, "Old Acquaintance" with Bette Davis and Miriam Hopkins. I'm quite sure that Davis is my favorite actress. There was some fine acting throughout the film, and I enjoyed it very much. Some very true to life incidents in the picture - for instance, Davis is waiting until 42 to get married and then when she decides to, her prospective groom (32 years old) tells her he's fallen in love with someone else - a younger girl. Of course, jealousy plays an important part in the picture. If you haven't seen it and it comes to a small neighborhood house, I advise you to go. I'm quite sure you'll enjoy it. Had a community sing film before the feature and that was fun. Especially when there was a special part for the girls and some of the boys would sing in a falsetto voice. I always have to laugh at that.

We had pancakes and eggs for breakfast along with wheatena. I used Karyl's jelly to good advantage on the cakes and eggs. Last night I had cheddar biscuits and jelly sandwiches, remember how often we used to have that at home?

There are some boys from another division staying with us for a while and they were all issued 1 bottle of Coke. I had a sip of one tonight, gee that was a touch of the US. We'll probably get some soon.

No more now, take care of yourselves and take it easy. Don't worry?

Love,
Charlie

Wednesday, December 13, 1944

Dear Folks,

Received two packages and a number of letters today. The packages were from Aunt Rose and the Bialos. Gee, I don't know how I'll ever be able to eat all the stuff. Aunt Rose's package was filled with canned goods - tuna fish, salmon, sardines, and surprise of all, *gefilte fish*.[222] The Bialos sent mostly candy. One package a week will sure be enough once this X-mas season is over.

Dad, I got your letter of the 3rd of December. You misunderstood me when I said money doesn't mean anything to me. I meant that at the present time I have no use for it and I would like Mom to spend it on her vacation. By now you know that my allotment of $33 is going to the bank monthly. Just have patience, it'll get there sooner or later. You know me better, Pop. Of course, I realize the importance of money and the independence one has when he has dough.

Got a nice letter today from Jo-Jo and Aunt Rose today. They mailed it December 3rd from Miami Beach; I do hope you get down there Mom.

I want to tell you all something. I remember how crazy you were with the radio. Mom would want to listen every half-hour and every commentator in the world had to be tuned in. Now, believe me, one news program daily is plenty - preferably the one at 11 PM. No one knows exactly what's going on and you can go batty listening to the radio every minute. This war could end in January and or might even end next January. No one knows and you'd be doing yourself a favor by not listening to the radio too much. And don't try to guess when this is over. Why, yesterday in the Stars and Stripes there was a story saying that the Navy believes the Japanese War will last until 1949. If you think I'm staying in the Army until then, you're mistaken. It's my own personal opinion that no one knows for sure the date of the end - just too many things enter into it. Let's hope it's soon.

E, thanks a lot for your letter of November 30th. I told you all I know about Artie. If he's driving now, that's new on me. We have men doing the same thing and they're okay. Of course, a shell can land any place so what is the use of worrying. He'll be okay.

Love and Kisses,
Charlie

---

[222] A traditional Eastern-European Jewish dish made from a poached mixture of ground fish - such as whitefish, carp or pike - and formed into patties. Often served as an appetizer on *Shabbat* and Jewish holidays.

Thursday, December 14, 1944

Hello again,

Saw an entertaining movie this evening, "Rosie the Riveter" was the picture and I got a few good laughs. You'd like it.

Got an old letter today, November 15th - you left out the 102 after the APO and consequently it was delayed. Be careful when you address the envelope. Don't rush to make the postman, it makes no difference if a letter is mailed the following morning. I know you do most of your writing at night and I can just picture Mom rushing to mail the letter before midnight.

Everything is okay and I'm feeling fine. It's pretty cold now and there was a slight frost on the ground this morning. Very little to write about, so I'll make this letter short. Hope I have more to say tomorrow night.

What do you hear from Artie, Sis?

Hope to go for a shower tomorrow morning.

Don't worry, am well and happy. Take good care of yourselves and don't work too hard.

All my Love and Kisses,
Charlie

Friday, December 15, 1944

Dear Mom, Dad, and Sis,

Received the package you sent on November 14th. It contained two big boxes of good chocolate, thanks a lot. It seems that the stuff mailed between September 15th and October 15th is coming over very slowly. I opened up the Cadeau assortment and the candies are delicious, thanks again, my dear friends.

Your lovely birthday cards also arrived today. They were mailed November 11th and probably hit a ship instead of an airplane. Just because they were late didn't take anything away from them. They were very nice cards, both Mom and Pop's and *Yenta's*.

There really is nothing to report. Didn't go for a shower today, expect to go tomorrow. It takes up an entire morning. Saw the dentist again this morning and he's doing some good work on my gums.

Oh, here's some news that will give you a chuckle. We have a big Christmas tree set up in the place we are staying and we even have the decorations that go with it. Tonight we heard carols sung over the radio so the Christmas spirit is really here.

How are the windows at home? All nicely decorated, I suppose. Please enjoy yourselves during the holiday season. You should be having all the fun possible. Just because I'm over here doesn't mean that you shouldn't have good times.

How are the Grandfolks? Tell me where they are so I can write them.

No more now, be good kiddies and take good care of yourselves during the cold spell. I'm always thinking and praying for you. I'm just fine and I wish you realize that. No need to fret about me, had chocolate cake for dessert tonight.

Love and Kisses,
Charlie

Saturday, December 16, 1944

Dear Mom, Dad, and Sis,

Another Saturday and that means the end of another week in the ETO.[223] Six more shopping days until Christmas, did business pick up for the holidays?

I received a package from Irene Witt today, it was indeed a surprise. She sent the stuff from New Orleans where she goes to college (Tulane). There was a fruit cake, Spanish nut toffee, and some prunes. Very nice of her, eh? No other mail.

Went for a shower today and took along clean clothes, so tonight I feel very clean. We manage to take showers quite frequently and that sure is a good break.

I looked over a bookcase in one of the rooms where we are staying. There must have been a high-school student in the family because I found a few Latin text-

---

[223] European Theater of Operations.

books along with the lesson books. All of the Latin looked familiar to me as it was the same stuff that I studied in high school. Also saw his geometry books and he was learning the same things that our high school students in the US study in geometry. It's too bad these people can't live without war, things would be so much better.

Read about Lupe Velez; isn't she - I should say, wasn't she - nuts. What price is fame? Thirty is a hell of an age to kill yourself. I think she should have gone some place incognito, have the baby and give it away. I wonder how many famous (well-known, is a better word) women do that? I remember seeing Velez in "Strike Me Pink" with Jimmy Durante about 9 years ago. If I'm not mistaken, Mom went with E and myself.

Everything is okey-doke. I'm feeling fine and am in good spirits. Take good care of yourselves and don't work too hard. You only have two people to take care of. E is taking care of herself and the Army is taking care of me.

Love and Kisses,
Charlie

Sunday, December 17, 1944

Dear Folks,

Just saw "Up in Mabel's Room" and it was a very funny picture. I saw it a few months ago but I don't mind seeing a picture twice, especially over here.

Enclosed is a $15 money order, it's the leftover from my pay and some old dough I had. It's for Mom's trip to Florida. The only reason I make it out for E is that it's easier for her to go to the post office than Mom or Dad. This is the fourth money order I've sent home. Have you received them all?

I don't know whether or not you got the pictures from Montfort. However, enclosed are some additional ones. I thought there were more of me, but my butcher friend must have lost them. You see, he just mailed them to me from France. The house is the place we lived in at Montfort. Everything is fine and dandy, I'm feeling fine, and all is well.

Take care of yourselves and best of luck.
All my love,
Charlie

Monday, December 18, 1944

Dear Mom, Dad, and E,

I'll have to stop eating some meals pretty shortly. No, I'm not ill, I just have so much stuff saved up from my packages that I'll have to eat some of the canned goods instead of our regular chow.

It's really not that bad, but the packages are coming in. Today I received two from Eadie and one from the Marshaks. Thanks loads, I'll drop Anna a line tonight. E, you pack the stuff so nicely. It's just like you - so neat. Artie has a nice home life ahead of him. All your selections just hit the right button. I put the fancy wrapping paper on our Christmas tree.

E, enclosed is a sports column from Stars and Stripes, I've heard the story before but I enjoyed reading it in the S & S. Say, wouldn't it be a deal if I were the Sports Editor of the paper?

I've been reading how good business is before X-mas, I hope you did your share. No more right now, be well and please don't worry; I'm just fine.

All my love,
Charlie

Tuesday, December 19, 1944

Dear Mom, Dad, and E,

There isn't a thing to report.[224] I haven't had any mail from you for a long while - just three or four days. However, another one of your packages arrived today and it contained a lot of cheese, thanks loads. It's really something to eat all of the stuff. Of course, I'm very liberal with it and I pass candy, etc. all around. Shirley Marcus sent me a nice box from Barnacinei. She's a swell girl and I think a lot of her. Nothing serious though, haven't gone out with her enough. Eadie's met her a few times.

---

[224] With the beginning of the Battle of the Bulge on December 16th, there is more happening in Charlie's day-to-day than what he lets on in his letters. However, the constraints of the censorship made writing of the military nature of events virtually impossible.

I had a can of tuna fish (Anna's) for chow tonight and it was real good. That's plenty for supper, had pudding for dessert. Everything is running smoothly. I was a little busier than usual today, I like it that way. It was warm again today.

How is the house? And the Grandfolks? I can use a few pairs of strong brown shoelaces (long), plain white envelopes, and brown shoe polish. Are you packing for Florida yet, Ma?

No more now, best of luck.
Love and Kisses,
Charlie

Wednesday, December 20, 1944

Dear Folks,

Not a thing to report this evening, feeling fine and everything is in tip-top shape. Had a can of sardines for supper, after I finish this line I'm going to indulge in a little of the cheese you sent me. Was kept fairly busy again today[225] and I'm getting along nicely with my new (it's old now) job.

I'm reading a fairly good book now, it's W. Somerset Maugham's "The Razor's Edge." Almost halfway through and I find it quite interesting. A lot of it is about Paris and that makes it all the more interesting for me. I wouldn't mind visiting there again, there is so much to see.

Just heard the 10 PM broadcast straight from America. It's the daily news of home program. It's pretty cold, eh? Keep warm and take care of yourselves. Mom, do you have your reservation for Florida yet? Hello, Pop. Keep smiling, Sis.

Love,
Charlie

---

[225] With the new mission assigned to the 102nd Division due to the German offensive, Charlie's section S-3 (in charge of operational planning and strategy) was understandably busier than usual.

Friday, December 22, 1944

Dear Mom, Dad, and Sis,

It was real swell to receive some mail from you. Eadie's V-Mail of December 4th and E's and Mom's letter on the new stationary (December 6th) and Mom's letter of December 2nd all arrived today. Thanks a lot.

I didn't get a chance to write yesterday, so don't expect a letter dated December 21st. You should get one for all the other days, though.

I've acquired a bed with springs. My mattress isn't very large but I put some blankets and a comforter on the lower part of the bed, so it's really comfortable. Boy, it was swell sleeping last night. I'm in a deep cellar and it's a pretty snazzy place.

Mom, don't worry about having more time to attend to me. There isn't a thing you have to do for me and just keep busy in the store, that'll suit me just fine. I know you're thinking of me all the time and I'm thinking of all of you always.

How many $10 bonds do you have? I'm so happy that you're clearing things up, you must feel great. I promise a big letter tomorrow.

Lots of love,
Charlie

Saturday, December 23, 1944

Dear Mom, Dad, and Sis,

I took a good hot shower this afternoon and I feel just dandy now. Got some nice, clean laundry back this evening, all pressed, so I'm in pretty good shape. I have one batch of laundry out now and when I get that back, I'll have all my stuff.

The papers must be full of war news these days. This may be a good chance for us to win more quickly, I surely hope so.

What a night this is back home. Saturday before Christmas, boy I can imagine all of the hustle and bustle. It's a nice long weekend and I hope you enjoy it.

Received a letter from Murray today. Buster will be 18 in May, and I guess they'll grab him right away. Murray says he's not like he was. Buster goes stepping with the gals, and if you recall, Murray never did until he was 21. I think Buster has the right idea, you're only young once.

Mom, you told me a while back that Morris expected to visit Belgium this summer. That's sure a big laugh now, maybe in '46 but not in '45 - that is his trip.

It's pretty cold now, but it's still not a white Christmas. Perhaps it'll snow by Monday. The German propaganda program plays the carols, so we hear all of them. I had the opportunity to visit Holland recently and people there prepare for the holidays just like us. Kids going home with trees, people carrying big packages, etc. And a loudspeaker with the Christmas songs. It's amazing how peaceful things are back in Holland - so homelike, etc. - and then after going into Germany, you're right in the middle of a terrible war. Why can't we all live in peace? That's the $64 question.

Expect turkey for the holiday and some cake or pie. The cooks have been saving sugar for the Christmas meal, and I think they're doing some baking. The cheese you sent was excellent, could use some more in the future.

That's all for now, take care of yourselves and be careful. I'm always thinking of you.

All my love,
Charlie

Sunday, December 24, 1944 - Christmas Eve in Germany

Greetings again,

Merry Christmas to you all. We just had the Protestant church services and I joined in the singing of the carols. There was plenty of cake, candy, etc. going around and I even had a good shot of gin. So it's been a merry X-mas - as merry as possible under the circumstances. The Commanding General of the Division was around today and wished us a Merry Christmas. He even shook my hand, a big deal, eh?

I still remember a X-mas many years ago when Mom came home late with E and my gifts. I think E got a big doll that time and we sneaked out of bed and took a peek at the presents. Do you recall that, Sis?

The radio is going full blast and there's plenty of good music. Trying to boost our morale, I imagine. A big meal is coming tomorrow, I'll write you about it tomorrow night. Oh yes, it's Sunday, another week gone by.

I hope you're all in good health and taking care of yourselves. My thoughts and prayers are with you.

Love,
Charlie

Monday, December 25, 1944

Dear Mom, Dad, and Sis,

Gee, I had a very pleasant Christmas Day. Slept until 9 and then had a delicious breakfast consisting of grapefruit juice, three pancakes with jams and butter, wheatena and coffee. Of course, it was a little late for breakfast but it pays to have friends in the kitchen.

Everything was slow and there wasn't much doing all day. At 12, we all were wished a Merry Christmas by the General, who was serving gin and grapefruit juice. We passed by with our canteen cups, I thought that was very nice. I even had two drinks as did everybody else, and then came Christmas dinner and was it good. I just can't imagine anyone having a better one over here.

We had turkey (2 helpings), mashed potatoes, sweet potatoes, cranberry sauce, filling, raisin bread, pineapple pie, chocolate-iced cake, and peaches. In addition, hard candy, two candy bars and a pack of cigarettes. Everything tasted swell and I certainly hand it to our cooks for preparing such an excellent meal. And as our extra special, we all had beer after the dinner. It's Belgian beer and it was fairly good.

Well, that was enough in itself to make the day a pleasant one but a USO show was still to be seen. A few of the boys in the Battery could attend and I decided to go. I'm glad I did because it was the best show I've seen in Europe. It was a Hollywood unit and it starred Frank McHugh and June Clyde and Mary

Brian. I've seen them all before in movies. McHugh was in "Going My Way" with Bing Crosby.

I came back at 4 and soon it was time for chow again and all I had was a little turkey, some sweet potatoes, cake and coffee. I've had enough food today for a long while.

Received a package today from one of my kids at Wakonda. I drop him a line occasionally and his folks sent me a box from Long Champs. Heard Bob Hope and Danny Kaye on a special variety show tonight. They're a funny pair.

That's all now. Be good and take care.
Love,
Charlie

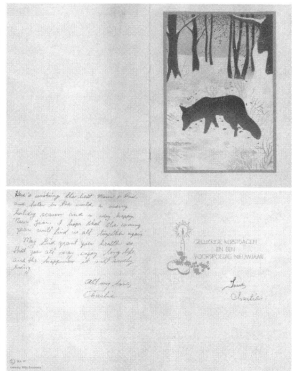

Holiday greeting card from Holland.

Tuesday, December 26, 1944

Hi Folks,

Very little to relate this evening. Had a pretty busy day and am learning a lot about my job. It's very interesting when there's real work to be done.

Breakfast is now served at 8 AM so I sleep until 7:50 or 7:55 and then run like hell. We have an additional man in the section now and we straighten things out in the morning and we both get a chance to wash up, it's pretty nice that way.

Eadie, I'd like to read Ernie Pyle's "Brave Men" and if you can find a pocket-size addition send it along, okay? Also, if you see some of the good novels in pocket-book form, I'd like to get a few. Sometimes I get a chance to read. Of course, there are days that I can't find time to open a book, but it would be nice to have some decent stuff around.

I hear that the "home-front" is all pepped up. It's too bad that it takes a setback to wake the civilians up.[226] I hope the current spirit lasts until we finish the job.

See any basketball games, Sis, or are you too busy? How's the NYU team doing? What good movies have you seen lately?

I hope you are all feeling fine. Mom, when are you going to Florida? Pop, have your new clothes yet? No mail for three days. Perhaps I'll hear from you tomorrow.

Regards to all.
Love and Kisses,
Charlie

Wednesday, December 27, 1944

Dear Mom, Dad, and Sis,

The news is taking a turn for the better now and I think we have the situation well in hand on the Belgian front.[227] Nothing to report from this courier. All is well and I'm in the best of health. It's not too cold - average about 35-40 degrees, and I like the crisp weather. Everything is frosted and most of the ground is white.

I finished "Razor's Edge" this evening. Enjoyed it. E, I think I could stand some professional literature of one sort or another. See if you can get an Accounting Journal - perhaps they're in the phone book and you might be able to get a sub-

---

[226] The initial phase of the Battle of the Bulge, with its successful surprise German advance, put the Allied forces into disarray.

[227] Referencing the Allied victory during the week-long siege of Bastogne. Outnumbered 5:1, Allied forces held the seven roads in and out of Bastogne until reinforcements arrived, thereby hindering the German offensive push.

scription. There is also a magazine called "Business." You might find it on one of the big newsstands in Times Square. I don't want to forget everything I know (or once knew). I'm also writing to school for a little material. Haven't the time for too much stuff

Had a good feast tonight. Cheese, peanut butter, jelly, and bread. Had a few sandwiches.

Am getting along fine, and I again ask you not to worry one bit. Take good care of yourselves.

All my love,
Charlie

Thursday, December 28, 1944

Dear Folks,

Everything continues to go okay. Had a treat today. I visited Holland and not only did I have a hot shower but I had a hot bath. Boy, that was the first time I was in a tub since I've been overseas. It was fun just stretching out and I remembered how often I did that back home. Gave myself a good scrubbing and put on clean clothes from field jacket to OD's[228] down to the cotton underwear I wear under my woolens. Dropped a big batch of dirty stuff to be washed and I should have that in a couple of days. You should see me with a crisp crease in my trousers.

Visited a few people I know in Holland and had a pleasant time. The American soldiers are sold on the Dutch. We all like them a lot. They, in turn, think the world of us, but when it comes to the British the feeling is entirely different. The Dutch just have no use for them, I found the same thing to hold true in France. Perhaps it's our good naturedness or generosity that impresses the Dutch, or it might be our similarity to them, but whatever it is we rate way over the British in their eyes.

---

[228] Olive Drab's, referring to military issued uniform.

Too bad that NYU lost by one basket against Tennessee on Christmas night. That must have been a good game, eh, Sis? We lost in the last forty seconds. Gee, those are real close ball games - just as I like them.

Say, E, here's something you might send me. I have a small leather toilet kit with a zipper. I'm sure you've seen them in the drugstores. The one I have is on its last leg and I certainly will be able to use a new one shortly. You should be able to pick one up for $2.50-$3.00. It's a football-shaped affair, more or less. If possible, get that kind. I have a cloth bag I can use, so if you have any trouble finding one, don't worry. I had the bag at Ft. Dix, and I brought it home on weekends, remember?

It's good and cold, but I'm well protected. Still no mail but I know you're all well. I pray for you every night and I'm sure God will look after you until I get home. How was the stuff Eadie got you for your birthday, Dad? I would have liked to purchase it myself - maybe next year. Just ate the rest of the cheese you sent, it was delicious.

Take care of yourselves and don't work too hard.
Love and Kisses,
Charlie

Friday, December 29, 1944

Dear Folks,

Two packages came through today but still no mail. One package was from you lovely people and the other was from Nelson Bros. They must have sent out a 3 lb. fruitcake to all their employees in the service and Charlie must have put my name on the mailing list. Your package was swell, as usual. Really go for that cheese and those Spanish Peanuts look good.

We had a double feature tonight. "Conflict" with Humphrey Bogart was an interesting picture, but "Hat Check Honey" was a stinkeroo and I quickly made my exit from the "theater" - the room in which I sleep.

After the movie, about five of the fellows, one officer and the Chaplain went to work on a "feast" consisting of the following items contributed by a few of us:

Sardines, boneless chicken, salmon steak, jelly, cheese, peanut butter, crackers, bread, and cookies. Some bill of fare, eh?

Am feeling fine, I hope you're all okay. Has the bank received any checks yet? Take care of yourselves and a very happy New Year.

Love and Kisses,
Charlie

Saturday, December 30, 1944

Dear Folks,

Absolutely nothing new to report. I like writing you every day but it's certainly hard to find material for my letters.

It snowed a little today and we'll surely have a "White New Year's." Everyone is in good spirits and there were quite a few snowballs in the air. There are a couple of kegs of beer to be washed on New Year's Eve and Day.

Another package came through today, it was from Mary Walker. Everything she sent was real nice and I'll certainly send her a letter. She included a lot of tasty items in her box, even had Campbell's Mushroom soup.

E, forgive me for the lack of personal letters, haven't got enough news to fill two epistles. However, I'll write to you shortly. Enclosed is an article from the Servicemen's Edition of the Daily Mirror. Murray sent it to me. Do you know the people?

That's all for now, best of luck.
Love,
Charlie

Sunday, December 31, 1944 - New Year's Eve

Dear Mom, Dad, and Sis,

Another mail-less day, when your letters do arrive, they'll come in batches.

I know what most people are doing back home at this time, at least the young ones who are planning a big night. They're either taking a nap in preparation for the night's festivities or else they're in a hot bath scrubbing up. Say, Pop, remember the trouble I used to have with that damn tuxedo? If it wasn't for you and Eadie I would have never been able to put the thing on. And I recall Dad trying to tie the box, wouldn't I look hot in a tux tonight?

I started this letter at 4 PM and now it's 11:15. We've had a swell evening. We all had plenty of beer and a bottle of Coca-Cola from the bottling company in Brussels. We had a big party all evening and it's just about breaking up now. We held it in the big room where the liaison office is and the enlisted men of the CP sleep. There were two bottles of champagne around and a bottle of cognac. Then we had cheese, tuna fish, deviled ham etc. Not bad for the Siegfried Line. There is a saying here now, "Sing and dine on the Siegfried Line." So now, a few minutes from the New Year, we're all feeling good. Wasn't too bad a New Year's Eve after all.

My only prayer is that 1945 will be the year of peace and that we'll all be to-gether again - that goes for Artie and myself and all the other boys. I'm sure that's what you are hoping for. May God grant us our wish.

I'm thinking of you and hoping for a Happy, Healthy, and Prosperous New Year for you.

All my love,
Charlie

E, some tea bags, okay? How's the piano, young lady?

I'm not too busy at present. Have everything I need. When I tell you I'm short of something in a few days I have more than I need. Remember me telling you that I needed envelopes? Well, now I have more than I'll ever use.

Go, you Russians, Go! Just like yelling at a football game, eh Sis? Berlin in a week, I hope. Then what? That's the $64 question. Take care of yourselves.

All my Love and Kisses,
Charlie

1945

Monday, January 1, 1945

Dear Folks,

At long last I got some mail from home, and it was Eadie's letter of December 11th that arrived along with a letter from Aunt Rose, and a very nice one at that. She sent me a $10 money order and I'll hold on to it for a while. We got paid yesterday for December and I'm having a few money orders bought. Did the War Bond come through this month? And how about the allotments? The only reason I need money is for an emergency - that is a pass to a big city and then to buy some little things – PX, etc. If I keep sending home my money, here's what I would like you to do.

When I accumulate a little dough in the bank, I want a traveler's check for $100, so if the war ends and we can travel or something else comes up, I'll have some money. Outside of that, I don't need money. Will wait a while for the traveler's check, but I would like it around May or June.

Had a nice day, we ate a big meal at 3 PM, and it was like our Christmas meal. We had turkey, string beans, mashed potatoes, corn, cakes and fruit cocktail. Everything is fine. Will write you tomorrow, Sis. Be careful on the streets.

Love,
Charlie

Tuesday, January 2, 1945

Dear Mom, Pop, and Sis,

A nice letter today from Mom dated December 12th. Don't bother too much about the packages, I'm better off without all the candy; an occasional one with cheese, crackers, and a little canned stuff will be fine. Oh, yes, if you come across some marshmallows send them, will you? It would be nice eating toasted marshmallows these winter nights. But go easy with all the candy.

It's very cold now, but I'm comfortable and it doesn't bother me. Another one of your swell packages arrived today. It's the one Eadie mailed on September 26, *Yom Kippur*. That sure did take long to get here, thanks loads. I'll have to start eating some soup, the box of Whitman's chocolate is certainly good.

I thought I might get to hear Hitler's speech on New Year's Eve, but I didn't. We laughed when we first heard him speak back in 1933, it's too bad we didn't stop him then.

Nothing else to report, it's the same routine and it's hard to find things to write about. I'm sending you a cable for your birthday, Pop. Don't let the telegrams scare you.

Love and Kisses,
Charlie

Wednesday, January 3, 1945

Dear Mom, Dad, and Sis,

Nothing unusual to report. It warmed up today and a lot of the snow and ice melted, so we have plenty of mud. It seems that mud must always be present.

Picked up some laundry today, it's nice to get pressed handkerchiefs and underwear. Incidentally, I can use a few washcloths. They come in handy when you wash out of a small pan or helmet.

Heard Bob Hope tonight, he had Bing Crosby as his guest; it was a pretty good program.

I tried some of the noodle soup tonight and it was delicious. It reminded me of Friday night so much, it's sure good stuff.

Visited Holland this morning and had a nice ride. Always enjoy going back there. Things are quite peaceful and you can forget about the war for a while. Then again, I know some people there and I pay them a visit.

I sure was surprised to hear about Hen Werlilim's mother. Gave me a good laugh, weren't the Brooklyn girls good enough for Sheldon?

Received a nice long letter from Karyl and she enclosed snapshots taken at 96th and Riverside Drive.

That's all, I'm fine and dandy. Take care of yourselves and be careful when you cross the streets.

Love and Kisses,
Charlie

Thursday January 4, 1945

Hiya Peoples,

Three nice letters from Mom dated December 22nd, 26th, and 27th. That last one was real quick, wasn't it? Mom, don't rush to meet the postman. It's just luck if the letter gets on a plane, so don't worry if your letter goes out in the morning. I can just picture you watching the clock with one eye and writing with the other.

I'm so glad that business is picking up and you're doing nicely. I can just see Dad smiling as he goes over the black book on Saturday night. I realize how valuable Mary is. Before you forget, the $7 tax is her responsibility, and you should never think about that. It's her obligation to the government and it has nothing to do with you. However, since you are doing well and able to clean up some old debts, I think you should hold on to her at all costs. Give her $45 a week; maybe that will please her, or is she out for more? I think the $25 bonus was very nice. Is she appreciative? At any rate, I think you should keep her, don't you think so, Pop?

Thanks for putting my money away. I really want all the money orders to go towards Mom and Dad's vacations, but if you won't accept them, the bank is the best place. Enclosed is a $10 order for Pop's vacation. How about using it towards that, Dad?

Mom, I'm safe, dry, and warm. That answers your worries in the December 27th letter, I haven't been shoved around. I don't know whether or not you get mail from Phi Alpha. If I have some extra dough, I'll mail it to them. However, don't let them hit you up for any dough. It's not necessary, I'll take care of it.

If there's any Kleenex or similar tissues on sale at home, get me a few boxes please.

Love,
Charlie

Friday, January 5, 1945

Dear Folks,

Hope you had a happy birthday, Dad. I sure want to celebrate it with you next year. What are the chances? Gosh, I wish I knew. Say Pop, you're 59, aren't you? You're going to live until 100 so you have a lot of birthdays to go. Many more happy ones and may next year find your son and your son-in-law with you.

Everything is the same. Mom wrote in one of the letters I received yesterday that she got six of my letters at once. From that, I gather that the mail situation is the same at home. No mail for a number of days and then a batch all together. Well, it's better that way than none at all.

A few of my buttons on my trousers are loose, so I'll have to do a little mending tonight. Would you like to do it for me, Mom?

We had a small PX yesterday and we all bought boxes of Weston's New Yorker Biscuit assortment, an excellent box of cookies. I was surprised to see them on sale at the PX. I'm eating some now and drinking grapefruit juice, good combinations.

All's well, I'm safe and sound.
All my love,
Charlie

Saturday, January 6, 1945

Dear Folks,

Got a swell V-Mail December 20th from "My sister who loves me very much." Isn't that sweet? E, you mentioned that Stellie just got out of the hospital; I didn't even know that she was ill. You probably told me about it in a letter that hasn't reached me yet. I hope she is okay. Please send Stellie and the rest of the Marshak family my best regards.

Glad you people had a visitor, probably kept you a little busy and took your mind off the war for a while. Both Mimi and Ellie are grand girls.

I'm glad the electrolysis treatments are helping you, E. Gosh, Artie will sure have a good-looking wife when he gets home.

It's late now so I'll end. More tomorrow.
Love and Kisses,
Charlie

Sunday, January 7, 1945

Dear Mom, Dad, and Sis,

Was just another day, although it was Sunday. That day used to mean a lot to me back home but now I hardly realize that it's "the Day of Rest." It was a little different in one respect, we got a cigarette and shaving cream ration (Red Cross) and we also received the European Theater of Operations Ribbon.

For the second day in a row we had our choice of Coca-Cola or beer with our dinner meal. On both occasions I took the coke. I think I told you that there is a coke bottling company in Brussels.

It's good and cold and we're having a pretty heavy snowstorm tonight. I hear that it's quite frigid in New York. I hope you're all taking care of yourselves. Be especially careful on the streets. I never forget how careless Mom used to be when crossing streets. I hope you are more cautious now, and that goes for the three of you.

Wojy (the fellow I've always worked with) went to a rest camp for two days and I took over the clerk's job in my section. He'll be back tomorrow morning. I should be going back for 48 hours in the not-too-distant future. The other Sergeant in the section goes on his pass tomorrow and I'll be taking over for him while he's away.

E, if you think you don't have news for your letters, just pity me, I have so little to write about. Why Sis, you can write about the new songs, movies, shows and numerable other things occurring on the home front. This Bacall dame is getting a big buildup, she went to Julia Richmond High School, you know. I'm glad NYU beat Cornell in the basketball game the other night, we must have a fair team. Wasn't CCNY's win over St. John's a surprise? I hope we defeat City this year. If you recall, I worked with a Bill Levine at Scaroon[229] (he was one of

---

[229] Scaroon Manor, an upscale hotel located in Schroon Lake in the Adirondack Park of Northeastern New York.

my waiters). Well, he went into the Army about two years ago and the other day I saw his picture in the Stars and Stripes. He's playing for CCNY again.

Nothing more right now, stay well and send my regards to all. What kind of suit and overcoats did you buy, Dad?

Love and Kisses,
Charlie

Monday, January 8, 1945

Dear Mom, Dad, and Sis,

A good couple inches of snow on the ground. It snowed a lot last night and started again this afternoon for a short while. I always enjoyed this weather back home. Over here its not so good, makes it hard to get around, etc.

Got my laundry back today. It's time for another shower and I'll take clean clothes with me and then take all my dirty stuff to the Dutch people who do it for me. Believe me, I'm well, comfortable and in excellent spirits. My Pop would say with that grin of his, "Only my son" if he could see how well situated we are. I should be the least of your worries.

Received two nice V-Mails from E, December 23rd and 26th. I certainly will write to Stellie, I'm sorry she's having so much trouble. I never did get to see Bernard Fillion. I called him up one night but he was out at the time. I left a message for him to call me, but he never did. Shortly after that he pulled out for the big show.

A Red Cross club mobile was a block away from us today and we went for some good coffee and delicious doughnuts. The girl nearest home came from Cedarhurst, another was from Los Angeles – I forget where the third was from.

Eadie, just you stay at home, let Eadie Davidson be in New Guinea. I agree with Artie, home with the folks and the Navy is the best thing. I'm not exactly sure what Artie wrote you. I work close to the old boy and am always in the same place, though.

Had roast beef and potatoes for dinner. For supper we had some excellent chicken, potatoes, peas, and cake. Not bad, eh? Three hot meals a day, every day.

We have an old accordion (belongs to some officer) in the room I live in and I played around with it tonight. Can get a fair tune out of it by playing the keyboard notes. Don't know anything about the little buttons.

That's all for now, gang. Take care and watch those slippery streets.
All my love,
Charlie

Tuesday, January 9, 1945

Dear Folks,

Received quite a little mail from home today. Have Mom's letter of December 20th and Eadie's of December 28th and 29th. So you're stealing my stuff, eh Sis? The family's journalist goes away for a while and sure enough you pop in as a substitute. A nice poem, E, and I'm enclosing it herein as you requested.

As long as you get a vacation, Mom, I'll be satisfied. I didn't realize that Grandma was still at home, I thought that she was in Florida. Didn't you tell me quite some time ago that she was going to go to Miami Beach? I'll write her tonight. Either Lakewood or Atlantic City would be nice, I think you might be able to do better in Lakewood, or am I mistaken?

Outside the two $10 money orders I sent to you (one for your anniversary - the other to E for Dad's birthday), I have sent home four for a total of $60. Mom mentioned that she deposited one for $15. Since then you should have received one for $20 (December 4th), $15 (December 17th) and $10 dated January 4th. I'm not worried about the dough, just wanted to make sure they all get to you. If you haven't received them, let me know and I'll forward the receipt and you can check. If you will use it for your vacation, I would be pleased. However, if you're against that, just buy some stuff you need or put it in the bank.

Thanks for attending to the stuff for Dad's birthday, E. Now I'm interested in what you bought him. I suppose I'll receive a letter telling me all about it shortly. I'm glad my letter reached you in time, I was afraid I might be a little late telling you to buy Dad a gift.

Since you plead for requests E, here goes. A request Mr. Postmaster - some cheese, a can of sardines or salmon or tuna fish, crackers, and anything else you want to send. Go easy on the candy, I like the bars and the boxes of chocolate occasionally. Say, Sis, that lunch you told me about, you know the day before Christmas, that all sounded good. How about sending me a sample in an olive bottle or a reasonable facsimile? How smart are you, Sis? Only time will tell!

All my love,
Charlie

Wednesday, January 10, 1945

Dear Folks,

Not much to report today. I read in today's Stars and Stripes that New Yorkers have been warned of a possible V-bomb[230] attack. Of course, it's possible but don't worry too much about it, and above all, if you have an alert, take cover and stay calm and collected. I'm not worried about it in the least. The news from the Pacific is excellent, isn't it? The landing on Luzon[231] takes us nearer our goal.

Heard from my friend, Nate Kelne today. He's in Italy with the Air Force. It's still cold and everything is still white. Good ice-skating and sled-riding weather.

Listening to the Bob Hope program now, it's probably the broadcast he had in the States last night. I think it's recorded and sent over to the ETO within 24 hours.

I'm in the best of health, I like my work and I'm doing okay at it. Hope you're all okay. How is Grandma and Grandpa? I wrote to Stellie last night, how is she?

All my love,
Charlie

---

[230] The V-1 flying bomb was an early German-developed cruise missile.

[231] An island in the Philippines.

Thursday, January 11, 1945

Dear Mom, Dad, and Sis,

Received your letter of November 23rd, December 27th and January 1st today, and was happy to read them all. Three were from Mom, and Dad wrote a letter, the November 23rd one. Of course, I realize that all the letters are from everyone and not just from the person who writes them.

So my father is going high-hat. Well, I'll be damned. Say, Dad, isn't Howard's good enough? I'm only kidding you, I got a lot of *nachas*[232] from Mom's letter telling about your trip to Canal Street. I hope you wear the stuff in the best of health. Boy, you sure must look like a million bucks. You, Mom and Sis, must be a pretty sight strutting around in your Sunday best. Mom, be careful you don't let Pop dress up too nicely, after all he's a handsome man and with the man-shortage back home, some woman might run after him and then where would you be?

That sure was a delicious anniversary dinner you had. Gee, 35 years. That's a long time, but we'll yet see 50 years together and more too. Right now I'm mostly concerned about getting home for your 36th anniversary. Sammy and Pauline - what a lovely couple, and what a lucky person you are Mom, to have Sam.

Dad, don't worry about Artie's new job. Driving a supply truck is not bad. Shells can land anyplace - front, back, east, west, so don't think Artie is bad off, that's a pretty good job.

We had a PX today and it was a decent one. Big box of cookies, sugar wafers, three candy bars, Kleenex, face towel - all for about 60 cents.

E, what are you doing for cigarettes? This is a good time to break your habit, or do you need your smokes? I hope and trust that you're not smoking a pipe.

They're selling cokes tonight until 8, so I better hurry to get mine. Coca-Cola in Germany, who would have thought it?

That's all for now, stay well and take care. Love to the Grannies, I wrote them last night.

All my love,
Charlie

---

[232] Hebrew: Pleasure.

Friday, January 12, 1945

Dear Mom, Dad, and Sis,

Received a nice package from you today. It was mailed November 17th and consisted of my old woolen gloves, figs, prunes and apricots, and some chocolate bars. Thanks a lot. No letters from you but I received some from a few friends.

My December's Reader's Digest has arrived, Sis, and I think it's the first December one to come in. That sure is a good subscription and look who provided it - good, old *Yentela*.

Heard a program from Belgium this afternoon and a lieutenant was interviewed. He told about a dog who was his company's mascot. His name, my dear Edith, was "Stinkie."

Working for Major Becker a couple of days while his clerk is on pass to the rest center. I'll go early next month, or so it looks now.

Am feeling fine, everything is grand. Had some Coca-Cola again tonight. Take care of yourselves. My prayers are with you all the time. Heard from Charlie Nelson today.

Love and Kisses,
Charlie

Saturday, January 13, 1945

Dear Folks,

The news certainly is encouraging, especially from the Far East.[233] Let's hope it continues.

Nothing new to report. I received another nice package from you today. Some cheese, Ritz Crackers, soup, etc. Thanks a lot. I'm going to go for the cheese and Ritz, first box of Ritz since I've been here.

---

[233] Possibly referring to the major events of the past few days. On January 9th, the Allied forces commenced a major battle of the Philippines Campaign, the Battle of Bessang Pass. On January 10th, the British Fourteenth Army captured the town of Gangaw in Burma. On January 12th, US warplanes attacked the Japanese naval base at Cam Ranh Bay, Vietnam and sank 40 ships, also sinking most of the ships in a Japanese convoy from Qui Nhơn, Vietnam.

It's another Saturday and you can't tell it by us. Boy, these weekends are sure different. At least in the States, even if you're a soldier, the weekend is a little change and Sunday is a day of rest. Except for the calendar, you can't tell Sunday from Thursday now.

Are you losing much of your hair, Dad, or is it staying in? Mine is just the same as when I left home. Have some good music on the radio now and a fine baritone is singing "*Pagliacci.*" Which reminds me, have you been to the Opera yet this season? Just switched the radio dial and now I have Frank Morgan's program on, some change, eh?

I came across an interesting book about the 1936 Olympics which were held in Berlin. I saw something similar a number of weeks ago but this book is more complete. Some excellent pictures of the track events and I had to laugh to see all of our colored boys who did so well. Hitler, at the time, was always denouncing the Negros, and our Olympic team visited Germany packed full with Negros, and sure enough they win most of the events.[234] That must have made Adolph hail.

The best picture, I think, is the one that shows three American flags over the Olympic stadium signifying a one-two-three victory for the USA in a major event. Pretty soon I hope three American flags will wave in Berlin.

Everything is swell and I'm feeling swell. Please take care of yourselves. How is your morale, Eadie? Don't worry, Artie will be home soon - this year, I hope and pray.

Love to all, and most of it to the three of you and the Grannies.
Love and Kisses,
Charlie

---

[234] Adolf Hitler viewed the 1939 Olympic Games as an opportunity to promote his government and ideals of Aryan racial supremacy. In the lead up to the Games, the official Nazi party newspaper, the *Völkischer Beobachter*, strongly advocated that Jewish people and Black people be barred from the competitions. However, when threatened with a boycott by other nations, Hitler conceded and allowed all to participate. Additionally, when hosting the nations of the world during the games, the Nazi party removed signs stating, "Jews not wanted" and similar racist and antisemitic slogans from the city's main tourist attractions. Famously, Jesse Owens, an African-American athlete, won four gold medals in the sprint and long jump events and became the most successful individual athlete to compete in Berlin, showing to the world the fallacy of the myth of "Aryan" racial superiority and physical prowess.

Sunday, January 14, 1945

Dear Folks,

Received your letter of January 3rd today and was very happy to indeed hear that you took care of the Youngs. I know how good you all must have felt. Fine work, folks, I'm real proud of you. You sure are accomplishing a great deal.

I realize that I'm pretty fortunate to be fairly young and it will be an advantage when I get back. Just look at the headstart I would have had if we didn't have a war. The news is excellent now. Boy, the Russians are sure going to town,[235] and things look rosier in Belgium.[236] I hope it continues.

My skin is improving and to tell you the truth, I don't worry about it now because there's nothing that I could do to help it.

Am back at my own job now. Everything is okay and I'm feeling fine. Ate the can of *gefilte fish* that I had tonight, was pretty good though not like yours, Mom.

Love and Kisses,
Charlie

Monday, January 15, 1945

Dear Mom, Dad, and Sis,

Hiya all doing, folksies? I'm just fine and am in the best of health, no change from yesterday.

Just finished a nice little party of cheese (the stuff you sent), Nestle's hot chocolate, and cookies. Very good indeed.

---

[235] Referring to the start of Vistula–Oder offensive of the Russian Red Army on the Eastern Front. During this offensive the Red Army completed a major advance into German-held territory, capturing Krakow, Warsaw and Poznan. By the end of the offensive push in February 1945, the Red Army had advanced 300 miles (483 km), pausing just 43 miles (69 km) from Berlin. Additionally, during this time the Russian Army liberated the concentration camps of Majdanek and Auschwitz.

[236] Though considerable fighting would continue until January 25 1945, by this time in mid-January the American forces stopped the initial German advance and launched their own counter-offensive. In every way, they were at the precipice of final victory of this campaign. On January 14, German Field Marshal Gerd von Rundstedt ordered a dramatic retreat in the Ardennes region, with the abandonment of the Houffalize and the Bastogne fronts.

I'm surprised so many people are against military training in peacetime. Of course, that's America, but nevertheless I believe it is a necessity. It's too bad we have to teach our youth the ways of war, but it would be a lot safer to have a strong, trained Army than a weak one if the time comes when we have to exert force. I think that the majority of the men in service are in favor of it.

Things are running along smoothly. We work in three shifts now: 8 AM to 5 PM, 4 PM to 1 AM, and 12 PM to 9 AM. At present I am on the 8-5 shift, a pretty good system when it works.

No more news at present, please take care of yourselves.
Love and Kisses,
Charlie

Tuesday, January 16, 1945

Dear Folks,

Mail is pretty scarce these days, but I take it for granted that you're all in the best of health and taking care of yourselves. The news continues to be excellent. Aren't the Russians making splendid advances? I hope we have a special reason to celebrate Eadie's and Mom's birthdays this year. Might be, might be!

Very comfortable. Visited one of the other sections tonight (in the same place but different building) and we had hot chocolate, toast and American cheese, and I played the piano for a while.

One of your packages arrived today and it contained a luscious fruitcake, 2 cans of sardines and other goodies (including the rock candy that Eadie put in). Mailed December 2 - pretty good timing, eh?

Go on duty at midnight tomorrow until 9 AM, that's for three days. Think I'll run for a shower tomorrow and also get a little laundry done. I'm going to try to get some pictures taken soon.

No more until tomorrow.
Love,
Charlie

Wednesday, January 17, 1945

Dear Folks,

Tried that fruitcake you sent in yesterday's package and it sure was good. Very fresh and tasty. Another package came in today and it was filled with cookies from Cake Master. E, you're crying for requests, so here is another one. Don't send out more than one a week, that's sufficient.

I still like the cheese and you can send some more of the cookies. Would like a box of marshmallows, if you can get them. Also send some crackers with the cheese. And, of course, I go for the sardines - if they don't cost too many points.

Feeling fine and dandy, go to work at midnight. Didn't get away for a shower today, so I'll go tomorrow morning when I get off duty. We have a little barber shop set up in a little room with chairs, mirror and a stove. Took a haircut today, get one about every three weeks.

The letter situation is very bad for everyone. There's probably a pile up somewhere.

That's all for now, folks. Stay well and God bless you all.

Love,

Charlie

Thursday, January 18, 1945

Dear Mom, Dad, and Sis,

It's 11 PM now and I go to work in another hour. Time goes pretty quickly at night, at least it did last night. There's a little work to keep busy at and you spend some time fixing up a snack, so you don't count the hours.

Went for a shower today and had a real good hot one. We have some fellows going every day and the boys always go to the same one and it seems that we're the only group that uses a certain room. That makes it very nice because it's not crowded and we can take our time. I shaved at the showers and also changed my clothes. After the shower I take my dirty clothes to the people I know in the certain Dutch town.[237]

---

[237] Heerlen, Holland.

After eating dinner, I went to bed and had a good eight-hour sleep. I didn't get up for supper, so after washing up, I fixed up some of the Lipton's noodle soup and ate a can of sardines. The soup is delicious. Please continue sending the noodle soup. Those sardines are also tasty and now with this occasional night shift, all the stuff you send will come in handy.

E, in case you want to know what Stellie thinks of you, I'm enclosing part of her recent letter. Don't tell her I sent it to you, as I don't want people to know that I relate what they write to me. Also received a nice V-Mail from Sam Young.

No mail again today, pretty soon I should get a handful of letters. The news continues to be excellent. Gosh, those Russians are sure travelling. I hope they get to Berlin on this drive, that would be the easy way to end the war.

When do you plan to go away, Mom? February would be about the best month, wouldn't it? You should have a good Easter rush this year and you want to be rested for that. Are you buying any ready-made garments? Is it possible to get a small line of hose for your customers, or is that out of the question? If you could work on those marvelous halters again, you should be busy in June and July, or is it too much bother? I know that Mom and Pop know best.

How is Stellie, E? I wrote her a letter and the next day I received one from her. What does Artie report? What movies have you seen lately?

No more news at present, will write again tomorrow. Are you getting all my letters? I write every day. Best of luck and God bless you.

Love,
Charlie

Friday, January 19, 1945

Dear Folks,

Your letter of January 5th reached me today and it was nice hearing from you after the short delay.

Just leave it to my Mother to fix up a good time. I'm sure Molly and Sam appreciated it and it sure was a quick, easy, and fine way to celebrate their anniversary and Dad's birthday. And I also know how you felt about things being cleaned up. I bet my Old Man was a proud son of a gun. Nice work, Mom and Dad, I told you that I received a V-mail from Sam that was before the anniversary. I dropped the Youngs a line last night.

How are your teeth coming along, Mom? That should be your prime concern at the present time.

Boy, nine letters from me at one time, I know just how you feel because at times I get a big batch from you at once. Mom, my spirits and morale are excellent, don't worry about that. I say my prayers every night and God is looking out for me and for the three of you and the rest of the family. I do not find it necessary to say, "My voice is smooth as velvet" etc. Remember that one, Eadie?

There was a movie tonight, "Till We Meet Again," but I saw that at home so I got a little more sleep. I go on the 4 PM - midnight shift tomorrow. That's about the best shift since you have practically the whole day for yourself.

There's a photo store in a small Dutch town and if I get the chance, I'm going to have my   picture taken. I'm not sure that I can go to the place, but if I do you'll have another picture of me.

I realize that the Grannies aren't getting any better. There's not much any of us can do, I just hope that they're as comfortable as possible. Where's Grandpa and how is he doing?

I heard from Nate Keline again, E. He's in Italy. Nate's a Staff Sergeant in the Air Force and has the Oak Leaf Cluster to the Air Medal,[238] he must be a gunner or radio man. No more now, take care of yourself in the bad weather you're having.

All my love,
Charlie

---

[238] The Air Medal is bestowed to members of the Air Force for single acts of heroism or meritorious conduct while engaging in aerial flight. The addition of the Oak Leaf Cluster implies preceding decorations and awards.

Saturday, January 20, 1945

Dear Mom, Dad, and Sis,

Hiya people's, how's by you these cold wintery days? You sure are having a spell of bad weather. I've read about the blizzards you had, how severe they've been. I hope it's let up by now. Do take care of yourself, especially when you're out in the streets. It must be very slippery. I know how Mom crosses the streets, so I do worry a little, be careful please.

I'm changing my living quarters. I've been living in a cellar for some time and I'm now in the process of moving into a nice little house right down the street from where I work. We've boarded up the place - we're using four rooms on the ground floor. Three rooms are for the men (we use one of them as a living room) and one is for two of our officers. We have a stove in each room and it's very comfortable. I have one of the rooms to myself for a while. I just set up my bed this evening, I'll move everything else tomorrow. You should see my bed; good spring mattress and over that I have a comforter, two blankets and on top of all that I have my bed roll. Some class!

I have a full mirror, an old-fashioned hall piece, and a little writing desk. There's a bureau in one of the rooms upstairs and I'm getting it down tomorrow. Now if I find a rug, I'll be all set. It's pretty nice, why don't you pay me a visit some day?

Two packages came in today. One was from Mollie Young and the other was from some people named Fletcher. Don't tell Mollie, but that jar of jam she sent broke in transit. However, her other stuff came through nicely - a box of soft candy, some nuts, and a package of figs, all very nice. Your package was excellent. Noodle soup, bouillon and four boxes of assorted crackers, and cheese. Thank you ever so much.

It's a few minutes to midnight and I'll be going to bed shortly. I'm now on the 4 PM shift. Probably stay on for one week instead of three days like we have been doing. I prefer changing every week.

Love,
Charlie

Sunday, January 21, 1945

Dear Mom, Pop, and Sis,

I have a cup of soup on my right and a cheese sandwich in my left. It's close to midnight and this sure reminds me of the midnight snacks I used to have at home. I'll be off soon and then I'll go to my nice new home. I spent a lot of time today fixing my room – scrubbed the windowsill, now who taught me that? It's in pretty good shape now. I have another little table with a few drawers, and I have a lace cloth on the top, nothing but the best.

Everything is swell, in fact I'm sure you can't realize how well off I am. I should be the least of your worries and I hope you have none. It's about time you stopped worrying about everything, Artie and I can take care of ourselves.

We had a little more snow tonight, but it's not any colder. Got a new pair of trousers today from Supply. I sure do have enough stuff. Was kept a little busy tonight but now I'm just waiting for the next man to relieve me.

Remember me telling you that I received the cookies from Cake Master? I didn't open one of the boxes until tonight, and I found out that it contained a delicious fine-looking fruitcake. Thanks a lot, it sure arrived in good shape. I passed it around tonight and everyone raved about it. I've emptied all of my packages into one of my drawers and it looks as if I have a small grocery store. If you visit me for dinner shortly, I'll be able to fix up a good meal.

We have an excellent generator, and it supplies electricity 24 hours a day, so we get plenty of light. I got hold of a December Esquire today. Most of the big mags send free copies overseas and we get them from Special Services.

The Colonel "adopted" a dog recently, so now we have a pet with us in the CP. It's a breed unknown in America. Right now the mutt is stretched out on his back with his feet in the air, it's the first dog I've seen sleep that way.

The night man is here now, so I'm going to bed. You'd be jealous if you saw my bed, it's just as good as Mom's. Be well, take care and don't worry. I love you all very dearly.

Love and Kisses,
Charlie

Monday, January 22, 1945

Dear Mom, Dad, and Sis,

Received ten nice letters today and about six were from you. I now owe you a big line, but I'll have to postpone it until tomorrow. It's getting late and I've been busy all evening, that is from 9:30 until now 12:15. I go on the day shift tomorrow, so I want to hit the hay. Thanks for all the lovely letters and for all the nice things you say.

Saw a fine movie this evening, "Rhapsody in Blue." I'm sure you must have seen it by now, I enjoyed it very much and I liked hearing all of Gershwin's music. The stadium scene certainly was familiar, and do you recall the 103rd Street and Riverside Drive street sign? It's too bad that he died so early in life as he surely had a lot of great work left in him. For some reason, the actor who portrayed Gershwin reminded me of Uncle Doc. I bet you all liked it and I can see my Mom crying away when he dies.

I'm safe and well. You should be proud of Artie, E. He's doing a great task.

More tomorrow.
Love,
Charlie

Tuesday, January 23, 1945

Dear Mom, Dad, and Sis,

Two more fine letters from you today and they are sure recent - one is from January 14th and it was postmarked the 16th, only one week and that's just about the fastest time possible. I just reread all of your letters, nine in all for the last two days, and I enjoyed every one. It was nice to get a few from you, Dad. It's true that Mom covers the news very well, but how about writing me without reading Mom's letters? Try it soon, it will be interesting. I hope all your wishes for the New Year come true, then things will certainly be okay.

I'm so glad that business is good and you're able to move around and do things. Now that the store is in good condition, here's what I think you should do. Both Mom and Pop should have the dentist give them the business so your mouths will be in perfect condition for the future. Do it now before too many other things pop up. I fully realize that your expenses are high and that it was necessary to clear up your obligations. But now that you're coming along, you should put a few bucks away occasionally. Get your clothes, no one deserves them more than my Mother and Father, clear up more of the little things, get medical and dental attention, and do all that with the plan that a little must be left in the bank.

Mom, I'm sure that the store doesn't need a lot of money. A good weekly cleaning and a frequent waxing job should make it look nice. The fixtures are okay and people now are more interested in getting their stuff than in how beautiful the place is. As long as it's clean and up-to-date, is all that matters. Let's see if you can budget yourselves so the bank sees you once a week, that would make me happy.

What are your plans for the Spring? You should try to keep the business going as nicely as it is. Those halters were a wonderful idea - or some of your real lightweight garments. I'm sure you are making plans now so you won't be caught short. Mom, this is the time to save a few bucks so don't make any bold investments in a big stock if you don't think it'll pay for itself above the cost, be careful.

Also remember this, the country will definitely have its greatest purchasing boom after the war. People want and need consumer goods. Try to hook up with a small manufacturer - put your label on and let them go fast over the counter. Forget your hand fittings except for the old-timers. Go real retail, if you know what I mean. For a year right after the war, I can't see why you won't be able to make $5,000 clean profit. Remember, it's going to be the day after the war is over. Just keep your eyes open and get anything you can and just dish it out. The boom should be good for a couple of years and I'm positive you can be in on it if you play it smart. That'll be the time to get hose, slips, and go big.

Mom, you can't do a great business by fitting everyone separately like you've been doing. It's good now, material is scarce, etc. But the way people will want to buy girdles, bras, etc. after the war, it would be foolish to fit for three lousy hours. For those few years, try to recall all of your long experience and cash in on all the tricks you've learned. Have a system, watch expenses, you don't have two kids anymore, there's just Mom and Pop, yourselves, to look out for. Start thinking about it now.

I'm in my little house sitting by the fire, there's another fellow in my room now and we have a nice set up. I'm well and comfortable. How's that, Mom? Relax, take it easy, for God's sake don't keep rushing like you always do. You're all doing grand, take time out to breathe and live.

The news certainly is encouraging, the Russians are only 165 miles from Berlin. Godspeed to them. Artie is out of any danger by now, may God watch over him all the time.

That Scaroon Manor postcard sure brought back fond memories, I wouldn't mind spending a couple of weeks there as a guest. No more now, take good care of yourselves and don't work too hard. I love you and pray to God to grant you long life, health, and happiness all the time.

Love and Kisses,
Charlie צודעק

Wednesday, January 24, 1945

Dear Mom, Pop, and Sis,

I can't help but feel optimistic tonight. The Russians are only 135 miles away from Berlin and they're still going strong. Gosh, wouldn't it be wonderful if they're in Berlin by the time you get this letter?

Everything is okay, no change. I understand why you hate the Germans so, but don't think that American-Germans are at fault to the same extent. Why, E, I'm surprised at you for staying away from Mary Wahler. Look how loyal some of our American-Japanese soldiers are. There are good and bad of every kind.

Heard from Charlie Zwerner yesterday for the first time in almost a year. He's still in England and is doing okay. Yes, E, that Mitch Hoehbery is the same one I know - Philadelphian. He graduated from OCS in August.

Had some cheese sandwiches tonight, used your cheese and it was real good. No more now, be good and take care of yourselves.

Love,
Charlie

Thursday, January 25, 1945

Dear Mom, Pop, and Sis,

All continues to go well on the Western Front. The news is still good from the East and I'm sure the Russians are making solid advances and won't be thrown back. It's just a case of how far they can go, I certainly hope it's to Berlin.

Nothing to report these days. Was a little busy today and go on the night shift tomorrow. I like that just about the best. Plan to go for a shower either tomorrow or Saturday.

One of the well-known "LIFE" photographers has been around lately taking pictures in the vicinity, his name is Bill Vandegrift or something like that. Kathrine Cornell and Brian Aherne are playing in "The Barnetts of Wimple Street" in some Holland town, but I haven't been able to get to see it. Two members of the cast visited us today, the man's name is McKay Norris, the girl's last name is Perry or something like that.

It's pretty cold, around 20-25 degrees. All is well, I'm well and safe.

Take care, will write more tomorrow.
Love,
Charlie

Friday, January 26, 1945

Dear Mom, Dad, and Sis,

Drinking some of your pea soup now and it is delicious. Didn't think it would be so good, but I was wrong. It's now 2 AM the 27th, but I'm dating this the 26th so it won't confuse you with my daily letters. It's very quiet tonight and there's not too much to do.

I think I told you when I first joined the Division that a boy I went to school with was in one of the artillery battalions. Remember we used to go around together at Camp Swift? Well, his mother is seriously ill and given only a few months to live (I think it's cancer). The kid has been trying to get home on a furlough but he didn't have luck. However, he just heard that he's going back as an orderly on a hospital ship and will get ten days at home.

His name is Seymour Rosenberg and he lives in Brooklyn. I went to see him today and he's going to phone you when he gets home. I don't imagine that he can visit you, too many boys want him to and ten days aren't too long. However, his brother lives at the Park Crescent Hotel at 150 Riverside Drive. I don't know his first name but he's single and has 1 room (help you find him). Seymour may stay there and if you care to, you might call them some evening. His mother is in Doctor's Hospital on York Avenue and the 80's. I think it'll be enough if he calls you and sends my regards. I sure wouldn't want to go back for that reason, although I'll be good and ready when the war is over.

Here I've been hoping that the Russians get to Berlin in a few weeks and in today's paper it says that they promised to get there by Spring! Well, I can wait a few more months with the millions of others. Maybe the Reds will fool us.

No additional news, everything is about the same. Received a letter from Mother today, it was written December 17th. Thanks for being so thoughtful about my packages. One from E, too, from the 14th of January.

There's a nice fire going and I'm comfortable. Be careful and take good care of yourselves. Send my love to the Grannies, I'm writing Eadie a letter right now.

All my love and kisses,
Charlie

Saturday, January 27, 1945

Dear Mom, Dad, and Sis,

For the first time that I can recall, I received three letters from you written on consecutive days: January 8th, 9th, and 10th. They were all V-Mails from Eadie, thanks a lot. In addition, I got five more epistles, including one from Anna.

The New York Herald Tribune resumed publication of its Pars edition about two weeks ago. Recently, we've been getting a copy a day late. I certainly enjoy reading it. It's the same font and type as the New York paper and it's written for civilians, not soldiers, so you get a different view that the Stars and Stripes presents. Many of the articles and editorials in it are reprints from the New York edition. I read tonight that it was zero degrees in New York City. I hope that the frigid temperature isn't bothering you too much. Be sure to take good care of yourselves.

Heard from Morty Marcus today for the first time in a number of months. He has about two more months until he is commissioned. That boy sure didn't get a break, I have no regrets because I didn't want to be a dentist.

Say, E, what program does Leah Ray sing on? I didn't know that she still performs, I've heard a lot about Katherine Dunham from the Brooklyn girl I go out with. She's a "student" of the dance and always raves about Dunham. I've seen some ballets but have never attended a performance of the modern dance, it should be good stuff.

So my telegram finally reached you, eh Pop? Too bad I didn't come along with it. I'll be sending more cables in the future, so don't worry when you see a telegram. It'll always be good news.

Took a shower this afternoon, and as usual, it was enjoyed. Had a real good supper - roast beef, spinach, browned potatoes, canned cherries and coffee. Eating well, feeling fine. Just take care of yourselves and don't work too hard and everything will be okay. The Russians are 91 miles away from Berlin today. Hope it's 75 tomorrow night.[239]

All my love to the best family in the world.
Love and Kisses,
Charlie

Sunday, January 28, 1945

Dear Mom, Pop, and Sis,

How did you spend this Sunday? Hope it was a pleasant one. If my Dad prepared the breakfast, I know you got off to a good start. Gosh, isn't he a talented man, Mom? Boy, it sure will be good to get some soft-boiled eggs for a change. Remember how I used to prefer scrambled eggs? Well, I'll settle for the boiled ones now. Does Pop still do the grocery shopping Saturday night, or has he been promoted?

---

[239] The movements and advance of the Russian Army were widely circulated in the US newspapers at this time, thus Army censorship didn't apply to this information.

Everything is the same and there's nothing new to report. A furlough plan to England has been put into effect for soldiers in the ETO, I don't imagine we'll get to go for a long while.

How are you feeling, folks, and you too, E? I hope the cold weather isn't getting you down. I'm in the best of health and spirits.

This is my last night on the night shift, tomorrow I go on at 4 PM. Just finished some potato soup one of the boys had. Also ate a peanut butter sandwich. Had a filling replaced by the dentist today.

Goodbye until tomorrow.
All my love,
Charlie

Monday, January 29, 1945

Dear Mom, Dad, and Sis,

Hope you're all feeling fine and are taking care of yourselves. Isn't it about time Mom went on her vacation?

We've had some fresh oranges and apples from the States recently. We've always been able to get apples in France and in Holland, but the California and Florida oranges are a real treat.

I had the chance of buying some gifts through the Army PX, so I bought you all some little presents. You won't get them for a couple of months. That will take care of Mother's Day, Father's Day, and for E, it's just a little reciprocation for all the packages she's wrapped up for me. I'll let the gifts be a surprise. I'm sure you'll like them. Let me know when they arrive and what you think of them.

Nothing much to report, it's a little past midnight and I'm ready to hit the hay. Send my love to the Grannies and the rest of the family. Be good and may God watch over you all.

Love and Kisses,
Charlie

Tuesday, January 30, 1945

Dear Mom, Dad, and Sis,

Received Mom's letter today written on January 2nd. The white wool socks also came through today, thanks a lot for both.

There's nothing new to report. I'm feeling dandy and everything is okey-doke. There's a big Red Cross center in the Dutch town we always visit, and doughnuts and coffee are served all day, I was in today and had some. Also took some clothes in to be washed. My gums are in perfect shape now, the dentist sure did a good job. The filling he put in the other day also feels good.

It's pretty cold these days, but I'm good and comfortable. Don't worry, everything is swell; food, work, etc.

Doing enough reading, get enough rest. Hitler spoke on the radio tonight,[240] he sort of conceded that Berlin is lost. Boy, those Russians will kill all those damn Germans, and that's okay by me. We would treat them too soft. Let the Reds massacre the Huns. News is good.

Love and Kisses,
Charlie

Wednesday, January 31, 1945

Dear Folks,

Just a quick line, it's 1 AM and I have to get up early for the day shift. Was in Holland again today and saw some of my friends. A club-mobile visited us in the morning and we had doughnuts and coffee.

Received Mom's letter of January 17th, same old Mummy - doing everything imaginable. Rest up a bit, Mom, don't strain yourself. You're no spring

---

[240] This was to be Hitler's last public speech, broadcasted on the twelfth anniversary of his ascent to power in 1933. Amongst other themes, in this speech Hitler declared that the struggle against "Jewish Asiatic bolshevism had been raging long before National Socialism came into power," but that he had strengthened the "natural resistance stamina of our people" to withstand the Jewish infection that sought to "systematically to undermine our nation from within." Hitler decried "The horrid fate that is now taking shape in the east" and called upon "every able-bodied German to fight with the complete disregard for his personal safety...to continue supporting this struggle with utmost fanaticism." (https://www.jewishvirtuallibrary.org/adolf-hitler-broadcast-on-the-12th-anniversary-of-the-national-socialist-regime-january-1945)

chicken anymore. Please have the teeth taken care of, that should be the number one item at present.

Heard from Murray today, he's still in Belgium and sends his regards to you.

Love and Kisses,
Charlie

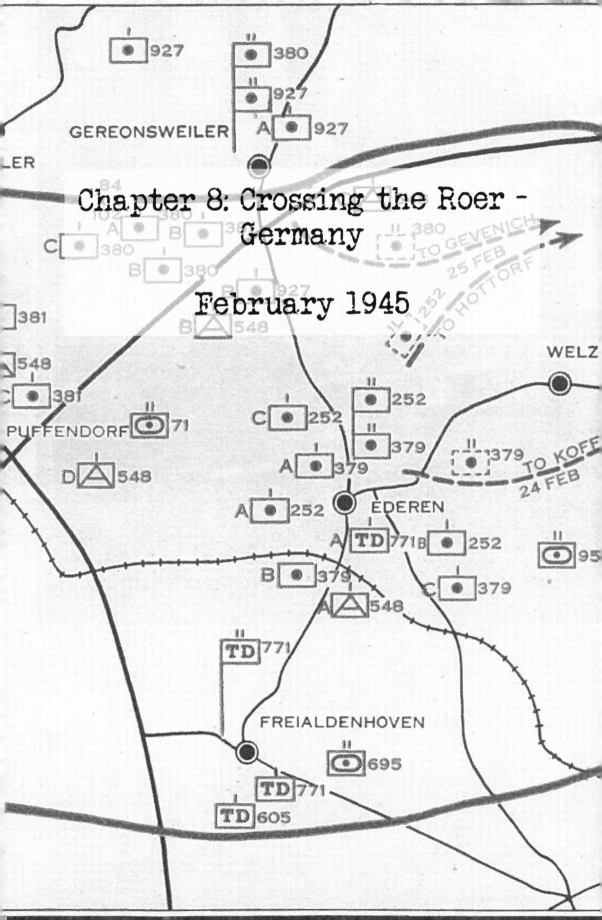

Chapter 8: Crossing the Roer - Germany

February 1945

The beginning of the month of February found the 102nd Division completing its training in preparation for its role in Operation Grenade, the coming assault across the Roer River and the advance towards the Rhine.[241] The Division's plans were abruptly thrown into disarray when the Roer River began to flood, rising four feet and consequently inundating the adjacent valley floor. By mid-February, the weather began to improve and with

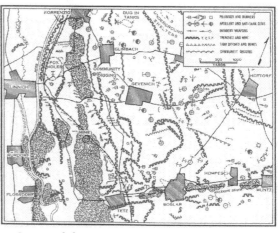

German defensive positions east of the Roer River.
(With the 102nd Infantry Division Through Germany,
pg. 124)

the waning of the turbulent flood conditions, the attack was set to commence with the sunrise on the morning of February 23, 1945.[242]

---

[241] With the 102nd Infantry Division Through Germany, pg. 93

[242] Ibid, pg. 116-120

After fierce fighting - in which the 102nd suffered 75 killed, 493 wounded, and 31 missing in action - the Division managed to cross the river in two locations and establish a bridgehead on the northern bank just one day after beginning their assault on the fortified German positions.[243] The next objectives on the horizon were to seize the town of Uerdingen and the Adolf Hitler Bridge, one of the most strategically important German routes of escape across the Rhine River.

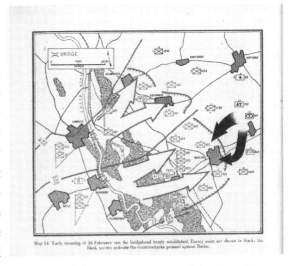

German defensive positions east of the Roer River. (With the 102nd Infantry Division Through Germany, pg. 124)

Finally, the Division was tasked with capturing the integral town of Viersen and Erkelenz, followed by the Niers Canal. The final capture would be the large industrial city of Krefeld, to be taken in the beginning of March 1945. When all was said and done, this objective would cover some 60 kilometers (app. 37 miles) from the Division's starting point before crossing the Roer River.[244]

Like the preceding months which saw heavy combat, Charlie and the Headquarters Battery continued progressing in step with the rest of the Division, to the rear of the front lines. His letters home did not speak to the tactical operations, rather they described the lighter aspects of day-to-day life and maintained focus on the health and wellness of the family he so cherished.

---

[243] Ibid, pg. 131

[244] Ibid, pg. 147

Thursday, February 1, 1945

Dear Mom, Pop, and E,

Everything is just perfect, working the day shift now and was through at 5 PM, then I had supper - broiled beef, potatoes, peas, raisin pie, and hot chocolate.

After chow I went to the PX and it was a good one this week. Bought Kleenex - don't send me any, I have plenty now - cookies and crackers, and some candy. From there I went to the supply room where I got my ration of one bottle of Coca-Cola.

Got to my "home" about 6:45 and washed up, read Stars and Stripes and here I am, sitting in my undershirt writing to you. A cup of grapefruit juice on my right, some cookies in my left, a nice fire going - what more could I ask for, other than to be home? I'm sorry that I didn't bring my moccasins over, that's the only thing I miss, but I didn't have room for them at the time.

Received a very nice letter from Artie today which he wrote from Luxembourg on January 26th. He even typed it and I take it for granted that he was inactive at the time. He said, "We have been experiencing freezing weather of late, but I am thankful to have a nice warm place to stay." That made me feel good. If you manage to get indoors, things aren't too bad. Stinkie's typing isn't anything to brag about; Sis, what's wrong with that dumbbell? Unless I'm mistaken, Artie is still taking it easy as of today. Have a pretty good idea of what every Division is doing and where it is.

My last three letters were a little skimpy, that's because I wrote them around midnight, just before going to bed. I'm afraid that I've spoiled you with these daily letters. I'm afraid to skip a day now, just hope that I can always write every day.

E's V-Mail of January 15th came in today, thanks Sis, you're so sweet. Oh yes, in your next package please include some tea bags, okay? How's the piano, young lady?

I'm not too busy at present. Have everything I need. When I tell you I'm short of something, in a few days I have more than I need. Remember me telling you that I needed envelopes? Well, now I have more than I'll ever use.

Go, you Russians, go! Just like yelling at a football game, eh Sis? Berlin in a week, I hope. Then what? That's the $64 question. Take care of yourselves.

All my love and kisses,
Charlie

Friday, February 2, 1945

Dear Mom, Pop, and Sis,

Some old mail caught up with us today and there were letters written on the 14th

Now It's Just 35 Miles to Go

Berlin Hears Guns As 3 Red Thrusts Advance on Capital

and 15th of December, Christmas cards from you and the grandfolks, and a package mailed the 19th of September. Thanks loads. The package contained some underwear, three envelopes of noodle soup, and about a dozen delicious brownies. I had a few of them tonight with some pineapple juice, thanks so much. There are some cornflakes and Wheaties around now and this morning we had cornflakes for breakfast. I have a box of Wheaties and I plan to eat them tonight with milk and sugar - yum-yum.

We cleaned up our house today and it looks very nice now. One room is set up as a "living-room" only. One boy was sleeping in it, but we moved his bed into one of the bedrooms. Now we have plenty of room for a washstand, mirror, chairs and writing tables - we also have a couch but it's not very comfortable. Plenty of food available and everything is simply fine. If you're worrying about me, you're crazy.

That's the boy, Dad. I sure want you and Mom to take good care of yourselves and I'm happy to hear that you are. People often comment how splendid looking you and Mom are in that picture I have. I certainly do remember those Christmases - Eadie's carriage - my first bike and the Sunday mornings when Sis and I would polish the stuff in the living room. They were pleasant days; I remember Mom sneaking in one Christmas Eve with the gifts and E and I getting up to get a look at them.

I hope the house is okay - especially with the money you put into it, as long as it's not costing you anything, it's okay. I'm not worried about it one bit. The weather has changed for the better. It's warmed up considerably but now we're plagued by our old friend, mud. Nice and sunny today.

News is excellent, I don't think the Russians can miss now. If only the fall of Berlin would end the war, but I'm afraid that it won't right away. These Russians deserve all the credit in the world. I wonder whether or not The Big Three Conference is in session yet?[245] I hope they do some good and make definite plans for peace, etc. What do you think about the row over Wallace?[246] He'll be lucky if he gets the job.

All my love,
Charlie

Saturday, February 3, 1945

Dear Mom, Dad, and Sis,

Received three nice letters from you lovely people. Two of them were dated January 7th and the other January 9th, thanks a lot. Glad to hear that everything is swell back at home and that you're doing so well. It sure makes me feel so proud of you all.

You're not kidding, Dad, about how great it will be to see you in your new clothes; I derive pleasure from everything my family does.

Not much news, tomorrow morning I'm going to Holland for a shower and to purchase a few things, if I have the time. Heard from Mimi today and she said you all look well and are feeling tops.

---

[245] Also known as The Yalta Conference, the Crimea Conference was the gathering of the heads of government of the United States, the United Kingdom, and the Soviet Union to deliberate the postwar reorganization of Germany and Europe. The three states were represented by President Franklin D. Roosevelt, Prime Minister Winston Churchill, and Premier Joseph Stalin, respectively. The location of the conference was near Yalta in Crimea, Soviet Union, between February 4-11,1945. (https://www.nationalww2museum.org/war/articles/big-three)

[246] Henry Agard Wallace (October 7, 1888 – November 18, 1965) was an American politician who served as the 33rd Vice President of the United States. In January 1945, Roosevelt selected Wallace for Secretary of Commerce. In this position, Wallace was expected to play a key role in the economy's postwar transition. The nomination brought an intense debate, as many senators objected to his support for liberal policies intended to boost wages and employment. After failing to block his nomination, Senator Walter F. George led passage of a measure signed by President Roosevelt removing the Reconstruction Finance Corporation from the Commerce Department, thereby impeding Wallace's ability to directly affect the country's post-war financial reconstruction. (https://wallace.org/).

The Russians are still pounding away, and I hope they break through very soon. I wonder what Hitler is thinking about these days?

No more right now, more tomorrow.
Love and Kisses,
Charlie

Sunday, February 4, 1945

Dear Mom, Dad, and Sis,

Spent a very nice Sunday. Change shift today and I go on at midnight, so I had the whole day to myself. In the morning I went for a shower and changed my clothes, came back in time for a swell dinner. We had fried chicken, potatoes, spinach, peaches and coffee.

How was the breakfast you made this morning for the family? I bet my omelets are still the best, remember how I used to flip them?

Took a nap during the afternoon and got up in time for supper. And this evening I've been taking it easy in my home reading and now I'm writing a few letters, not a bad day, eh? Just finished a good snack of cornflakes, peaches and cream.

Does Artie complain of a cigarette shortage? I have some extra cigarettes and I was going to mail them to Artie but I'm afraid that they'll never get to him. However, if he needs them, I'll send a carton to him.

Received Mom's letter of January 10th. I assure you that I look forward to all your letters just as much as you do from mine. E, thanks for the letter about indoctrination for Return to the US. Certainly, very funny and I got a big kick out of it, so did the fellows.

Irene Witt (the girl from Georgia) sent me a Valentine's card, isn't that sweet? I correspond with five girls - Shirley Marcus, Karyl Steiner, Ann (from Brooklyn), Zelda (the sister of one of my campers at Wakonda) and Irene. That's not too much, is it? Get an occasional letter from others. I write regularly to Murray Goldblatt, Al Rosman, Artie, and occasionally to Morty Marcus. Then, of course, every once in a while, a letter comes through from a friend. All in all, I have a fairly good correspondence. Your letters are the favorites.

It's still fairly warm and muddy as ever. There's plenty of cold weather left, though. Hope it has warmed up a bit at home. That was certainly some cold spell you people had.

I have a nice red silk scarf made from a German parachute we found. Still haven't worn the blue sweater you sent, so you know I'm warm and comfortable. God bless you all.

Love,
Charlie

Monday, February 5, 1945

Dear Mom, Dad, and Sis,

Nothing startling to report this trip. I could have seen the movie "Jamie" this evening, but I was sleeping and didn't know that we were going to have a picture. When I'm on the night shift I usually go to bed at 1 PM and sleep to about 10. I can go to bed in the morning and sleep to 4:30 PM and have the evening to myself. I change around quite frequently.

Since I missed supper tonight, I fixed up a nice little bite when I got up at 10 PM. I had grapefruit juice, Wheaties, and two sardine sandwiches on toast. Very good. Got a big batch of clean laundry back today and now I'm set for another stretch.

I haven't heard from Stellie recently, I imagine she's back at school. I hope she's getting along okay. Did I tell you that I received a letter from Mimi the other day?

The noodle soup is ready to eat now, so I'll close the letter. Be good and please take care of yourselves. I'm comfortable and content. God bless you all always.

Love and Kisses,
Charlie

Tuesday, February 6, 1945

Dear Maw, Daw, and *Yenta*,

How's by you these days, folksies? Hope you're all in the best of health.

Under separate envelope I'm sending home the red silk scarf I have. It was made from the pure silk of a German parachute we captured. The chute was cut into small pieces and then the pieces were dyed red. Wear it if you like, E, but save it for me. It's one of the few souvenirs I have.

Enclosed is a $25 money order. If you need the dough, you're welcome to it. Otherwise, please deposit it for me. I should be getting near the $200 mark.

With this warm weather, we're getting quite a bit of rain, not too good for the ground.

The Russians are off again and now that they've crossed the Oder River,[247] they should be on their way.

Received a marvelous package from you today. Everything I like: cheese, crackers, sardines, fruitcake and figs. Had a swell party tonight, what a great family I have.

Love and Kisses,
Charlie

Wednesday, February 7, 1945

Dear Mom, Pop, and Sis,

It's late so this will have to be short. For a while most of my letters will be brief, as I'm being kept quite busy. However, you can depend on that daily letter whenever possible.

Got some swell mail from you today and I'll answer some of it tomorrow morning when I have some free time.

It's very warm, close to 50 degrees. One o'clock now (AM, February 8th) and I just had a can of your sardines and I washed up. I'm very comfortable and con-

---

[247] Only 69 kilometers (app. 43 miles) from Berlin.

tent. Never worry about my morale, it's always tops. With a family like you at home, who wouldn't always be in a good frame of mind?

On the 4-12 shift now and it keeps us going, I like it that way. The boss handed me a few bouquets tonight and the Colonel pawned a few drinks for all of us.

Everything is fine; I love you all very dearly, *Pessa, Shmiel* and *Yenta*.

Love and Kisses,
Charlie

Thursday, February 8, 1945

Dear Mom, Pop, and Sis,

It's 1:30 PM now and I have a few hours to myself before going to work. Since I wrote such a brief line yesterday, I feel I owe you a longer one this trip. I'll try.

Slept until 9 AM and then toasted some bread. Had a marmalade spread and then on the next three pieces of toast I finished up the cheese you sent me. Did all this in my house, some luxury, eh? For dinner we had roast beef, potatoes, string beans, peaches, bread and coffee, and it's only a Thursday.

Three fine letters came from you yesterday. One from Mom and Dad dated January 25th, one the 29th and another the 31st of January - that just took one week. Yes, Pop, the news is favorable. You didn't guess quite right about the Russians being in Berlin when your letter reached me. However, I hope it's just a matter of days. Don't get too optimistic folks, even if Berlin falls, we may have quite a bit of fighting left to do.

Mom, you say that after business your time goes to writing letters and listening to the radio news. Gosh, don't tell me you still tune in to all those *kibbitzers*.[248] All they do is confuse you since everyone says something different and they all have different point of views. Why don't you just listen to the 11 PM newscast? That's your best bet. And also, once you hear the news in one day, it's the same the rest of the day. So why waste your precious time? There are so many other things you could be doing.

---

[248] Yiddish: One who offers opinions.

As for all of your going out and enjoying yourselves while Artie and I are over here, why that's just what we want you to do. We're over here so you people can continue your way of life and I'd be very disappointed if you stay at home pining away. You've had so little fun out of life, that it's about time you did step out. So do me a great favor and keep stepping.

My next money order will be for the express purpose of purchasing three tickets to a Musical Comedy or Opera for Mom and now a show for Pop - I'd like you to see "Up in the 70's," "Bloomer Girl" or one of the other hits. If you want to, Sis, buy the tickets now and I'll send you the dough real soon. Don't forget, that's what I want, so please do it. Close the store early occasionally, you just can't go on like you are without a let up. You'll make the final sale a day later, Mom, don't rush so.

You never mention Grandpa in your letters. Is anything wrong? Let me know if there is - after all, he was an old man. Send him my love. How's Grandma doing? Is she living alone in the apartment?

How is the coat turning out, the one Mom is having remodeled? Boy, what a classy three you must be. Nothing else right now, will write again tomorrow. Please take care of yourselves and don't work too hard.

All my love and kisses, God bless you.
Charlie

Friday, February 9, 1945

Dear Folks,

Very little is happening, so it's really tough to get out these daily letters. I hardly know what to tell you except that I'm feeling swell and that everything is okey-doke.

It's 4 PM now and I'm just about ready to go to work. Tomorrow I go on at 8 AM. It's still warm but there are signs of the weather getting cold again. There's a brisk wind today and the day is exceptionally clear. That's always good because then our Air Force can do some work.

Finished your fruitcake last night with some coffee. That was sure a good piece of cake. I bet you're tired of buying fruitcake, they certainly became popular during this war. I bet there isn't a soldier in the Army who hasn't received one at one time or another.

What do you hear about Artie? I'm just about due for a letter from him.

No more news right now, take good care of yourselves and have some fun. God bless you all.

Love and Kisses,
Charlie

Sunday, February 11, 1945

Dear Folks,

Had a nice Sunday and it was topped off with a swell package from you - Nestle's Hot Chocolate, two boxes of cookies, and figs. Thank you a lot, just had a little party and all the stuff was good. We had roast chicken for dinner today and roast beef for supper, so we have our share of chow.

It rained most of the day but that doesn't bother me. I'm still in the same place and living in my little house and I'm quite comfortable.

Heard from Murray Goldblatt today and he's still in Belgium, no other mail today.

How's everything at home? I hope it's not too cold anymore. Excuse the briefness of this letter, but I'm just about set to go to bed.

Love and Kisses,
Charlie

Monday, February 12, 1945

Dear Mom, Pop, and Sis,

I received the fastest letter yet from you today, it was written the 6th of February, last Tuesday and it was postmarked February 7th at 1:30 PM. Boy, isn't that some time? That one certainly came air mail. I was surprised to hear that you haven't had any mail for a week. As you know, I write every day and I always imagine my letters arrive daily at home. However, they must get to you eventually. Do you keep them in date order? Also got your January 23rd letter and E's V-Mail of January 24th. Thanks for all of them. I'm glad that Dad enjoyed a pleasant birthday, I want to celebrate it with him next year.

I didn't know that you had an opera singer for a customer. That must have made *"Il trovatore"* so much more interesting - that is knowing someone is the cast. How were your seats?

It's still moderate temperature, around 40 degrees. Saw "Our Hearts Were Young and Gay" tonight and enjoyed it. I read a condensed version of the book. More tomorrow.

Love and Kisses,
Charlie

Tuesday, February 13, 1945

Dear Mom, Dad, and Sis,

Another day gone by without too much to report. I'm on the night shift now and I had the day for myself. Went into Holland this afternoon and took a good hot shower and put on clean clothes. Had a couple of hours to kill so I walked around town, met a few people and had a good time. The weather was beautiful today, quite warm, and a little sun for a change.

Did that boy, Seymour Rosenberg, call you up yet? I imagine that he's home by now. He'll tell you how things are and after speaking with him I hope you won't do any more foolish worrying.

Gosh, there's really so little to write about. My letters must be terribly dull, but I know that all you want to hear is that I'm well and comfortable - and that I am.

How's the piano coming, E? You'll have to play for me a little too.

God bless you all.
Love,
Charlie

Wednesday, February 14, 1945

Dear Mom, Pop, and Sis,

It's the same old story and that doesn't bother me one bit. Had a big feast in my house tonight. Fixed up that Mrs. Grass noodle soup you sent, had tongue sandwiches, cheese sandwiches and grapefruit juice. Still in the house we fixed up and am very comfortable.

We recently started to have movies every day. In the afternoon, men from the battalions attend the show and in the evening it's for the Battery. This evening we had "Bermuda Mystery" which was a fair picture, pretty good to have a daily movie.

Read all about The Big Three meeting and I'm convinced that the groundwork for future peace has been laid. Frankie, Joe, and Winston certainly accomplished a great deal during their confab. I hope their plans materialize, especially those concerned with the speedy defeat of the common enemy.

Had a picture taken by a very small camera last month. I'm holding the print but enclosed you'll find the negative. Be sure to have it enlarged and then have some prints made. As it is now, you can hardly see my face.

Mom's letter of February 3rd arrived today. I understand that there's very little we can do about the Grannies. 75 is pretty old and if they keep as comfortable as possible, that's all we can hope for.

Heard from Jo-Jo again, that kid writes a very amusing letter. He has an excellent sense of humor for a 12-year-old.

Glad to hear that you're taking care of yourselves and eating well. Don't worry about not having enough help, Mom. You just have to get the customers to take their time. Say, Pop, who gets you those sandwiches from across the street now that I'm gone? Are you still a big *fresser*?[249]

Nothing more to relate right now. I'm feeling fine - hope you are all okay. Take care and be careful. God bless you always.

Love and Kisses,
Charlie

---

[249] Yiddish: Glutton, heavy eater.

Thursday, February 15, 1945

Dear Mom, Dad, and Sis,

Another uneventful day has passed. I'm feeling fine and hope you are all in the best of health. Saw the movie, "Laura" tonight and it was a very good mystery picture. Gene Tierney plays the lead and she is excellent. Two straight mysteries, we're due for something light tomorrow.

How is Uncle Moishe? I often think of him and the rest of your family, Pop. Send them my regards. And how is your *mishpucha*,[250] Mom?

Did a little playing on the field organ this evening. Say, E, for some of the popular songs how about writing out the chorus in keys, like the trolley song is E E E D C D E E A E D C D etc, just do the melody and the middle part and then I'll have the whole song. I'd like to play "I'll Walk Alone," some song about a "Dolly," also the middle of the Trolly song. I can still pick up tunes, but I don't hear the melodies often enough. What's your favorite tune now? Could you give me the notes for "Embraceable You"?

We had another pleasant day, fairly mild. Have you been to the dentist yet, Mom? I'm afraid that I know the answer, please attend to it. And how about that vacation?

After you have the negative enlarged (I sent you one yesterday) please send me a few prints (about five). I'd like to send them to a few friends.

The press and Congress seem to be in accord with the recent conference. I'm especially glad that Congress is supporting Roosevelt in all his peace and post-war plans, that means a great deal.

No more now, take care of yourselves and God bless you.
Love and Kisses,
Charlie

---

[250] Hebrew: Family

Friday, February 16, 1945

Dear Mom, Dad, and Sis,

Five swell letters from you today ranging from December 24th to February 9th. Your letters are always the best. Mom should be on her vacation by the time this letter reaches you. Hope Dad was able to get away for a weekend, let me know what you did.

E, I sure got a kick out of that letter your friend wrote requesting things for me, good sense of humor. I'm surprised that Mom didn't have you take home loads of cutting over the Christmas weekend, Pop. Is she getting soft? You sure have bad luck with your letters, Dad. The girls mailed theirs on February 9th and I got them today. You wrote yours on December 24th and it just arrived today. Don't you know the postmaster?

There really isn't too much to report. I'm feeling fine and love you all very dearly, hope we'll all be together soon.

Love and Kisses,
Charlie

Saturday, February 17, 1945

Dear Mom, Pop, and Sis,

It's Saturday night and at least I'm hearing some good music with a set of earphones. Here's how it works. Somewhere along the line a switchboard operator has a radio, and all the operators plug in on it. My operator receives it and I put on a set of earphones, and he plugs me into the board, so I get the benefit of the music and no one is disturbed. We still have our own radio but it's close to 12 AM and too many people are sleeping. I imagine around 20 fellows are listening in on this one program; some system, isn't it?

I went in for a shower this afternoon and as usual had a pleasant time. It's always nice to get some place where you can see and speak to civilians and just see people living a natural life. Visited some friends in the Dutch town with three friends and we had coffee and a delicious prune pie. Our boys bring these people little things whenever we have a chance, and I imagine that they have quite a bit stored up. There are 8 kids in the family and one of the girls, about 11, had one arm blown off by a German shell. These are the people that usually do my laundry. After spending some time with civilians in a place that is now quite distant from the war, I hate to go back to Germany.

One of our officers, a Major, got a lucky break. He joined us about three months ago and he has about 30 months of overseas service. He's supposed to leave for a 30-day furlough in the States on the 23rd of February. He has a daughter who he's never seen and don't you think he isn't plenty excited. Of course, we're all waiting until the 23rd to see whether he actually goes or not. I hope I don't have to be overseas 30 months before I get home.

The events in the Pacific are certainly encouraging.[251] They must be way ahead of schedule if they're already in Japanese water near Tokyo. For some reason, I don't think that that war will last as long as some experts predict. And once we get going here, I hope we can finish things in quick fashion.

There's not much more to tell you right now. Tomorrow morning, Pop will fix some scrambled eggs for you and I hope you enjoy them. How's the Swiss cheese these days? They must be charging a fortune for it. I wonder why the Army doesn't serve lox and bagels - don't they know what's good, Dad? Aren't you looking forward to the day when I'll make you one of my super deluxe omelets? Boy, I'll flip that thing all over the place.

I'll be writing you again tomorrow, take good care of yourself. God bless you.
Love and Kisses,
Charlie

Sunday, February 18, 1945

Dear Mom, Dad, and Sis,

Didn't get my mail until late yesterday and I received no less than 14 letters with 11 of them from you. Boy, I stayed up until 2 AM reading all of it. I won't be able to answer the letters specifically because I'm on duty now and all my mail is at the house. Thanks for it all. With such a wonderful family, how can a fellow miss?

---

[251] On February 16, the US Navy launched its first Aircraft Carrier raid against the Tokyo area.

I sure enjoy all those little clippings you've been enclosing in the letters, E. Who is supplying you with the material? I noticed a strange handwriting on the items from the New York Herald Tribune; are some of the girls at your office giving you stuff?

Muriel DeVos, a married woman now and one of the girls in the neighborhood, dropped me a line (I had sent her and the hubby a Christmas card). She gave me some interesting news. Sally Sager and Sally Ellerstein (E may know the names) will be mothers shortly. God, Pop used to tell me not so long ago that those girls were cockers[252] and here they are prospective mothers. Time certainly passes. Most of the girls in our neighborhood who I went out with are now married. Muriel's husband is at Ft. Belvoir, Virginia, awaiting assignment. She asked about your hubby, E. I used to tell her about Artie. Boy, I used to brag to everyone about my sister.

No more to write now, am feeling fine and am in excellent spirits. Don't worry about my chin, folks, it's always up. Be good, take care of yourselves and don't work too hard. I love you all very much.

Love and Kisses,
Charlie

Monday, February 19, 1945

Hiya Folks,

Thanks for that lovely Valentine's card. You must think I'm pretty good. In that big haul of mail from you there were letters from January 21st to February 8th. Pop, don't worry about me taking too many drinks. I know enough about liquor, when I tell you that we had some stuff you can be sure that I only drink a sensible amount.

I was glad to see in today's Stars and Stripes that the weather is improving and that there are signs of spring. We had a beautiful day just like May and I think our winter is over. If so, we were very fortunate because we had a mild winter. There were very few actually cold days and the temperature never went below 15 degrees.

---

[252] Pampered and indulgent youngsters.

Thanks for sending me the notice from the bank. I assume that the allotment checks are coming in steady now. Before long, I should have over $200, or am I off my figuring?

Mom, I'm also looking for the day when you can tuck me in, love me up a bit and take me to Schraffts,[253] even though I don't like that place. I'll take you there for a vanilla soda.

Your interviewing work sounds interesting, Eadie, and I understand how tiring it can be. That survey is probably for the post-war plans of the Navy Officer Reserves, etc. isn't it?

Nothing else new over here, I'm fine still in my house on Adolf Hitler *Strausʊ*.[254] Take care of yourselves and start putting a little dough away for yourselves. How's the Mt. Lebanon business?

Love and Kisses,
Charlie

Tuesday, February 20, 1945

Dear Mom, Dad, and Sis,

Received two speedy letters from you today. One was from Mom and Dad written on February 11th and the other was from Mom written on February 13th, thanks for all the stamps you've been sending. They always come in handy.

Yes, the news is good, but look, we're still fighting and we will be for a long while. Too bad Chernyakhovsky[255] was killed in action, he was an excellent General, but the Russians will find a good replacement, I'm sure.

Pop, you stated in one of your lines that I've dropped off a bit and I assume you're referring to my correspondence. If they're short it doesn't mean I'm lazy,

---

[253] Local Restaurant

[254] German: Street

[255] Ivan Danilovich Chernyakhovsky (June 1907 – 18 February 1945) was the youngest-ever Soviet General of the Army. Twice awarded the prestigious title of Hero of the Soviet Union for acts of leadership during World War II, he was killed in action at age 37. His wounds were received outside Königsberg, during his command of the 3rd Belorussian Front. (www.britannica.com/)

just that there isn't too much to write about. And I've been writing daily so you will be getting them all sooner or later.

I'm going to the Rest Center tomorrow morning for two days. I expect to have a pleasant time, I don't know how much "rest" I'll get. Take care of yourselves and don't work too hard. Send my best to the Grannies.

Love and Kisses,
Charlie

Wednesday, February 21, 1945

Dear Folks,

It's 5:30 now and I'm waiting for supper to be served. I'm at the Rest Center in Holland and it's certainly nice to get away for two days.

Got here at 10 AM and I spent the morning visiting some friends. I came back in time for dinner, believe me it's really something to sit down to a meal and be waited on. Some Catholic Sisters run the place and they make things as nice as possible. There are nice clean tablecloths, good china, and the food is cooked very tasty.

Went for a dance this afternoon - first one in Holland - and the girls have sure learned how to dance well. A soldier band supplied the music, and doughnuts and coffee were served – two Red Cross girls were in charge, one was from Brooklyn, no less. Just finished dinner and I'm going to another dance. Good rest, isn't it?

Tell you about it tomorrow.
Love,
Charlie

Friday, February 23, 1945

Dear Mom, Pop, and Sis,

Didn't get time to write yesterday - I was too busy "resting." In my February 21st letter I told you that I was going to a dance that evening. It turned out to be a very nice affair. I met and danced with some girl who told me that the family was giving her brother a birthday party, and I should come over to her house after the dance.

My friend and I went to her home and she has a very nice family - two brothers who speak good English and nice parents. The home was a very comfortable one, and when the mother asked us to sleep there we accepted immediately. You don't know what a great feeling it is to live in a civilian home for a while. Well, during the evening we had beer, pies and cakes, coffee, tea, real nice. When we were shown our room - that topped everything - a well-furnished boy's room with two beds, clean sheets, etc. It was great. We were also invited to stay over the next night (last night) so yesterday morning we took our bags to the house from the Rest Center (only cots there!).

Slept late yesterday morning and then went for a shower and shampoo. After a good dinner at the rest home, we borrowed two bikes from the family we lived with and had a nice afternoon bicycling around and visiting some friends in small towns. It was a gorgeous sunny day and we had loads of fun. We returned to the sisters for supper and we had the surprise of some entertainment while we ate supper. A Dutch boy, a marvelous accordionist, and a soldier - a guitarist - played songs and sang. A Dutch girl sang "I'll Walk Alone" with a heavy Dutch accent, it was very good.

After supper we rode over to our friends on the bikes and spent a nice evening at home *kibbitzing*,[256] talking about America and hearing terrible stories about the Nazi's occupation and the good work the underground did.

Got up at 9 this morning, took a haircut and before I knew it, I was back in the Fatherland. All in all, I had a very pleasant time. Now I'm quite busy. Heard from Artie today, he's still in Luxemburg.

God bless you.
Love and Kisses,
Charlie

---

[256] Yiddish: Chatting.

Saturday, February 24, 1945

Dear Folks,

Hiya doing, peoples. For various reasons, I've been quite busy lately, but I have a little time now to drop you a line. I sure got back from my rest at an important time. There's been quite a bit of work the past few days.[257] I'm feeling fine and am still enjoying the comfort of my little house.

The weather is grand, we've been having sunny days and I hope it keeps up that way.

Enclosed is a $15 money order. Use it if you want, deposit it otherwise.

There's very little I can write about now, my two-day rest seems like an ancient thing already. I'll drop the Grannies a line tonight, without fail. I've been neglecting them of late.

Think even more of the Dutch now after living with some for a while. One of the boys in the family I stayed with used to be a runner. His brother printed the underground paper during the German occupation. The Gestapo paid him a visit once but couldn't pin anything on him. These people think the same way we do - are interested in their families, jobs, homes, etc. Many of the young Dutch people want to come to America after the war. After seeing their lovely homes and pretty good conditions (in peacetime) I doubt if many would be able to do better for themselves in the States.

That's all for now. Take good care of yourselves and don't work too hard. Mom, when are you going away? Have your teeth fixed yet?

Love and Kisses,
Charlie

---

[257] The 102nd Division began their crossing of the Roer River on February 23, 1945. The preceding days were understandably busy for Charlie and the other members of the S-3 section, who were responsible for combat operational planning.

Monday, February 26, 1945

Dear Mom, Pop, and Sis,

All's well, but there just isn't time for much letter writing. The weather is pretty nice and I'm feeling swell. I hardly know what to write at the present time as nothing much is happening outside of a military nature. Read your newspapers, that's all I can tell you.[258]

Had three good hot meals today, good hot water to shave with. Things aren't bad at all. Sleeping indoors all the time and getting enough sleep.

No more now, regards.
Love and Kisses,
Charlie

Wednesday, February 28, 1945

Dear Folks,

Everything is just fine; this is my second letter[259] to you today so you see that I'm not too rushed. Sitting in the CP now, it's 11 PM - nice fire going, electric lights, a good-looking rug on the floor - what else could I want? It's living like kings these days, anything we see is ours and some of the people have left (out of necessity) in quite a hurry.

I could have so much stuff - souvenirs, etc. if I had the time to pick it up and room to carry it. Clothes, food, liquor, this part of Germany wasn't hit too badly and they seem to have had everything they wanted.

What I'd like to do is blow up every house we leave behind, some of them are too nice for the Krauts. Pop, I could dress you and me in good fashion for ten years with some of the fine clothes I've seen. I'd like to send some stuff to Jo-Jo; swastikas, German uniforms, etc. but I haven't the time or facilities. I'm seeing it all and I'll tell you all about it when I get home. But, believe me, it's some-

---

[258] At this time, the 102nd Division completed the crossing of the Roer and established their bridgehead. They continued their assault against the towns of Hottorf, Hompesch and Erkelenz.

[259] Unfortunately, the first letter of this date has been lost.

thing to go into these homes and take over. In fact, in some the fires are still burning, it's no longer rare to see truck drivers wearing top-hats, derby's, etc.

After all, I don't think I was too bad with my letters recently. I usually will be able to drop a line every few days, even when things travel fast. Got a nice mattress for tonight, oh it looks so soft that I think I'll end now and go to my bedroom and sleep. What a life!

I love you all, as if you didn't know, I'm just fine - moral and spirit is high. On to Berlin!

Love and Kisses,
Charlie

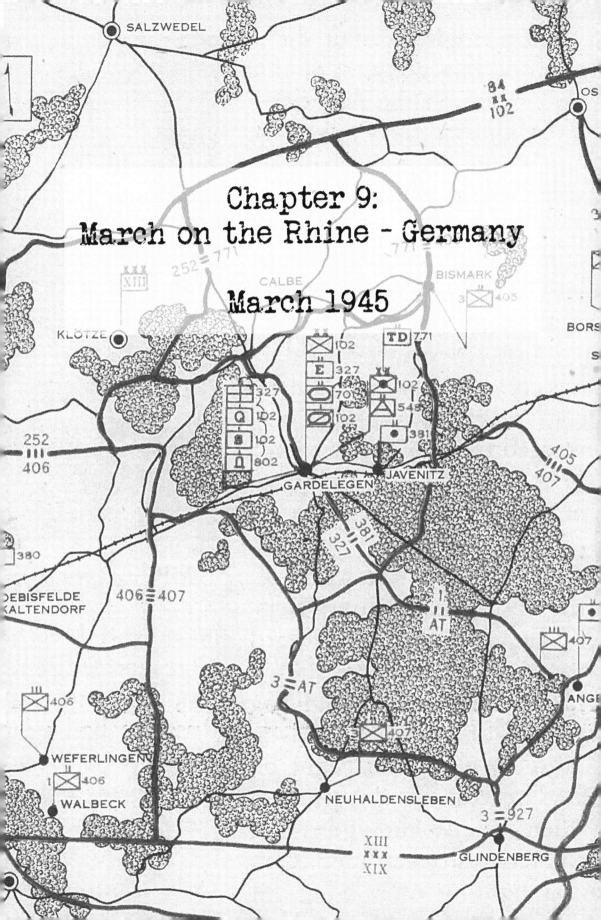

Chapter 9:
March on the Rhine - Germany

March 1945

From February 23-March 3, 1945, the Division advanced 53 kilometers (app. 33 miles), seized 83 towns/villages, 3 cities, and captured 4,187 prisoners. The Division's attack on the city of Krefeld abutting the Rhine River commenced on March 2, 1945. By the next morning, the 102nd Division was in control of the southern two-thirds of Krefeld, and contact had been established with the 84th Infantry Division in the

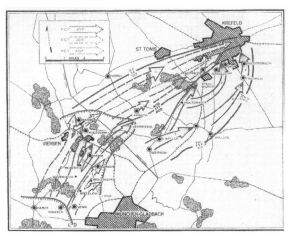

102nd Division's attack on Krefeld." (With the 102nd Infantry Division Through Germany, pg. 166)

north. Two hours later, Krefeld was officially pronounced captured. This battle was not without its losses, for the Division suffered a total of 1,888 casualties: 178 killed, 1,219 wounded and 351 non-combat casualties.[260]

---

[260] With the 102nd Infantry Division Through Germany, pg. 167

After the capture of Krefeld, the Division was introduced to its first experience with a Military Government in the heavily populated areas between Erkelenz and the Rhine. The technique of Military Government was to maintain as civic an organization as possible until the initial stage of the occupation was complete. Essentially, the objective was to return as many city functions as possible back to civilian officials.[261]

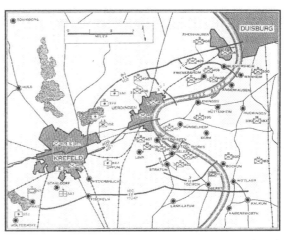

Division's defensive sector on the Rhine River." (With the 102nd Infantry Division Through Germany, pg. 174)

However, the immediate goal was to maintain calm, assure equal distribution of food and ensure the maximum operations of public services.

Additionally, since the Division was engaged in steady fighting since its arrival in Europe, at this time they received orders to remain in the Krefeld area and conduct a program of rest, rehabilitation, and training. These orders took the Division out of front-line combat for the first time since early November 1944. To facilitate this program, a liberal system of leaves, furloughs, and passes were initiated and during the remainder of the month of March, some 267 officers and 2,239 enlisted men were allowed to depart on leave to rest-centers in Holland, Paris, Brussels, the French Riviera, the United Kingdom, and the United States.[262]

From after the fall of Krefeld until the Division's crossing of the Rhine River in the beginning of April 1945, Charlie and the Headquarters Battery moved into quarters in the Northeast sector of the city. During this period, the Allied path to victory was crystallizing from dream to reality. And all roads home led through Berlin.

---

[261] Ibid, pg. 171

[262] Ibid, pg. 175

Thursday, March 1, 1945

Dear Mom, Pop, and Sis,

Received Dad's letter of February 23rd, and of course, I was very glad to hear from you. The mail has not been very good recently.

Irene Witt told me her father was going to New York, but I didn't think he'd call you up this trip. After all, it's quite some time since I saw those people. I correspond with Irene fairly regularly but that's all there is to our friendship. Perhaps you could have invited Mr. Witt out to dinner, but don't worry about it.

Nothing of interest to report. Things are quite routine. Am going to bed early tonight as I go on duty at 5 AM. Just finished reading the February 5th issue of Time. That magazine certainly covers every topic thoroughly. Send my regards to all.

Love and Kisses,
Charlie

Friday, March 2, 1945 - From Germany on a Kraut typewriter

Hi Folks,

Been seeing quite a bit the past two days and have stopped at two interesting places. Yesterday we put up at a brewery, of all places, and what a time it was. The company bottled everything from cognac to wine with some excellent brandy in between.

I didn't have many drinks - just sampled a little of the stuff, and since I knew I was taking it away from some German it tasted all the better. Spent last night in a nice home - the civilians were put out before we got there and, in some instances, fires were still going when we moved in.

Was on the go again this morning and tonight we're in a swell place that used to be a wholesale distributor of groceries, feed, etc. Most business establishments here in the small places have residences close by and if you don't think we're living in style, you're sadly mistaken.

The place we're in now has a central heating boiler and we have that going, and we attached our generators to the house's circuit so the whole place has electric lights. We had a little bad weather while moving yesterday, but outside of that, things couldn't be better. And we're getting there also, aren't we? Just think, only one more barrier until we can start going for Berlin, that's okay boy.

One of these days I'll take time out to write you a real long letter about everything I see, the people, etc. But for the time being, I just want to write you so that you don't worry. I'm eating all sorts of good food that was bottled and left behind. Why, I had strawberry and milk last night and have also tasted cherries, pears, string beans, peas, etc. The Germans will be surprised to see what a hungry bunch of men the American army consists of when they return to their homes.

Have a swell bed for the night - two comforters on top of a soft mattress, blankets galore, steam heat and a nice breakfast of wheat-cakes to look forward to in the morning.

E, the only main difference between typewriters is that the Y and Z are in reverse positions. It's no longer strange to see the boys riding around in civilian autos, motorcycles, etc. The American *Soldat*[263] - good guy (they used to say in Holland).

That's all for now, a real long letter next time I promise.
Love and Kisses,
Charlie

---

[263] German: Soldier

Saturday, March 3, 1945

Dear Folks and Eadie,

Hiya all doing? My letters are a little more regular now, aren't they? They should be that way for a little while.

Everything is just fine. I'm still settled in the warehouse I told you about in yesterday's letter. I have a swell room fixed up and am living with two other fellows. We have nice rugs on the floor, good mattresses and comforters, a table with clean white cloths, dishes, towels, and a sink. Quite snazzy - I hope it's a few days before we leave here.

The town I always visited in Holland was Heerlen, and the small place where I had many friends was Heerlerheide, a very nice place. Was only a short way from Maastricht but never got a chance to visit there. My home in Germany for that long period was Beggendorf, near Geilenkirchen.

Eating well, thanks loads for your latest package. I got it today; pecans, cheese, crackers, all very good.

Love and Kisses,
Charlie

Sunday, March 4, 1945

Dear Folks,

Received three nice V-Mails from E today. Thanks loads, kid, and I realize why you don't write every day. However, Sis, you should try to pen a line to Artie daily without fail. I'm sure you can stay up the ten extra minutes at night if it means a letter to him.

Things are fine at the present time. In fact, everything has been okay straight along. At times, we did a lot of moving, some of it in bad weather, but we always had warm places for the night with beds or mattresses.

Right now in this warehouse, I have just about the best set-up I've had since overseas. I'm in a swell room, good stove, electric light, sleeping with two sheets, plenty of jarred fruit, wine, the contents of packages from you and from Aunt Rose. Just try to picture the table I'm writing on. A nice clean white cloth is covering it and on the table I have the pecans you sent in a candy dish, the party crackers in fine cut glass dishes, jam in a regular serving dish, a butter plate filled to the top and a pitcher of water. This really is the life.

The civilians are treated fairly but sternly. They are allowed on the streets between 12-1 PM and 3-4 PM, at all other times they must be in their homes. In the town I'm staying in there are plenty of civilians and none are causing any trouble. This place hasn't been damaged very badly and the city is quite attractive and has all the latest facilities, etc. That made us wonder why they ever fell for Hitler and brought all this hardship upon themselves. It's no fun to be put out of your house and be forced to leave most of your belongings behind. Many Germans have had to do that lately.

It rained a lot today, on the whole the weather was quite favorable during the recent push.

I'm in perfect health and feeling fine. Would like to cross the Rhine tomorrow. Be well and take care of yourselves. How are your piano lessons coming, E?

Love and Kisses,
Charlie

Monday, March 5, 1945

Dear Folks,

Hello again from my warehouse home in the heart of the Fatherland. This morning we let two women pick some stuff in the garden and I had to explain something to them in my very bad German. That was the first time I ever spoke to a Kraut. If you don't stay on alert all the time, they try to get your sympathy and as soon as you start to become personal in your conversation, they try to take you for a ride. At least that's the observation I've made. In the short time they're allowed out I suppose they have enough to do, because they scurry about getting water, food, etc. Military government is already set up here and the civilians are ruled by that organization.

I sent Jo-Jo a package today consisting of a Nazi flag, a German garrison cap and a few other little things I picked up recently. A kid Joe's age will get a kick out of the junk, but I won't bother sending any of it home. You people are grown-ups, remember. I have enough time to write now and I certainly owe a lot of letters, but I just don't have the ambition to get down to some heavy corresponding. After my incoming mail falls off, I suppose I'll hurry up and answer all the mail. I sent my fraternity a ten-dollar money order today so I'm cleared up with that.

Heerlen will always have a place in my memory. That's the Dutch town we always went to when we were in Beggendorf. I visited there quite frequently and spent my two-day pass there. I also passed through Maastricht at one time but didn't have the opportunity to spend any time there. That's the largest city in liberated Holland and it's really a modern town of some 50-75,000 inhabitants.

Say, E, if you have any old clothes you plan to discard or if any of your friends do, I'd like you to mail them to this certain family in Heerlerheide that was very nice to me. It's that family of eight kids I wrote you about, and one of the daughters had an arm blown off by the Nazis. Find out the particulars at the post office and I'll send you the address soon. In the package include a dollar fountain pen - it's hard for the kids to get them over here. And if you don't have any clothes, you might send them any type of package - something like you send me - okay? There are a number of boys in the family and I think I'll tell Aunt Rose to send them Jo-Jo's old stuff. He certainly wears out a lot of clothes. I also saw Linnich, a town you probably read a lot about, and I travelled through Geilenkirchen, Aachen and Julich.

Artie is moving quite rapidly these days. I hope he's doing okay. Things are a little better in these larger towns and cities. There's always a place to stay at night and it's much better traveling in these big places than through open fields, etc. Our Division Commander sent the troops a letter of commendation today praising us for our recent work, etc. and saying that there is no better Division on the Western Front. I imagine he's a little prejudiced, but I'm inclined to agree that we have a pretty good Division. It's nice to know that you belong to a good organization, one that can do a job.

There's nothing more that I can report now. Living real nice, had tea at 4 PM today with toast and jam. Tonight, had more cheese with some of that Lipton's noodle soup. Everything is swell, I assure you. We're catching our breaths now and we're all comfortable.

No more until tomorrow. How's my mail coming through? I think I only missed a few days during the whole drive. Take good care of yourselves, I hope you enjoy the show E bought tickets for. Enclosed are some pictures of a few Krauts who hit the road before we arrived.

Love and Kisses,
Charlie

Mia Crousen

Tuesday, March 6, 1945

Dear Folks,

Things continue to be okay and I haven't a thing to complain about. Our chow is good, living conditions very comfortable and of course, this rest is very welcomed.

Am in my suite now and it's really neat. Good light, clean table, with nice chinaware. It would do your heart good to see the way we're living. Why, in a few days we expect to have running water from the city supply and gas in addition to the steam heat. This is a good way to fight a war. Right now I have the water heating for coffee and I'm going to make some toast and eat a can of salmon that Aunt Rose sent. I'm on duty from 2-5 AM but I don't go on again until 4 tomorrow afternoon, so it's not bad.

Yesterday I wrote about sending some of E's old clothes to these people in Holland. If you want to do it, Sis, the address is Mia Crousen- Gravenstraat 30, Heerlerheide, Limbourg, Holland.

Nothing much to write about. Pretty quiet and the occurrences are routine. I'm healthy, happy and content, just hoping that all this comes to a speedy end.

Be good, kiddies and take care of yourselves. Mom, did you even do the things you promised me you would - take a vacation and go to the dentist?

Send my regards to all, received a nice letter from the Kanes.

Will report again tomorrow.
All my love,
Charlie

Thursday, March 8, 1945

Dear Folks,

Twelve letters today and the five best were from you. Thanks a lot for the mail and for the stamps. The dates of the letters ranged from February 18th to February 28th. Saw "A Tree Grows in Brooklyn" tonight. There's a big theater in the center of town and the Army took it over. Movies are shown twice a day, so for a while I should see some pictures. I enjoyed the movie version of "A Tree" but I believe I found the book more interesting. The novel held my interest throughout, while I found the movie dragging along at times. The scene in which Katie Nolan is awaiting her baby is excellent and it's the first time I've seen so much about the trials and tribulations of childbirth on the screen. Very good acting throughout.

It's a little cold these days, but I'm very comfortable. Took my first shower in a couple of weeks. There's a quartermaster shower unit in the field nearby. They set up showers in big tents and heat the water, it's not bad at all. I feel real clean now and have fresh clothes on. No more now, take care of yourselves, will write again tomorrow.

Love and Kisses,
Charlie

Friday, March 9, 1945

Dear Folks,

Hello again, how are you feeling these last few winter days? At last spring is approaching, and with it, I hope victory. Isn't that wonderful news about the First Army crossing the Rhine?[264] I hope we all get across soon.

Received your V-Mail of February 20th today, Sis. Don't worry about writing, I understand that you're kept busy. Whenever you get a few extra minutes, just drop me a line and that will be just swell.

Went to the theater in town this afternoon and a Special Service Company gave a fine stage performance - good band, singer, etc. Then we saw Gloria Jean in "Destiny" and that was fairly good, so it was a good three hours of entertainment.

Heard from the Youngs today. Everything is okay here, take good care of yourselves and don't work too hard.

Love and Kisses,
Charlie

Saturday, March 10, 1945

Dear Mom, Pop, and Sis,

Another week coming to a close, and at least it's seven days closer to victory. I agree with you, Pop, that the Germans are licked on every side but we all have to get in there from the sides to deliver the knockout blow. Let's pray it is real soon that Hitler and Co. will have to yell, "quits."

Went to the movies today and saw "Swing Down Low" or something like that with Benny Goodman and Orchestra, Linda Daniel and Jack Oakie. It's a light musical and entertaining enough to serve its purpose.

---

[264] The Rhine River, measuring approximately 766 miles long with an average width of 1,300 feet, stands as a natural defensive line against invasion of Central Germany from the west. The US Army Corps of Engineers judged the river completely unfordable, even at low tide, and the Germans had either destroyed or were prepared to destroy every significant bridge along the river. On March 7, the US First Army crossed the Rhine at Remagen and established a bridgehead to support further offensive actions into the heartland of Central Germany. (With the 102nd Division in Germany)

I wasn't too happy to hear that you took over the house. I'm afraid it's too much work and there's not enough in it for you to fool around with and knock yourselves out. But you know best and I hope it works out okay. Please don't become slaves to the damn place. How's the neighborhood now? Are the tenants making any more money?

Are those pictures the sailor took ready yet? I'm anxious to see them. Don't forget to send me a snapshot of yourself, E.

Nothing more to report now. Please take good care of yourselves and don't work too hard, it doesn't pay.

I'm feeling fine, in the best of spirits - there's a bottle of wine on the table. *L'Chaim!*[265]

Love and Kisses,
Charlie

Sunday, March 11, 1945

Dear Mom, Dad, and Sis,

Spent an uneventful Sunday. Everything is okay and our existence now is becoming like the life we led before the drive.

You know how friendly I am with children. Well, it's entirely different with the Kraut kids. They all try to be friendly and say hello, but I ignore them and so do most of the fellows.

The other day some ex-slave laborers came to our place to take away sugar and some other stuff from the warehouse. They are the foreigners the Germans imported to work on the farms and in the factories. Some of the poor devils have been here for five years. Most of the ones I saw were Polish and the one guy I spoke to came from Warsaw. He got a kick out of the fact that you were born there. (Not you, E, just Mom and Dad).

No more right now, take good care of yourselves and don't work too hard. Whatever became of those vacations?

Love and Kisses,
Charlie

---

[265] Hebrew: The traditional Jewish toast, "To life!"

Monday, March 12, 1945

Dear Mom, Pop, and Sis,

Living in a new place now and although I hate to admit it, these homes are really something. We're set up in a beautiful residential section you could compare with Riverside Drive in Wilkes-Barre, the best part of Flatbush, Westchester, etc. Gosh, these rich Krauts knew how to live. I was really surprised to find such luxurious homes, and we're taking advantage of them, believe me. I have a very nice room, good springs and mattresses.

There really isn't much to report. Wojy, the clerk I've always worked with, goes to Paris on a pass tomorrow and I'll take over for the few days he'll be away. That'll change my routine a bit.

The weather has been rather mild of late and that helps a lot.

No more right now, I'll try to write a little more next time.
Love and Kisses,
Charlie

Tuesday, March 13, 1945

Dear Folks,

All's the same, there's so little to write about it's pathetic.

Lily Pons and Andre Kostelanetz[266] are in the vicinity and tonight they had dinner with our General. Tomorrow they're coming down to the CP in the morning and in the afternoon, Lily is going to sing, and her hubby is going to lead a GI Orchestra.

This town is full of civilians and the main part of town is just like any other - people walking around, riding bikes, etc. Some of the girls are quite pretty but

---

[266] Alice Joséphine Pons (April 12, 1898 – February 13, 1976), known professionally as Lily Pons, was a famous French-American operatic soprano and actress. In 1944, Pons suspended her season at the Metropolitan Opera in New York and instead performed with the USO, entertaining troops with her singing. Her husband, Andre Kostelanetz (December 22, 1901 – January 13, 1980), was an orchestral music conductor/arranger and directed a band composed of American soldiers as accompaniment to her voice. During 1944-1945, the pair took the stage at military bases in North Africa, Italy, the Middle East, the Persian Gulf, India, Burma, China, Belgium, France and Germany. (wikipedia.org/wiki/Lily_Pons).

as I told you before, we don't even notice them. The rule says $65 fine but believe me if you're caught fraternizing, it's much worse than that. In Stars and Stripes there was an article about a Warrant Officer being fined $350.

No more now, the weather is grand.

Love and Kisses,
Charlie

Wednesday, March 14, 1945

Dear Mom, Dad, and Sis,

Lily Pons and Andre Kostelanetz paid us a visit this morning. She looked very well - slacks, big field overcoat - and he also looked okay. I always knew she spoke with a French accent, but I never knew that it was so heavy.

She picked out a target on the maps, and then went to one of our battalions to pull the lanyard of a gun (the chain that shoots the shell). She wrote a message on the projectile - "Catch this, Hitler - Lily Pons." She didn't seem to have any airs about her, very simple and plain. You'll probably see pictures of her and if it says anything about Artillery, you'll know that it was with us, they may not mention the 102nd.

It's real spring weather and I hope it keeps up. I'm feeling swell, hope you're all okay.

Love and Kisses,
Charlie

Thursday, March 15, 1945

Dear Folks,

A swell package arrived from you today, thanks loads. It contained a big fruitcake, a box of cookies, a big box of those chocolate cookies and some chewing gum. I may have asked you for this once before, but I could use some Kolynos toothpaste in your next package. A tube or two will be plenty, right now I'm using Squibb's and I hate it. By the time you send the Kolynos we'll probably have some, but it's worth the try.

Everything is just fine, feeling swell and living quite luxuriously. I hate to think of the Pacific after this. Oh me! I read that some Congressman said the war will be over in a few days. Wasn't that a ridiculous statement.

The weather is sure grand. What kind of Spring are you having? Be good and take care of yourselves, don't work too hard.

Love and Kisses,
Charlie

Friday, March 16, 1945

Hiya Folks,

Say, Pop, yesterday was income-tax day and I'm wondering how you made out without the help of your son. Did you have Kaufman fix up the form? Did you show enough profit to have to pay a tax or were the figures still in the red? Incidentally, every January I used to figure the gross and net income - expenses, etc. - what were the figures this year, or haven't you had the chance to figure it up yet? Are you sure you added correctly, Dad? Better let Mom check. Remember, Mom does things best - like dictating letters, doesn't she, Dad? What a wonderful woman Pauline is.

E, how are your piano lessons coming along? It's too bad that you lost so much of your skill that you had to get a teacher, but now let's hope you regain your old finesse and keep it. That's too valuable an accomplishment not to treasure very highly.

Saw a March 5 issue of Time Magazine around, that's the fastest we've ever received a copy.

Mom, did Irene's (*Razel's*) husband ever get inducted? If so, where is he and what is he doing? I remember he got a deferment for a while. Bertram Goldblatt will be 18 in May. I hope he gets in the Navy as he desires. Send them my regards when you speak to them.

No more now, I'm fine and dandy and feeling swell. Plenty to eat and drink (more wine than Grandma ever made). Don't worry, I'm not drinking too much.

Take care of yourselves.
Love and Kisses,
Charlie

Saturday, March 17, 1945

Dear Folks,

I finally made the Lily Pons concert this afternoon and it was marvelous. A GI orchestra from the First and Ninth Army with Kostelanetz conducting, Theodore Paxton as the pianist and Pons's flutist - I don't remember his name - comprised the show. The USO really came through this time with a great program.

Lily sang "The Blue Danube," *"Estrolito," "Ave Maria,"* "Summertime" and *avia* from *Rigoletto* and an English folk song. She was in fine form and she sang beautifully. It reminded me of the operas I've seen her in and also a concert she gave at Lewisohn Stadium - I went with Mom. She wore a red polka-dot gown with red trimming around the top and a red skullcap. She carried a green handkerchief - which could have been for St. Patrick's Day.

The band, which was pretty good, played "American Patrol," "Rhapsody in Blue," a melody of Victor Herbert's songs and "Stars and Stripes Forever." All in all, it was a very entertaining program and I enjoyed hearing Pons immensely.

The weather continues to be nice and I'm in great spirits and good health. As long as you take care of yourselves, things will be okay. Be good, don't work too hard.

Love and Kisses,
Charlie

Sunday, March 18, 1945

Dear Mom, Pop, and Sis,

I'm a real veteran now since I'm entitled to wear one gold stripe on my sleeve, indicating six months overseas. And I see men over here wearing five and six stripes, oh heavens, God forbid. Spent a nice quiet Sunday doing nothing much. I'm not working very hard these days and there's very little to do.

Before we crossed the Roer we used to get back to Holland, and of course, I'd then have something to write about. Now we just don't do anything except stay where we live so it's even difficult to dream up things to write about.

Say, E, what kind of story made the rounds when Dinah Shore had a baby? How are the Marshaks, Sis? Still see them a lot? What do you hear from "Stinkie"?

No more now, take good care of yourselves and may God bless you.
Love and Kisses,
Charlie

Monday, March 19, 1945

Dear Mom, Dad, and Sis,

Seven swell letters from you today and it's just about a week since I heard from you.

Mom, I'm sure glad you didn't butt in about Charlie Zwerner. It's none of our business and if the kid wants to do it, it's up to him. I don't see why Aunt Rose is getting all excited about it. I wish him a lot of luck and that's all I have to do with it. I don't see anything so terribly wrong with it, even though I wouldn't do it myself.

I'm glad Mollie Zwerner got a child. I wrote to her yesterday and guessed that she had a boy. But a girl is just as good, eh Pop? Where is Muttel living now? He's in pretty bad shape, eh?

I received another swell package today, and it contained some hard candy, a can of nut tidbits - very good - and a can of peanut candy. Thanks loads, you sure are swell people.

E, thanks ever so much for the subscription to Time Magazine, you're such a sweet sister. No kidding. Say folks, did my presents ever reach you? I bought a little something for the three of you and you should be getting it shortly. Let me know when they arrive.

I've read that there's an acute meat shortage in the States. I know you'll get along so I'm not worried. However, is it as bad as they say it is?

It was a beautiful day and I took some pictures. E, if you can buy some 616 films, please send me a few rolls.

I love you all very much, regards to the Grannies.
Love and Kisses,
Charlie

Tuesday, March 20, 1945

Dear Mom, Dad, and Sis,

Received some real old mail today from December 9 and December 11 and a recent one dated February 23. Yes, E, we still get Stars and Stripes, but I like to read clipping from other papers occasionally.

This afternoon I went to a band concert that was just so-so and a lousy movie, "Action in the East" or something like that. This evening we had a movie in the battery, "Sensations of 1945"- another mediocre film.

We have the baseball gloves out and during the afternoon we play catch a little. I hear you're having some good warm weather. I hope you're all feeling well. Don't work too hard on the building, I hope you're not running those stairs. Take good care of yourselves, I love you very much. God bless you.

Love and Kisses,
Charlie

Wednesday, March 21, 1945

Dear Mom, Dad, and Sis,

The first day of Spring, Tra-la, la, Tra-la, la. The weather was very appropriate and I played a little baseball to make it really feel like Spring. We found some excellent athletic grounds which were used mainly for soccer and track. We're quickly putting them to use as a baseball diamond. Our baseball is a strange game to the Germans and whenever we play it, the kids watch very intently.

Thanks for the pictures, E. I'm now waiting for a snapshot of you and also the prints of the pictures the navy boy took of the family. Use your camera more often on Sunday, this is good weather now for picture taking.

Everything is fine, feeling swell and am in good spirits, just hope that this will be the Spring. Enclosed is an article from the Stars and Stripes.

Love and Kisses,
Charlie

Thursday, March 22, 1945

Dear Folks,

Everything continues to go along nicely and there's nothing startling to report. Received a nice letter from Artie today and he's just fine. Walked around the neighborhood a bit this afternoon and there are certainly enough people here. Many of them go about their business as if nothing was wrong. A lot of stores are open for the civilians under the jurisdiction of the Military Government.

How are you feeling? I just about finished my furlough this time last year. I hope next March I'm home on permanent furlough.

There's really no news. Excuse the dull letter. Take good care of yourselves and don't work too hard.

Love to the Grannies.
All my love,
Charlie

Friday, March 23, 1945

Dear Folks,

Everything is just fine. I could stand a little more mail from you, but it'll probably come in a batch shortly.

There are hot baths and showers available in town and I'll be going one of these days for a bath, of course. It's funny to see how spoiled we are. If there isn't any bathing facilities, a shower becomes a luxury, but as soon as there are plenty of showers and baths everyone wants the tub. I can't blame them, can you?

Say, Mom, I'd like you to mail me that traveler's check now. I'd like to have it handy - not that a pass is imminent, but just in case I do get a chance to get to a big city. Have it made out for $100, and when I receive it I'll mail you the cash I have on hand and you can deposit that.

Feeling okay, hope you're all in good health. Take care, please.

Love and Kisses,
Charlie

Saturday, March 24, 1945

Dear Mom, Dad, and Sis,

After reading the day's news I couldn't blame anyone for feeling optimistic.[267] Gosh, it's marvelous and this could be the home stretch, everyone is making advances. I can imagine how excited you people are back home. Well, I for one hope this is the beginning of the end.

I saw a picture this evening that was a little different and quite entertaining, "Mr. Winkle Goes to War" with Edward G. Robinson. Got a letter from Stellie Marshak today. She doesn't seem to be so sure about graduating in June.

The weather continues to be excellent; the sun has been quite strong. Feeling just fine, please take care of yourselves, I may be home any year now.

Love and Kisses,
Charlie

Sunday, March 25, 1945

Dear Folks,

A package of dried fruit arrived today, thanks loads. I imagine you're short of requests, so I'll ask for some cheese, a couple of cans of sardines and some cookies.

The Division band has reformed and this afternoon it gave a concert at our CP out in the garden. Isn't that nice, a band concert outdoors on a Sunday afternoon? A number of Krauts gathered on the outside to listen to the music and some of the bums even applauded at the end of the numbers.

Played a couple of games of volleyball this evening after chow, life is really pretty good now.

---

[267] Most probably referring to the following events: On March 23, US and Filipino troops captured San Fernando on Luzon in the Philippines, and the Indian 20th Infantry Division took the city of Wundwin in Burma. Additionally, on March 24, the successful airborne attack of Operation *Varsity* was launched. Involving more than 16,000 paratroopers and several thousand aircraft, it was the largest airborne operation in history to be conducted on a single day and in one location. Varsity was part of Operation Plunder, the Anglo-American Canadian assault led by Field Marshal Bernard Montgomery, crossing the northern Rhine River and from there entering Northern Germany.

The news continues to be excellent, I can't see how the Germans can last much longer. Only time will tell.

Mom, why don't you make a break for your vacation now before it's too late? You'll be in the midst of your Spring season shortly and then you surely won't want to go.

(With the 102nd Infantry Division Through Germany, pg. 273)

Speaking of vacations - The Riviera in France is now at the disposal of the US Army and one of the boys from the Battery is going there tomorrow. I believe it counts as a furlough and it's for seven days' duration. That would be a nice place to go, wouldn't it?

We're still having that nice weather. I hope it continues as it certainly lets our Air Force out, we see plenty of planes around.

Everything is just fine. Had some good chicken for dinner today. Nothing for you to worry about. How's Mollie and the baby girl? Got my March Reader's Digest today, thanks to you E.

Love and Kisses,
Charlie

Monday, March 26, 1945

Dear Mom, Pop, and Sis,

Received a nice letter from Mom dated March 14 and a short note from E, along with the World Telegram's sport page. The envelope was postmarked March 21, that's five short days and the fastest delivery yet. God, you might as well come over and visit me for a few days if mail comes so quickly. Thanks for the stamps enclosed in your letter, Mom, and thanks for the paper, Sis.

I hope your bridge work came out okay, Mother. I can imagine what a rough job the extractions were and I'm sorry you had to undergo such a painful job. However, perhaps it was for the best and your health will benefit by it. Now I think you're due for your well-earned vacation.

You're all doing a splendid job at home. I realize that you have only one experienced girl in the workroom, and that's all the more credit for you. Mom, don't forget to mail me the traveler's check shortly. Don't hesitate to use the money I send home if you have any need for it.

I'm on duty until 1 AM. I just cooked some green-pea soup - that about ends my supply of soup. You can send some more if you wish.

Saw a good movie this evening "The Thin Man Goes Home" with William Powell and Myrna Lay in the old series that I've always enjoyed. Two very good performers, I think. Things are swell, still in those nice houses. News is marvelous.[268] Artie is on the go again, he's okay, not meeting much stuff. God bless you and love to the Grannies.

Love and Kisses,
Charlie

Tuesday, March 27, 1945

Dear Mom, Pop, and Sis,

All's well and there's nothing much to report. Played a couple of games of volleyball this afternoon and went to work at 3 PM; very quiet of late.

Tonight, I went over to another battalion's place and there was a little jam session. A pianist from the Bronx, from the Artillery (I know him very well), a violinist from Molt Street, a trumpeter from East Orange, New York and a guitar player from New York City (72nd Street) played all the popular songs and it was swell.

Received the March 19 copy of Time Magazine; that's pretty good time, Eadie thanks to you.

---

[268] On March 25, the Battle of Remagen ended in Allied victory and the Red Army began the Bratislava–Brno Offensive in Slovakia. On March 26, the Battle of Iwo Jima in the Pacific Theater ended in American victory.

The weather isn't as nice as it has been, it's a little chilly now and the sun has been AWOL for two days. I'm feeling fine and dandy. Hope you're all in good health, how's the teeth, Mom?

God Bless you and a Happy Passover. We're having services tomorrow. Take care of yourselves.

Love and Kisses,
Charlie

Wednesday, March 28, 1945

Dear Mom, Dad, and Sis,

This sure is a nice *Pesach* considering the present conditions. The holiday started this evening with a big *Seder* service conducted by our corps. As a conservative estimate, I'd say that at least 1,500 men attended. All the tables had white tablecloths and chinaware. There was a nice main table for the chaplain, the Corps commander, and a few other two-star generals. They gave short speeches at the end of the meal and services.

The service itself was the regular one we have at home on *Seder* night, except that it was cut down a lot (like I used to want Pop to do). Some kid said the Four Questions and we sang the traditional songs including *Addir Hu*. Enclosed is the program. Of course, the meal couldn't be elaborate on account of the size of the crowd, and we were content with the *matzos* and fishcakes, string beans, pineapple and coffee. The *matzos* were made by a Bonn Co. in London, they're darn good. I brought back a whole box of them, and I've been eating quite a lot with some butter I have, no salt around.

It's of great significance that a Jewish service can be held in public in Germany. Tomorrow morning for our service we're re-dedicating a building that once housed a synagogue.[269] All of the big Temples have been ruined but this place is next to a cemetery, and it is believed that burial services were held in this building. I'll be going tomorrow and there's another *Seder* tomorrow night which I may attend.

Re-dedication ceremony of the synagogue in Krefeld. (With the 102nd Infantry Division Through Germany, pg. 177)

You'll never guess who I met at the *Seder*. After the services a voice called, "Charlie Fletcher" and was I surprised to see Herbert Monavitz (the baker on 89th and Amsterdam Avenue). I knew he was getting close to 18 but I had no idea that he was already overseas. He's in one of the infantry regiments of my division and he looks very well, he just joined us about three weeks ago.

I have a fraternity brother in another division that wasn't in the services tonight and I had hopes of seeing him. I met some boys from his Company and they said that at the last minute he changed his mind and decided not to go. I told them to tell him to come to services in the morning so I may see him then.

Received a nice letter from Charlie and June, I always get a kick out of his letters. Feeling fine and dandy. How were your *Seders*?

All my love to you, a happy Passover (a little late),

Love and Kisses,
Charlie

---

[269] The first documented Jew living in Krefeld was recorded in 1617, with a synagogue later built in 1764. During the 1800's, the community grew from 308 to 2,000 individuals (1.9% of the population). When the Nazis rose to power in 1933, there were 1,481 Jews living in Krefeld. In November 1938, during *Kristallnacht* (the Night of Broken Glass), the two synagogues were attacked and ruined. During the war, 1,374 Jews were deported from Krefeld to the East, the majority to Theresienstadt concentration camp. (www.jewishvirtuallibrary.org/krefeld)

Thursday, March 29, 1945

Dear Mom, Dad, and Sis,

Spent a very enjoyable day, this first day of *Pesach*. Went to services this morning and it was quite gratifying to see such a large gathering in an old synagogue. I was really surprised to see the building standing right near the cemetery. The Jewish star and some Hebrew words were still on the outside of the place and the inside wasn't too messed up. They fixed it up nicely with small green trees, the service was the regular affair.

The cemetery, as you can imagine, is in pretty poor shape. The damn Germans wrecked many of the tombstones and on another they took the ornamental metal. The chaplain told us that as late as last year, some elderly Jews took their own lives instead of being deported by the Gestapo. Their graves are marked by small wooden sticks, and I saw them.

Received a nice batch of mail today, one letter from Mom dated the 20th of March and a V-Mail from E written the 15th. Remember the faculty advisor we had on the Bulletin – a Doctor Winning? Well, he entered the Army as a Major, and from a letter I received from him today I learned that he's now a Lt. Colonel. He's in charge of a Military Government detachment with the 7th Army.

Also heard from Howie Kane, who is in Hawaii, and he seems to be having the time of his life. Jo-Jo the Great wrote me another humorous letter. I enjoy hearing from him a lot. Went to *Seder* again this evening, and it's just like home - the second night is not as good as the first.

No more now, take care of yourselves.

All my love,
Charlie

Friday, March 30, 1945

Dear Folks,

Nothing much to report today. I read about the hot weather you're having, 81 degrees in March is really something. It's been cooler here this past week than earlier in the month, and we're also having some rain.

I'm reading the book, "Strange Fruit" and it's fairly good. The authoress doesn't offer any solution for the problem, and since the problem has been presented so often, she really doesn't accomplish very much.

Saw Bob Hope in "The Princess and the Pirate" and I was quite disappointed, not nearly as good as his other pictures.

Feeling fine and living well. For breakfast this morning I had two fried eggs, corn flakes and coffee - ain't bad.

Love and Kisses,
Charlie

Saturday, March 31, 1945

Dear Mom, Dad, and Sis,

Everything is just fine, if this excellent news continues things will be great.[270] That 4th Armored is sure going in high gear, eh E?

I received E's nice letter of 13 March and also her V-mail of 21 and 22 March. Thanks for all the mail, Sis, very kind of you.

No, I don't have the organ anymore but instead, I played the two songs you sent me on a Steinway. Fair exchange isn't it? I haven't any letters from Artie on hand but the ones I get from now on will be forwarded to you. I got the pieces down pretty well on the piano. Send some more if you have the time. It was great to hear that you're practicing the piano studiously, please keep it up.

I've been to the Tavern on the Green - as recently as last August, and I did enjoy it a lot. It's a very nice place to spend an evening. It's swell that you and Sim get out together occasionally.

Folks, I'm so glad to hear that you're feeling well and going strong. We want to have some good times for a long while after I get home, so take care of your-

---

[270] Between March 28-March 31, the following significant events occurred: The Soviet 3rd Belorussian Front achieved the almost complete destruction of the German 4th Army, with some 80,000 killed and 50,000 captured. Additionally, The US 80th Infantry Division captured the city of Wiesbaden in Central Western Germany. Lastly, the 2nd Shock Army of the 2nd Belorussian Front captured the city of Danzig, a city situated on the Baltic coast of northern Poland.

selves. Just think, by 1948 I should be home for good. Pessimistic, ain't I? Well, if I get home sooner I'll be in for a real surprise. Artie should be home after V-E Day,[271] E. I doubt whether he'll go to the CBI,[272] it's hard to predict the end of this/next week/next month - God knows. However, I think it'll be by July 1, time will tell.

The weather is still cool and drizzly, could use a little sun now. Still living in luxury.

Love and Kisses,
Charlie

---

[271] Victory in Europe.

[272] China-Burma-India Theater.

— Nicht übertragbar —

Ausgabe D

ugsberechtigungssch

für den Ausgabe- oder nachfolgenden

über

ein Liter Brennspiritus

smonopolverwaltung für Brannt

Berlin

ltig mit Stempel der Ausgabestelle und

rfallene Bezugsberechtigungsscheine wir

Ersatz gewährt.

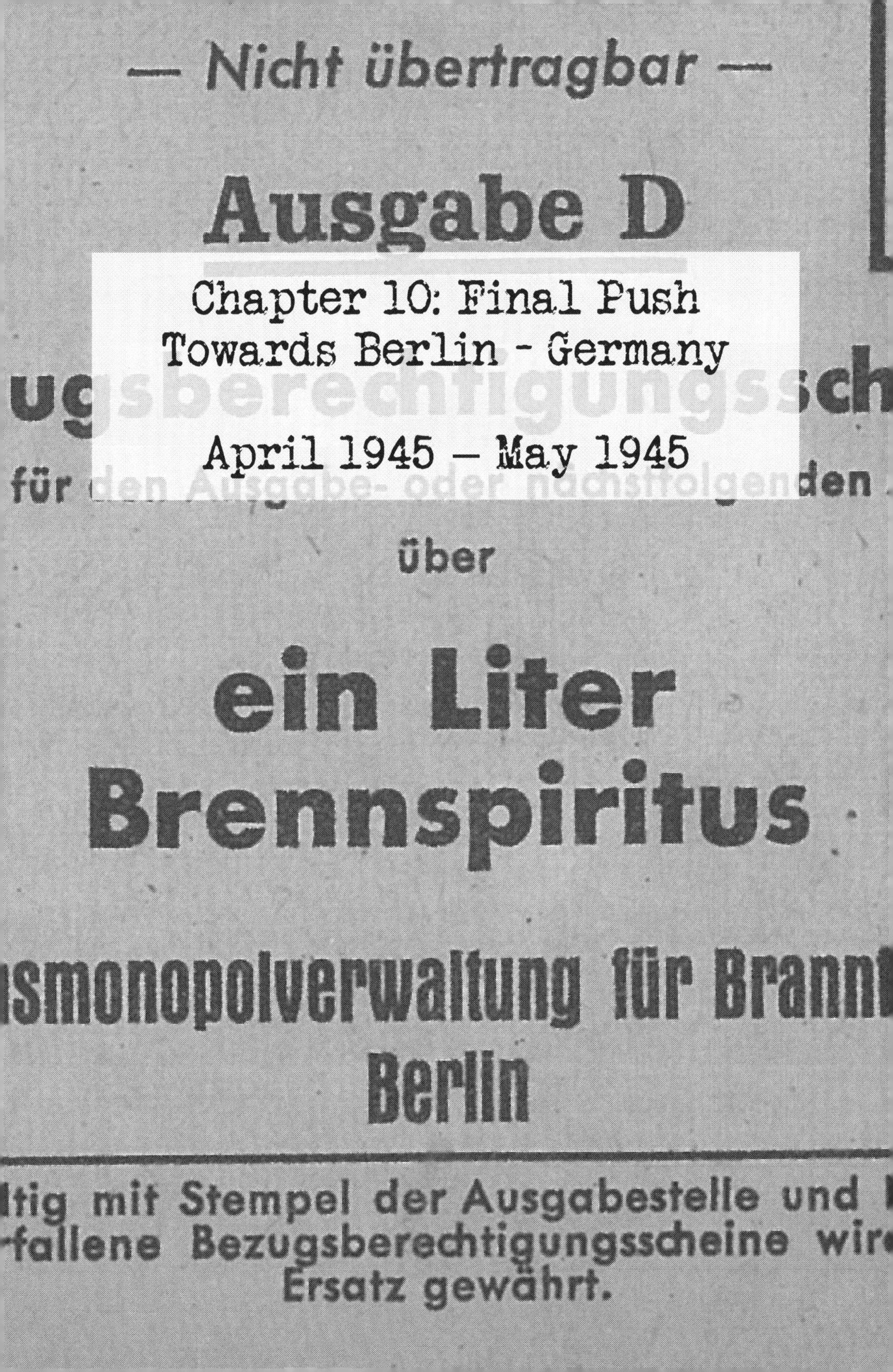

With the Allied victories of the previous months, the beginning of April 1945 set the stage for the ultimate victory of the European campaign. After being relieved of its defensive positions between Duisburg and Dusseldorf, the 102nd Division began its journey north in a convoy of some 1,750 vehicles to cross the Rhine River at the town of Wesel.[273] The Division crossed the Rhine on April 4, 1945 and some five days later, elements of the Division had reached the Weser River and with it, took control of more than 160 kilometers (app. 100 miles) of German heartland.[274] The days of April 9-11 saw the Division travel another 56 kilometers (app. 35 miles) to reach the Leine River, this slower pace than the previous advance due to stiff German resistance in the town of Wesergebirge. With that victory in hand, the Division continued and covered the 177 kilometers (app. 110 miles) between the Leine River and the Elbe River in only three days.[275] The Division's last military engagement of the war took place on April 21, 1945 near the town of Stendal, abutting the Elbe River. From this point onward, the Ozarks patiently waited for the Russians to complete their advance from the East, hunkering down some 125 kilometers (app. 77 miles) from Berlin. A German counterattack on the Division's

---

[273] With the 102nd Infantry Division Through Germany, pg. 186

[274] Ibid, pg. 188

[275] Ibid, pg. 206

perimeter commenced on April 21, but with Hitler's suicide on April 30, the enemy lost its will to fight. Berlin fell just five days later to the Russian Army on May 2, 1945, while the 102nd Division watched the final battle of the war in Europe unfold at the town of Tangermunde from its position on the Elbe River. On May 7, 1945, the Division accepted the surrender of the Ninth and Twelfth Panzer Armies, numbering a total of 71,000 troops. The news of the war's end and V-E Day - Victory in Europe - came to the men of the 102nd Division early on the morning of May 9, 1945. With the new day's dawn, they began their next tasks as part of the Army of Occupation.

During this time, Charlie followed the rear of the Division, leaving the city of Krefeld on April 4, arriving in Munster on April 12 and finally reaching the town of Bismark by April 15. All told, the Division covered some 395 kilometers (app. 246 miles) in the span of 14 days. By early May, the Headquarters Battery moved to the German town of Gardelegen, the site of a horrific massacre just days before.

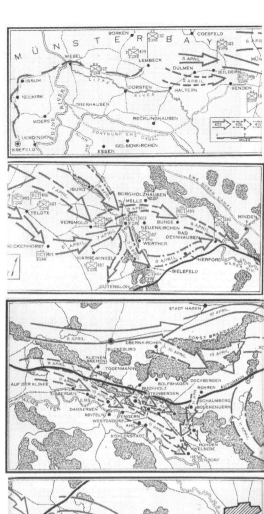

The Division's crossing of the Rhine and advance through the German heartland." (With the 102nd Infantry Division Through Germany, pg. 188-197)

459

After the surrender of Gardelegen, the men of the 102nd Division came face-to-face with the German atrocities of the Holocaust. While conducting a routine search of a surrounding Luftwaffe airfield, the members of the 2nd Battalion 405th Infantry regiment found several prisoners uniformed bodies pierced with bullets near a large stonework hay storage shed.[276] After closer inspection of the exterior of the building, the men opened the large doors of the shed and were witness to the slaughter inside. More than 1,000 prisoners had been forced inside the building, and then with the doors barricaded, the gasoline-soaked straw was set on fire.[277] Just seven prisoners managed to escape, one of them a Hungarian Jew named Bondo Gaza, who told his story the men of the Division and stayed on as an interpreter.[278]

On April 21, 1945, the local commander of the 102nd Division ordered "every available male citizen" of Gardelegen to give the murdered prisoners a proper burial. Over the next few days, the German civilians exhumed 586 bodies from the trenches and recovered 430 bodies from the barn, placing each in an individual grave. On April 25, the 102nd carried out a ceremony to honor the dead and erected a memorial tablet to the victims:

> *Here lie 1,016 Allied prisoners of war who were murdered by their captors. They were buried by the citizens of Gardelegen, who are charged with the responsibility that these graves are forever kept as green as the memory of these unfortunates will be kept in the hearts of freedom-loving men everywhere."*[279]

During the burial ceremony the Division Chief of Staff Colonel George Lynch addressed the German civilians at Gardelegen with the following statement:

> *The German people have been told that stories of German atrocities were Allied propaganda. Here, you can see for yourself. Some will say that the Nazis were responsible for this crime. Others will point*

---

[276] With the 102nd Infantry Division Through Germany, pg. 186

[277] United States Holocaust Museum, https://encyclopedia.ushmm.org/content/en/article/gardelegen

[278] United States Holocaust Museum, https://collections.ushmm.org/search/catalog/irn513319

[279] With the 102nd Infantry Division Through Germany, pg. 216

[280] United States Holocaust Museum, https://encyclopedia.ushmm.org/content/en/article/gardelegen

to the Gestapo. The responsibility rests with neither—it is the responsibility of the German people.... Your so-called Master Race has demonstrated that it is master only of crime, cruelty and sadism. You have lost the respect of the civilized world. [280]

Memorial tablet to the victims of Gardelegen. (With the 102nd Infantry Division Through Germany, pg. 214)

Local citizens bear witness at Gardelegen. (With the 102nd Infantry Division Through Germany, pg. 213)

Sunday, April 1, 1945

Dear Mom, Pop, and Sis,

Spent an uneventful Easter Sunday and April Fool's Day.

Finished "Strange Fruit" tonight, the book was pretty good - nothing extraordinary, though. Lillian Smith wrote it very interestingly, I think.

Saw "A Woman In the Window" this evening and that was excellent. That's the picture that you and Simmy saw, isn't it E? Edward G. Robinson is really a fine actor and Joan Bennett also gave a fine performance. It's the first time I've seen her in a long while.

Nice mail from you today. Dad finally came through with a letter. I'm glad my letters help your morale. Mom, I hope you're feeling well and that the teeth are okay.

More tomorrow.
Love,
Charlie

Wednesday, April 4, 1945

Dear Mom, Dad, and Sis,

Have been on the move like crazy the past few days and this is my first opportunity to write. We get on the truck and go on as short as ten minute's notice, and sometimes I wonder if anyone knows where we're going. But it's been interesting riding through Germany, and I've kept comfortable always. The roughest I've had it is sleeping on a floor, but most of the time there's a bed or a mattress. A few nights (like tonight) have been spent in a farmhouse and milk and eggs are aplenty. This afternoon we had a good hot meal consisting of meatloaf, lime beans, potatoes, and apricots. So, even though we're kept on the go, things are okay and there's nothing to worry about.

Those marvelous pictures arrived today and they're sure great, every one of them. Thanks loads, I must have looked at them about four times already. I sure have a good-looking family. How was that chicken you were cooking, Sis? Artie will go wild over the pictures - his wife isn't too ugly. Boy, Pop, you certainly practiced your smile.

Received a nice batch of mail today, including four from you. I wish I could answer it all but I don't have too much time. E, I hope I'm an uncle right after the war. I'm all for it. How's your extra job, Pop? Any trouble collecting? You ought to see me throw the Krauts out of their homes so we can get in, I'll be good at dispossessing people. As soon as I have a few minutes I'll write another letter.

Love,
Charlie

Thursday, April 5, 1945

Dear Mom, Pop, and Sis,

All's well. I saw the Stars and Stripes for the first time in a number of days and the news is still very encouraging.[281] Some units are 155 miles from Berlin and just a few weeks ago it was 300 miles.

Living in a nice house tonight - mattress, running water - it's right near the farm I told you about yesterday. This morning I fried three eggs and grilled some American cheese from a ration and drank a few cups of milk. Tonight our kitchen served a good hot meal.

Got to speak to two Russian girls who have been working on this Kraut's farm for three years. There are so many slave-laborers around and the roads are cluttered with them.

On the move and I like it, because that's the only way to get the war over with. I've spent some time in Viersen and Krefeld, the latter being a very large city. This Rhineland and Ruhr Valley is very beautiful country, especially the farmland and open country. The towns and cities are wrecked completely, some I think as bad as St. Lo.

---

[281] Since the beginning of April, the following battles and operations resulted in Allied victories: Operation Roast led by British Commandos pushed the Germans across the River Po and out of Italy; The 6th Guards Tank Army of the 3rd Ukrainian Front captured the Hungarian city of Sopron on the Austrian border; The 102nd Division and other elements of the Ninth United States Army captured the city of Münster and the US Third Army took the city of Kassel some 380 kilometers (app. 236 miles) from Berlin.

All these Germans deny being Nazis, the people I had to put out yesterday cursed Hitler and claimed they never wanted the war. But that's all a lot of baloney, you can't trust any of them, and of course they'll all say they were never Nazis and hated Hitler.

Feeling okay, getting enough rest. Take care of yourselves. That news about Walter's house and the special apartment is good news, E.

No more now, best of luck.
Love,
Charlie

Friday, April 6, 1945

Dear Folks,

Here I am again. I'm not doing too badly with my letter writing considering the situation. Usually, there's only time for one letter and you know who gets that.

In a nice spot for the night and we'll be very comfortable. Got some eggs so I'll do a little frying tonight. Passed through a very large town this afternoon[282] and believe me, I hardly saw one building intact.

About the happiest people here are the foreigners. Today some got on the road en masse, headed for home and half were drunk. It seems as if they had a big celebration with some GI's. Although a great deal goes on every day, I can't write in detail because of censorship rules. I can say that I'm safe for a very good reason and there's nothing to worry about.

The people we put out today must have thought they'd never get their home back because they were trying to take everything. I explained to them to lock up the stuff they wanted as it would only be for a short while that we would occupy their homes.

A lot of these Krauts still think Germany is winning the war, can you imagine that? And of course, America started it. Gosh, what can you do with people

---

[282] Likely referring to the town of Münster, Germany.

like that? Most of the Germans concede us victory, but I'd like to know what they're thinking. What a terrible people.

Love and Kisses,
Charlie

Saturday, April 7, 1945

Dear Mom, Dad, and Sis,

Everything is fine and dandy. In a new place tonight and it's very nice. Have a big bed with another fellow. We have an idea that we'll be here for a day so we're sending some laundry out in the morning. I went out to find someone to do it for my section and I came across some Catholic sisters who said they would be very glad to do it.

This is the last region where Nazism isn't at its strongest. From now on, Germany will be really Nazi. The Rhineland and Westphalia are predominantly inhabited by Roman Catholics and industrial workers who were never too pro-Nazi. It's different now.

I'm going on guard now, so I'll have to close.

Love and Kisses,
Charlie

Sunday, April 8, 1945

Dear Folks,

Had a nice Sunday, stayed in one place and that was a pleasant change.

Took our laundry out this morning at 9. The Sisters (Lutheran) have a well-equipped place and by this evening all the stuff was done and pressed nicely too. It all came out good and that was sure a quick job. Two girls from the Girls Home the sisters run did all the work and I wanted to give them something. However, after I gave them a little soap, I saw one of the old maids take it away. That bummed me up but I didn't care to make a fuss.

For breakfast today we had grapefruit juice, fried eggs, Wheaties, and coffee. "Chicken every Sunday" held true again, also potatoes, corn, soup and peaches. Pretty good, eh?

You can't imagine how many Russians and Poles are here. They have some stories to tell. You can't talk to them too freely because the non-fraternization rule also applies to them (just for security sake, etc.) However, most of the boys pass a few words with our friends.

One said that up to ten days ago the Krauts were still *heiling Hitler*, but as soon as we were near the town that baloney was stopped. Also, the Germans never treated these laborers any too well, but as soon as they saw how friendly the Yanks were to them they changed their attitude. Now the "*Russkas*"[283] are telling their German bosses to go to hell. Most of them are still celebrating and are slightly stewed all day. I can't blame them; three years is a long time to be a virtual slave.

The farm certainly is very beautiful, oh so much better than these bastards deserve. Many of the civilians are still haughty and walk and talk with that real German air. You know, they're winning the war (many actually believe that).

Well, that's about all this trip. My shift tonight is 2-5 and it's 3:30 now. Just had three scrambled eggs and toast, very good. No mail from you in over a week but none has reached any of us yet, soon maybe.

Be good - take care of yourselves, regards to the Grannies.

Love,
Charlie

Monday, April 9, 1945

Dear Mom, Pop, and Sis,

You should see the mansion we're staying in tonight. Real East Side townhouses. I imagine a couple of families lived in there. The one I sleep in has at least 30 rooms - nice beds, rugs, toilets, etc. Everything is intact here, light, gas - these homes are the most modern I've seen in Germany. Gas refrigerators, up

---

[283] Russians.

to date plumbing, etc. The Germans are lousy, but I'm just telling you that so far, I've seen beautiful scenery and some nice homes.

Slept real well, little cool now. Took a bath last night, real movie bathroom - dressers, chairs etc. Feeling swell. Wrote Artie yesterday.

Love,
Charlie

Tuesday, April 10, 1945

Dear Folks,

All is well. Traveled a bit today but didn't mind it. Had three hot meals and the weather was lovely, so it was like an all-day picnic.

Tonight we're in another big house owned by a regular Army officer and boy, are we finding souvenirs. If I get the chance, E and Jo-Jo will get a nice package. I have a nice 2 room set up with another boy, nice beds, etc.

Had some Kraut sardines tonight and they were tasty. Pictures, stories, all about the military here - this guy was a big shot.

Feeling fine, got your miss-you card, Sis, thanks.

Love,
Charlie

Thursday, April 12, 1945

Dear Folks,

Just finished a good dish of fried eggs and fried potatoes - it's 1 AM now and I go off at 2. Have a swell bed tonight and I'll sleep like a log.

Travelled a bit during the morning and saw some real ruined towns. I've been through Munster, a place that really got a going over. Picked up some souvenirs, I think I told you - will try to send them home. This is real Nazi-land. Everyone is a member of the party, and I will certainly follow your advice of not having anything to do with them.

Received three letters from you dated March 23, 26, 30. Mom, please don't ask me about the money going to the bank. That's an automatic deduction and I have nothing to do with the time it's sent, etc. Those checks usually catch up.

I'm glad the apartments are going fast. Of course, it's a good thing to hang on to, but I hate to think of you knocking yourself out over it. Did you get your teeth yet, toothless Ma? I hope you're fixed up now, because it sounds like such a big job and I'll be happy to hear that it's over.

Got your card from The Tavern on the Green, Sis. Thanks. Received a nice letter from Dean Schiffer today, will send it to you when I answer him.

Take care and love to the Grannies.
Love and Kisses,
Charlie

Friday, April 13, 1945

Dear Folks,

I was shocked to learn about the President's death.[284] Not much comment here, a little too busy I imagine, but to me it meant a great deal. This was a hard time to lose the country's leader and in my opinion Roosevelt would have seen the peace business through to the end. However, he's laid the groundwork for the United Nations and peace, and I hope every American tries to achieve the goals he had in mind. Truman will be the headman now, but I think Hopkins, Wallace, Baruch[285] - that is, Roosevelt's men - will be behind the curtain. Well, we lost one of our greatest men.

Nice house again, did you see that the 9th Army is only 67 miles from Berlin? Stopped in a doctor's place for lunch and a pause and tonight we're in a dentist's home.

---

[284] On April 12, 1945, President Franklin Delano Roosevelt died at the age of 63 after suffering a stroke. Though in declining health since 1940, this been kept secret from the public and his death was met with shock and grief across the world.

[285] Harry Lloyd Hopkins, FDR's closest advisor on foreign policy and his chief ambassador to British Prime Minister Winston Churchill. Henry Agard Wallace, 10th US Secretary of Commerce, and Bernard Mannes Baruch served as the president's appointee as special adviser to the director of the Office of War Mobilization.

Your Time Magazines are coming in nicely, Sis. Murray G. is now in Germany.

No more, I'm fine, don't worry about the packages.

Love and Kisses,
Charlie

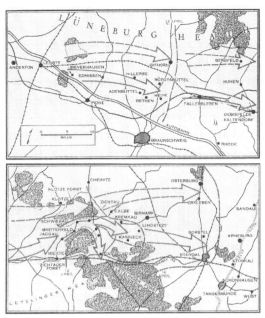

102nd Division's movements from April 12-April 14.

Sunday, April 15, 1945

Dear Folks,

Everything is just fine and dandy. Catching my breath a bit and I spent the last 30 minutes re-reading your mail of the past ten days. Yes, Dad, I often think of that day when I'll get home - I imagine everyone does.

Living in a small hotel[286] and have a nice soft bed. Quite an old-fashioned (my pen is on the blink, so I'll finish on the typewriter) place but it's comfortable. Took some dirty clothes out today and they should be ready tomorrow.

Have really had a good sight-seeing tour of Germany recently and I've seen just about all I want to see. The part of Germany I'm in now is pretty poor - a lot of small villages without industry and very little farming. This is Hitler's territory more than any other part of the country.

This hotel must be the hub of all activity in town. It has a bowling alley, a theater, and a kindergarten on the premises. There is so little to write about that even I'm surprised. You see, we have so much happening and we're kept busy but very little that's occurring is allowed to be written at this time.

I've seen truckloads of prisoners going to POW[287] cages and they certainly look like a licked bunch. I read today that some German POW's in the States went

---

[286] Charlie is now located in Bismark, Germany.

[287] Prisoner of War.

on strike because their cigarettes didn't arrive on time; isn't that something! We freed some British POW's and the stories they have to tell are horrible.

I'll have enough to tell you when I get home. This typewriter also seems to be on the blink. It's 5 AM now, please excuse the brief letters of late. As soon as we settle down I'll try to write better ones.

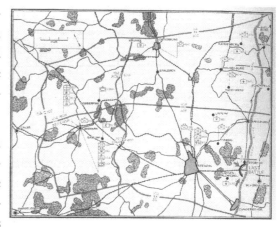

*The Division's positions along the River Elbe."
(With the 102nd Infantry Division Through Germany, pg. 219)*

Send my love to the Grannies.
What do you hear from Artie? Be good and take care of yourselves. A very nice package arrived today - fruitcake, asparagus soup broth, etc. Thanks loads, you're all so swell. Don't worry, I'm just fine.

Love and Kisses,
Charlie

Monday, April 16, 1945

Dear Folks,

I can see right now that this stationery isn't for me. It's just too long and I get scared by looking at it; how I'll ever be able to fill it up, I don't know.

Two nice letters from Mom and one from Sis today. Mom, I'm not going to have my money sent here, all I need is that one $100 and with my regular pay I'll have more than enough. Thanks for the $10,000 check—at least it looks good. Who said Pauline Fletcher couldn't sign a 10 grand check?

Things look great, I hope we keep going until it's all over. Heard Truman on the radio tonight and he sounded pretty good. Not a bad speaker, needs a few lessons on emphasis, etc. but he speaks clearly and has a pleasant delivery - no FDR though.

Thanks for your review on "Amber" - I can see that it's a good time-waster, E. Gosh, Sis, I have no idea what's to be after Germany capitulates. I wouldn't think that Artie would have to go to the Pacific, but who knows, time will tell.

You should see the lovely pictures I got from Karyl Steiner today.

All's well, still in my small hotel. Feeling fine, take care of yourselves.

Love and Kisses,
Charlie

Tuesday, April 17, 1945

Dear Mom, Dad, and Sis,

Heard from the three of you today. Thanks for the letters and the stamps. I look forward to your lines as much as you do for mine.

E, I took care of that little favor already. I sent Lt. Davis a Nazi armband and a real German bill (money). I have accumulated a lot of other stuff as I told you, but it's not easy to mail stuff home now. They're sort of tightening up on that. I hope those two things will suffice. How are your chances for a raise? If your work is done by commissioned WAVES[288] is there a chance for you to get a commission or is it too late?

Of course, you don't want to leave New York and don't even think of going into the WAVES as an enlisted woman. The only reason I mention all this is that it would be good if you could get a commission and do the same work.

See Dad, Eadie does have talent. Mom, I hope your teeth feel better, you'll get used to them.

Thanks for your encouragement, don't worry about my spirits.

Love and Kisses,
Charlie

---

[288] Also known as Women Accepted for Volunteer Emergency Service, WAVES was the women's branch of the United States Naval Reserve during World War II.

Thursday, April 19, 1945

Dear Mom, Dad, and Sis,

Received a nice letter from you today, Mom. You and Dad are sure doing a good job with the house and all I hope is that your efforts are rewarded. I'm quite sure they will be.

There's not much to write about these days. I'm well and comfortable in this small hotel, the weather is grand, plenty of good food; if I were home, things would be excellent.

We had a PX ration today and we could buy grapefruit juice, peanuts, cokes and film. I bought a roll that fits one of the boy's cameras and I'll take some shots in a few days. It's very difficult to have the film developed.

Way behind in my correspondence and if I want to continue getting mail, I had better do some writing.

Take good care of yourselves. Don't worry about not hearing from Artie, when he moves like he has been there's no chance to write.

Love and Kisses,
Charlie

Friday, April 20, 1945

Dear Mom, Pop, and Sis,

All's in hand on the Western Front.

Received your letter with the note from the bank, Mom. I'm sorry if it's causing you trouble - the money order for $100 will be just as good as the traveler's check. Have one made out for $100, that's better than smaller ones.

We're having a movie tonight, "Stormy Weather" with Lena Home, Bill Robinson, and an all-Negro cast. It's a pretty old picture but I haven't seen it, I imagine it'll be entertaining.

Shirley Marcus sent me a nice package from Miami Beach. Some good fruit candy and pecan candy, very thoughtful I say.

Be good, I'll write again tomorrow.

Love,
Charlie

Saturday, April 21, 1945

Hello again,

I saw "Stormy Weather" last night and it was entertaining, as expected nothing to it except singing, dancing, etc. This evening I saw "Saratoga Trunk" with Ingrid Bergman and Gary Cooper, two excellent performers. However, there was too much thrown into the plot and that led to a little confusion, but on the whole it was a decent film.

Thanks for all the telegram sports sheets, Sis. The ones you sent certainly had enough about NYU's basketball team. I received a release from George Shiebler, NYU's Sports Publicist, and it contained some interesting items about people you and I know. I sent it to you. One item: Len Bates, now 2nd Lt. Bates, glad that he finally made it.

Wrote to Art yesterday. Folks and E, the way he's been moving it's just impossible to write so don't worry about him.

I see that Ernie Pyle got knocked off.[289] He was foolish to go back to war after getting out safely from the ETO. He'll be remembered as the outstanding columnist of this war.

Feeling fine, everything is swell. Take good care of yourselves. How are your teeth, Mom?

Regards to the grannies and the rest of the *mishpooka*.[290]

All my love,
Charlie

---

[289] Ernest Taylor Pyle (August 3, 1900 – April 18, 1945) was a Pulitzer Prize–winning American journalist and war correspondent, noted for his reporting about American soldiers during World War II. He was killed by enemy fire on Iejima (then known as Ie Shima) during the Battle of Okinawa.(https://www.nationalww2museum.org/)

[290] Yiddish: Family

Sunday, April 22, 1945

Dear Folks,

A furlough list was published today and I'm third on the list, which means that once quotas come in, I'll be getting away for a 7-day rest plus travelling time.

At present, furloughs are given to Great Britain and the Riviera. If I have any choice in the matter I believe I'd select London, but I'll take whatever comes along. Dad, if you have the address of your cousins, send it to me. I'd get a kick out of visiting them if I get to England. Also, Mom, send out the money order pronto, please. I have Charles Bialogora's address and if I do go to London, I'll try to contact him. I understand that the Riviera is very nice, so wherever I get to go I'll have a good time.

Everything is okay. I'm working the night shift tonight, once every 4 nights. The news is certainly encouraging, eh?[291]

I've heard rumors that the Russians and the US have linked at one point, it's bound to happen shortly. The Reds might have a little trouble going through Berlin, but now that they're in the town I think its fall is only a matter of time.

Rained again today and it's pretty cool, not like the nice weather we've been having. Doing a little reading, am quite comfortable in this hotel.

Be good - take care of yourselves, don't work too hard. Did your gifts arrive, Mom and E? I know Dad received his, what about you?

Love and Kisses,
Charlie

Tuesday, April 24, 1945

Dear Folks,

The sun made its appearance again today and it looks like we're in for some nice weather. This typewriter is quite bad, so excuse the mistakes.

---

[291] The encouraging news of the previous days: On April 20, Soviet artillery began shelling Berlin, and the Seventh United States Army captured the city of Nuremberg. The battle of the Ruhr Pocket ended in Allied victory on April 21, with some 317,000 German troops and 24 German generals taken prisoner.

I'm glad you liked the gift I sent you, Sis. Use the stuff in good health and I hope Artie can see it soon. Now when Mom gets hers that'll complete the set I sent out. I hope you like your present, Mom, it looked pretty good in the catalogue, as if you can tell by that.

Very little is happening and that makes it quite difficult to find stuff to write about. We're all anxiously awaiting the Russians and everyone is on the lookout for them. I wonder if they're going to bring any vodka with them? That sure is a potent drink.

We're eating well and living comfortably, we'll have to get accustomed to a different kind of life if we ever go to another theater of operations.

The Russian slave-laborers here are really sweating out the Red Army, they'll probably have some celebration.

The Peace Conference opens tomorrow, and I hope it does accomplish its mission.[292] Too bad FDR won't be around, but that's the way it is. I thought the people at home would act the way you described it. Over here there wasn't much discussed, perhaps the military isn't as sentimental or emotional as the civilian population. I, though, did feel that we suffered a real loss.

The picture "Atlantic City" is being shown tonight and I think I'll go even though I heard it wasn't too good.

That's all for now. I'll have to dig up some material to make these letters more interesting.

All my love,
Charlie.

---

[292] Referring to the United Nations Conference on International Organization (UNCIO), also known as the San Francisco Conference, was a summit meeting of delegates from 50 Allied nations, resulting in the establishment of the United Nations Charter. President Truman addressed the delegates by telephone: "You members of this Conference are to be the architects of the better world...In your hands rests our future. By your labors at this Conference, we shall know if suffering humanity is to achieve a just and lasting peace. Let us labor to achieve a peace which is really worthy of their great sacrifice. We must make certain, by your work here, that another war will be impossible."

Memories from Bismarck, Germany.

Wednesday, April 25, 1945

Dear Mom, Dad, and Sis,

I saw "Atlantic City" and it wasn't too hot. The sight of the boardwalk and the hotels reminded me of all the summers I spent there. It was gorgeous today, real summery. Still nothing happening.

I took a bath this evening and I feel swell now. Have had my clothes washed and all my stuff is clean now. One thing about these Krauts, tell them to do something and they'll do it; that's military discipline. I'd like to tell them to kill themselves.

Love,
Charlie

Thursday, April 26, 1945

Dear Mom, Pop, and Sis,

I'm living in another town[293] nearby our old place. Accommodations are very good and we're all settled. I have a nice five-room apartment with a bathroom with 3 other fellows.

There's running water, electric lights, bathtub, gas (a few hours a day), and a stove that heats up the entire apartment for free. No $70 a month to the landlord, that's not bad, eh?

The nice weather is still with us. Had a delicious dinner of steak, potatoes, peas and peaches today. Our food is still very good.

I'm feeling fine, everything is swell. Just don't worry.

Love and Kisses,
Charlie

Friday, April 27, 1945

Dear Folks,

All's hotsy-totsy. Received three nice letters from "toothless Pauline." Thanks loads, Mom, your mail is certainly encouraging.

E, I know you thought a great deal about FDR but I didn't believe his death would affect you so. Perhaps you wanted a good emotional outlet, eh? I felt very badly myself, and I can see why you took it so hard.

Sis, you're right about mail not going out when the action is fast moving. I wrote nearly everyday during our advance but I know the letters didn't go to our APO[294] for a week at least. The APO isn't always available. I trust that Artie's letters are coming in now.

Have a nice piano in my apartment, perhaps I'll practice a little. Nothing to worry about, we're having the life now.

Take good care of yourselves.
All my love,
Charlie

---

[293] Gardelegen, Germany.

[294] Army Post Office.

Saturday, April 28, 1945

Dear Folksies,

There's nothing much to report.

Went on duty at 1 AM, so last evening I took a hot bath and got to sleep about 8. I'll sleep some more this morning when I get off duty. It's something to have a tub right in your apartment; we have to make a fire to heat the water, but it's well worth it.

We're sort of settling down here and the life isn't bad at all. Our staff is doing some military government work and I may be able to do some things along that line.

I could use Carrie 3 times a week to clean the apartment, see if she'd be willing to come.

That boy, Seymour Rosenberg, who called you up, is still at home. It seems that no more soldiers are being shipped to the ETO and some have been home over 100 days. He'll probably go to the CBI[295] shortly.

I'm feeling swell, skin pretty fair, should improve now with the better washing facilities.

Received a nice package from Aunt Rose; if you need a request, send some cookies please. Going tomorrow to have my new stationery printed.

Love and Kisses,
Charlie

Sunday, April 29, 1945

Hello Folks,

This is the snazzy stationary I told you about. Not too bad for an old Kraut job, is it?

Nothing much of interest. There is a movie in town now and I'll go down one of these evenings. It turned chilly again and it's just about comfortable with a

---

[295] China-Burma-India theater.

field jacket. We'll have our share of hot weather, though. I understand it never really gets too hot here and the nights are always cool, I hope that's right.

Pretty soon we'll be having organized athletics in the afternoon, that'll give us some exercise. No more now.

Love and Kisses,
Charlie

Monday, April 30, 1945

Dear Folks,

What with all these peace rumors at home, you people must sure be excited.

I do hope that shortly one of them turns out to be the truth. I wonder if the people will have enough strength to celebrate after all the false starts? Just take it easy, it may come tomorrow and then it may take a few weeks.

There is so very little to write about that it's pathetic. I'm doing a bit more typing now and since we're pretty well settled, I'll be more of a clerk than I've been in recent operations.

It's still surprisingly cool. I gave my laundry away and tonight I'll take another hot bath, with the clean clothes I'll be %100 "*sauber*,"[296] *versteh*?[297]

You'll be getting some snapshots as soon as the prints are developed. I'm glad my mail finally reached you, folks. It should be steadier now. I do hope you've heard from Artie, I'm anxious for your sake. I'm confident that he's okay.

Take care of yourselves.
All of my love and kisses,
Charlie

---

[296] German: Clean

[297] German: Understand

Tuesday, May 1, 1945

Dear Folks,

Saw a fairly entertaining picture last night, "Blonde Fever." Nothing to do with the war and that of course is always a good factor. Tonight "Tall in the Saddle" is showing and I think I'll pass that up.

The news of the junction between the US and Russian Armies was very welcomed. Everyone has been waiting for that for so long. Before long, I imagine there will be a link-up straight along the line. From what they say, the Russian soldier is crazier than the American GI - and that's something.

Just heard the news about Hitler dying.[298] Very sketchy report and I don't know how official it is. All the radio said was that Hitler had fallen in Berlin after directing the defense of the city. It was a German radio broadcast, so I'm not too sure. Well, that's one gangster out of our way, but for my money he got out much too easy. I know you agree with me on that score.

Alan Jacobs must have become ambitious because he actually wrote me two V-mails. He's in Texas now, as usual expects to go overseas, is well, and sends his regards to you all. A lot of the men in this town are wearing ties to the movies in the evening. Oh, won't that be something if we'll have to put on ties in Germany.

The weather stays cool but I expect Old Man Sun will get to work shortly and warm things up. It's about time, how is it at home?

That's just about all for today, will write again tomorrow. Is my mail coming through all right these days? Send my love to the Grannies - I'll drop them a line soon. Have fun and don't worry. Mom, do send out that money order shortly.

Love and Kisses,
Charlie

Thursday, May 3, 1945

Dear Folks,

---

[298] Reichssender Hamburg's Flensburg radio station erroneously declared that Adolf Hitler had fallen in Berlin while "fighting for Germany." In fact, Hitler committed suicide in his Berlin bunker on April 30, 1945.

Received a nice batch of letters today for which I thank you. E, I received a note from the Davis fellow saying that he received the small swastika I sent.

Dad, you sounded pretty low in spirits and there's no need for that at this time. Most of the boys in uniform that you see are back from overseas and the only way they get home is being wounded twice, close to two years overseas, combat fatigue (psycho cases) and serious home trouble. Thank God, I don't qualify on any one of those things. Don't forget Dad, most soldiers who are able have been shipped over. Of course, the Air Corps and a few of the service forces have some men, but that's the Army. I consider myself very fortunate and in no way envy the boys at home. Of course, I'd like to be there myself but that just can't be.

Pop, do you know that as a conservative estimate, close to 35 percent of the boys I did Basic with are dead and a good 60 percent have been wounded? I haven't a kick in the world and if you and Mom look at it that way, I'm sure you'd feel better. You've taken my being away splendidly straight along and I'm sure you'll continue to do so.

E told me that Mom's gift arrived and I'm glad Sis asked to wear it. That means it must be pretty nice, but don't forget Eadie, it's Mom's. I knew the Mother's Day card would arrive early but I didn't want to take any chances.

I have to stop now, more tomorrow.

All my love and kisses,
Charlie

Friday, May 4, 1945

Dear Mom, Pop, and Sis,

The mass surrender of a few million German soldiers at one clip is indeed encouraging. Denmark, Netherlands, and Northwest Germany are now through with war and it's beyond me how much longer the Krauts in the South and in Czechoslovakia can resist. Personally, the outlook is very promising.

I saw Jascha Heifetz in concert of the 3rd. He was excellent, say is Fritz Cuisler still living? I know that he was ill and then recovered, that's a year or so ago.

481

Heifetz played "The *Staccato*", "*Ava Maria*", "Gypsy Airs", "Introduction to an Overture", some of Bach's "Prelude" - a pretty good concert.

Last night I saw "A Song to Remember." I imagine you've seen it, if not, be sure to go.

All's well, love and kisses,
Charlie

Saturday, May 5, 1945

Dear Mom, Dad, and *Schwester*,[299]

Wie geht es ibnen, gut, yah? Ich ben sehr gezund und ich hoffe dass ist der gut.[300] That's my German lesson for the day. If I had a suitable text this would sure be the time to learn the language.

E, I replied quickly to your request for a souvenir for Lt. Davis and now I have a favor to ask. In the house, somewhere, (probably in the hall closet), there are a few German textbooks. Pick out a couple, be sure one has the grammar and vocabulary. If you can't find the books, please go to Barnes & Noble and buy a good text, their review books are quite good. Do this soon Sis, I'll appreciate it.

Did I tell you that I saw "Blonde Fever" - nothing to compare with "A Song to Remember." "And Now Tomorrow" played here but I couldn't get to see it. I understand that it was pretty good.

Still quite cool for May. I'm so glad you heard from Artie. I'm sure he's okay and will always be able to take care of himself. Take good care of yourselves and don't do any worrying. There's just nothing to worry about now.

Send my love to the Grannies, how are they these days?
Love and Kisses,
Charlie

---

[299] German: Sister

[300] German: How are you, good, yes? I'm very healthy and I hope you are well.

Sunday, May 6, 1945

Dear Mom, Dad, and Sis,

I'm happy you like the gift, Mother. Wear it in the best of health.

It must have been great to get personal regards from Artie's friend, I've always told you that he's okay.

There was supposed to be a concert by the Division band this afternoon, but it was postponed on account of inclement weather. A whole crowd of Krauts had gathered and they seemed disappointed when the program was called off. I can just picture the Russians giving a concert at the Town Hall for the Germans.

The news is so encouraging. We've had a pretty big prisoner haul lately,[301] you may have read about it in the papers.

A swell package arrived from you today, thanks ever so much. Good creamed corn, candy, salted nuts, my hair brush, asparagus soup, etc. It's still a treat to receive the packages, keep them up. In your next one, please include Kolynos toothpaste along with the usual goodies.

Take care of yourselves, God bless you.

Love and Kisses,
Charlie

Monday, May 7, 1945

Dear Mom, Dad, and Sis,

Well, it looks as if it's all over but the shouting.[302] Now to get on with the next task and finish the complete job and go home. Things do look rosier now, how the Japs will survive more than a year is beyond me. But it's much too early to predict such things, I just hate to be optimistic.

---

[299] On May 7, the 102nd Division, though not directly participating had "courtside" seats at one of the final actions of the European campaign, the Battle of Tangermunde Bridge. This was an engagement between the Russian Red Army and German forces along the River Elbe.

The weather took a turn for the better today and it was warm and sunny for the first time in weeks. There's actually very little to write about. I haven't seen any Russians, but they're not too far away.

I read an old Life Magazine with an editorial, "Salute to the Armies." The Third Army was cited as one of the best, and of course, the 4th Armored was mentioned as its best division. Artie won't speak to us commoners.

That's all now, take care of yourselves.

Love and Kisses,
Charlie

Tuesday, May 8, 1945

Dear Folks,

By now you've heard the great news and I can imagine how good you're feeling.[303] It's marvelous in my opinion, and although we're not celebrating on a very large scale, I hope you are. After all, we've defeated a major power and our task is now half-completed.

We had 3 high-ranking officers (POW's) in our place today and one said that he heard the Armistice was signed. I said there was no armistice and he looked quite puzzled. I went on to say it was unconditional surrender, that is something entirely different.[304]

Now all we can do is await further developments, but the conclusion of the German war makes things look so much better. I heard Churchill speak today but was unable to get Truman on the air. I didn't think much of Churchill's speech, but for an announcement of V-E Day I don't imagine the speech had to be very good.

Took a hot bath tonight. Feel very well and am grateful to God tonight for protecting me through this war.

---

[303] Victory in Europe Day, celebrating the formal acceptance by the Allies of Germany's unconditional surrender of its armed forces on Tuesday, 8 May 1945, marking the end of World War II in Europe.

[304] An "armistice" is a mutually agreed temporary cessation of hostilities, whereas an "unconditional surrender" is a complete cessation of hostilities by the surrendering party in which no guarantees are given to them.

God bless you - E, my hope is for Artie to get home real shortly and me to follow soon after. Take care of yourselves, Mom and Dad.

Love and Kisses,
Charlie

The Division's positions on V-E Day." (With the 102nd Infantry Division Through Germany, pg. 243)

Wednesday, May 9, 1945

Dear Mom, Dad, and Sis,

Well, it's official now. Yes, Germany is *"Kaput"*[305] and we've forced the devil to his knees. I must agree with you, E, that Hitler got away too easily. But you couldn't expect a man like him to take his own medicine.

Mom, there must be some way to send money over here. Many boys get dough. E, please help Mother checkup. If you have the $100 in cash you might be able to put a traveler's check somewhere other than the bank. Also I think you can cable it from Western Union – or if necessary, a money order with an address in the States (that's not too good an idea). But do send it soon. This furlough may come up at any time and I'll be short.

I hope you had a pleasant Mother's Day, Ma. You certainly deserve all the good things that God can grant. Don't worry so about me, I take care of myself, I'm not depressed in the least. The sight of those bodies[306] did not make me bitter (except for the first few hours after seeing it) and I'm in excellent spirits. So please don't harp on that in your letters.

How about a line, Dad?

Love and Kisses,
Charlie

---

[305] German: broken and useless; no longer working or effective.

[306] Referring to the massacre at Gardelegen.

Thursday, May 10, 1945

Hello Gang,

How goes it today? We're getting our first taste of hot weather and it was noticeable on account of the extreme change.

These German women really went for Hitler's baloney on the birthrate. Everyone has kids, I've never seen anything like it. Young, old, married, unwed - all wheel baby carriages. What a birthrate they must have had these past few years. In addition, there are numerous youngsters around 10-15.

Say, Mom, if you can get money orders in small denominations, send the $100 that way. Otherwise cable or get the cash and buy a travelers check at some agency. We're having it pretty nice now, not much changed for us since it's been quiet here for over a week.

E, you mentioned that the 4th wasn't mentioned for a long time, but it came up again recently. Why, you didn't read about the 102nd for over 6 weeks and we certainly weren't coming home. Dreaming doesn't hurt, Sis. I think you'll see Art pretty soon, I hope so.

Saw "Objective Burma" yesterday and thought it was very good.

No more now.
Love and Kisses,
Charlie

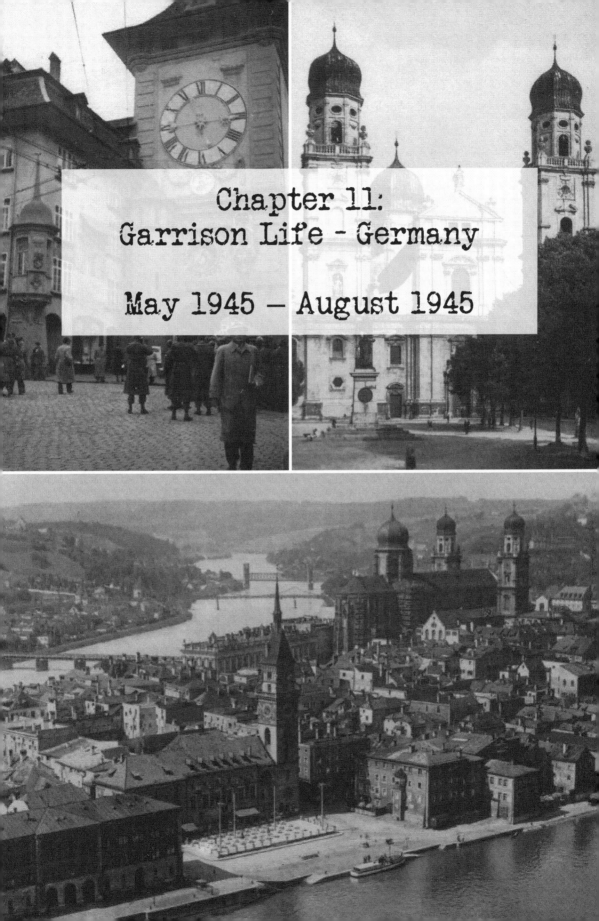

Chapter 11:
Garrison Life - Germany

May 1945 – August 1945

There were four well-defined stages of Occupational Duty for the men of the 102nd Division between May 1945 until their eventual return to the United States in March 1946. The first stage was in Altmark, the area controlled by the Division on V-E Day. After being relieved by the British, the Division then moved to the second phase with the occupation of part of Thuringia, where-after being relieved by the Russians, the Division traveled to Niederbayern on the Danube. Finally, the Division moved to the Bavarian province of Franconia for its longest and final stint of Occupational Duty.[307]

While in Altmark during the month of May, the Division was responsible for the care of 120,000 prisoners of war and 64,000 displaced persons. June 1945 found the 102nd in their second phase in Thuringia. During this period the Division uncovered in the vaults of the Ichterhausen Prison, twelve tons of documents from the Reich Ministry of Justice detailing the Nazi Party's rise in Germany, cases tried by the highest German courts, and detailed death reports from concentration camps, including Dachau.[308] Additionally, during this time the Division took on another major project to apprehend and rehabilitate the many German scientists who contributed to the German war effort. In July 1945, the Division moved yet again to the Niederbayern district, where the

---

[307] With the 102nd Infantry Division Through Germany, pg. 240

[308] Ibid, pg. 242

men guarded some 60 installations and manned 116 roadblocks, while assisting the displaced persons and refugees.[309]

During this time, Charlie and the Headquarters Battery of the 102nd Division Artillery were located in Gardelegen in the month of May, moving to Friedrichroda for the month of June, and finally settling in Passau for July-August 1945. Victory in Japan on August 15, 1945, and the subsequent reorganization of many units in the European Theater based on the Point System, led to Charlie's transfer from the 102nd Division Headquarters to the Third US Army Engineers in the southeast German town of Bad Tölz, Bavaria, in September 1945.

After the surrender of Germany in 1945, the fate of every soldier was determined by the Point System. Officially known as the Adjusted Service Rating Score, it was developed in order to implement a fair system to decide which soldiers would stay in Europe for Occupational Duty, which would be transferred to the Pacific theater, and finally which soldiers would be sent back home to the United States.[310] Every soldier accrued points according to the following rubric:

- One point for each month of service in the Army;

Displaced persons in the area of Altmark." (With the 102nd Infantry Division Through Germany, pg. 199)

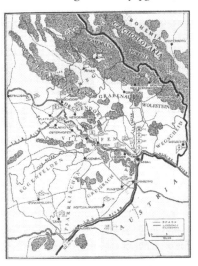

102nd Division's positions in the occupation of the Niederbayern province of lower Bavaria." (With the 102nd Infantry Division Through Germany, pg. 246)

---

[309] Ibid, pg. 244

[310] National World War II Museum, https://www.nationalww2museum.org/war/articles/points-system-us-armys-demobilization

- One additional point for each month of service overseas;

- Five points for each campaign;

- Five points for a Medal for Merit or Valor;

- Five points for a Purple Heart;

- Twelve points for each dependent child, up to three dependent children.[311]

In his letters, Charlie lamented his frustration at the inconsistencies of the Point System. However, in hindsight, the System shows that the Army actually discharged soldiers at a rapid rate. By the end of 1945, more than four million soldiers had returned to the United States. Between the months of September - December 1945, the Army discharged an average of 1.2 million soldiers per month. By June 1946, the military suspended the Point System and instead discharged all servicemen who had finished two years of service. With the official ending of the United States Army de-mobilization on June 30, 1947, the Army had decreased to just 684,000 soldiers from the eight million who were involved in active service in 1945.[312]

---

[311] Ibid.

[312] Ibid.

Friday, May 11, 1945

Dear Mom, Dad, and Sis,

We're certainly having typical summer weather now. I have a little porch outside of my apartment and I cleaned it up this morning. I'm going to pick up a beach chair somewhere and then I'll be able to take some good sunbaths.

There's very little to write about. We're leading a garrison life, more or less. Our Captain went to a party given by the Russians along with the General. He told us all about it and it's some story. All this about the Reds drinking enormous quantities of vodka is the truth. Girl MP's directed traffic on the roads. At the dinner, course after course was served and in addition to vodka, champagne, cognac, and wine were served. There was a toast a minute and that calls for emptying the glass, not just sipping.

I've seen one or two Russian officers; there's going to be a reception here Wednesday and we'll probably see more then.

I'm just fine.
All my love,
Charlie

Saturday, May 12, 1945

Hello again Family,

Had another warm day and I'm quite sure that this summer weather is here to stay.

Did you get to see the atrocity pictures they're showing at home?[313] I understand that most of the theaters showed them. It's certainly not a pleasant thing to witness but I think every American should see it. It's something beyond the comprehension of most Americans and perhaps if they see these atrocities with their own eyes they'll actually believe that things of that nature were commonplace here. And then more Americans will have a better idea of the ruthlessness and barbarity of these Germans.

---

[313] Films of the concentration camps.

One thing impresses me greatly, and that's the apparent freedom of guilt that all the Krauts have. They don't think they've done a thing wrong and it will be a pretty tough task to convince them they have. They blame all the murders and purges on the SS and claim they "couldn't do anything about it." That's an old familiar phrase, "couldn't do anything about it."

Feeling swell, I don't know exactly how this point system will work but I have about 43 points and I figure (roughly) that Artie must have around 70. Took a nice sunbath, I have my bathing trunks with me. Had a good bath this evening, all's well. Take good care of yourselves, there's surely nothing to worry about now.

All my love,
Charlie

Sunday, May 13, 1945

Dear Mom, Dad, and Sis,

I hope you had an enjoyable Mother's Day, Mom. Did my flowers get delivered today? I asked Karyl Steiner to take care of that, more of a surprise than if Eadie purchased them.

What do you hear from Artie? He must be settled by now and I hope you're getting a lot of mail. Where did he end up? Czechoslovakia, wasn't it? I read in Stars and Stripes that the American soldiers say the Czech girls are the prettiest in Europe.

The May 7th Time Magazine arrived today and it contains loads of material, that was sure a splendid present, Sis. I look forward to it each week. The May Digest also came in today, thanks to you.

Joe Nelson wrote me and said that Grandma is in Clifton Springs; where is that, near Wilkes-Barre? How's Grandpop making out? I must write to them soon.

We had another glorious day, in fact, it was a bit too warm for early May. There's nothing much happening. I'm feeling fine. Now that the war in Europe is over you should be relaxing a bit, at least not worrying constantly about Artie and me. We're quite safe now, I doubt whether any of our troops will experience any trouble from the civilians. They don't have any fight left and also, they're aware of the consequences which are quite severe.

No more now, take good care of yourselves. Are you going out any?

Love and Kisses,
Charlie

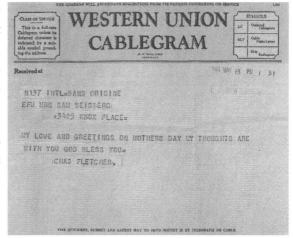

Monday, May 14, 1945

Dear Mom, Dad, and Sis,

Received the money order today for which I thank you loads. I'll be looking for the other one soon. Mom, I told you the money is for the furlough when I get one and it will be spent mainly for a good time. So don't fret about spending it foolishly, it may sound as if it isn't going for a good cause, but as far as I'm concerned all I spend on myself during a rest period will be well spent.

A splendid package also came in from you. It contained a delicious fruitcake, chicken broth, etc. thanks very much. In your next package please include 2 or 3 undershorts size 40 (don't die, Pop, they're more comfortable that size).

Take good care of yourselves.

Love,
Charlie

Wednesday, May 16, 1945

Hello Folks,

Another swell package from you and it's great. Anchovies (I love them), tuna fish, fruitcake, etc. I can always go for that. Thanks for the toothpaste, send more next time please, along with a good toothbrush.

There are some Polish Jews in this town[314] and I must have met them all yesterday, about 51. The majority have been in concentration camps for over five years and they certainly have some stories to tell. One boy claims he's a nephew of Sholem Ach, and all of them have relatives in the States (New York is the

Charlie with Jews just recently liberated from Nazi concentration camps.

home of most of the relatives). They're just about getting to look good, some American troops have been feeding them very well. They've got pretty good living quarters. God knows what'll become of them. The Poles treated them terribly and none want to go back there. When you see something like this, you begin to realize why Palestine[315] would be such a grand place. These people actually have no place to go. They all speak Yiddish and I understood them, just like hearing my Old Man speak it. A lot came from Warsaw and they say it was a terrible place for the Jews. Going to see them again with our doctor and dentist.

Saw Russian officers today driving to a reception; looked very nice, clean, pretty different uniforms and medals.

That's all now.
Love and Kisses,
Charlie

---

[314] Gardelegen, Germany; the location of the 102nd Division Artillery Headquarters.

[315] Palestine was still under the stewardship of the British Mandate Government Authorities at this time, but it had a flourishing Jewish community and political structure. Throughout his adult life, Charlie was an ardent Zionist, giving of his time and resources to Jewish and Israeli causes.

Thursday, May 17, 1945

Dear Mom, Dad, and Sis,

We're having an old-fashioned rainstorm tonight - the first of the Spring season and it's lightning and thundering like no one's business.

Thanks for your card on Mother's Day, Mom. You think of everything, don't you? Went to the movies this evening and saw "And Now Tomorrow." It played here before but I missed it. Not a bad picture, the soundtrack was very bad and that took a lot away from the film. However, the acting was good and I enjoyed it very much.

Do you know, folks, I'm not worried about one thing - except your health and your lives. Take good care of yourselves, please. I want both of you to be in excellent condition when I come home. I don't worry about the business, I don't give a damn about the house. As long as you two are okay, then I'm content. And of course, Sis, that goes for you too.

Went swimming this afternoon. 'Twas fun, the water a bit too cold.

That's all for now.
Love and Kisses,
Charlie

Friday, May 18, 1945

Dear Folks,

Nothing much to report today, the weather is still lovely although it has cooled down a bit.

I went down to see those Jewish people again last night and I took our doctor along - a Grand Concourse boy. It was *Shevuas*[316] yesterday and the women had noodles made and some delicious cheesecake. Some soldiers had a baker make "*halle*,"[317] and it looked good to see that bread again. Our Dentist is also a Jew

---

[316] The holiday of *Shavuot,* commonly known in English as the Feast of Weeks, is a holiday that occurs on the sixth day of the Hebrew month of *Sivan* marking the revelation of the Torah to Moses and the Israelites at Mount Sinai.

[317] *Challah* bread, a traditional bread of Jewish origin, usually braided and typically eaten on ceremonial occasions such as Shabbat and major Jewish holidays.

The site and victims of the German atrocities at Gardelegen.

and I'll take him one of these nights. Incidentally, the Corps Jewish chaplain had services yesterday morning and most of the Jewish civilians attended. All the stories we heard are true. These people have seen the things with their own eyes, and in many cases these people suffered the horrible atrocities we could hardly believe.

Incidentally, our mail is no longer censored by the Battery. There is still a base censorship in effect but they only spot-check and probably will only censor

[318] See Historical Introduction to Chapter 10.

very few letters in the future. So, if I write a little more freely don't worry. I never had to restrict myself when writing to you. I even forgot after a while that our mail was read, you get used to the idea of someone reading your letters.

The movie "Tall in the Saddle" is playing tonight. I didn't see it when it played last week because I was afraid it might be very bad but the boys say it's pretty entertaining and I think that I may go this evening. Must continue to catch up on my correspondence, I'm still very far behind.

No idea of what's going to happen. We're living in the town of Gardelegen, about 80 miles west of Berlin. It's not a bad town, not wrecked at all and I told you about our comfortable quarters, etc. This is the town in which I saw those 1,000 people burned to death (on the outskirts of town).[318] It was the SS and Gestapo that committed the atrocity, however. These Germans need such a drastic re-education. You have no idea of how stagnant their minds are and how used they are to have people do their thinking for them. Yes, it's all a very big job.

Take good care of yourselves, will write again tomorrow.
Love and Kisses,
Charlie

Saturday, May 19, 1945

Dear Mom, Pop, and Sis,

Another day, another week. Not a darn thing to tell you.

I saw "High in the Saddle" this evening and it was a real Western, plenty of action and laughs. It's very quiet now and we're not doing a thing. In fact, it's an exceedingly lazy life. Tomorrow is our first real day of rest. We're supposed to be off on Sunday, and I'll let you know if we actually are.

Have a little red wine tonight and it's very good. Eating some sardines, chicken, etc. The water is good and hot now and I'm going to take a real Saturday night bath.

Take it easy, be well and God bless you.

Love and Kisses,
Charlie

Sunday, May 20, 1945

Dear Mom, Dad, and Sis,

Hope you're spending an enjoyable Sunday. Say, you have a good little camera; how about taking some pictures on these lovely Spring days? I took 8 shots this afternoon and they'll be coming to you as soon as I can have them developed. Sis, if you haven't bought me any 120's yet, change that to 616; the boys in my section have two 616 Kodak cameras.

It's a beautiful day and also a restful one. Slept until noon, had a good dinner, bathed, took pictures and now writing letters in my apartment. Received your May 11th line today, Mom. It's highly improbable that I'll meet that Mrs. Young, but there's always the possibility. You might see me yourself before too many months. Can never tell what'll happen in the Army.

What does Artie write, E? Does he expect to stay here or go to the CBI? Bernard Fillion's Division is passing through town today and what a racket that is. I don't know where they're going.

The "Keys of the Kingdom" is playing today and Monday; I may go this evening, I don't know yet. That's about all I have to say right now. I hear that furloughs will be starting again in a week or so, I hope so. I've been waiting quite a while.

Send my regards to all the family. How are the Grannies doing?

Take care of yourselves. Are my monthly checks reaching the bank? How about my $10 War Bonds?

Love and Kisses,
Charlie

Monday, May 21, 1945

Dear Mom, Pop, and Sis,

E, I met Bernard Fillion today for a few minutes and it was certainly a surprise. I told you yesterday that his outfit was passing by. Well, this evening about 5:30, the 77th Medical Battalion trucks were going through and they halted for a while. I asked some fellow if he knew Fillion and he said he was in a weapons carrier 10 trucks to the rear. So, there I was and it came as a complete surprise to him. He said he heard from you recently, E. Looks pretty well.

Pretty nasty today, slight drizzle. Nothing much happening. Going to visit my Jewish friends now. I have 33 points, oh me.

No more now.
All my love,
Charlie

Tuesday, May 22, 1945

Dear Mom, Pop, and Sis,

I'm so glad that Mother's Day turned out so nicely. I didn't expect the cable-gram to arrive exactly on the 13th, but all Mother's Day cables must have been held up for delivery on Sunday. Karyl Steiner chose the flowers and I'm happy you liked them. I asked her to send roses, she told me she picked nice ones. Now, Pop, if you were a sissy, I'd send you pansies for Father's Day but I know you wouldn't want me to.

Last night was a most enjoyable one. I visited the Jews in town and had deli-cious *bubkas*.[319] Not as good as yours, but I told them it was better than my mother's and *buba's*[320] *bubka*. We sang all the Hebrew and Jewish songs - Dad must know them all because a lot of these people come from the same part of Poland as Pop. We also sang *Adon Olam*,[321] *Ain Kelohanu*,[322] *HaTikva*,[323] and others, the names I don't know. I can sing all the tunes without the words, just carry along.

The Jews gave a party for the German *Bringmeister* (mayor) last night and he had just left before I arrived. One of our officers is in charge of these displaced persons and he said the Jews will be allowed to stay for a while, at least. That made them all feel fine. Names like Spielman, Borenstein, Tachman - all famil-iar.

No, E, I don't know what's going to happen to me. We're leaving this place shortly, but I have no idea of our destination.

---

[319] A *babka* is a sweet, braided bread or cake which originated in the Jewish communi-ties of Poland and Ukraine. It is prepared with a yeast-leavened dough that is rolled out and spread with a filling such as chocolate, cinnamon, fruit, or cheese, then rolled up and braided before baking.

[320] Yiddish: Grandmother.

[321] Jewish liturgical song.

[322] Jewish liturgical song.

[323] Poem and national anthem of Israel, written by Naftali Herz Imber in 1877.

No more right now, visiting there again tonight. Take good care of yourselves.
All my love,
Charlie

Wednesday, May 23, 1945

Dear Folks,

Another rainy, nasty day but that doesn't bother me. Have the apartment nice
and warm for the evening and I plan to take a good hot bath. There's really very
little to do these days, just hang around the office, usually take off a couple of
hours a day.

If things were more sure we'd probably have the education program the Army
has planned,[324] but I guess no one actually knows what's going to happen. As
I see it, we may occupy an area in the US Zone for a while and then ship back
to the States, probably for the trip to the CBI. But then again, I have no foundation, whatsoever, for my prediction. Personally, I'd prefer staying here for a
long, long time. Right?

We've all been interviewed for this education program, it looks like a real Army
"snafu"[325] to me. I may be an instructor in business subjects at a battalion
school. I stated that I'd like to go to a University study center (Oxford, Cam-
bridge, Sorbonne) but I doubt whether those programs will ever start. The
Army talks too much about education, special services, athletics, etc. and does
too little.

Incidentally, now that I write everything I please, don't have my letters printed
anywhere. I know of many families who send their son's letters to newspapers,
magazines, etc. That's a good way to make trouble and I know you have no idea
of doing anything like that, but I just want to make sure.

Did you get your coat yet, Mom? Wear it in good health. Pop, you should be
getting a spring suit, shouldn't you? A medium price suit (Howards, etc.)
should be smart enough for the warm weather. Please try to buy one.

Everything is just fine, feeling fine, eating well.

---

[324] The Information and Education program, see Historical Introduction Chapter 12 for more
details.

[325] Situation Normal, All Fouled Up.

Take good care of yourselves.
Love and Kisses,
Charlie

Thursday, May 24, 1945

Dear Folks,

In tonight's Stars and Stripes, four divisions were named as going to the Pacific via the US next month and thank God we weren't in the first batch. The 95th, 86th, 104th, and 97th Divisions are the one's scheduled to leave in June. We came over after three of them so I imagine we may be pretty well up on the list. But no one knows, so what's the use of speculating?

Learning to drive a jeep, had two short lessons today and did very well. I think it's a lot of fun, that's because it's something new, I guess.

Still a little cool and nasty. Had six British boys in the apartment last night. I think I told you they're taking over from us.[326]

No more now. Received a swell package from you today. Marvelous cookies, sardines, etc. Oh, what a lovely family I have.

Love and Kisses,
Charlie

Friday, May 25, 1945

Dear Mother, Father, and Sister, (Formal today)

How's by you all? I hope you're all feeling okay and everything is alright.

Still a bit cool for the end of May. Quite a few Englishmen around now in preparation of relieving us. I understand that the city we're going to is quite large[327] and we're going to live in a big hotel that's in good condition. That doesn't sound bad.

Right now I'm guessing that I'll be home for Labor Day, but this guessing game isn't always right. E, don't hope that Artie comes home quickly. The

---

[326] The 102nd Division was in the process of being relieved by the British 52nd Division before being transferred to occupational duties in Thuringia.

[327] Charlie and the Headquarters Battery of the 102nd Division Artillery were to take up residence in the town of Friedrichroda.

longer he's in the ETO the better his chances of not going to the CBI, and that's what you should be mainly interested in.

Going to visit my Jewish friends tonight, it's Friday and we'll probably have services (a good *davening*[328] session).

Love,
Charlie

Saturday, May 26, 1945

Dear Mom, Pop, and Sis,

Had an enjoyable time last night. I visited the Jewish people and as I thought they would, they conducted Friday night services. And, boy, do they *daven*, just like all the religious people back home. They don't need books, they know it all by heart. I really get a kick out of going to their place, but that's considered fraternization - can you imagine that?

The other evening the MP's[329] picked up some boys for going there and now I'm a little hesitant. I'll be careful, don't worry. Another week gone by, a pretty easy day tomorrow - Sunday. Went to services this afternoon but the chaplain never showed up. A real Jewish 1:30 it must have been.

Take care of yourselves.
All my love,
Charlie

Sunday, May 27, 1945

Dear Folksies,

A very quiet Sunday to say the least. Slept a great part of the day and feel quite refreshed.

I ate the last can of Portugal Sardines I received, and they were delicious.

Winding up our affairs here. Have to get two pairs of pants from a tailor, they're new and were a little too big. I think I'll squeeze one more laundry in, we're leaving Thursday and that should give me time.

---

[328] Yiddish: Prayer.

[329] Military Police.

Nothing else right now. E, I haven't Adam's exact address. He told me you owed him a letter. Try c/o PO, Normoyle Field, San Antonio, Texas.

Love and Kisses,
Charlie

Tuesday, May 29, 1945

Dear Folksies,

All's well in Deutschland. Got a lot of sun the past two days and now I have a nice little burn. Played volleyball yesterday afternoon and in the evening I saw "To Have or Have Not" with Lauren Bacall and Bogart. Enjoyed it and she is quite terrific.

Now we're not moving until June 1st, there's always changes in the Army.

There's very little to write about. We're loafing, not much work. Everything is just fine and I'm feeling swell.

Sis, you're not forgetting the package and those people in Holland, are you? Let me know if you've sent it.

That's all until tomorrow.
All my love,
Charlie

Wednesday, May 30, 1945

Dear Folksies,

A little nasty today, but that's to be expected. After yesterday's sunny day it comes as a letdown. Received five letters from you, thanks a lot. Glad you sent the German books, one or two would have been enough. I have a good chance to learn German well because I'm here, that's the main reason I want the books. Sorry it's not for the Army of Occupation.

Mom, we're getting plenty to eat, don't worry about that. The Army will be cut down last, if it's necessary at all. Please send 616 film and Kolynos.

No more now.
Love and Kisses,
Charlie

Life in Gardelegen, May 1945

COSMOLINE
CP

Views of Friedrichroda

Saturday, June 2, 1945

Dear Folks,

Excuse the slight delay, but the past two days have been quite busy with moving and setting up.[330] Travelled all day yesterday and it was a pleasant trip except for a little rain. Saw a lot of Germany and this central part is really beautiful, no doubt about it. Passed through Magdeburg (all wrecked, but good), Halberstadt, and Blankenburg. We're 9 miles or so from Gotha, the nearest large city.

This place is exquisite. It's a summer resort town in the mountains and we have a couple of hotels and rich private homes. Typical Catskills or Blue Ridge. I'm in a hotel with my own room, very nice bed, sink, closet. More amenities in Gardelegen, but no complaints.

The swimming pool here is the nicest I've ever seen. It's real Miami Beach or Hollywood stuff, 16 feet deep, 3 diving boards, the highest about 25 feet. There are athletic fields galore. Too many damn hills, the whole town is hilly and walking is fatiguing. Still occupied getting settled, more tomorrow.

All my love and kisses,
Charlie

---

[330] Friedrichroda is located in central Germany, some 272 kilometers (app. 169 miles) southwest of Gardelegen.

Tuesday, June 5, 1945

Dear Folks,

On my way to Paris for 3 days. Will write soon.

Happy Father's Day, Pop. Train leaves now.

Love,
Charlie

Monday, June 11, 1945

Dear Folks,

Haven't written for a week or so and you'll please excuse, eh? But as you know I've been to Paris for a three-day pass. I imagine you received my cable. There certainly is no time for letter writing while in Paris for 72 hours.

Left Germany last Tuesday morning at 4:30. We caught the train at this town Tuesday evening at 7 PM, and we hit Paris at 1 PM on Wednesday. We pulled out of Paris Saturday night at 8 PM and came here 1 PM yesterday. Our trucks hadn't arrived, so we stayed overnight and we also have today to ourselves. We should be on our trucks tomorrow morning. It's quite a miserable trip, wooden seats all the way, etc. the train too.

The Red Cross provides the room and Mess in Paris and it's pretty nice. You're own your own for the rest of the things. I took an excellent sightseeing trip and did a lot of touring by myself. Went bike-riding one afternoon and saw some interesting sights.

Unfortunately, I couldn't meet Artie this trip, I did send regards via some other 4th Armored boys. They were of the opinion that the 4th will be occupation troops and in today's papers it says that the 3rd and 7th Armies will remain here. So that'll be a break, E, and Artie must be real close to 85, so he is set.[331] I hope they lower the score to 81 or 82. If you're correct about those 57 points, Artie has at least 82 because the 4th Armored has 5 stars. That's what some fellows told me.

---

[331] At this point in time, 85 points made a serviceman eligible to be sent back to the United States and formally discharged.

In Paris I saw the "*Folies Berg-ere*," a burlesque on a little higher level than ours. Beautiful scenery and gorgeous costumes. The women didn't impress me as much as they did last September.

FOLIES - BERGERE
VENDREDI SOIREE
Fauteuil de Balcon
N°
PRIX 92.00
Timbre en compte avec le 1 00
TOTAL 93.00
Prière de conserver ce ticket pour être présenté à toute réquisition N° 04803
Watelet Arbel 8 JUIN 1945

Nothing much to this place, pretty poor town now although it probably was prosperous before the war. Last night I saw "Winged Victory" and this afternoon "Dough Girls"- tonight I'm going to a GI nightclub.

No news from my outfit, still in the same place though. Will write as soon as I get back to the Battery.

All my love,
Charlie

Tuesday, June 12, 1945

Dear Mom, Dad, and Sis,

Well, we're still in Belgium. Four of our trucks came in yesterday and we thought we'd leave this morning. However, the drivers took off to Aachen for some reason or other and we're still waiting. Liege is only 10 miles from here and I may visit there this afternoon. We have to meet again at 1:30 but I doubt very much whether we'll leave then. I'm glad I have some extra dough because you just have to have money even to breathe. The $75 you sent came in very handy.

It looks like we'll be coming home real soon. I wish we knew for sure. I hate this business of guessing and "sweating it out."

I should have loads of mail when I get back to the Battery. I'll have to do plenty of writing.

Had a splendid time last night at the GI nightclub in town. It's a very nice spot, an excellent 15-piece civilian band, singers, dancing with nice Belgian girls and beer and orangeade. The police check the girls at the door, they have a "good" list and a "bad" list, some fun, eh?

How are the Grannies?

Take good care of yourselves.
Love and Kisses,
Charlie

Charlie at the GI Night Club in Verviers, Belgium.

Friday, June 15, 1945

Dear Folksies,

All's well. Major Becker's clerk went to Paris and I'm working for him while the man is away. Very quiet, sit and read and write, etc. Things are so good now that I'm afraid it can't last. Outside of 3 hours' guard every third night or so, we don't have a blessed detail and the morning hours of "work" go by rapidly. Then the afternoon is spent playing ball or swimming.

We all put on ties for supper and our meals are good. When we go out at night we wear our OD caps, real garrison now. The weather turned nice today and I hope it lasts. Took some more snaps today and I'll mail them shortly.

Enclosed is a souvenir from Paris, Mom. The hanky is for Ma and the picture is for Pop. Hope you like it.

All my love,
Charlie

Saturday, June 16, 1945

Dear Mom, Pop, and Sis,

Here I is again, ain't I a good boy?

I was thrilled to learn about Ellie's and Larry's marriage and I'm sure happy that she got her man. It's too bad things couldn't have gone off as originally planned, but now that they're wed let them have a life of "real *nachas*"[332] - how's that, Pop?

Two grand packages arrived from you today and they contained just about everything I could desire. Fruitcake, swell cookies, anchovies, etc. thank you very much. Had an easy day. Was on guard last night so I slept until 10 and then "went to the office," took off about 4:30 PM and had a hot bath.

This evening there was a barrel of beer on the porch of the hotel in which we eat, and while waiting in line we all helped ourselves, some fun, eh? You can't imagine how comfortably we're living. We get three good meals, no food shortage for us, I only hope you are eating as well. Pop, is Mom starving you to death? I hope you can still eat bread with your soup, Dad.

E, here's a job for you. Of all the pictures I send home I want you to save one copy for me so I can have them for my family. Please do that because I know you and the folks will want copies and I don't want to be without any snapshots.

All my love to you all,
Charlie

Sunday, June 17, 1945

Dear Folks,

Here it is Sunday afternoon, and I just finished a very enjoyable dinner and ate some of your delicious cookies as extra dessert. For chow we had goulash, mashed potatoes, peas, pears, and cold chocolate drink. No, I didn't get up for breakfast, in fact I slept until noon. This is a tough life, eh?

---

[332] Hebrew: Pleasure or satisfaction.

There's a USO show here today and I'm going to the evening performance at 7:30. The theater in town is very modern. The man who owns it lived with his family in Houston, Texas for ten years. The acoustics are excellent and it's quite a relaxation to see a movie there.

I met an old lady who lived on East 86th Street for ten years and returned here in 1938. Can you imagine anyone being so stupid as to leave our great United States of America? I bet everyone who did is regretting it now. But they're no different than these other Krauts. If they had the real American spirit, they would never have left our shores in the first place, right?

Do you know that I haven't been in our pool yet because it's just too cool. I never experienced such a June - real chilly, little sun. Today we have the sun but there is a very strong wind, so I guess swimming will have to wait for a while.

You probably read the story about the next four divisions to go to the Pacific via the States. Another two, the 4th and 9th Infantry Divisions, were also mentioned. So, we're not in the next batch. I'd really like to know just when we're going home, or just what'll be. However, it's not the Army's policy to tell you what you want to know, as if you didn't know that by now.

I'm up in the office now. We don't work on Sunday, but I dropped by to see whether or not Major Becker needed me. There might be a little work so I'm hanging around for a while.

No more news now. Today is your day, Pop, and I hope the ladies are treating you nicely. Many more Father's Days and next year I hope you'll have your son with you.

Best wishes, all my love,
Zudek Leibish ben Schlemiel

Tuesday, June 19, 1945

Dear Mom, Pop, and E,

Not a blessed thing new. Was on guard last night so I slept until noon today and now I'm just hanging around the office with nothing much to do.

It's a real beautiful day, quite warm, but a lovely breeze. I don't think it ever gets actually hot in this part of Germany.

While on guard last night with another guy we had a picnic. I opened a can of sardines that Aunt Rose had sent along with some asparagus soup from you. I heated the soup in the kitchen and it was delicious. Then we had some of your fruitcake and finally the other boy made the contribution of a Schnafft Chocolate bar.

You can continue sending packages until the post office won't accept them. They usually refuse packages 30 days before a unit is to leave the ETO. You might send some sardines and salmon, that's just if you need a request. I'm not being greedy, I know you need all the food you can get.

Be good and take good care of yourselves.

All my love,
Charlie

Wednesday, June 20, 1945

Dear Folks and E,

Another beautiful day and if I didn't have CQ duty I would have gone swimming, perhaps tomorrow. Put in more or less a full day in the office but it consisted mainly of reading Time and the Reader's Digest, thanks to Mrs. Marshak.

The 4th Armored is officially an Occupation Division,[333] Sis, so you can breathe easy now. Enclosed is the article from the Stars and Stripes.

The two small pictures enclosed in this letter were taken by Major Becker at Buchenwald, one of the Nazi's terror camps. They show plainly the stoves in

---

[333] One of the Divisions officially tasked with occupation duty in the American Zone of occupied Europe.

which the people were burned to death. If you look closely (get your magnifying glass, Mom) you can see ashes etc. and little details. The other shot is of the barrels in which the ashes were stored. For 30 marks ($3) a family can buy the ashes of a member of their family. Some German culture, eh? The other shots are more pleasant, and I hope you enjoy them. Don't forget, E, save me some.

We may move from here, damn it. But it'll be to another part of Germany.

Love and Kisses,
Charlie

Thursday, June 21, 1945

Dear Mom, Paw, and Yenta,

How's by you "*heute*"?[334] One of these days I think I'll surprise you and write a letter in German. I don't know any of the grammar, but I manage to speak it pretty well.

Having another easy day in the office. I haven't been able to get out in the afternoon for athletics or swimming, but as soon as Major Becker's clerk comes back I'll be getting out. Now I write letters or read. What do you hear from your honey, Sis? How's his morale? I'm positive he'll be home for good by winter. So keep up the chin for a few more months.

---

[334] German: Today.

Say, Mom and Pop, I have a question to ask. I want a little advice. Uncle Mendel has helped you out a lot, but only on one occasion have I personally borrowed money from him. If you recall, on one Christmas vacation in Wilkes-Barre ('41 or '42) I asked him for $100 so I could register for the Spring Semester.

Now, he said that he didn't want it back when I offered to repay him. I have the dough now and do you think I should send him $100? That sum means nothing to Uncle Mendel. There are a few sides to the question. Perhaps he'll think I'm softening him up for a post-war loan, etc. which I don't want any part of, or other things. Talk it over and let me hear what you both think about it.

Be good, have fun. That's some parade Eisenhower had, eh?[335]
Love,
Charlie

Friday, June 22, 1945

Dear Folks,

Not a blessed thing new. Slept until 12 today, as I was on guard last night. Then I left the office at 4 PM - a real rough day, eh? In the evening there was a double feature "Between Two Women" and "Sunday Dinner for A Soldier" - both were fair.

E, remember I told you about points being added after May 12? Well, the Army is "snafu-ing" again and that's been changed. I believe when the new score is announced you'll go by the May 12 score, but then for future dates you can add points. 80 is a good total anyway, I'm enclosing the article from Stars and Stripes to confuse you a little more.

Did a little pair of wooden shoes reach you yet, Sis? I sent them from Verviers, Belgium. I'm glad you liked the last box of souvenirs. Divide the coins up with me. The reason for the different kind of stuff is that I got it all is this Colonel's house and he was a pretty big hot-shot.

Love and Kisses,
Charlie

---

[335] Victory Parade held in New York City on June 10, 1945.

Monday, June 25, 1945

Dear Folks,

I took a vacation from writing this past weekend, so you'll please excuse. Enclosed is a photo I had taken recently here in a studio in town. Any good? One is coming for you, Sis.

Went bathing yesterday morning before dinner and it was swell. The day was warm and the water felt very refreshing.

Got letters from the three of you today, thanks. There's one thing I'd like to straighten out, you continually say that you hope I get a break—school or another assignment. Don't you realize that I'm very fortunate to be in this Battery and I'll be content to finish up with them? Of course, there are better jobs, Stars and Stripes or an office in Paris - but there are also plenty of worse jobs. If it's my luck to go to the Pacific, why, I'll just go. Unfortunately, I'm a soldier and have to do as told. But those are the circumstances and that's that. And sooner or later most men in rear offices who haven't seen combat will be transferred, I at least saw combat from a pretty safe place. Since overseas I haven't had one rough day. Ate C or K rations about 4 days out of about 240 days. After leaving France, did not sleep outside once. The Pacific may be rough, but if the others can do it, so can I. Thank God, I'm so well taken care of.

Please feel the same way. Many times I think of trying to transfer, go to school, etc. But know I'm too well off to fool around. I would never want to leave my present job unless it was for something certain, and nothing is certain.

Had two big helpings of delicious chocolate ice cream tonight at supper. Eating well and feeling fine. Major Becker's clerk came back yesterday so now I have some more time for myself. I go on guard now for a little while and sleep tomorrow morning.

All my love and kisses,
Charlie

PS: I have enough pictures for the family and will send them out soon.

Tuesday, June 26, 1945

Dear Folks,

Had a very nice day. Took the morning off because I was on guard last night and in the afternoon I went out for athletics (played volleyball) and then went swimming. Not too rough a day, eh?

"Roughly Speaking" with Rosaline Russell was shown tonight. I didn't get to go but it's being shown again tomorrow and since most of the boys say it's good, I think I'll go. There is a circus in Gotha and may go to see it one of these evenings.

We're still waiting for the word to move. The Russians are definitely moving in but just when, we don't know. But until we do leave, we're taking advantage of the nice set up.

That's about all. Enclosed are a few more snaps. You should have a small collection by now, eh?

Love and Kisses,
Charlie

Wednesday, June 27, 1945

Dear Folks,

Quite a bit of rain today but I was indoors all the time. Very little work, as usual.

Received a few letters from you today. Glad you got to see Eisenhower, Mom. That was an historic day. Did he drive slowly outside the store or wasn't that part of the parade? He seems to be a very sincere man.

Well, the San Francisco Conference is over,[336] and I think it's a good step in the right direction. We must all forget petty differences and concentrate on the big thing, maintaining peace for all time.

---

[336] Referring to the conclusion of the United Nations Conference on International Organization (UNCIO), commonly known as the San Francisco Conference, a convention of delegates from 50 Allied nations which resulted in the creation of the United Nations Charter.

E, what town is Artie near? Stars and Stripes hasn't given the location of the 4th Armored for a long time. Sweat it out, kid, it can't be too long.

Saw an excellent movie tonight, "Roughly Speaking" - that mother certainly reminded me of my own Mom. Have you people seen it? You'll probably cry a little but it's worthwhile.

That's about it, for now.

Take care of yourselves, try to send some 616 film. Don't worry for me, Mom, I'm very content and satisfied. Please get that into your head.

Love,
Charlie

Thursday, June 28, 1945

Hello People,

Nothing new. Went to a USO show this morning and it was pretty good. It's cooled off again and it's really pretty chilly. This is about the coolest June I can remember.

I'm glad to hear that Paul Young is at school. It must be at Fontainebleau, as that is near Paris. I have no reason to go to an Army school as I have my job and am trained for it. Paul is probably going to clerical school or classification school. I'm not positive I'm right but I'm pretty sure that's what it's for.

Haven't heard from Molly and Sam in a long while, I suppose I should drop them a line soon. How is Armette, should be quite the young eligible lady now. Is Ira Fogelman honeymooning? I'm quite convinced that married life speaks to me and although I haven't the slightest idea whom it will be, I will be ready as soon as conditions permit.

On CQ tonight, reading a good book, "Yankee Lawyer" an autobiography of Ephriam Tutt, a pretty well-known lawyer. That's all for tonight.

Love,
Charlie

Daily Life in Friedrichroda, June 1945

Friday, June 29, 1945

Dear Mom, Dad, and E,

No news at all today. Played volleyball this afternoon but it was a bit too chilly for swimming. The German books arrived today, thank you. I'll try to use them about one hour a day, and perhaps if I'm here another two months I'll be able to talk it pretty well.

In yesterday's letter Mom asked if I get cauliflower? Well, just for dinner today we had some for the first time. Isn't that a coincidence?

No more now, I'm feeling good.

Love and Kisses,
Charlie

Sunday, July 1, 1945

Dear Folks,

Well, our time here is drawing to an end. The advance party left this morning, and we leave tomorrow or Tuesday, so that's that. I'm very sorry to leave. For a few days we're going to be near Bayreuth[337] and we'll be living in pup-tents again. Then we're to go further south to a permanent location. It'll be "fun" living in tents again, first time since Normandy.

Mom, there's one thing about your letters that still bothers me. You continuously say, "Keep your chin up, be optimistic, you're just losing a few years, etc." Mom, I've told you repeatedly that I'm in the best of spirits, I'm always smiling and happy, that I'm not pessimistic in the least, etc. So please lay off that stuff.

Slept until 10:30 this morning and then I shaved and showered. Had a delicious dinner, steak, French fries, corn, coffee, and peaches. Hope you are still eating well.

All my love,
Charlie

---

[337] City in Southern Germany, near the border of Czechoslovakia.

Monday, July 2, 1945

Dear Folks,

Just a short line before I go on guard. We leave here tomorrow morning at 10:30.

Edith, I'm sorry that I have been unable to send a cable for your birthday as yet. Our APO moved a few days ago and we have no mail or cable service. I plan to send Pop ten dollars so he can take you out for the 26th celebration. You, Mom, and Dad. Why, Sis, you're almost an *A.K.*[338] I'll be a bit late, but please excuse me.

Rainy, nasty weather. I'm all packed, in addition to my duffle bag I have a foot-locker; I travel in class. Feeling swell and everything is fine.

Have more pictures when I settle down. Perhaps no letters for a few days. Don't worry, can't get shot at anymore.

Love and Kisses,
Charlie

Wednesday, July 4, 1945 - Munchberg, Germany

Hello Folksies,

Happy Fourth to you. We're going to have a day off tomorrow to celebrate the holiday. It was supposed to be today but since we just arrived here last night, there was a little too much work.

We had a nice trip down, lots of rain but the truck was covered. Boy, the people in Thuringia Province were sorry to see us go.

This is in Bayern Province now and it looks okay. The town is small and we're not allowed out yet, so I can't tell you much about it. We were very fortunate to land in a textile factory. Most of the Division is living in tents. I have a good cot so I'm comfortable. We have a very nice Mess Hall and shower facilities are good. Only thing is that it rains a lot and is very nasty.

That's all for now, we'll be here about one week.

---

[338] Yiddish: *Alter Kaker,* elderly person, old timer.

Love and Kisses,
Charlie

Thursday, July 5, 1945

Dear Mom, Dad, and Sis,

Had a real lazy day. Got up for breakfast at 7 and then did a little reading and brushing up on my German. From 11-12 I took a nap and then had a delicious dinner: steak, French fries, green peas, crushed pineapple and coffee.

Went for a ride on the *Autobahn*[339] highway in the afternoon, and after we got back played ping-pong until about 5. Then a shower and shave was in order and I felt refreshed.

Very little to do, we're just waiting until we get the word to go to our next area. We're going to be in the vicinity of Passau, deep in the heart of Bavaria.

General Keating, the Division Commander, is in the US now and our old man, General Busbee, is at Division so we're not troubled with a General officer. Keating went home with General Simpson and he should be back soon.

All my love,
Charlie

Friday, July 6, 1945

Dear Mom, Pop, and Sis,

More rain again. This place is sure reminiscent of Normandy. We've had about three hours of sun in the four days we've been here.

I finally got a little information regarding our future and I imagine you'd be interested to hear it. From official sources it has been learned that we're sched-

---

[339] The *Autobahn*, officially *Bundesautobahn*, is the federal-controlled access highway system in Germany, famous for the lack of a mandated speed limit. First designed in the mid-1920's, construction work on the not yet completed autobahn system relied on forced workers and concentration camp inmates during WWII. As of 1942, only 3,800 kilometers (app. 2,400 miles) out of a planned 20,000 kilometers (app. 12,000 miles) of autobahn had been completed.

uled to stay in and around Passau[340] until February 1946. Then we are to go to the US and be placed in the "strategic reserve" which you may have heard about. That means more garrison and I imagine a lot depends on the progress of the Japanese War. So, it looks pretty good. At least, it doesn't mean immediate action in the Pacific. All this was official as of 4 July. There's no way of telling when or if plans will be changed.

Pop, enclosed is a ten dollar money order and I want it spent on a little celebration (late as it may be) for Eadie's birthday. I'm sorry it's tardy, but I couldn't get the money order earlier. Go to a show or to a movie and dinner or whatever you want to do. Please do it quickly.

That's about all, taking it easy and eating well. Not a thing to worry about, I'm very content.

Take good care of yourselves,

Love and Kisses,
Charlie

Saturday, July 7, 1945

Dear Mom, Dad, and Sis,

We've had no mail all week and we don't expect any until next Wednesday. Our APO has been moving and it's already down at the new area. I hope to get a big batch next week.

More rain, of course, but the sun made an appearance for a few hours late in the afternoon. There's a movie in town and I plan to go tomorrow afternoon. "The Unseen" is playing and it's supposed to be pretty good.

Eating very well here, we have some excellent cooks and when they do get the rations, they certainly put out good chow.

Eadie, you know what my wishes are for your birthday. I hope it's the last you spend without Artie, and as a belated present I wish that he'd get home soon.

I'm just fine and dandy.

All my love,
Charlie

---

[340] Passau is a city in Lower Bavaria, Germany on the Austrian border. During World War II, the city housed three sub-camps of the infamous Mauthausen-Gusen concentration camp: Passau I (Oberilzmühle), Passau II (Waldwerke Passau-Ilzstadt) and Passau III (Jandelsbrunn).

Sunday, July 8, 1945

Dear Folks,

Woke up to a very beautiful day and surprisingly enough it remained so. There wasn't any rain at all the entire day and that is something. Studied German in the morning and had a good meal at noon. In the afternoon I went to see "The Unseen" with Joel McCrea, Gail Patrick, and Herbert Marshall. It was a good movie, a psychological murder.

Very little else doing. Spent the day reading. Just finished "Earth and High Heaven" and I enjoyed it. It's about a Jewish-Canadian who falls in love with a Gentile girl who is very wealthy and a socialite. It gives the pros and cons of marriage, and it's made into an interesting story - the girl's father ignoring the boy, etc.

We're leaving here Tuesday morning at 5:30. Boy, that means an early rising. It's the first time we're getting away so early. We've always managed to leave a position about 10 or 11, but this time they got us.

Love and Kisses,
Charlie

Wednesday, July 11, 1945 - Passau, Germany

Dear Mom, Dad, and Sis,

Arrived here last night after a 12-hour ride. It was a nice day for traveling but it was quite dusty.

We're set up in a wonderful CP,[341] a former bank or insurance office. Plenty of desks, etc. right in the center of town. It will make a good headquarters for the next half a year or so. Our living quarters are not so hot at present. The 83rd Division Artillery has been here a long while and they, of course, have the better accommodations but they are scheduled to leave this area on August 1 and then we'll have everything we want. The 83rd HQ Battery is in a grand hotel, room for every man and we're getting that on the 1st. Now we have a nice

---

[341] Command Post.

room, I have a cot, it's a bit crowded but clean. We're eating with chinaware, so it's not bad.

There are 40,000 DP's[342] here and the town is packed. I don't know the normal population but it's a pretty big place. An old town and it's located very nicely, Austria and Czechoslovakia are a stone's throw. Perhaps I'll get to visit there in the next few months.

More tomorrow, I'm feeling swell. Out of 11 reserve divisions we're number 10 on the list, so it's highly improbable that we'll ever fight the Japs. Good news, eh?

Please take it easy now, it's hot at home.

All my love,
Charlie

General Charles M. Busbee at the Division Artillery Headquarters

---

[342] Displaced Persons: Displaced Persons Camps in post–World War II Europe were created out of necessity in Germany, Austria, and Italy, primarily for refugees from Eastern Europe and for the former inmates of the Nazi German concentration camps. At the end of WWII, more than 11 million people had been displaced from their home countries, with about seven million in Allied-occupied Germany.

Thursday, July 12, 1945

Hello again,

There's very little to report. We're settled down and it's just that old routine again. There's not too much work although right now I'm busy bringing our files of Army regulations, War Department circulars, etc. up to date.

The weather is perfect, and I hope it stays nice. This is the first place we've found July weather. I never thought I'd see the "Blue Danube" but it's right here in town. Not too impressive, just not the time for sailing on the Danube.[343]

Received a few of your letters but I think more are still to catch up with me. I better start writing more letters to my friends if I want to keep getting mail.

In town you see just about every nationality represented. There are Czechs, Russians, Poles, Hungarian, Romanians, etc. I imagine there are some Jews, but I haven't located any yet.

Well, that's about all this trip. There won't be much to write about now, it's the same old story every day.

Are you closing on Saturdays or are you just too much afraid of being shut one day? Mom and Pop, get away for a rest, it doesn't have to be Atlantic City or a big trip.

Love and Kisses,
Charlie

Friday, July 13, 1945

Dear Mom, Pop, and Sis,

Another lovely day and I think we're set now for a streak of good weather. Took a little ride around town this afternoon and very shortly I plan to go visit Austria just to say I've been there.

---

[343] The Danube River is the second-longest river in Europe, after the Volga in Russia. It flows for 2,850 kilometers (app. 1,770 miles), through much of Central and Southeastern Europe, from the Black Forest into the Black Sea.

Shower facilities aren't too good in town but I think I've found a fair place and I'm going tomorrow morning.

I certainly don't like the idea of being in Patton's Army.[344] Of course, it doesn't make much difference, but he really goes in for "chicken." For instance, now we're only allowed to wear helmet liners, no garrison caps at all, our brims have to be varnished - all little stuff and it doesn't bother me, but it's surprising how petty a high-ranking general can be. I'm trying to get a definite location of Artie's outfit, and if it's at all possible, I'll visit him. Of course, it may be too far away.

Nothing much else to report. Don't believe everything you read about the Education Program in the ETO. It's being run on a very small scale now and we don't have any classes as yet. It's another Army snafu, I think.

I'm feeling fine; nothing to worry about, sleeping and eating well.

All my love,
Charlie

Saturday, July 14, 1945

Hello Folks,

The end of another week, they sure do fly by. I wonder how long we'll stay here? You know, it's supposed to be our definite area but I've learned that nothing but change is definite in the Army. But it appears to be quite definite that we'll be in Europe until January at least.

No, Mom, I don't blame you for praying that I won't go to the Pacific, I now feel as if your prayers have been answered. With the marvelous progress we seem to be making in the Pacific,[345] I doubt if we'll ever get there. As it is now, there are about 20 divisions ahead of us to fight the Japs.

---

[344] George Smith Patton Jr. was a General in the United States Army, famous for his strict discipline and no-nonsense approach. He commanded the Seventh United States Army in the Mediterranean theater of World War II, and the Third United States Army in France and Germany. After Victory in Europe, during the Allied occupation of Germany, Patton was appointed military governor of Bavaria, until being relieved of his position on September 28, 1945 (https://www.history.com/topics/world-war-ii/george-smith-patton).

[345] Japan was to surrender in little over a month, on August 17, 1945.

Yesterday, I told you I'd look up Artie's location. Well, I discovered he was no more than 60 miles away and in a jiffy I started to call him up. Lines were busy but I eventually got him. I couldn't speak long as it was 12 o'clock and I had to go with the truck to the Battery to eat, but we made an appointment for a 12:50 call and I got him in about 40 seconds. He's a little disappointed about those 80 points, but that's natural. His living conditions are good and he sounded well. Isn't that something, call him up anytime I want. I have to go through 5 extensions, division, corps, etc. but I can get him okay. A little hard to hear, but what the hell. Now, I'm going to try to visit him. It's not too easy to get a vehicle, so I may hitchhike down. I'll let you know if I can get to see him.

"The Corn Is Green" is playing tonight and I'm looking forward to it. With Bette Davis in it, it's sure to be good.

Love and Kisses,
Charlie

Sunday, July 15, 1945

Dear Mom, Pop, and Sis,

I received another batch of mail from you today. Glad you had a nice 4th of July. I think Molly and Sam Young make good company for Mom and Dad, and you should go out more often.

Thanks for your opinion about repaying Uncle Mendel. I'll think it over, don't say anything and as soon as I get a hundred together, I'll make up my mind. I think I'll do it.

Was supposed to have the day for myself but the fellow on CQ hit the guard list and I had to take the CQ. That's not bad because there's nothing to do but sit around and read or write letters.

It's beautiful today and this morning I climbed a hill and got a beautiful view of the city and also a good sunning. I hope we find a decent place for swimming. A lot of people go in the Ilz River and that may be a good place. I'll wait until the Division approves a place. I don't go bathing in water that hasn't been inspected.

Well, that's about all, I repeat again that there's very little to write about. Regards to all.

Love and Kisses,
Charlie

Monday, July 16, 1945

Hello Folks,

Had a very warm day but we're having a real thunderstorm tonight and I believe it'll cool things off a bit. I just came back from the theater. I saw "A Christmas in Connecticut." Nothing much, but it was entertaining.

There really is very little doing and therefore very little to write about. We're eating well, quarters are comfortable and if I were a civilian and at home, everything would be fine. But this really isn't bad. I'm quite content.

Mom, it'll soon be birthday time and I wish you every bit of happiness that you desire. You, more than anyone else I know, deserve it. Perhaps now that you are "maturing" and growing up you will have more pleasant days and a better life. May this also be the last birthday you celebrate without your son and son-in-law. Happy Birthday, Mom. I'd send a cable but we haven't been able to for the past few weeks. I'll try.

Love and Kisses,
Charlie

Tuesday, July 17, 1945

Dear Mom, Dad, and E,

Weather continues to be lovely and everything else is also okey-doke.

Jack Benny's show was here today, and it was very good. Ingrid Bergman is a beautiful and gracious woman, she did some of her lines from Joan of Arc - the play she'll appear in on Broadway in the Fall. I met her after the show and she is one actress who has natural beauty. Marta Tilton did some very good singing, and a real cute one from the show, "Follow the Girls" - she can still put them over. Larry Adler performed on his harmonica and he is a wizard. He played

Fitz's Second Hungarian Rhapsody and that's a feat on the harmonica. And there was also a good GI band from some Armored Division.

There's quite a gas shortage right now. Of course, it just cuts down on pleasure riding, etc. so it's not serious. As far as I'm concerned, let them send all of the gas to the Pacific.

Enclosed is a 20 mark note that Ingrid Bergman autographed, please save it for me, E.

All my love,
Charlie

Thursday, July 19, 1945

Dear Folks,

Not a blessed thing new. General Patton is going to be in Passau the 24th, and the 83rd Division will probably parade for him. The MP's are now trying to get things in shape and they stop everyone who is not in the proper uniform, etc.

I'm trying to figure out a way to get over to Artie. I don't think I can get a vehicle for the sole purpose of going to Landshut. The best bet is hitchhiking but there's some rule about staying out of another Division's area, and I'll have to check into that. Art called me last night but I wasn't in. He wants me to call back at 11:30 and I'll do that.

It continues to be nice and everything is in good shape. Get a little mail from my friends but I'm not as good a correspondent as I used to be.

Well, that's all for now. Take good care of yourselves. Still think you should close on Saturdays during August.

Received a very nice package from Charles and June today.

Love and Kisses,
Charlie

Saturday, July 21, 1945

Dear Folks,

Had a little fun today. Third Army conducted a search for weapons in the homes and we had to do it in our area. It was kept secret and when we started at 5:30 AM, the Krauts were certainly surprised. Of course, we didn't find any guns, one or two knives, that was all.[346]

Artie told me that he's going to try to visit me tomorrow, I hope he can make it.

About the homes I went into today. My group had a poor district but there was no need for the homes to be so dirty. I thought that Germans were pretty clean but I'm inclined to think differently now. Most of the Krauts tried to be friendly and many were the offers of *schnapps*,[347] etc.

Thank you so much for your two latest packages. What swell people you all are. Everything is just swell. The cookies were grand. If you need a request, Sis, I'll be able to eat more cookies, anchovies, or whatever you send.

Love,
Charlie

Sunday, July 22, 1945

Dear Mom, Pop, and Sis,

I took a few days off from letter writing. I'll do that every once in a while, because there's just nothing to write about and then again I get a bit tired of writing at times.

Today was Sunday and it was a bit civilianish. I had a visitor - Artie Marshak. I expected him this morning and I was waiting for him in our CP. He came up with a friend and a driver in a jeep. It was a little after eleven by the time we got to the Battery and we all washed up. Chow wasn't served until 12:30 so we sat

---

[346] Though Charlie may have come up empty handed, the operation as a whole was successful. In this initiative, 1,837 citizens were apprehended for possessing either improper credentials or none at all. Among the weapons uncovered in the Division's area of operations were 2 machine-guns, 211 rifles, 10 pistols, 92 swords, bayonets, and daggers, and 8 grenades. Additionally, $5,000,000 worth of opium was confiscated from the Hungarian Navy anchored in the Danube. (With the 102nd Infantry Division Through Germany, pg. 247).

[347] Alcoholic Beverage.

around our room and I had some olives June sent and cheese from you with crackers. So, it was very nice. Dinner was good and the boys sure enjoyed it. Artie claims we get more and better food than his Company does.

We took the jeep out in the afternoon and rode along the Danube for a while and snapped a few shots. Then we decided to go to Austria and it was a lovely ride. Austria is a very lovely country, and we rode for quite a while before stopping at a beer garden and drinking a couple. We took some pictures there and I hope they come out okay.

We got back a little before chow and just sat around talking. Supper was also good and the boys just left to go back. I think they had a nice day, it's always good to get away from your own place.

Art is looking very well. Much better than when I saw him last September. He's in pretty good humor and has high hopes of being home next winter. He's still as nice as ever, E. We get along fine together.

That's all now. Artie sends his love to all of you.

Love and Kisses,
Charlie

Tuesday, July 24, 1945

Dear Mom, Pop, and Sis,

Receiving a little mail from you, thanks a lot. Mom's last letter told me of how optimistic Artie was on July 5th. Well, there is still a lot of strong talk of lowering the point score to 80, so perhaps he will get home soon. At any rate, E, you know he's coming home in good condition and a little earlier or later won't mean too much. After seeing all these mutilated German men, I realize how lucky Artie and I are to be in such good condition.

Did I tell you that the other night we had an all-German stage show? The 83rd Division Artillery got the talent together and we hope to keep it up. There's an excellent 15-piece band, a few good dancers, several accordionists, comedian, magician, etc. It was quite entertaining.

The weather continues to be nice. It warms up quite a bit in the afternoon but it doesn't bother me. That's all for now, more tomorrow.

Love and Kisses,
Charlie

Thursday, July 26, 1945

Hiya Folks,

Received July 18th and 20th's letters from Ma. If it wasn't for you, Mom, my take of mail would be very slim. I'm glad that my July 11th line was reassuring. Now with the marvelous news about the Jap War[548] I'm more confident than ever that I won't get to the Pacific.

Mother, my nerves haven't been affected one bit by the war. It's still the same. In fact, I'm still the same person who went away September '43. Artie and I talked about this business of re-adjusting and we both agree that all we need is discharge papers and a civilian suit and we'll be ready to play the part of normal American citizens. Have no fear about that.

I don't understand why E doesn't tell Artie she's buying a beaver coat with her own money? It's about time that you stopped buying things for your children and Art doesn't expect you to get clothes for E anymore. That's their problem now and I think that Art realizes that he and E must pay their own way now. You certainly deserve a coat, Mom, but perhaps a Persian lamb is a bit too expensive. However, you know best on that matter. Incidentally, didn't Ellie give E a beaver jacket?

I appreciate your trying to mail a package to Holland. Maybe the post office will accept them soon. I'll write the people.

That's about all. I missed writing yesterday as I was on guard. Tonight, I'm CQ. It's nice and warm. Feeling fine and everything is swell. Take good care of yourselves, be careful during these very hot days. You can't become millionaires in one week.

All my love,
Charlie

Thanks for the stamps. Request: in your next package enclose some face soap please, also any other goodies that you can manage to acquire.

[548] TOn July 24, the United States Third Fleet began the bombing of Kure, Hiroshima. In this action, the Allied navy sank most of the surviving large warships of the Imperial Japanese Navy.

A Sunday afternoon out with Artie

Saturday, July 28, 1945

Hello Folksies,

I hope you had a pleasant birthday Maw. Next year it will be nicer, I think. You should have your two boys home by then.

I met a soldier today who left this part of Germany 20 years ago and he just visited his mother and father. They didn't recognize him at first (he's 33) but they were overjoyed at seeing him. That's some experience, eh?

We're becoming sharpies. We just got Eisenhower jackets[349] and now we're getting the Ozark on our helmet liners. I think the insignia looks nice on the front, but no, the Division Commander wants it on the right side and that's where it'll be. They're also taking our names off.

Everything is pleasant. I'm doing a lot of typing. I told you I'm typing out a German course. This I&E program is just a lot of noise. The quotas to the civilian universities are negligible and the other courses are no good at all.

I'm just fine, hope you're all well. Love to the Grannies.

Love and Kisses,
Charlie

Sunday, July 29, 1945

Dear Mom, Dad, and Sis,

All is well on this last Sunday in July. It's a lovely day and I just finished a delicious chicken dinner. I'm going to spend the rest of the day writing letters and reading a little. One of the fellows got a book, I forget the exact title but it's about the Russian people. I'm going to start it today.

I spoke to a Russian Lieutenant in our headquarters yesterday. He came to help us send some more Russian nationals home. I told you we had a lot of DP's (displaced persons) here and we're trying to send as many home as we possibly can. Many don't want to go back to their homes and that makes the job quite difficult.

---

[349] Developed for the US Army personnel during the later stages of WWII, The Eisenhower jacket or "Ike" jacket, officially known as the Jacket, Field, Wool, Olive Drab, is a type of waist-length jacket named in honor of the General.

Too bad the dumb Japs didn't accept our surrender terms.[350] Now we'll really give them everything we have and that's plenty. Gosh, that country will be "*ka-put*" after this is over.

We're supposed to move into the hotel on Thursday, that's good. Although things aren't bad at all, now.

All my love,
Charlie

Tuesday, July 31, 1945

Dear Mom, Dad, and Sis,

Here's the end of another month. Just received my pay and I'll send Uncle Mendel a money order for $100 shortly. It's cooled off considerably, but I think it'll warm up again real soon. The nights are always cool and that's conducive to good sleeping.

Went to the movies this afternoon and saw "The Great John L." It's all about the prize fighter John L. Sullivan, and it's entertaining to say the least. It should help to cure some people from drinking excessively. Sullivan was just about to go to the dogs when he stopped "indulging." I'm thankful that Pop isn't a drinking man. Perhaps I get my moderation from him.

We move into the Eisenhower Hotel tomorrow afternoon. It's an easy move, just our living quarters. The CP is remaining in its present location.

That's all folks,

All my love,
Charlie

---

[350] On July 26, 1945, United States President Harry S. Truman, United Kingdom Prime Minister Winston Churchill, and President of China Chiang Kai-shek released The Potsdam Declaration, or the Proclamation Defining Terms for Japanese Surrender. This statement called for the surrender of all Japanese armed forces with the ultimatum that if they failed to do so, the result would be their "prompt and utter destruction." (trumanlibraryinstitute.org/wwii-75-marching-victory-17/)

Wednesday, August 1, 1945

Dear Folks,

We moved as scheduled and the hotel is certainly nice. There are a lot of Hungarian women working around the place and they cleaned it up before we moved in. We always clean up a place before leaving but our new quarters are always left dirty.

I'm in a large room facing the street. Three men (including myself). We all have good beds and there's enough closet space and room to move around. It's a little too much like civilian life - got a bed lamp, dining room on the main floor and hot running water, oh me! So, once again, I'm very comfortable.

Will call up Art today, perhaps make arrangements to see him soon. The pictures we took didn't come out well at all. I'm disappointed, probably didn't have the camera set right. Will enclose them in a line to E.

It's still cool, coolest August I remember. Be good and take care of yourselves. Glad Dad got away, now your turn Mom.

Love,
Charlie

Thursday, August 2, 1945

Dear Folks,

Settled down in our new home and it's mighty satisfactory. All I have to do is find some sheets for my bed and I'll be okay. The bed is very comfortable.

I just read the news that the point score is to remain at 85 for the time being. Well, Sis, that's too bad but you still have to be grateful. Even if the score was lowered it would take months before all the men could get home. Perhaps early in the Fall they'll lower it.

It's still pleasantly cool here and the days are comfortable. Some change from New York August, but the hot ones are yet to come, I guess.

Have a $100 money order for Uncle Mendel and I'll send it out today. I'm in CQ tonight and I had letters to write, loads of letters.

Bob Hope is due here early next week and he's going to put up at our officer's hotel. He may eat with us a few times, thrill - huh?

Nothing else now, be good, take it easy, and take care of yourselves.

All my love,
Charlie

Sunday, August 5, 1945

Dear Mom, Pop, and Sis,

I was sure thrilled to receive Dad's letter from the Mountains. Boy, the Old Man got away at last. I guess the last time you were away, Pop, was when we went to Lakewood. I hope you enjoyed yourself and that the weather turned out better. I hope that Mom is now on her vacation. Please, Ma, get away soon.

I'm glad you got a bag with the dough I sent home. That will always come in handy. Eadie's gift of a housecoat is also a dandy.

Had a pleasant day. General Busbee inspected the hotel and our rooms yesterday. Tomorrow General Keating, the Division Commander, is inspecting the Artillery and he may very well visit the Battery. So we're getting up at 5:45 to prepare, real Army.

Glad to hear that everything is going along okay. E, don't be blue.

I love you all a little bit.

Love,
Charlie

Monday, August 6, 1945

Dear Mom, Pop, and Sis,

I have a new job for the time being and it looks like a good one. Special Services for the Artillery has grown by leaps and bounds and there was a need for a clerk-administrative, keep payroll for the actors, etc. Yesterday afternoon when I got back from the Bob Hope show, Major Becker told me to report to the Special Service Officer and here I am.

It's a good deal in a way. Our office is in one of our theaters and it's nice and clean, freshly painted. There's plenty of work and I'll be kept quite busy. I don't mind that, though. A 1st Lt. is in charge and he's a go-getter. Really accomplished a lot, I'll let you know more about it later.

Was disappointed with the Hope Show. I think he was a little vexed. He had to make two plane trips down. He came in a C-47 the first time and there wasn't a suitable field here so they had to go back to Regensburg and come down again in a smaller plane. And then, the lights were *kaput*, the loudspeaker snafued, so I guess he wasn't in too good a mood to perform. Jerry Colona was along and some lesser lights.

That's all now, take it easy. Mom, tell me about your vacation, you better get away this month.

All my love,
Charlie

Tuesday, August 7, 1945

Dear Mom, Dad, and Sis,

Everything is getting along okey-doke. I'm kept quite busy on the new job and I like it. We run a lot of stage shows, movies, boat rides, etc. and the office is usually bursting with activity.

Had my first German lesson yesterday and I'm quite ahead of the class since most of the men are just starting. There's very little to write about, it's the same stuff every day. I'm eagerly awaiting word that Mom is on her vacation. One of the boys is on his way home for emergency reasons and he may give you a ring, he lives in the Bronx.

The Army is sure getting a lot of criticism these days. I guess that's the natural reaction in a peace-loving country after a long war. Some of our senators are sure lambasting the War Department, and I'm with them on a lot of points.

I'm quite content, living and eating well. Be good and take care of yourselves. E, try your best to go away with Mom.

All my love,
Charlie

Wednesday, August 8, 1945

Hiya Gang,

Thanks for a swell package. A big fruit cake, cheese, candy and soup. Who has the best family in the world?

I'm sorry Mary took her vacation before you got away, Mom. However, be sure to go away as soon as she returns, and no maybe about it.

Well, the news is certainly coming in fast and thick. First, the new atomic bomb and then Russia's declaration of war on Japan. Boy, things are progressing rapidly. I can only give the Japs about three months now. That bomb is a devastating thing and it's just about the beginning of new things to come. Don't you think so? They certainly have to control such a "weapon." Can you imagine such a thing wiping out a whole city?

Everything is fine here, feeling swell, little rain tonight.

Send my best regards to all.
Love,
Charlie

Friday, August 10, 1945

Dear Mom, Pop, and Sis,

It's a beautiful day and everything is coming along nicely. I'm in such an optimistic frame of mind now that I think the Jap war will be over by the time I get back to the States. I think the Japs have had just about enough and are ready to throw in the towel.[351]

I just called up Artie, but the connection was very poor, and I couldn't hear him. I would like to repay his visit, but I can't get a vehicle for that purpose, and I don't particularly care for the idea of hitchhiking.

We're having a boat ride tonight on the Danube, it should be pretty nice.

---

[351] On August 6, the United States B-29 Superfortress *Enola Gay* dropped a uranium-235 atomic bomb on the Japanese city of Hiroshima. With that city brought to its knees, just three days later on August 9, the B-29 bomber *Bockscar* dropped a plutonium-239 atomic bomb on the Japanese city of Nagasaki. The two bombings killed between 129,000 and 226,000 people, majority of whom were civilians.

This afternoon we're having a parade. We've had no practice whatsoever and I'm afraid to think of how bad it's going to be. A few decorations are going to be awarded. No, I'm not getting any - I don't want any.

Well, that's all now. E, I'm not forgetting your anniversary. Next year you'll have Artie for a grand celebration. Best of luck to you and heartiest congratulations.

Love and Kisses,
Charlie

Saturday, August 11, 1945

Dear Mom, Pop, and Sis,

I'm eagerly awaiting final word on Japan's capitulation. Rumors are plentiful but nothing official has come through yet, so we're still keeping our fingers crossed. Isn't it all so wonderful? Many people expected the end of Japan soon after V-E Day, but I doubt whether anyone foresaw such a speedy end. The Army announced yesterday that 3,000,000 men will be released in the first year after the defeat of Japan. Well, it might still be a long time for me, but this is the beginning of the end now so it's okay.

The boat ride was nice last night. It rained but that didn't bother us as we were inside. The ship was a very good one, quite modern, I believe it was Hungarian at one time.

Hal McIntyre and his band are going to play here on Friday. Patton is also coming here again this week. I'm quite sure the men would rather have McIntyre than Patton.

Everything is just fine. I'm CQ tomorrow so that takes care of a Sunday.

All my love,
Charlie

Sunday, August 12, 1945

Hello Again,

If I were the Japanese Council, I would surely accept our peace terms. And I think they will accept any minute now. In a way, it's advisable to allow them to keep Hirohito,[352] through him we will be able to do more administering, etc. and the people will take it as a matter of fact if the Emperor directs so and so. I consider him more as a pagan God than a politician or statesman. It was never our intent to destroy a people's religion, so I'm not against allowing him to remain. However, all the war criminals in Japan should be brought to trial, what a relief this will be for the entire world.

Mom, get your vacation now. You might be kept very busy this Fall. Don't celebrate too much when the war is all over. I don't want you to get too severe a hangover or become a drunkard. I know it's very difficult to find a suitable apartment (cost, etc.) but perhaps you could find a little larger place in not too an expensive house so Mom and Pop can have a bedroom and I could have a small den-room or hole in the wall for myself. Then a nice living room and kitchenette is all we'd need. E won't be with you people too long. They'll really start sending the men home after V-J.[353]

Love,
Charlie

Monday, August 13, 1945

Dear Mom, Pop, and Sis,

Nothing much has happened lately, still awaiting final word. The Japs are surely taking their time. I just heard a broadcast and it said that an answer is expected momentarily. Well, I'm ready.

We had a variety show tonight and it wasn't too bad considering it was comprised of a bunch of gypsies.

---

[352] Hirohito was the 124th Emperor of Japan, ruling from 1926 until his death in 1989.

[353] Victory in Japan.

The weather is okay. To be truthful there's not a thing to report, same old life. Ate some good sardines today with tomato juice. If you need a request, I could use cookies, cheese, etc.

Not working too hard, start on this payroll business shortly.

Really nothing more now. Will try to write more tomorrow. We have a little kitchen in the theater and the *Frau* just made some delicious fritters, very delicious, not as good as Mom's though.

Love and Kisses,
Charlie

Wednesday, August 15, 1945

> *Glory Halleluiah! Sholom Aleichem!*
>
> *Got zie dank! Vos ich ker*[354]

Well, this is it and I'm certainly thankful. Even took out my little prayer book this morning and read a few passages. I can imagine how joyous you must be. I heard a re-broadcast of the celebrations in Times Square, that must have been some jubilant crowd. Did you have a few good drinks? I have some wine, but I'm saving it for our Battery party Friday night.

Your job is still good for a while, isn't it, Sis? Artie's chances now look better, but don't count on anything. No one knows what's what now. Not too much celebration here, we're still in the Army, maybe that's why.

No more right now. Thank God it's over and we're all safe and sound. Regards to all.

Love and Kisses,
Charlie

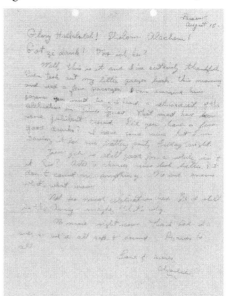

---

[354] German: Thank you God!

Friday, August 17, 1945

THE WAR IS OVER, ISN'T THAT GREAT?

I CAN HARDLY BELIEVE IT.

Dear Mom, Dad, and Sis,

Now that the war is over, I'm taking it a little easy and if I don't write a letter everyday don't get excited. You'll get plenty of mail from me, but perhaps every now and then I'll skip a day or two.

Today is our Victory Day holiday and we're all loafing around. Had breakfast at 8, dinner at 12:30 and supper will be at 5:30 tonight. We're having a party and a 15-piece band will play. In addition, Hal McIntyre is playing in the Auditorium at 8 PM and I think I'll drop in to hear him.

The other night, Wednesday, I had to go to a party on the boat. The Special Service Office always has to have one man on the boat for supervision of the band, etc. It was a nice dance and a good buffet dinner. Monday night my section has its party at the town's only night club. Some rough life, eh?

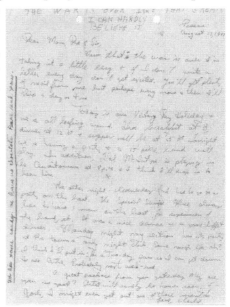

I think I'll put in for a two-day pass so I can get down to see Artie, probably next week.

A great package from you yesterday. Why are you so good? Artie will surely be home soon, E. Gosh, I might even get out one of these months.

Love,
Charlie

Saturday, August 18, 1945

Dear Folks,

What a SNAFU Army. After getting all set-up here and making everything permanent, we get the word to move. We're supposed to leave next week and in typical Army fashion we're going back to the vicinity of Bayreuth (Munchberg) where we stayed for a week on our way down here from Friedrichroda. It's over 100 miles away and believe me, we're all bummed up about it but there's not much we can do.

The 83rd Division is coming back here and I understand that the 4th Armored is also moving in. Really no need for two divisions in this area.

Everything else is okey-doke. The move won't be hard as we'll shuttle our stuff and have enough time. It's warmed up a bit to let us know it's still August.

Nothing else new. Mom, let's hurry up and get away for your rest.

Love to all,
Charlie

Monday, August 20, 1945

Dear Mom, Pop, and Sis,

We're here for another two weeks yet, so the move will come around September 5. We'll be near Coburg and Bayreuth and we relieve the 9th Armored Division which is slated to go home shortly. It still looks as if we'll be here until the first of the year but I think the truth is that no one knows exactly when we'll head for home, but it should be early next year.

If you have to sign a new lease this Fall, please consider a larger place in another house. E will be going to her home any month, probably in the late Fall or early winter, and there'll be the three of us. It's not so necessary to be in such a swanky house. On 87th Street between Amsterdam and Columbus there are some good middle-class apartment-houses. See if you can get anything there.

I could use a little dough, since I sent Uncle Mendel the $100, I've been broke.

Love,
Charlie

Wednesday, August 22, 1945

Dear Mother, Father, and Sister, (formal today)

Lovely day and I may go on a boat ride at 10 AM. It's 9 now and I may have to take one of our bands out to the boat. The day ride is from 10-4, that'll be a nice way to spend the day.

Nothing much new, I'm afraid our next location will be Munchberg, the place we stayed for a week. I didn't think much of the place then, perhaps it was too crowded. The 83rd Division Artillery is coming back today so we'll be crowded for a while.

I'm back from the boat ride and I had a pleasant time. Nothing to do but collect the money for the band and see that they play enough. Pretty soft, eh?

Well, that's all for today. More tomorrow.

Love and Kisses,
Charlie

Thursday, August 23, 1945

Dear Mom, Dad, and Sis,

I got a real big batch of mail from you yesterday, thanks a lot, you lovely people.

Aunt Rose was very thoughtful to send you $100 for a vacation, Mom. God knows, it should only be used for that and for nothing else. I'm still awaiting word that you're on vacation.

Spoke to Murray Goldblatt today. The connection was good for a few seconds and then it got very bad. However, we got to exchange a few words and he said everything is okay. Buster is in Mississippi.

Oh yes, Uncle Mendel dropped me a line and told me it was nice to be remembered. He bought me a $150 bond with my money order.

Everything else is okay. If everything goes well, I'll be off to see Art this weekend.

Love and Kisses,
Charlie

Tuesday, August 28, 1945

Dear Mom, Pop, and Sis,

Got back okay from my visit to Artie. I left there yesterday morning around 9 and I got back here at 1:30. Had a nice stay with him. He's got most of his weight back and Mother, he still has his color, so don't worry.

I sincerely hope that Mom and Sis are on their vacation now. I hope you did right by putting that $100 check toward your coat, Mom. I would have liked to see it go toward your vacation, but let's hope it all works out well.

The weather has surely warmed up a lot. It's been a funny summer. Cool up to the last two weeks in August and now hot as blazes, oh well.

Keeping busy in the office, eating well. E, what are your plans concerning an apartment?

Love and Kisses to *Pessa, Shmiel* and *Yenta*,
Charlie

Wednesday, August 29, 1945

Hello Gang,

Things are beginning to pop now. All men in the division with 65 points are scheduled to leave within a week, the same things as in Artie's division. Men with less than 45 (I have 38) may also leave in the near future but there's nothing definite on that. Once they start counting, I'll have around 46 but I don't know what good that'll do me. All we can do is wait, at least now it's only a matter of time, no more war involved or Pacific.

It's sure hot. Quite a surprise after the cool summer. Pop, now that you had a vacation you must be going stronger than ever. I imagine you're cutting until 3 AM every morning. Be sure that the Old Lady gets away.

We'll start moving in another week, don't know exactly when. Will let you know.

Take good care of yourselves.

Love and Kisses,
Charlie

Thursday, August 30, 1945

Dear Mom, Pop, and Sis,

Another real hot day, how is it back home now? I bet you're still spending a lot of time down at the Drive, Dad.

Was Charge of Quarters last night and got a good night's sleep. There isn't anything to do on that job but hang around.

We start moving Saturday and I expect I'll be here until the 5th or 6th or thereabouts. In a way I'm sorry to leave this place, good set-up, etc. but it may be better in a small place. The winter is going to be pretty rough and it might be bad in too large a town with so many people going hungry and cold, etc. At least in a small town you don't have so many people to contend with.

I have to work in the CP tomorrow because the other two clerks will be away.

Feeling fine, everything is swell. Take good care of yourselves.
Love and Kisses,
Charlie

Friday, August 31, 1945

Dear Folks,

Well, I have some good news concerning Artie. He's going to the 16th Armored Division, the same division that our 65 pointers are going to. The 16th Division is in Czechoslovakia now and it is scheduled to leave for the port on September 7th and its shipping date is supposed to be September 28th. Now, all that was told to us by our Battery Commander last night and he got it from the Division Commander. So if all this poop is correct, Artie will be home early in October. I called Art last evening and gave him all this information. All he knew was that he was leaving this morning (Friday) for the 16th Division. Well, I hope that all works out.

As for myself, it was a little bad news. All men with less than 45 points may be in the Army of Occupation, for how long no one knows. I already have 8 points coming and that gives me 46, but by then they may raise the requirement for going home. We'll have to wait and see. I wouldn't worry about it if I were you.

All my love,
Charlie

Snapshots of Passau

— PATTON   September 5
Bad Tölz
(near Munich)

Hi Folks,

Well here I am — just me the above address and your letters will ... this morning & had a nice 130 mile ...

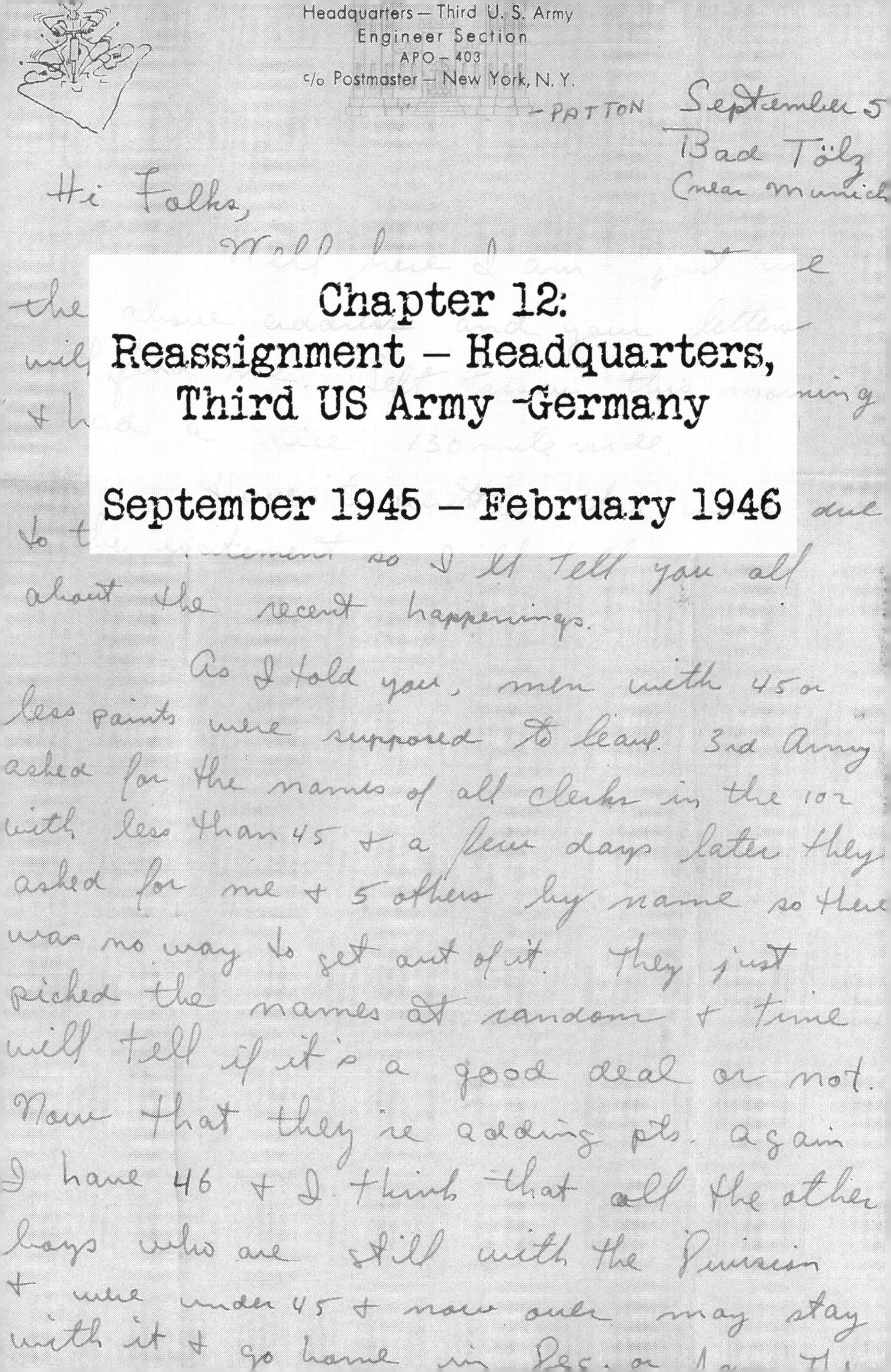

... so I'll tell you all about the recent happenings.

As I told you, men with 45 or less points were supposed to leave. 3rd Army asked for the names of all clerks in the 102 with less than 45 & a few days later they asked for me & 5 others by name so there was no way to get out of it. They just picked the names at random & time will tell if it's a good deal or not. Now that they're adding pts. again I have 46 & I think that all the other boys who are still with the Division & were under 45 & now over may stay with it & go home in Dec. or Jan. ...

After his reassignment based on the Point System, Charlie arrived in Bad Tölz, Germany, some 45 kilometers (app. 30 miles) south of Munich on September 5, 1945. There he was assigned to the Engineer Section, Headquarters Third US Army. During this time, Charlie was stationed in the now repurposed SS-Junkerschule, an officers training school for the Waffen-SS that had been established in 1937.

The US Army Engineers played an integral part in the occupation and reconstruction of post-World War II Germany. The US Zone of Occupation in Germany covered about 47,000 miles, contained few industrial resources and only two major cities—Frankfurt and Munich. In July 1945, the Zone comprised about 19 million people, including many refugees from Eastern Europe.[355] In addition to administrative roles, the Engineers were also assigned the task of assisting in reconstruction of infrastructure destroyed during the war. No small task, seeing as 81% of all lodging units in the US Zone were either completely destroyed or severely damaged. The city of Frankfurt, which served as Headquarters of the American military government, had only 44,000 of 177,000 residences left standing.[356]

---

[355] Building for Peace, US Army Engineers in Europe 1945-1997, pg. 12

[356] Ibid. pg. 7

Throughout this time, Charlie served in the administrative section of the Engineers. Among other duties, he was responsible for the troop assignment and allocation to the Information and Education Programs in Europe. These Information and Education Programs were part of the United States Armed Forces Institute, which was established in 1942 with the goal of enabling soldiers to continue their education and prepare themselves for life after the war.[357] While on Occupational Duty, American soldiers had the option of taking courses in specialized army-training centers, correspondence courses, or in-person attendance in participating civilian universities throughout Europe. Indeed, the Army had secured quotas for 32,000 soldier-students at thirty-five European civilian colleges.[358] In terms of the scope of this project, some 27,114 correspondence courses were processed during 1945, and a total of 21,799 students had graduated from their eight-week course by the time the Army training centers were closed in 1946.[359]

---

[357] How to Plan, Organize and Promote an Off-Duty Education Program - Headquarters, Army Service Forces, 1945 pg. 13

[358] The US Army in the Occupation of Germany 1944-1946, pg. 330

[359] The American Military Occupation of Germany 1945-1953, pg. 106

Saturday, September 1, 1945

Dear Mom, Pop, and Sis,

Gosh, how time flies. Another September here and I can hardly imagine it. This time last year I was enjoying one of my last weekend passes at home. Oh well, I'll be there one of these months.

We're having a beer party tonight in honor of the 20 men who are leaving to-morrow morning. There'll be a few drunk soldiers around, I'm sure - don't worry, I won't be one of them.

Yesterday I saw something quite humorous. Two jeeps were passing by - the first had a gas can attached to the back and one of the people in the second jeep was sounding a siren - a real big racket - well, it was a wedding procession. A nurse and some GI officer, I couldn't see. On the back of the 1st jeep there was a big sign which said, *"Just Married - she got him this morning, but he'll get her tonight."*

Love,
Charlie

Wednesday, September 5, 1945 - Bad Tölz (near Munich)

Headquarters- Third US Army

Engineer Section

APO-403

C/O Postmaster- New York, New York

Hi Folks,

Well, here I am – just use the above address and your letters will find me. Left Passau this morning and had a nice 130-mile ride.

Haven't written this week due to the excitement, so I'll tell you all about the recent happenings. As I told you, men with 45 or less points were supposed to leave. The 3rd Army asked for the names of all clerks in the 102nd Division with less than 45 points; a few days later they asked for me and five others by name so there was no way to get out of it. They just picked the names at random and time will tell if it's a good deal or not. Now that they're adding points again I have 46, and I think that all the other boys who are still with the Division and were under 45 and now over, may stay with it and go home in December or January. Then again, they may have to go someplace too. I'll tell you about the others when I hear from them.

As to how long I'm here for - can't venture a guess. But here's the thing. This is a great deal as far as an assignment - I'm in an Army HQ (Patton is in the same building), and that's just about the best set-up, although good old HQ Battery was good enough for me.

I'll go into detail about living quarters and facilities tomorrow, I'm tired now. But we're housed in a former OCS[360] school for SS troops and the facilities are marvelous, everything in one huge building. Got a cot, took most of my junk from Passau, glad I did. Nice Mess Hall, tablecloths, etc. Chow, well only one meal so far and just fair, but I'll reserve my opinion. Close to 100 WAC's,[361] about 500 soldiers all told. I'm used to smaller groups and the privacy that goes with it, but I'm happy.

All is well.
Love,
Charlie

Thursday, September 6, 1945

Dear Mom, Dad, and Sis,

I must say that an Army Headquarters lives in grand style. Our set-up isn't of a homey nature, no homes or hotel, but this SS school is really something. I'll try my best to explain the place although I haven't seen all of it yet.

The main building is a huge rectangular structure - I guess it's over ½ mile around. There's everything I need in the one building. I live on the 2nd floor in a nice spacious room with six other men, just down the corridor is a shower room with hot water. About two minutes' walk from my room is the Engineer Section. There's a laundry, tailor, barbershop, a huge theater, game room, library, day rooms, pool, PX - well, everything. Just about 100 yards from the big

---

[360] Officer Candidate School.

[361] The Women's Army Corps.

building is an NCO club, music every night and drinks, champagne, liquor, gin, etc.

I visited the town tonight and it's pretty nice. It's about the size of Gardelegen. The Red Cross Country Club is about the nicest I've seen. A gorgeous club house with beautiful grounds, doughnuts, coffee, music. Very little to do with the German girls, no beer halls going or dancing parties with the Krauts.

My job is interesting. Oh, first I'll tell you about this morning when we reported for duty. Two men had to go to 3rd Army rear in Munich and I didn't like that, since I was here, I wanted to stay put and everything looked well. I was chosen after the Personnel Officer looked at the records or after he looked at my shaped head; that's better, eh Pop?

I'm in the administrative section of the Engineer and I'm doing the Information and Education work. Get quotas for Army Engineer troops, go through the applications - and I do the work - no officer telling me when or how. In fact, enlisted men are the bosses in my section. I really like that set-up. They give you credit for having some brains.

I'm happy, big GI band at the noon day meal. Chow is okay.

Love and Kisses,
Charlie

Friday, September 7, 1945

Happy *Rosh Hashanah*,

Two years today, my dear family, I've been an *Americanisha Soldat*. I can still remember Mom and Pop sending me off that Monday morning in 1943. Mom even tried to sing "Johnny, get your gun." This should really be the last New Year I'm away from home, don't you think? The Army is sending a lot of men home and my turn will eventually come.

Artie is all set now, in the Stars and Stripes it says that men with 85 points will be in the States by October 31. Hold tight, Sis, any day now. Are you making any plans for an apartment? I think you should, although I realize how difficult it is to find anything. However, I remember you telling me about Walter saving you a place in his house. Is there anything to that now?

We're about one mile away from town but there's bus service and plenty of other vehicles. I went in for a short while this evening. I tried to get into Munich tonight for the services[362] but I couldn't catch a ride. I'll do my best to go tomorrow, it's a good 1 ½ hour trip to Munich.

My job is good and I'm very well satisfied. I'm in charge of all the I&E[363] stuff for the Engineers. Once I get settled down here, I'll try to go away for a course myself. Right now I want to establish myself in the office; what a shape head, eh Dad?

Many fellows still wear their old patches on the left shoulder, but I think I'll put on the 3rd Army patch and put the Ozark on the right side. After all, I'm in a new outfit and I may as well get accustomed to it.

This place is very much like a camp in the States. You have to go out a gate to get on the street, pass, etc. It's beautiful though.

I'm feeling grand. Love to all, most love to you three.

Happy New Year,
Love,
Charlie

Monday, September 10, 1945

Hiya Gang,

Had a swell time yesterday and I know you'll excuse the lack of a letter.

We are supposed to work on Sunday mornings from 9-12, but yesterday about seven of us got a vehicle and went to Garmisch-Partenkirchen, about 30-35 miles away. It's the town where the highest mountain in Germany is and it's a good spot for sightseeing. There is a train going to the top of the mountain, the *Zugspitze*, at 9 and 10 AM. We arrived at 10:15 but we caught up to the train at the only other stop. It took us way up and it was quite chilly. It was the first time that I've ever been on the top of a real high mountain and it was an interesting experience.

---

[362] *Rosh Hashanah* Synagogue services.

[363] Information and Education.

I went to the very top on one of these cable elevators that we see in the movies. It's about 10,000 feet. The day was very cloudy so I couldn't see too much. When it's clear you can see Austria, Italy, and Czechoslovakia from the peak. So I'm beginning to see a little, I hope we can get away soon again, I'd like to get down to Berchtesgaden.[364]

From now on, all we have to do on Sundays is report in at 9 and then we can take off a few minutes later. And with the two additional afternoons off, things aren't so bad.

I'm enjoying my work very much and I am very well adjusted here. The class of boy, as an average, is a little better here and I

Charlie in Berchtesgaden

get along very well with everyone. When things get settled (old men leave and low-pointers come in) I'll try to get away to London for a week. Please send me $100 soon, take it out of one of my blanks that I signed. I'm sure to go somewhere soon and I don't want to be caught flat.

Incidentally, I'm quite sure that I'll be here Christmas, so you don't have to worry about not sending packages. Just let them come.

All my love,
Charlie

---

[364] A municipality in the district Berchtesgadener Land, Bavaria, in southeastern Germany, near the border with Austria, 180 kilometers (110 miles) southeast of Munich.

Wednesday, September 12, 1945

Dear Mom, Dad, and Sis,

All's well in the foothills of the Bavarian Alps. The scenery here is just gorgeous. We're right at the bottom of all the mountains and it's very scenic country. I'll try to send home some pictures shortly.

I was off this afternoon and I took a few shots of the Headquarters, hope they come out okay. Enclosed are some pictures of the *Zugspitze*, I wrote you about in my last letter.

I just got through speaking with Artie, we had a good connection and he certainly sounded happy. He said that the 16th Armored goes to Le Havre this Sunday. Stinky will be home by October 15th at least, and a civilian by November 1st. Happy Day, eh *Yentala*?

Gee, I haven't heard from you people in a week now. I hope the letters catch up to me soon. I called the mail clerk to give him my new address so I should be getting some mail shortly.

Life here is quite comfortable. Barbershop in the place, POW's who were barbers in civilian life do the work. Shines are free, so I won't have any trouble keeping my shoes shined. It's not compulsory though, I was afraid that this place would be very GI on account of Patton, but surprisingly enough it's not. No strict uniform rules, etc. Not as much carrying on as down in the Battery but it's still a good deal. Take in laundry whenever you want, etc.

My work is coming along nicely. I have some more men to send to school tomorrow and that necessitates my choosing them from the application blanks turned in and notifying them, etc. I do some thinking here, that's why I like it.[365]

Love and Kisses,
Charlie

---

[365] Not only did Charlie "do some thinking," according to his military separation record he supervised the work of the Administration Section of the 3rd US Army Engineer Headquarters and managed the work of six clerk typists and helped prepare correspondence for the army engineer. Additionally, he handled personnel problems for all the Engineer Units in the 3rd Army.

Garmisch and the Zugspitze

Thursday, September 13, 1945

Dear Folks,

Had another busy day and accomplished a lot. Filled up all my quotas for the various schools and also secured extra quotas for some of the men. There was an I&E meeting today and all the staff sections except for the Engineers failed to fill their quota. See, your sonny is on the ball. Of course, I could get myself in on some school now, but I want to hang around a little. Do you think that's the wise thing? I'm settled on the fact that I want to go to London and I'll fix myself up with a short course there. I might go to an I&E school in Paris for three days very shortly. I hope you're getting a money order.

Tonight I saw Bing Cosby in "Here Come the Waves." The other evening I saw "God for My Co-Pilot" - or is that repeating myself? It gets real cold at night already, I can see that we'll need plenty of coal this winter.

I'm just fine. Mother, if you didn't get away for a week, I'll be quite angry.

Love,
Charlie

Friday, September 14, 1945

Dear Mom, Dad, and Sis,

Listen to my evening and then think of how good things are for me. Had steak for supper and then layed on my bed until 8 reading the Stars and Stripes, Yank, and The New York Herald Tribune (Paris). I decided to take a shower so I went to the pool room and soaked in the hot water. Then I went for a dip in the beautiful pool, right in my "house." After the dip I could choose the movies, gym, ping-pong, beer hall, library, etc. without going outside. Boy, what a rough life. I could stay here 30 years (what a lie). But I want you to know that I'm really living nicely and you shouldn't have a worry in the world about me. I'm well taken care of until I get home.

I have a suggestion for a Christmas present. I could use a bathrobe. It will come in handy for going down to the pool or to the showers, etc. Don't make it too good, in fact a cheap one is preferable for here. Send it out shortly, a wool one or a Turkish kind. Thanks loads. I'm quite sure I'll be here at least until February, probably till Spring or Summer.

Love and Kisses,
Charlie

Sunday, September 16, 1945

Dear Mom, Pop, and Sis,

Received a cablegram from Aunt Rose today wishing me a Happy New Year, very thoughtful, don't you think? She had my new address already, that's fast work.

A rainy Sunday. We gained an hour's sleep as we turned the clock back one hour at 1 AM. I don't like the idea of reporting for work on Sunday even though there's not too much to do. It's close to noon now so I'll be through soon. Some officer just donated a bottle of champagne to four of us and we'll knock that off before chow. Incidentally, that officer is a Jew - Lt. Silverman - the warrant officer is also Jewish, there may be one or two others but I'm not sure.

Plan to make a quiet Sunday afternoon, just like *Schmiel* enjoys. Perhaps write a few letters, take a dip maybe, and then a movie. Oh, what a hard life.

Well, it's bedtime now, and here's what I did. After chow went for a little walk and then took a snooze. I slept through the show but at 4:30 one of the boys woke me and told me to get dressed. We had two cars to take a bunch of us to the Recreation Center at Tegernsee. I heard a lot about the place, but this was the first time I had a chance to go.

ell, it's something beautiful, a real country-club deluxe as you can well see by the enclosed circular. Nothing is too good for the soldier and the evening meal of soup, hot biscuits, roast beef, dessert and coffee was excellent. There's a beautiful lake with sailboats, etc. and a few ping-pong tables. I played a few games on the terrace.

After chow, we lounged around on big soft couches and shot a little pool (billiards). So the day was very enjoyable, have to get out to the place more often. As it is now, our section can send two men for two days every day. So I'll be going out every two weeks for a couple of days. Not bad, eh? Oh, it's rough in the ETO.

How was *Kol Nidre*?
Love and Kisses,
Charlie

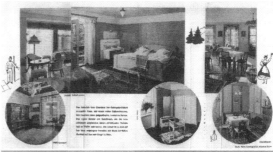

Monday, September 17, 1945

Dear Folks,

Nothing to report today. Still keeping busy on the I&E program. Selected 25 men to go to Shrivenham University in England and tomorrow I'll have to write the letters making it official and getting them on their way.

I bought a beautiful pair of boots today, brand new and a perfect fit. They're German shoes and a fellow who is leaving tomorrow sold them to me for $5.40. I borrowed the dough. I'm polishing them up before I wear them, pretty sharp-looking leather.

Still waiting for my mail to get here. Think I'll phone the mailman in the old place again. Please take care of yourselves. Getting ready for Art?

Love and Kisses,
Charlie

Thursday, September 20, 1945

Hiya Gang,

Things are just dandy. Some more high-pointers left yesterday, and I took over a lovely two room suite with a complete bathroom. I share one room with another fellow from the 102nd and two others live in the other room. We have a kitchenette right in the wall. It was an officer's apartment in the days of the SS. So once again I have excellent living quarters.

The weather has been gorgeous lately. Real warm days with little, if any, rain. I hope it keeps up a while. As soon as I get some dough, I'll try to get away on furlough or school.

Nothing else right now.
Lots of love,
Charlie

Wednesday, September 26, 1945

Dear Folks,

I have good news today; I'm going to leave this afternoon on a splendid trip. I managed to get a quota to the University of Glasgow for a one-week course in Political and World Problems. I couldn't get permission to take a longer course, so I settled for this.

I fly to Paris this afternoon and tomorrow I fly to London. From there I take a train to Glasgow. Boy, I'm seeing the world! I'm on my own so I'll be able to spend a few days in London and in Paris, in addition to the week in Glasgow.

Once again I have to explain the money situation. You tell me the bank hasn't received my allotment. This is the twentieth time I'm telling you that I have nothing to do with it. I never see the dough, it goes from Washington to the 86th Street Bank. Understand? It might take months to get there, but it should arrive sometime. If not, I have to write to Washington about it. I'm not spending it, I never see the dough, okay?

Now about the $100 I'm asking for. I'm broke because I scrapped everything together for Uncle Mendel. I don't want and I won't take your $100, thanks; I want my own from the bank. I don't need your money, I'm 21 and you need everything for yourself. Just take a withdrawal slip and send me $100 - fast, please. To this address. I'll have the letter when I return from the trip.

This is probably the last time I'll ever be in Europe and of course, I'm going to try to see everything I can. Can't blame me, eh? I'll still have a furlough this winter.

E, see that the $100 (mine and not the folks) is sent out soon. All the dough I get is $32 a month and that cares for PX, money I've sent home, and little things I pick up, a bottle of wine or champagne now and then.

All my love, you sweeties, I'll write soon.
Love,
Charlie

Wednesday, September 26, 1945 - Marseilles, France

Hello Gang,

Excuse the V-Mail but I have no other paper now. Couldn't get a plane to Paris so I came here instead. Will try to get a plane to London tomorrow, but they're all very crowded and have long reservation lists. Well, I'm on my way, at any rate.

I enjoyed the flight very much. It was my first time up and it was a B-17, some beautiful plane. We averaged 200 miles an hour and I got from Munich to Marseilles in a little over three hours. By train it would have taken me at least twenty-eight hours. I wasn't afraid at all and my stomach took it well, I even napped for 1 ½ hours. It's a great thrill looking down through clouds to pick out a city. Went over Nice but couldn't land there. I'm having fun.

Love,
Charlie

Monday, October 1, 1945

Hello People,

Your globetrotting son is now in the land of the Scots and a very nice place it is.

I left Marseilles on Thursday morning and arrived in Paris in time for lunch. I had a pleasant stay there and I remained until Saturday noon. Then I took the plane for Prestwich, Scotland, and I landed about 5 PM. So, I've been here ever since.

I report to my class this evening at 7 PM. I'll be living in a house at the University, and it should be an interesting experience.

This is a splendid country. When I got off the train (from an air base to town) Saturday evening I could have sworn that I was in the States. Everything's the same outside of the Scott brogue. All the stores are opened, although people are very heavily rationed.

They have their share of Jews here and the first girl I met at the Red Cross turned out to be a Jewess. I visited the *Shul* this morning. Incidentally, the girls are very attractive, and everyone is quite friendly. I met a music student yesterday and we visited the art gallery together and, in the evening, I went to her home. She played the piano and did very well. Chopin's "*Polonaise*" (pronounced like Mayonnaise), some of Fritz's stuff. A soldier (mostly Air Corps) who has been stationed here for three years really has nothing to complain about. It's a touch of home.

You should see the two-decker busses and trolleys. Wasn't that a sight for sore eyes? I'll be here until next Sunday or Monday and then I'll be off for London.

Will write again tomorrow. The telephone situation is too rugged for me to attempt a call. Have to be on hand for close to twelve hours and then you're still not sure.

Toodeloo for now,
Love,
Charlie

Saturday, October 6, 1945

Dear Mom, Dad, and Sis,

Simply having a wonderful time and enjoying every minute of it. My course was very interesting and I'll send you the schedule of it shortly. We were treated royally all the time.

Attending a wedding in Scotland. Charlie is in the center, fifth from left.

Last Monday night I moved into a house right near the University and we lived there for the week. Real style, nice beds, delicious meals, teas, receptions, and one dinner given by the British Council at the best hotel in town. The council is more or less a goodwill agency. We even were given a tea reception by the Lord Provost of Glasgow (mayor).

Well, I met a nice chap at the big dinner and through him I met a nice girl and a small crowd. There was a wedding scheduled for Friday and I was invited. We left Glasgow yesterday morning by train and then took a steamer across the River Clyde to the Island of Bute. The name of the town is Rothesay and we're at a small hotel run by the bride's mother. The wedding was Friday afternoon and the weather was so beautiful that it was held out on the lawn. We had a fine dinner and in the evening a real good party.

It's Sunday now and I'm waiting for the 4:55 boat back to the train station. It has been a real civilian weekend. The people have all been very hospitable, nice beds, good home cooked food, pleasant company. Just like the old days.

I'm heading for Loch Lomond to-morrow, and in the evening I'm going to Edinburgh. Tuesday night I'm catching the London train. I'll stay there till Saturday or Sunday and then go to Paris and then "home" to Bad Tölz.

Feeling great.
Love and Kisses,
Charlie

Monday, October 8, 1945 - Drymen, Scotland

Dear Folks,

Continuing to have a superb time. I came back to Glasgow from Rothesay last evening and I immediately took off for this place - the American Red Cross Hotel near Loch Lomond "On Bon-Bonnie Banks."

This is another beautiful place. I was tired this morning, so I slept until 11. It was gorgeous and it was the ideal time to visit the Lochs. Now it's lunch time and it's beginning to rain. I'm boiling mad but I've had my share of nice weather. I should have gotten up early today.

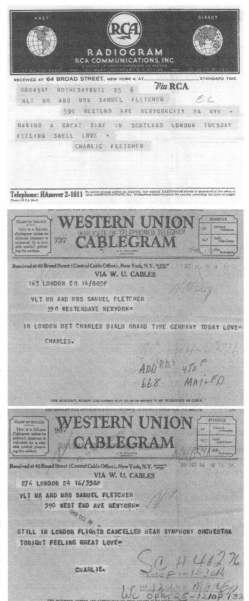

This hotel is just like a civilian one. Very quiet, nice people, snack bar, nice lounge with fire.

The scenery is out of this world, really magnificent.

All my love,
Charlie

Thursday, October 18, 1945 – Bad Tölz, Germany

Dear Folks,

I'm back "home" again and my letters will certainly be more regular again. Thanks for putting up with me the past three weeks. I hope my few cables kept you aware of my location.

Finally managed to get a plane ride yesterday and we took off from London at 11:45 and arrived in Munich 3 ½ hours later, very good time. Then it took me 5 hours to get to Bad Tölz (35 miles), that was due to the wait for a jeep. I had a huge stack of mail awaiting me and most of it came from you three ducky-wuckys. Thanks for writing so steadily.

The money-order was received, and I'll hold on to it for future furlough. I managed to finance this last trip by a few "business transactions." I was indeed surprised to learn that only one $33 check has been received. I went to the Personnel Office in Munich this afternoon and told them the story. They will write to the office which handles that stuff in the States and check on it. I'm not worried about it as I never got the money and therefore it's due me and I'll eventually get it. Incidentally, that one $33 check that did come, to whom was it payable and when did you receive it? That information might be useful, so please let me know if you can think of it. Incidentally, how are my $10 War Bonds coming? Do you receive them every month?

When I returned yesterday, I received official notice of my promotion to Sergeant Technician Fourth Grade. The order came through on October 1 and I knew about it but I wasn't positive, so I didn't say anything about it. I now get a gross pay of $93.60. $78 base pay + 20%, it's a $14.40 raise and until my allotment to the bank is straightened out, I'll hold on to the extra dough and perhaps send it home every now and then. Money is of little value here. I do intend getting a portrait painted by an expert artist in town and perhaps have a few suits made, etc., if possible. Did I tell you that I picked up a lovely blue slip-over in Scotland?

Thanks for all the packages. Whew, what a slew of them. I caught the Holland one and sent it off to my friends there. You can forget about that for a while. However, there are two more families I'd like to send a little something, so mark "civilian" on a couple of future packages, nothing perishable.

UNKNOWN SINGER TRIUMPHS

At Albert Hall

MISS JOSEPHINE SYREY,
Daily Mail Picture last night.

By Daily Mail Reporter

SIX thousand people at the Royal Albert Hall, London, last night acclaimed a new star—a coloratura soprano who had held them spellbound by her perfect singing of two operatic arias.

Josephine Syrey, appearing with the London Symphony Orchestra, was known to none in the audience and to no one in the orchestra.

Mascagni's pupil

Late last night at a West End hotel Miss Syrey told me the story of her career. "I was born in France but have never sung in France," she said.

"My mother, who was a very good singer, first taught me. Then one day Mascagni, composer of 'Cavalleria Rusticana,' heard me sing, and taught me himself.

"At the age of 18 I made my first public appearance in opera in Germany, in Czecho-Slovakia both in opera and in concert.

"I came to this country just before war broke out, and have been here ever since. Tonight was my first real public appearance in England, although I sang at a charity concert at St. Ives, in Cornwall, a few months ago."

Mr. Vere Laurie, of the Imperial Concert Agency, said : "She walked into my office one morning and asked for an audition. She sang several operatic arias, and I knew at once that I had a rare discovery."

Ralph Hill, Daily Mail Music Critic, who attended the concert, writes :

Here is a singer of outstanding gifts and promise. Miss Syrey displayed a voice of superb quality in every note of its wide range.

Furthermore, every phrase she sings is delivered with the utmost musical feeling, and her technique as a coloratura singer is as brilliant as it is impeccable.

Well, I'm anxiously awaiting word that Artie got home. I've read that the 16th Armored is arriving in the States but it'll be "official" when I hear it from you. I do hope he gets his discharge shortly. What's new on the apartment situation? I appreciate the difficulty in securing one but I'm confident that the agency in your building or Mr. Roberts will be able to find something. E, don't hold out for a marvelous spot, take anything now so at least you and Art can have your own place.

I can't begin to tell you about my wonderful trip. It lasted exactly three weeks, just as I had planned. I did want to hit Paris on my return trip, but it was impossible to fly and I didn't relish the boat and train ride, so I flew direct to Munich.

Charles Bialo came down Friday evening and we met Saturday morning and spent two pleasant days together. He's a very nice fellow and was exceedingly hospitable. He took me to dinner a few times and we took in an excellent show, "While the Sun Shines," on Saturday night. On Sunday we had lunch together, visited some of his friends, went to Hyde Park and then to the movies. We had dinner in a Jewish restaurant and passed the evening at some young friend's home. Charles was expecting Morris this coming weekend, but I couldn't stay long enough. He is the exact image of Morris and is very much like Paul. Plays the piano quite expertly.

Had a full seven days in London and took in four shows and one symphony concert, a review is enclosed herein. Spent twelve days in Scotland and found both Glasgow and Edinburgh very nice. Loch Lomond is a thing of beauty. London is a real big city with plenty to do. Heard Isabel Baille, soprano, sing at one of the daily lunchtime concerts at the National Art Gallery, a splendid idea.

The weather was ideal throughout, very lucky indeed. Expected miserable days but hit a good streak instead. Travelling is quite an experience. It's the only way to know people and learn about foreign countries. I saw all the sights in London, toured through Westminster Abby and saw Buckingham Palace, etc., very nice.

Things are normal here, Germans still alive and kicking. I'm feeling fine. I realize I'm lucky to be in such good health after such a great war and I'm thankful and content. Don't worry, I'm waiting patiently.

Regards to all. How is Grandpop? You only mention Grandma! I'd like to know everything.

Love and Kisses,
Charlie

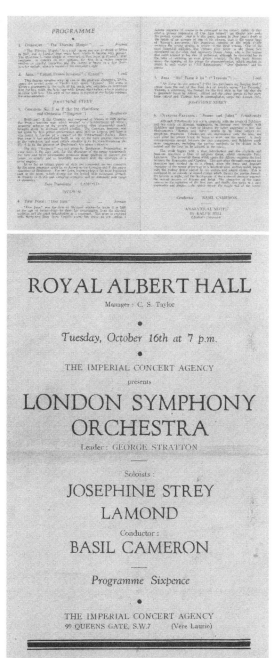

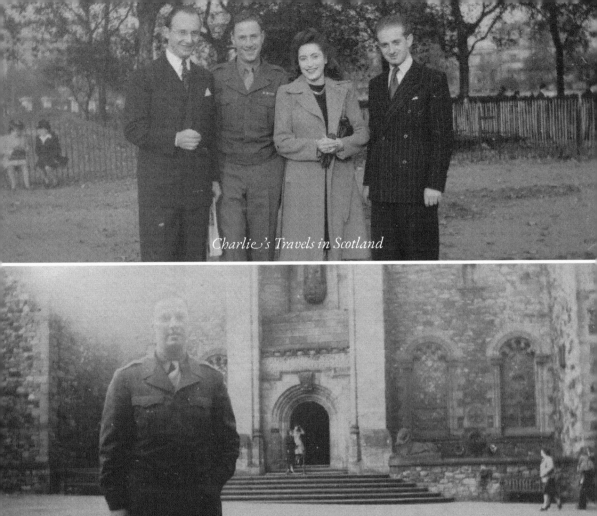

Charlie's Travels in Scotland

Friday, October 19, 1945

Dear Folks,

Received more mail from you today.

Dad, I didn't fly for the thrills. It's been a long time since I did things just for a thrill. I flew because it's the best way to travel over here. It would be foolish to go by rail and boat from Germany to Scotland for only a week stay, wouldn't it? And then again, air transportation in a very few years will be the common rule rather than the exception.

I'm sorry that E's had no luck with an apartment. I hope she holds out against Anna's wishes. It would be pathetic if they settled, even for a few days, at the Marshak's. For once and always, Artie should know he's on his own and forget his mother's apron-strings. He's a swell guy and should realize that he and E are living their own lives.

The weather has been brisk and clean, the nights are cold but I've been staying in. That's all right now, I'm a bit rushed catching up with things.

Regards to all.
Love and Kisses,
Charlie

Sunday, October 21, 1945

Dear Mom, Pop, and Sis,

Well, it must be great, Sis, to have her husband back.[366] I bet they're acting like a honeymoon couple. I'm anxious to hear all about it.

I've just finished a very humorous book, "Parm Me" by Arthur Kober. It's written in Jewish dialect and it's very entertaining. You'll enjoy it.

We were supposed to have a football game today but the team from Berlin couldn't get air transportation so it was cancelled. I took a stroll into town and then came back to my suite.

---

[366] The 16th Armored Division, where Artie transferred after the cessation of hostilities in Europe, returned to the New York Port of Embarkation on October 13, 1945 and was de-activated at Camp Kilmer, New Jersey on October 15, 1945.

A lot of men from the 102nd Division with 60-65 points were transferred to the 79th Division for the trip home. Just a few days ago they were transferred back to the 102nd, no shipping space at the present time. Can you imagine how angry they all are?

Soldiers aren't fit for Occupation Duty. We're all inclined to be too soft and lenient and that's no good. A good civilian force would be much more suitable. I just read that the Yanks are "strolling with the Jap girls in the parks of Tokyo." That's just about the last straw, but we all knew that it would be that way.

Thanks ever so much for all of your grand packages. That salmon is simply marvelous and all the other stuff is good. That's about all now, I'm feeling well. I'll stay around here until December 1 then try to get a furlough.

Lots of love,
Charlie

Monday, October 22, 1945

Dear Mom and Pop, (Sis in on her own now)

Went out this morning with the Personnel Officer (the Jewish Warrant Officer) on an inspection, so that killed half the day. One of our units is going home soon and we checked the records.

Another one of your excellent packages arrived, yum-yum.

How's the weather at home? It's been fairly mild here but any one of these days I expect winter to break loose in all its fury. Nothing much doing, I'm back in the swing of things, taking it real easy. I've signed up for piano lessons and I take my first one Monday at 8 AM. Now I'll get a German teacher and I'll be set.

I'll keep my letters coming, Dad. I know you enjoy the mail as much as I do. Did Morris Bialo leave New York yet? I'm quite sure he won't get here but he will get to Antwerp. That's all for now. Take good care of yourselves. How are you both feeling?

All my love,
Charlie

Tuesday, October 23, 1945

Dear Mom and Pop,

All's well here. I hope that the same is true on your home front. Seems to be a lot doing back in the States, what with the labor unrest, atomic bomb discussion, etc. Things should settle down soon. This is the first tough period President Truman has encountered and I'm interested in the performance he gives.

Our new General, Truscott, is quite a different man than Patton. He is very quiet and seems to be getting after all known-Nazis. He doesn't bother us at all. Social life in Tölz is nil compared to the other towns I've been in, that is, beer halls, dancing, shows, etc.

Did you get to see Charlie Zwerner? How does he look? I hope his wife gets to the States soon, but it will be another six months at least, I'm afraid.

Been taking it easy. Should exercise more, so I might start playing basketball, and take an occasional dip.

No more today, best regards to E and Art.
Love and Kisses,
Charlie

Wednesday, October 24, 1945

Dear Folks,

I'm Charge of Quarters tonight so I'm taking it easy in the office and trying to catch up with some mail. It's a tough job because I'm months behind.

Drew my overcoat this week and the tailor is putting on the patches and stripes and pressing it up a bit. I had most of my stuff cleaned since I came back, so I'm in good shape.

A couple of the fellows and myself are planning a trip to the Brenner Pass[367] this weekend. If we're lucky we'll be able to get into Italy. This Saturday I'm off at noon and free until Monday morning, I get that every other week. In addition,

---

[367] The Brenner Pass, some 136 kilometers (app. 84 miles) south of Charlie's base in Bad Tölz, is a mountain pass through the Alps which forms the border between Italy and Austria.

we get one afternoon off plus Sunday afternoon. We still work from 9-12 Sunday morning. Really no reason for it.

I've enclosed a few pictures I took before leaving. I hope to have some from my trip soon.

Take care of yourselves. Tell E to put these pictures away for me. Aunt Rose has certainly been marvelous. What a lady!

Love and Kisses,
Charlie

Sunday, October 28, 1945

Dear Folks,

Just came back from a lovely weekend trip. Was off yesterday at noon and we went to Garmisch, the place I wrote about before. It's mainly a winter resort town, renowned for its skiing. We stayed at the classy hotel run for GI's and it was deluxe. Catered to a very wealthy class before the war.

This morning we took a trip into Austria (French occupied) and after going through Innsbruck and getting to the Brenner Pass, we got into Italy. You're not supposed to go over the border, but a British guard let us by. So that's another county I've been in. We stopped at a small town, Vipiteno, for a dinner and had some good soup, chicken and wine. Your צודיען is getting around. We spent the afternoon driving around Italy (penetrated in about 35 miles). In this territory there are many Austrians and Germans. All the scenery is beautiful, some peaks are snow-covered but it's still a little too early for all the mountains to be white.

I enjoy the long weekends, especially when we can get a vehicle. There's quite a bit to see here abouts. Now I've been in Scotland, England, France, Belgium, Holland, Germany, Austria and Italy. Before I'm through here I should get into Czechoslovakia and Switzerland.

We missed supper last night and don't think it wasn't nice to get to my suite and make some hot soup - the vegetable, which is delicious. I also opened a can of sardines, and they were tasty.

Austria, Fall 1945

I can use more soup, remember the noodles in packages from last winter? And also the small can of vegetable, etc., the cheese, sardines, salmon, tuna, etc., will also come in handy. Chow hasn't been too good of late and I get an appetite around 10 PM.

Well, my lovelies, all my fondest wishes for you. Hope E is okay. I imagine they're staying at the Bretton Hall[368] until they find a place. Regards to Artie and the folks. Where is Grandpop?

Love,
Charlie

[368] A residential hotel on 2350 Broadway, spanning from West 85th to 86th Streets.

Monday, October 29, 1945

Dear Folks,

I was very happy to learn that Art arrived home safely. I still haven't received a letter describing his homecoming in detail, but I imagine Eadie will write a big line shortly.

It was a surprise to learn that you gave the apartment to Art and E, even for a few weeks. I should think that a hotel would be a good place for them for the short time. Both of you are getting older and that business of travelling to work, something that you avoided all during your lives, is quite ridiculous and uncalled for. I know you mean well, Mom, but that's carrying things too far. After all, Art and E have some money of their own and they certainly have the right to spend it, especially now at such a joyous time.

Please don't think I'm throwing a hamper on things. It's been a great thrill to me too, to see Artie over here and know that he was going home to my sister. But there's no reason in the world why you had to leave your home. That's the way I feel about it, no hard feelings.

The weather is very unseasonal, real summery and that means snow or rain real soon. Work is still pretty slow, I'm keeping interest though.

No more now, all my love. Artie should write when he gets a chance.
Love,
Charlie

Wednesday, October 31, 1945

Hello Folks,

The weatherman is sure upset. We're having summer days now and some people say it may keep up this way until Christmas. The real cold months here are supposed to be February, March, and April. In fact, last May when the Americans came here, there was a lot of snow on the ground.

Nothing much doing. I told you I met a fraternity brother who is stationed in Munich. I invited him out for the weekend and we should have a good time. Mail is pretty poor these days. A couple of days always go by before I hear from you. I know you write as often as possible, so don't worry.

How are Art and E making out? They must be having happy days. I haven't heard from Sis since Artie got home. I realize she must be pretty busy.

I'll be waiting for your mail telling me all the latest news. I'm feeling fine, all is well here. Your packages are swell, keep 'em coming when you can.

Love,
Charlie

Thursday, November 1, 1945

Dear Folks,

Just look, another month here already. It won't be too long before you'll be seeing my ugly puss again.

It's 5 PM now and I'm just hanging around until the C-2[369] comes in. Had a fairly busy day, still sending some men to school but that entire program has let down quite a bit.

Took my first piano lesson this week and I'm doing some finger exercises. Still looking around for a capable German teacher. I speak the language fairly well now.

In another month or so I plan to go to Switzerland. That'll be a swell trip. I would also like to get away at Christmas time. Perhaps I'll go to this place at Garmisch, the ski resort.

Everything is okay. My roommate is on his way to Berlin. He's delivering some maps to the Berlin District HQ.

No more right now, take good care of yourselves.

All my love,
Charlie

---

[369] Staff Officer responsible for Command and Control Operations.

Friday, November 2, 1945

Hello, You Lovely People,

It's anniversary time again and you know my wishes. If they ever came true you would be floating on velvet. I hope you spend many more years together and I know it's safe to say that at the next anniversary, I'll be with you. That's for sure.

I realize why you're jealous, folks, but remember that most of the men getting out now have been in at least a year longer than I. Also, it's not nice to be jealous of other people's good fortune. I'll get back safe and sound, and that's more than some other mothers and fathers sons will do.

Pop, you're elected to take Mom out on the enclosed $10. Take in a musical show, please, and also have a bit in some restaurant. Also, Dad, give the Old Lady a kiss for me. Isn't she fortunate in having two men with such fine-shaped heads?

Take care of yourselves.
All my love,
Charlie

Monday, November 5, 1945

Hello Folks,

Had a very nice weekend right here at "home." My friend from Munich came down on Saturday evening and he stayed over until Monday morning. We had a lot of old times to talk about and we had a pleasant time.

Another week begins today. A year ago yesterday we were in Germany for the first time. Gosh, time does fly, where does it all go?

Artie and E dropped me a nice line recently and I'll answer them today. Boy, Artie must be real proud of his civilian suit. It would be nice if they could get away for a while before Art goes to work. But they know what they're doing.

It's quite foggy today and I think we're in for a little rain. I'll be comfortable, though. I'm off this afternoon and I think I'll get off a couple of letters. Took my 2nd piano lesson yesterday, still doing exercises. How does Charles Zwerner look? Send him my best regards.

That's all for now.
Love,
Charlie

Tuesday, November 6, 1945

Dear Folks,

All's well here in Bavaria. *Vie gehts alles in New York? Mein Deutsch ist gut, nicht wahr? Heute war nicht schon,*[370] it drizzled a little bit and was quite chilly.

Aunt Rose has sent me two tasty packages from Altman's. I'm getting a little reserve for the winter months. As it looks now, I won't be on my way home for at least five or six months (March or April). If there is a possibility of getting a discharge this month and then taking a civilian job for six months, I'm going to do so. I'm investigating the possibilities now. Doc Winning from New York University is a Lt. Col. in Military Court, and I wrote him a line today. The only difference is that I'll be a civilian during the remainder of my stay here, more money and no longer a soldier.

Everyone who gets one of these civilian jobs must have the number of points necessary for discharge but there is a chance that some low-pointers may be able to get out. I'm not looking for a job here, but if this thing goes through, I'll make a little money before coming home and it won't entail my staying here any longer than if I remained in the service. We'll see what happens, it all takes a lot of time and loads of red tape.

Right now it's pretty slow. This evening I think I'll practice the piano and write a few letters.

Did Charles Zwerner go out to the coast yet? He must have changed in the few years he's been away.

Enclosed are some pictures taken on my recent trip. Please save them, I'll send copies to the Bialos soon.

Lots of Love,
Charlie

---

[370] German: How's everything going in New York? My German is good, isn't it? Today wasn't nice.

Thursday, November 8, 1945

Hello Folks,

It's quite a task composing a letter these days.

My roommate is still away in Berlin. He'll probably have interesting stories to relate. Gosh, the men stationed there are making piles of dough. I wouldn't mind being there for a few weeks.

Did I tell you that I plan to go to Switzerland early in December? That should be an interesting trip. This weekend I'm going to Garmisch, that's the big skiing town. I've got to try out those darn things this winter. Don't worry, I'm not going to go on any hills, just on level ground.

Well, that's all for right now. Take care of yourselves.

Love,
Charlie

Saturday, November 10, 1945

Dear Folks,

Another weekend beginning today, and I'm ready to take-off soon for Garmisch. We have hotel reservations there and we may even be able to stay over until Monday night on account of the holiday.

My friend came back from Berlin and he had a nice trip. He and I pooled some cigarettes and without bothering to deal direct with the Russians or Germans, he made $500. He sold a carton of cigarettes to some American soldier stationed there for $50 and that GI can sell them to a Kraut for $100. It's very difficult to send money home or else there would be a gold mint made.

As it is, I have two $100 money orders, one is enclosed and the other will follow in the next letter. Please bank them, unless you need the dough.

It's Saturday afternoon in Garmisch now and I'm having a splendid time. We're having gorgeous weather, plenty of snow, the same hotel as last time with excellent food. Met a British soldier who's driving some British and American Secret Servicemen and we went for a ride this morning up into the mountains.

We stopped at Oberammergau, the place where the Passion Play (all about Christ) is held every ten years. A very historic town, visited the famous theater and also the church which is very beautiful.

I should have gone skiing today but I slept late. Perhaps next time I'll take it in. My weekends here are just great. The GI's are finding out how nice it is and are crowding in, but there's room for a very large crowd.

The Jewish Warrant Officer left for home yesterday and if he has a chance while in New York, he'll give you a buzz. He's a very nice guy, name is Mr. Kranzberg!

Send my love to all, a very big letter tomorrow.

Love,
Charlie

Monday, November 12, 1945

Dear Mom and Dad,

Came back this morning from Garmisch. The ride takes 1 1/2 hours and it's quite pleasant. Two of the boys were afraid they would have to work today so we returned early. As it is, no one is doing anything. It's a fulltime holiday and I'm taking it easy in my apartment reading and writing.

I receive very little mail these days, outside of yours. The main reason, of

Inside the Oberammergau Church

586

course, is that I don't do much writing. Ever since the war ended I haven't had the desire to do a lot of corresponding.

Mom, I realize how you feel on that touchy subject you discussed in a recent letter. Some people are funny and there's nothing you can do about it. It won't be that way for me.

Pop, how the hell are you? Your letters are scarce but I imagine the Old Lady has you cutting 20 hours a day. Oh, what a fine shaped head!

I'm feeling fine, a bit old, too, facing this 22nd birthday. Oh my, I'm getting old.

There's no more of interest now. Enclosed is another $100 money order. Please bank it all, your worries about your children should be all over. E's husband is home and he'll look after her. All you should worry about is *Pessa* and *Schmiel*, I mean that.

Love,
Charlie

Wednesday, November 14, 1945

Dear Mom and Pop,

Things are running along as usual. I'm having a busy week as I'm acting as Chief Clerk for the section. You see, the Master Sergeant is in the hospital and the assistant is away at school so I had to take over. I'm waiting for one of them to return, as I'm not particularly interested in contending with so many headaches. There's quite a bit attached to the job and it should be a supervisory one. However, this week we're shorthanded and I have to do much of the work myself. It's interesting, though, and I don't mind being the boss for a couple of days.

I'm going to Switzerland about December 1st. I'll be on the lookout for watches, if I can get enough money together. I have the dough but you can only convert a certain amount. I'm deliberating now whether I want to be in Switzerland for Christmas or here. I'll have to make up my mind.

Taking it easy, can't wait until my turn comes to go home. It won't be too many months.

Love and Kisses,
Charlie

Friday, November 16, 1945

Dear Mom and Pop,

How are you two lovebirds today? I hope that you're both in good health and that the winter isn't too severe for you. It is plenty cold here already and I imagine we still have the real frost ahead of us. It looks like another snowstorm soon and we will have all the snow we want within the next few weeks.

Art must have started work by now. Did anything come through on that apartment the kids thought they had? I think it was a cousin of Artie who was going to Florida for the winter and was willing to let Art and E use it. I hope they find something soon.

All this news about lowering the point-score soon and possibly discharging by length of service all sounds very good, but it doesn't mean much. There is such a tremendous backlog of men waiting to be sent home that all a new system would mean to the men overseas would be eligible for discharge and no way of getting home. For the men in the US, it would be a good break. I'm still thinking about Federal Service here for six months, if I can get it now. I'll still get home in the Spring and I'll come home like a human being. But there's nothing definite on it yet. I'll wait a couple of days and if I don't hear from Doc Winning, I'll start my application by myself.

I was off this afternoon and didn't do a thing. I sent two fellows to Munich today to pick up some fur and sheepskin pelts we requisitioned. I plan to sew mine in my field jacket and that will make it very warm. I think I'll have one extra to wear as a coat and also enough waste material to make a pair of gloves.

There is very little to write about. They're still bringing more people up here from Munich and the place is getting much too crowded, but what can you do?

I'm reading a funny book now, "High Time" by Mary Laswell. I think it is one of the best-sellers now. I read her old book, "Suds in Your Eye," quite some time ago.

There's nothing else tonight, excuse the short note. More next time, I hope. Still plan to go to Czechoslovakia this weekend, so perhaps no letter until Monday.

Love,
Charlie

Monday, November 19, 1945

Dear Folks,

Came back late last night from the trip to Pilsen, Czechoslovakia.[371] It was a pretty rough ride, but it was worth it. The roads were good, but last evening the fog was very heavy and we had to be very cautious. Instead of the return ride taking six or so hours, it took nine.

On Saturday we stopped off at Deggendorf, Germany and we left there at 9 AM Sunday for Pilsen. We arrived there at 11:30 and had a delicious meal (fried chicken) at the Corps Headquarters. We toured the city and then parked our jeep and walked around. Of course, one can't see much in a couple of hours on Sunday, but I can say that I saw Czech people going to the theater, walking their babies around, etc. The stores are fairly well-stocked and there is enough food, not plentiful by any means though.

These people have a strong hate of the Germans, can't blame them after seven years of occupation. All Germans still in Czechoslovakia must wear yellow armbands and collaborators have white armbands. The language is quite difficult and very similar to Russian. The GI's who were stationed there had a good time. But as in all places, there are good and bad people.

Another promotion came through for me on November 15th. The Warrant Officer, Mr. Kranzberg, fixed me up before he left. It's a Technician Third Grade rating and my pay is $96 + 20% = $105. Once I start drawing that pay, I'll send some money orders home for the bank. I'm still considering what is

---

[371] Some 342 kilometers (app. 212 miles) northeast of Bad Tölz.

the fastest way to get home and it may be in the Army. In that case, I'll forget about a civilian job. Some of those positions sound attractive but they turn out sour.

Well, you kiddies are going to celebrate an anniversary this week. Best of luck, congratulations and future happiness. You know I always wish you the finest of everything.

Enclosed are a couple of snaps we took on our trip to Italy; I'm wearing the overcoat in the group picture. That's the first Italian town one hits after going through Brenner Pass.

Best to *Bubba*, hope she is ok.

Love,
Charlie

Pilsen, Czechoslovakia

Trip to Italy, 1945

590

Tuesday, November 20, 1945

Dear Folks,

How are you the day before your צודעקם 22nd birthday? Boy, time does fly, doesn't it? I wonder if I can still get in bed with you Mom, or sit on your lap? I'm an *Alter Kaker* now.

 plan to have a big feast tomorrow night. My roommate's birthday is on the 22nd so we're dining and celebrating together. The menu will be soup, anchovies, turkey, and hot beef stew with potatoes. Dessert will be tea, fruitcake and a little liquor. During the meal, we'll have the bottle of red wine I picked up in Italy. I'll let you know how it comes out.

I sent you lovebirds a telegram for your anniversary. I hope you get it in time.

Right now I'm waiting to use the piano. I had a lesson on Monday -I'm not going to be much good at it but it gives me something to do.

As a birthday present for myself I expect to go to Garmisch for Thanksgiving dinner and stay there until Sunday evening. That'll be a nice four-day pass and then on December 1 I'm going to Switzerland for my furlough. Last trip to England didn't count as a furlough, so I have this one coming. My fraternity brother from Munich is going with me so we should have a great time. I'm looking forward to it, it should be a grand experience.

That's all now, Mom and Pop.
Love,
Charlie

Friday, November 23, 1945

Dear Folks,

I got myself away for four days and I celebrated Thanksgiving here. Gee, what a marvelous meal. The menu is enclosed. It took about two hours to serve the feast and during the entire time there was music and entertainment.

Left Bad Tölz yesterday at 9 AM and we checked into the Alpenhof Hotel here at 10:30. You know, everything here is free. Meals, room-dining, horseback riding, everything. Yesterday afternoon we went out to see King Ludwig's castle.

On the way we had a flat and we stopped at an Engineer Company. They had their turkey at 1:30 and we were invited, so we had two turkey dinners yesterday.

The castle is very beautiful, it's a copy of the palace at Versailles and there is a miniature Hall of Mirrors, etc. I drove the jeep and I did pretty well at the wheel.

I'm staying here until early Monday morning, it's nice to get away this way.

My Birthday dinner sure turned out swell. The food was delicious and also the soup.

This morning I slept until 9 and then went horseback riding. I'd like to go ice-skating but there aren't any skates available. We should get some soon. There's not enough snow for real good skiing but I'll get my chance at that soon.

It's a rough life, Switzerland next Saturday. I hope I get two nice watches for you.

All my love,
Charlie

Monday, November 26, 1945

Hello Folks,

Back home again. Left Garmisch this morning at 8:45 and was back at Tölz at 10:10. Very little work today, really loafed throughout the day.

Received your telegram and E's and Art's, thanks for your wishes. A nice package also arrived and true to form, it was very attractive and appetizing. Charlie and June also sent me a package for Christmas. We're due for some more snow as the weather has warmed up and that's usually the sign of a flurry.

At 7:30 this evening I went horseback riding in the riding hall. It's an instruction period and the hall's a large stable with soft dirt and mirrors (so you can watch your form). I'm to go Monday, Wednesday, and Friday from 7:30 to 8:30. It was a lot of fun tonight.

I missed my piano lesson yesterday morning and I'll have to arrange another hour now. Well, that's all for today. I'm getting ready for my Switzerland trip.

Love and Kisses,
Charlie

Thursday, November 29, 1945

Dear Folks,

Not a thing new to report. Everything is running along smoothly and I'm in the best of health.

I cleaned up some junk the other night and got a package together to ship home. Please hold on to the stuff as it's part of my "memories." A lot of it is pictures and negatives and I'm going to put them in a scrapbook.

There's a bottle of perfume in a couple of white socks. That's Mom's Christmas gift. Pop, since you won't be jealous, the bayonet is your Christmas present. I also enclosed a couple of books, my hairbrush (I have another one) etc. When my turn to go arrives, I want to be in streamlined shape. I'll send one more package with odds and ends a little later on.

I'm just about ready to leave for Switzerland. I have to pick up some clothes and borrow a suitcase; today is payday, so I'll get enough dough together. Took some more pictures yesterday. You'll get them soon.

Be good, take care of yourselves.
Love,
Charlie

Friday, December 7, 1945 - Montreux, Switzerland

Dear Folks,

I'm very sorry that our connection was so poor this morning, Mother. It was a thrill to hear you say "Hello, Charlie" but after that I couldn't hear very well. Of course, I was extremely disappointed but that was our luck. Some calls go through splendidly, others poorly.

Well, now that I know that Dad has been to the hospital, we can start doing things. I've had no letters about it so all I know is what you told me on the phone. Here's how you can help things.

Have the Red Cross send a telegram describing conditions at home, don't have to recommend a furlough or disapprove one, just have them say that Dad is 59 or 60 (I forget) and that he has been ill in the hospital, etc. and that you are aging and are diabetic, etc. If they don't think conditions warrant a furlough, send it anyway - but don't let them recommend. Leave it up to the Commanding General, Third Army.

As soon as I get back, December 12 or 13, I'll start my own letter through and state that the Red Cross report is on its way. The Warrant Officer got home with no Red Cross telegram and it came later just describing his wife's condition, no recommendation on furlough. We'll do our best and see if I can get home. Have the Red Cross bring out your age, hard work, only son, etc.

I'm having a fine time. We visit Geneva tomorrow and on Sunday we go to Basel for our last two days.

I hope you both are feeling well, please take care. I'll be home soon and then things will be okay. Don't worry about me, I'm feeling fine.

Regards to all, love to Grandma.
Love and Kisses,
Charlie

Saturday, December 15, 1945 - Bad Tölz, Germany

Dear Mom and Dad,

I received two more letters and I'm indeed relieved to learn that Dad is in no danger. I wasn't pleased about you sending a letter to the Congressman from our district. I don't think very much of those methods; first, definitely does no good and second, I've served on my own until now and I'd like to get home on my own. Of course, if the Red Cross can get me a furlough I'd be very grateful, but this business of crying to a Congressman is something entirely different. No harm done, but don't keep writing to him.

Before I forget, I want to pay for the phone call home. In yesterday's letter I enclosed a check for $52, before depositing it please take out enough to cover the cost of the call. In addition, if you need the dough, keep it.

Everything is coming along okay. Working a little lately because one of the other fellows is away to school.

How are you these days, Pop? Please keep resting, sorry I couldn't give any of my blood.

No more now. I'm taking it easy here this weekend. Send my love to Grandma, regards to E and Art.

Love and Kisses,
Charlie

Monday, December 17, 1945

Dear Mom and Dad,

There's nothing new to report, everything is running smoothly.

I went skiing yesterday and it was loads of fun. Believe me, there's a lot of work attached to it and you can't beat it for exercise. We only went down one hill and I did okay. Don't worry, we don't go jumping through the air as you see in the movies. We kept walking across fields for practice. Climbing hills is quite a feat. I was a tired man when we came home.

Had a field jacket fixed up with sheepskin and it turned out very nice. It keeps me warm.

No reason to stop packages unless the Red Cross gets a furlough for me. Redeployment has slowed up a bit and 50-54 pointers aren't due to leave until January 15. So, I won't leave until February, sometime. Of course, one can't be sure. Your packages are sure swell, they're all appreciated.

Take good care of yourselves. Pop, how's your condition?

Love and Kisses,
Charlie

Tuesday, December 18, 1945,

Dear Mom and Dad,

I hope everything is okay at home and that Dad is progressing nicely. I'm aware of your need for me to return now and I am equally anxious to get home now to help out in any way I can. However, it's not as easy as it sounds. I've never received a cable from the Red Cross, so I take it for granted that they did not approve an emergency furlough at the present time.

E and Art suggested a request for discharge on account of dependency and that's a possibility. But before I do anything about it, I need an affidavit or a statement from a doctor merely stating that Dad is in the hospital, that he needs loads of rest, and that it is not advisable for him on account of his age to do much work. Also, if Dr. Elisberg could write about Mom being a diabetic, etc. that might help. In addition, Mom, you could have E write a statement that it's impossible to continue the store without Dad's help and that my presence would help matters as I am familiar with the routine, administration, and purchasing supplies for the store. Have that notarized.

Enclosed you will find a draft copy of a letter that I'll submit (or something similar) once you give me some affidavits and an okay on the letter. I want everything in writing on our part to be on the up and up. Correct the ages if they're not correct and also correct the letter or add to it. It's very difficult to get out on dependency now, but it's worth a try.

Consult with Art and E on this, and tell Art this is the same thing as hardship. I don't want to go ahead without hearing from you as we might make different statements, etc. and that will mean trouble later on. I think you have the general idea of what I need, so I'll wait to hear from you.

Everything over here is okay. I was off this afternoon and I took it easy. I'm on CQ this Sunday afternoon and that cuts the holiday weekend down a bit. However, I plan to go to Garmisch on Monday morning and stay through until Wednesday morn. Then for New Year's I'd like to get away for three full days.

Most of the boys have moved up to the attic or into barracks, but it looks like we'll be able to hold on to our apartment. We're going to get an extra man but it will be worth it. You see, they are consolidating Headquarters now and everyone is moving to Tölz, so the living quarters are now needed for office space.

On or about 1 Dec 45 my father was taken to Mount Sinai hospital in New York City after recurring attacks caused by stomach ulcers. Doctors have stated that on account of his advanced age, 60 years, he will be required to rest for a few months before any treatment can commence. It is expected that an operation will be necessary. **This is the second time in two and one-half years that my father has been hospitalized. In 1943 he underwent a hernia operation at the Veterans Hospital in New York City.**

3. My father's illness seriously handicaps my mother who is dependent on a small retail business run jointly by my parents. At 58 years of age, my mother can no longer work in the store on a full-time basis . She is a diabetic and is under a doctor's care. The store is the only source of income which my parents have. My presence at home would greatly aid the situation as I could take my father's place in the business and also take care of my mother who is now alone at home. The necessity of my return home is extreme as the sole source of income of my parents is in danger and the health and age of my parents is such that my discharge would be of great value to them.

Section III   AR 615-362.

I'm not so worried about Dad because from what Mom and E write everything is under control and it's definitely not heart trouble.

Love and Kisses,
Charlie

Thursday, December 20, 1945

Dear Mom and Dad,

The discharge news is certainly encouraging. All 50-pointers will be eligible for discharge on December 31. That seems to indicate that most all 50's will be on their way home by the first weeks of the new year. So it can't be too long for them to get to the 46ers. If you can't do anything now about an emergency furlough or a dependency discharge, don't be disappointed because I'll be home in a couple of months anyway. My guess is that I'll be home sometime in March; take it for what it's worth.

I'm having the Red Cross contact you to discuss a dependency discharge. It's better to work from your end because you'll have to supply the affidavits, etc. I gave Artie some more information and he'll talk it over with you. Don't knock yourself out trying to work it as I'll be home soon enough now.

Be good and take it easy. I may hold your watches, so don't look for them. I'll tell you if I mail them.

That's all for now.
Love and Kisses,
Charlie

Friday, December 21, 1945

Hello Folks,

Received two packages today and they're beauts. I'll let you know when to stop them but for the time being I can use the goodies. Especially good was the boned chicken. We had some last night with some mayonnaise and it certainly was delicious. Incidentally, if you can purchase some, I would like you to send a jar of mayonnaise in your next package. That's a tasty delicacy that we rarely see.

Everything is okay. Our brief warm spell seems to be over because this evening it is real cold. We'll probably hit some more snow just before Christmas.

How are you making out, Pop? Hope everything is okay. Send my love to Grandma. Tell her to be patient a little longer and she'll see her grandson.

That's all now.
Love and Kisses,
Charlie

Sunday, December 23, 1945

Dear Folks,

Here it is Sunday afternoon and I'm stuck with Charge of Quarters. No complaints though, because this is the first Sunday I've been tied down for ages. And tomorrow I'm taking off for Garmisch to spend a couple of days, so things are okay. Our New Year weekend is also a long one and I plan to spend four days in Garmisch.

Nothing very exciting going on. Quite a few Christmas trees around and a little joviality, but that's as far as the Christmas spirit goes.

Too bad Patton had to die the way he did.[372] I never had much use for him but everyone has to admit that he was one of our greatest field commanders. Some of the men from HQ are being sent to Luxembourg for the funeral.

The weather is very nice, we're still "snowless" except for the mountains. This recent warm spell took all our snow away. Listening to some beautiful music now. Just heard the Nelson Eddy program.

Love,
Charlie

Thursday, December 27, 1945

Hi Folks,

Hope everyone is in good health. Thanks for your letters, Mom. The mail has been pretty bad lately, but your lines keep coming in.

Well, Pop, another birthday is just about here. I have that gorgeous watch I bought for you in Switzerland. I'm sorry I didn't get it to you in time but better late than never. If I get around to it, I'll mail it home in a wooden box. I'm mail-

---

[372] After being injured in a car accident on December 9, 1945, General Patton passed away on December 21, 1945, at the age of 60.

ing out a small box tomorrow. In it you'll find a good German fountain pen. Mom, your gift will be a nice hand painting. Please save the other junk for me.

Enclosed are some pictures I snapped in Switzerland; they didn't come out too well as the weather wasn't very favorable. My roommate visited some Germans near Passau (he was also in the 102nd) and he came back with 30 eggs. We had soft-boiled ones for breakfast today and were they good.

Love,
Charlie

Saturday, December 29, 1945

Hi Folks,

Boy, it's snowing to beat the band. It was fairly warm last night but this morning we woke up to see a completely white-covered countryside. I'll probably get some skiing in this weekend.

I still have a couple of eggs left and for breakfast today I had grapefruit juice, rice flakes with milk, two soft boiled eggs, toast, jam, and tea (all in my room of course).

Mom, there's nothing to be afraid about those money orders totaling $250. All that money was approved by an officer and it's okay to deposit it anywhere.

This snowstorm will delay the mail some more, how are the letters and affidavits coming along? Did the Red Cross give you any assistance? That's a good way to get out now if it goes through. If it's turned down, don't raise a storm. I'll get out on my own one of these years!

I'm staying here in Tölz for the weekend. Garmisch would be nice but we'll have a Section New Year's Eve party and we should have a good meal New Year's Day.

Well, I sure hope that Dad is well. I realize Grandma's condition and I hope she's able to hold out a while longer. Regards to all.

Love and Kisses,
Charlie

Monday, December 31, 1945

Hi Mom and Dad,

Well, I'll be damned, another year has passed into history. And what history it is! Quite a few events of '45 will take their places alongside the biggest occurrences of all time. You and I are living in an eventful era. I hope things settle down for a while now, let us catch our breath.

Taking it easy today, really don't know what's in the wind for tonight. The Section is planning a little brawl and I'll probably end up there. The officers heard we were throwing a party and they contributed 15 bottles of vodka, brandy, and cognac. Oh, my aching back! In addition, we have beer, cokes, wine, and plenty to eat.

It's very beautiful in Tölz now. We have oodles of snow and everything is blanketed in white. We're situated in a valley, so with the big white mountains all around us we're really surrounded by towers of snow. All very picturesque.

Happy New Year once again.
Love,
Charlie

1946

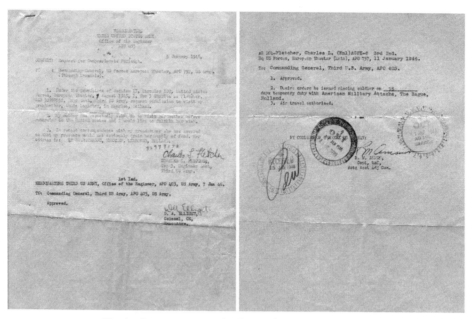

Charlie's request to visit his "Grandmother" in Holland.

Wednesday, January 2, 1946

Dear Mom and Dad,

Back to work again in 1946, two days gone. Gosh time flies.

Nothing much going on in the office. I may take a trip to Holland late this month, if I can get away. You know, I have a "grandmother" living there and I should like to see her before going home. I have no particular reason to go there but I would like to get away for a while and that seems to be the best bet.

I have some good friends in Heerlen and Heerlerheide and they continually ask me to visit. My French friends in Montfort also have invited me, but I can't get all over.

Incidentally, my roommate and I sent Christmas packages to two families in Holland and one in France and they all acknowledged receipt. I was a little skeptical about them getting through.

All's well, hope you are okay. Happy Birthday again, Pop!

Love and Kisses,
Charlie

Thursday, January 3, 1946

Dear Mom and Dad,

Guess what? I got up enough ambition to go skiing again and I had loads of fun. In fact, I think I showed a lot of improvement over the last time.

A few weeks ago, you realized how optimistic I was about redeployment. Well, you know how things change. All of the sudden, movement of troops to the States has slowed down. Even though 50's are eligible for discharge, 50 pointers in our Headquarters won't start the trek home until early February. So now, I'm not expecting anything but the worst, but it can't be later than March - the month I predicted quite sometime ago. I'll be alive and healthy, though, and that's what counts.

Love and Kisses,
Charlie

Friday, January 4, 1946

Dear Mom and Dad,

Happy Birthday, Pop, and many more too. How's the shape of your head these days? How often are the times I thank God for having your shape head. I think myself very fortunate.

It's good and cold here. I'm very lucky in one respect, we don't have any guard duty. It's pretty rough spending a couple of hours outdoors, especially knowing the war is over. We have a battalion of MP's and they do all the guard.

Just finished Cronin's "Green Tears" and it was a good book. I don't think I'll go to Garmisch this weekend - just hang around, ski a little, perhaps.

I can use some cheese, salmon, and as a treat, please send a little tuna fish. Unless things change quickly or if my discharge comes in from Washington, I'm afraid I'm here until early March. But that's just speculation, as you know.

I hope you are all in good health. Mail has been very poor for everyone. Sometimes I don't hear from you in days. So don't get excited when you don't get my letters.

I've straightened out the allotment deal and in a couple of weeks the bank should receive some checks. Go by there sometime next month and see if any have come in. Incidentally, how are my War Bonds coming in? Let me know if they're not, because this is a good time to check.

That's all for today, take it easy.
Love,
Charlie

Sunday, January 6, 1946

Dear Folks,

The news last night was anything but good. General McNarney[373] made some statements about redeployment and the main point was that after the 50-pointers go out, we shouldn't count on going home just because we become eligible on points or length of service. I think that's a very terrible thing. Just because a man is in the US he can get discharged when he had the required number of points, but if he is in Europe he can't even expect to go to the States. McNarney said that usually a soldier might depend upon going home three months after he becomes eligible.

The reason for all this is that enough replacements haven't been sent over by the War Department and it all goes back to the failure of the Draft Boards to induct sufficient number of people. It's understandable that they need a close-out force here, but it's hard to conceive why men over here for so long must do the job while men who have never been overseas and have little time in the States are being discharged. Well, that's the way it goes.

It's hard to say how all this applies to me individually. After February, 50,000 men will go home on points and service each month in addition to 40,000 for other reasons (furlough, re-enlistment, etc.). When they get down to 46, God knows, but McNarney said that all closeout men should be out of Europe by July 1. I really don't expect to be stuck that long, though.

---

[372] General Joseph Taggart McNarney (August 28, 1893 – February 1, 1972) served as Military Governor of occupied Germany and as Commanding General of the United States Forces in the European Theater and Commander in Chief, United States Forces of Occupation in Europe.

Redeploying by Points Ends; 50,000 Will Sail Each Month

Now it would be lovely if that dependency discharge comes through. I really think it is a deserving request on your part. I received two letters from you yesterday, December 18 and 24. I imagine all the letters got to Washington by the 1st of January, so we should know something shortly.

You might as well keep up those delicious packages for a while, unless you know something definite. Give E the dough and let here make them up. Yours are very nice but Eadie has a little more time. Can use sardines, cheese, soup, etc. Leave out the anchovies please, I don't go for them so much.

Love,
Charlie

Slowdown Ascribed To Draft's Failure To Supply Troops

FRANKFURT, Jan. 5—Redeployment on the basis of points has ended. Many men with point scores in the fifties now face one to three months more duty in Europe.

Military necessity now will determine the rate at which ET veterans will be returned home.

Shipments for January have already been determined, and the changes will not affect any men already earmarked for shipment or processing in preparation for shipment.

Only about 50,000 men per month will be sent home from Europe during the next six months.

A permanent occupation force of 300,000 men thus will be reached by next July 1.

The slowdown in redeployment is due to the inability of Selective Service to provide the required number of replacements.

Arrival of replacements may make it possible to send more than 50,000 men home monthly, also, a culling of theater needs may reduce the number of men needed, thus allowing them to be returned to the States.

These facts were announced today by Gen. Joseph T. McNarney, the theater commander, and Brig. Gen. George S. Eyster, USFET redeployment chief, on the heels of disclosure in Washington of a new War Department mobilization plan.

Need for Troops Overseas Is Put Before Shipping

(A United Press dispatch from Washington said Lt. Gen. Joseph L. Collins, former corps commander in the ET and now Army director of information, announced that the rate of demobilization and redeployment would be slowed down six months.

(Collins was quoted as saying the point had been reached where the need for troops overseas, rather than the availability of shipping would be the controlling factor determining the rate at which overseas veterans would be brought home and discharged.)

(He said that as a result troops from all theaters would be taken to the U. S. at the rate of 300,000 a month.

(When, at the end of six months, 1,800,000 more have reached the U. S., Army strength overseas will have been reduced to the "planned minimum" of 767,000.

(Collins said that if all available shipping were used, 1,800,000 could be brought home in three months But he said, according to the United Press, this would cripple the Army's occupational functions.

Slowdown Is Due to Lack of Replacements

(Collins also announced a lowered estimate of total Army manpower requirements as of July 1. The new figure of 1,550,000 is a reduction of about 400,000 from estimates made last September. Collins said the reduction resulted from a culling of estimated needs in all areas.)

McNarney emphasized that the slowdown of shipments of European Theater veterans to the States was due to the lack of replacements in the theater. He said Selective Service was to have provided 50,000 replacements monthly, but this figure had been more than 10,000 short each month. Eyster said approximately 23,000 replacements were overdue in the ET

(On Oct. 10, USFET announced that 135,000 replacements would arrive in the ET by Jan. 31 to relieve the 48 to 59-point group The announcement said that 20,000 troops were expected by the end of October.

(This estimate was cut on Dec. 21 to a total of 87,000

(Continued on Page 9)

Monday, January 7, 1946

Hello Mom and Pop,

All the redeployment news is pretty lousy and instead of griping about it, I'm enclosing a couple of articles from Stars and Stripes. The statement by General Collins[374] that very few men overseas now heard a shot fired is a lot of baloney. Nearly everyone with 35 points or over saw action.

---

[374] General Joseph Lawton Collins (May 1, 1896 – September 12, 1987) was a senior United States Army officer. During World War II, he served in both the Pacific and European Theaters of Operations. At this point in his career, he was Director of Information (later Chief of Public Information) of the United States Army.

Redeployment by Points Is Ended; 50,000 Men Sail Home Each Month

(Continued from Page 1)

replacements expected by the end of January, with 65,100 due to arrive in Europe by Dec. 31, according to USFET G-1, in Frankfurt.

(By the end of October, however, only 188 replacements had arrived at Le Havre and none at other ports. Statistics from Le Havre showed that 33,116 replacements arrived there in November and 16,092 in December, while 10,477 came through Bremerhaven in December, making a total of 59,873 up to the first of the year. Marseille and Antwerp, the only two other redeployment ports, reported that no replacements have passed through.)

50,000 Close-Out Troops a Month Will Go

The present theater troop strength, McNarney said, was 616,000 men. Of these, he said, 316,000 were engaged in "close-out" duties such as disposing of German prisoners and surplus property and in maintaining law and order in some areas.

Starting this month McNarney said, the close-out force would be reduced by an equal monthly figure over a period of six months ending July 1 (thus, 50,000 per month, making a total of 300,000 to leave by July 1). Transportation for the return of personnel in this close-out force had been arranged, he said.

"No transportation required for the return of military personnel will be used for other purposes," the Theater Commander said.

Eyster emphasized that men to be shipped home would be selected on the basis of points or length of service, whichever criterion was set by the War Department.

(Reports on the War Department announcement Saturday night did not indicate there was a change in the current system, which has been based both on points and length of service. The War Department had said that on or about March 20 it would discharge men with two years of service.)

A "liquidation and manpower board" has been established to check into every activity in the theater to determine whether there were any nonessential jobs and possibly to eliminate them if found, McNarney said.

"No soldier will be retained in Europe longer than absolutely necessary," the Theater Commander promised.

While January shipments already have been determined, Eyster said, they have not been estimated for February and March. He said it was not possible to predict when all men in the 50 to 60-point bracket would have cleared the theater. High-pointers, he said, would continue to receive priority.

Force to Be Static July 1

It was expected, McNarney said, that approximately 20,000 to 25,000 men monthly would be shipped home as replacements arrived. These homeward shipments, he said, would be in addition to the expected 50,000 monthly reductions in the close-out force.

By next July 1, he said, the occupation force would be at static strength. It would at that time consist of a highly-mobile, armored constabulary force of "first class troops."

(This constabulary force, he said, would be supported by a mobile force of three infantry divisions and Air Force units. The constabulary force, he said, would patrol the entire occupation zone in armored cars. Approximately 62,000 Air Force personnel would be included in the occupation force.)

Should the new "liquidation and manpower board" determine that further reductions in the theater close-out force could be made beyond the estimates given today, McNarney said, "we will request additional shipping of the War Department to take these extra men home."

Shipment of war brides already has been provided for, he said, and they "will be shipped home, but not to the disadvantage of any eligible U. S. soldier who can be spared from the necessary tasks at hand."

The redeployment and demobilization plan was given by McNarney and Eyster at a special conference called by the Theater Commander and attended by members of the Theater General Staff.

Everything is okay. I really have no complaints except that I'm not at home. I'm willing to spend a couple of months more here but then I want to go home *schnell.*[375]

Mail continues to be bad. Hope everything is okay. Pop, *vie gehts?*[376] Send my regards to E and Art. I'll write them soon.

Love and Kisses,
Charlie

[375] German: Quickly.

[376] German: How is it going?

Tuesday, January 8, 1946

Dear Mom and Pop,

I hope you're getting all my mail, as I'm writing almost every day.

On Saturday, January 5, I mailed you a small wooden box containing the two watches I bought you while in Switzerland. One is for Mom, the other for Dad. Hope you like them, I pray that they get to you all right. I got tired of holding on to them and it's just as much a chance to carry them home in all the hustle-bustle as it is to mail them, so I took the chance. Please let me know when you receive them.

Just because you haven't received any money orders lately doesn't mean that I'm not holding on to my dough. I have two money orders totaling $110 and I have about $70 in cash. I'm holding on to it for a while in case I get away again. My gross pay is now $115, after deductions I receive $68. I'll start sending some home soon, though.

Nothing else to write. Everything is okay. Don't beat up your Congressman too badly. Everyone seems to be writing to someone about this redeployment. I'll get home one of the Spring months, so be patient.

Love and Kisses,
Charlie

Thursday, January 10, 1946

Dear Mom and Pop,

I received your New Year's letter today. Now that you got all the letters into the War Department, all you can do is wait and see what happens. As far as Dr. Winning goes, Mom, I can make more deals in ten months than he can make in two weeks. There's no way to get home from here. It must come from the States.

I hardly approve of all the demonstrations taking place in Europe and the Pacific. I believe something should be done to get high-point men home and bring over replacements, but this demonstrating business should not go on in the Army. The people at home are the ones to shout, not the soldiers.[377]

Everything is just fine. I could use some packages when you get a chance. Perhaps some are on the way, so I shouldn't ask. Please let me know if my War Bonds are coming through, also tell me if the watches arrived safely.

It's very mild now but there's plenty of winter ahead.

No more today, regards to E and Art.
Love,
Charlie

Saturday, January 12, 1946

Hello Again,

Gosh, there's so little doing that it is a tough job to compose a letter.

First, I recently sent home a package with a silk scarf on the top. If you go through the pictures, pick out the ones of a young woman and a baby. They don't belong to me, but they were misplaced by one of the fellows and I'm quite sure I had them in my bunch. It's a Dutch woman and in one is her grandmother. If you can find them, send them back, otherwise forget it.

I think I'll go to the movies this evening, "Captain Kidd" is playing. Just finished "Canal Town," a good book written by Samuel Hopkins Adams. It's about a young doctor who goes to Palmyra, New York in the early 1800's to start practicing. The Erie Canal was being built then and the author tells an interesting story. Now I'm reading Bowen's "Yankee from Olympus," the biog-

---

[377] Responding to the perceived sluggish pace of demobilization in December 1945 and January 1946, US servicemen launched a protest insisting a more efficient and timely discharge process. This was replicated across all areas of operations, as more than 20,000 American soldiers marched in Manila, Philippines demanding to return home. Another 20,000 demonstrated in Honolulu. Three thousand joined them in Korea, and 5,000 in Kolkata. In Guam, 3,500 Air Force troops organized a hunger strike, while 18,000 soldiers collected money to send a cable to journalists making their case for repatriation. Despite these widespread perceptions, the Army actually demobilized its forces at an impressive pace. By the end of 1945, the War Department had returned more than four million servicemembers to the United States. And between September and December 1945, the Army discharged an average of 1.2 million soldiers per month. (washingtonpost.com/history/2021/11/11/world-war-ii-mutiny-protests-veterans & nationalww2museum.org/war/articles/points-system-us-armys-demobilization)

raphy of Oliver Wendell Holmes. I read a condensation of it quite some time ago.

We're having a little snowstorm for a change. We lost practically all of our snow.

I don't think I'll go away this weekend. I expect to leave for Holland early in February and I'll have enough travelling then. On that trip I'm going to try to hit Paris, Brussels among other places.

That's all, mail just came and five letters came in from you and E.

Love and Kisses,
Charlie

Sunday, January 13, 1946

Dear *Schmiel*,

Was Machst du? [378] איך בין געזונט

Gee, I think I've forgotten my Yiddish. But once you start dictating with Mother's help, I'll do okay. That's strange isn't it, you could never dictate a letter without Mom's assistance. What's the matter, Dad, don't you know enough Jewish?

You must excuse me for not writing very much to the Hospital. I have been writing to Mom regular and I know you get to see those letters. Also, save this line for Mom.

In one of your letters, Mom, you say that every time you hear the elevator or the doorbell rings unexpectedly you think it may be me. Mom, you ought to cut that foolish business out. You'll know when I'm coming home and there's no chance in the world that I'll walk in out of a clear sky.

There's nothing I can do about getting home except re-enlisting and getting a furlough. You know how quick I'd do that, don't you? If the War Department doesn't approve a discharge, we'll just have to wait. If anything pops up before then, try to get me an emergency furlough, because once I'm in the States I'll never have to go overseas again and I probably would get a discharge. I saw a

---

[378] Yiddish: How are you? I am healthy.

copy of the letter the Doctor wrote and it looks very good. I swear that should have gotten me an emergency.

Please don't think I'm on pins and needs about you getting me home. I know you're doing your best and don't knock yourselves out. If I can get home now, so much the better; otherwise, I'll just have to wait and I'm living nicely and not "suffering" from want or anything.

I'm glad Charles Bialo got to the States okay. He must have had a rough voyage. Have you met him yet? What do you think of him? I found him to be a very sociable and a pleasant person.

We had a wet snowstorm but it's all over now. Enjoying a quiet Sunday, we've got our working Sunday mornings down to every third week. Well, that's all for now. Pop, be a good patient and take care of yourselves.

The only thing about this redeployment is that men should continue to be drafted so a steady flow of replacements can be sent to Europe and the Pacific. We need men here and the Army has sent home a huge number of men. My only desire is that soldiers in the States should be sent over to relieve the men who have been here so long. I'm in my 17th month now, I hardly approve of all these demonstrations.

Love and Kisses,
Charlie

Monday, January 14, 1946

Dear Mom and Dad,

Yesterday's letter was addressed to Dad at Mount Sinai[379] and I hope you received it. I can't understand the poor mail service, Mom, but by this time it should be cleared up. Today I received some letters from you dated around January 5th.

If the snowstorm we're having keeps up, we'll be snowed in before long. It started yesterday evening and except for a few hours, it's been coming down in great flurries.

---

[379] Hospital.

Had a grapefruit a couple of times lately. I imagine that the food will improve right along. It was pretty poor during the redeployment rush.

Nothing much doing these nights or days, for that matter. I saw "Captain Kidd" the other day and it was pretty good. Tonight I plan to write some letters and read "Yanks from Olympus." It's a pretty good book.

Love,
Charlie

Tuesday, January 15, 1946

Dear Mom and Pop,

The entire redeployment situation is clarified now after today's War Department announcement. According to the revision, I should be home on a boat by April 30, give or take a couple of weeks. How do you feel about that? Three and one-half months more. Not too bad, since the date seems to be pretty definite. Let's wait until April 30 and see what gives.

This is really snow-covered territory now, and there's plenty of cold to go with the white stuff.

There's really nothing to report. I saw "Human Comedy" last night and it was excellent. I missed the picture when it first came out and I'm glad I got to see it. Micky Rooney and Jack Jenkins give superior performances.

I hate to end now, but I'll be damned if there's anything else to write about.

Take care of yourselves,

Love,
Charlie

Wednesday, January 16, 1946

Dear Mom and Dad,

How cold it is these days. But I'm very lucky. I don't have to go out at all unless I want to and in the apartment it's always very warm.

Had a nice breakfast today. Prunes, oatmeal, eggs, potatoes, toast, and coffee. The food is slowly improving. I think I'll take a swim this morning. We're supposed to exercise one hour a day and since the pool is in the building, it's a convenient way to spend the hour.

Last evening I watched a hockey game in Tölz, just for a few minutes though since it was so cold. There's an outdoor ice rink in town and it's lighted up at night.

I hope the UNO works out all right.[380] We've had enough war in this world, let's have peace for a change. The present conference seems to be going along nicely enough.

Not a thing in the world is new, I'm feeling fine. Regards to all and hope you are okay.

Love,
Charlie

Thursday, January 17, 1946

Dear Mom and Pop,

My furlough to Holland has been approved and I'll take off round February 1. I expect to go to Paris first and I'll spend a few days there. While in France I'm going to visit the family I know in Montfort L'Amaury. I also plan to visit Brussels.

I believe I have to report to the Hague, Holland's capital, before proceeding to Heerlen and if that's the case I'll be able to go to Amsterdam and Rotterdam. It's unfortunate that I'm seeing all these famous cities while they are suffering from the aftereffects of war, but it's better seeing them this way than not at all.

Charles Bialo gave me the address of a cousin of his who lives in Paris, I'll look her up when I get there.

Very little work these days, taking it good and easy and doing a little reading.

Love to all, most to you.
Charlie

---

[380] The General Assembly of the United Nations opened in London on January 10, 1946, with the United Nations Secretary-General selection.

Saturday, January 19, 1946

Dear Mom and Dad,

Another week swiftly coming to a close. I think I'll take off to Garmisch this noon. It's 9 AM now and we're all in the office trying to look busy, but there's actually very little to do. General Truscott[381] was supposed to come around to the section this morning, but I think he's in Nuremberg, so we all tidied up for nothing.

I'm reading "The Gauntlet" by James Street and so far interesting. Very little to write about, believe me. I'm getting a few things ready for my trip, but I won't be leaving until the end of the month. We still have loads of snow but it's not so cold now. Maybe I'll do a little skiing this weekend.

Well, I'll end now.
Love and Kisses,
Charlie

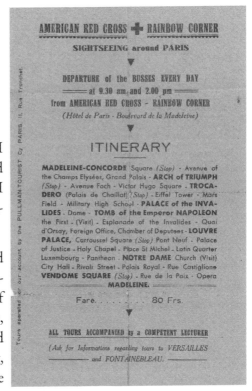

Monday, January 21, 1946

Hello People,

How's everything coming along? I hope you're okay. I haven't received any letter dated after 6 January, so I don't have all the current information.

There was a big story in Stars and Stripes today about hardship discharge becoming more lenient. If you still are trying to get me home, I'd advise you to check with the Red Cross on the new January 15 ruling, also send me the duplicates of the

---

[381] General Lucian King Truscott Jr. (January 9, 1895 – September 12, 1965) took over command of the Third Army from General George S. Patton on October 8, 1945-April 1946. This command included the Eastern Military District of the US Occupation Zone of Germany, which consisted primarily of the state of Bavaria. At this time, he was Charlie's commanding General.

letters you submitted to the Adjutant General's Office and I'll see if anything can be done over here.

Enclosed is a $37 money order; use it if you need it, otherwise please bank it for me. Also, tell me if my War Bonds are coming through. By any chance did my allotment check hit the bank yet?

I had a swell weekend in Garmisch, came back this morning at 11.

Love,
Charlie

Tuesday, January 22, 1946

Dear Mom and Dad,

Received two big letters from you, one dated the 6th of January. I'm glad you got the perfume, Mom, use it in good health. I'm sure you and Dad will like the wristwatches once they reach you. My friend's wife received her watch already and it was in good shape. Please let me know when you get them.

I sent the $250 money orders in two different letters. The two $100's that you received on the 29th of November were part of the $250. I'll check on the receipt for the other $50. The other stuff seems to be in order, so that $50 money order is about the only thing up in the air.

You won't have to go for the watches, they'll be delivered right to the house. It doesn't pay to register the packages.

Yesterday I sent a $37 money order. It was signed by Robert H. Lovening who sent it for me. If you need it, don't hesitate to use it. Please mention something about my War Bonds so I can check on them if they aren't coming in.

Feeling fine, a little busy this week. Take care of yourselves. Everyone writes that you're looking like a million bucks, Dad. Keep it up.

Love and Kisses,
Charlie

Wednesday, January 23, 1946

Hello Folks,

Was off this afternoon and took a little nap before doing a little tidying up around the room.

The other night I saw "The Polly's Sister" with Betty Grable and it was very entertaining. I'm still reading "The Gauntlet" and it's good.

It's warmed up a bit and it's quite comfortable outdoors. It's already getting light early in the morning and our days are longer.

The Krauts were very fortunate to have such a mild winter. Of course, it can still get cold, but I think they've got the winter beat. It helped us out also in our occupation job. There's not very much more to relate today.

How's your head shape, Pop, after staying in the hospital so long?

Love,
Charlie

Thursday, January 24, 1946

Dear Mom and Pop,

Although there isn't anything new to tell you, here I am again. I understand that they're going to move this headquarters to a more centrally located place, but it's not going to be effective until May or June. By that time I'll be a civilian so I'm not worried about that. I think Nuremberg is under consideration since that city is just about in the center of the US Zone.

It's still fairly moderate. I watched a hockey game outdoors last night and I was warm except for my feet. What's new in New York? You didn't get to see the

---

[382] Held on January 12, The New York City Victory Parade of 1946 took place to celebrate the victorious finish of WWII. The parade was escorted by 13,000 men of the 82nd Airborne Division and also included Sherman tanks and other armored vehicles, such as self-propelled howitzers, and a fly-by of a formation of glider-towing C-47s. The parade, beginning at Washington Square, marching up Fifth Avenue, was estimated to be four miles long. (. The All Americans in World War II: A Photographic History of the 82nd Airborne Division at War)

parade of the 82nd Airborne Division put on,[382] did you? That must have been something to see.

I think I'll take off from here on February 1 or 2 for my trip. I hope it's a nice one, as it'll probably be my last in Europe.

That's all for now, take care.

Love,
Charlie

Saturday, January 26, 1946

Dear Mom and Dad,

Here I is again with nothing much to write about. I'm on duty this weekend so I'll have to hang around, I assure you that there won't be much doing. I got my orders for the trip and I'll leave here on Friday or Saturday the 31st or 1st. I'm going to Paris first and I spend three days there, and then I'll go to Brussels.

Mom, don't worry about the packages. I'll let you know when to stop sending them. Last night we had a little feast and the sardines and salmon you sent came in very handy.

I think I'll do a little skiing tomorrow. The weather is very nice, not cold. Really nothing more. My best regards to you all.

Love and Kisses,
Charlie

Sunday, January 27, 1946

Dear Mom and Pop,

No skiing today due to the mild weather. There are too many bare spots on the hills and it wouldn't be wise to attempt skiing. I went to the Red Cross instead, and there was a radio broadcast plugging the March of Dimes.[383] Two bands played and it turned out to be a pleasant afternoon.

---

[383] The March of Dimes is a US nonprofit organization dedicated to improving the health and wellness of mothers and babies. It was first established by President Franklin D. Roosevelt in 1938, as the National Foundation for Infantile Paralysis, to combat polio. (www.marchofdimes.org)

Gosh, there's really so little doing that it's a struggle to get enough down for a letter.

We've been getting some decent meals lately and with your packages I have more than enough. Last night I had some asparagus soup and it was tasty.

Did the watches reach you yet? I hope they get through okay.

Going to clean up all my work this coming week, so I can take off all caught up.

Love,
Charlie

Monday, January 28, 1946

Hello Mom and Pop,

Here it is, the last week in January, how time flies.

Keeping a little busy, getting everything in shape - but I'm not breaking my back, I assure you.

Saw a good movie this evening, "The Spanish Man" with Maureen O' Hara. It was a little different for these times and quite entertaining. I'm reading "Northwest Passage" by Kenneth Roberts, so that takes care of that phase of my activities. I usually manage to take a dip a couple of times a week and that gives me a little exercise.

It started snowing again this evening, but it doesn't look as if it will last long. Nothing more doing at the present time, leaving here around Saturday.

Take care of yourselves.
Love and Kisses,
Charlie

Wednesday, January 30, 1946

Dear Folks,

Boy, is it snowing! We're really having a little storm and it's something beautiful to watch, everything so white.

I got the letter with the doctor's affidavits, and they look okay. In fact, I think I may try to get a quick trip home on them. They just changed that business of emergency furloughs again and now I can get one. Of course, I might not be able to get it but it's worth the try just on account of traveling to the port by myself. And then once I hit the States I'll get discharged with my points and service or from your dependency discharge request if it is approved. I'm leaving on my trip Saturday and by the time I get back, I should have some word.

At any rate, it can't be long before I get home since the 48 pointers are leaving here for a carrier division on February 20. The 102nd is also sailing in February and how nice it would have been to go home with my own division.

I'm sure now that you received all my money orders except for $50 and one for $37 that I just mailed. The $250 was broken down to two $100 and one $50, and that's the one that is missing. I have the receipt number and if you still haven't received it, I'll start a claim through.

By now my watches must have gotten home and I hope you're wearing them in good health.

No more news now. Good luck and take care of yourselves.

Love and Kisses,
Charlie

Saturday, February 2, 1946 – Munich, Germany

Hi Folks,

I'm just about ready to leave for Paris and this starts my winter "European Tour." I came into town late yesterday afternoon and was put up splendidly for the night by the Town Major. These town majors in all the big cities are under the Army Engineer. The people here have a beautiful home and are very hospitable. Dinner was good and served nicely. Much better than staying in transient billets, ask Artie. Boy, does your son get around.

My application for emergency return home was approved by the Third Army and now it goes to Frankfurt. I should know shortly. The boys are going to send me a telegram to the Hague in Holland and inform me of the decision.

I'm feeling great and am looking forward to a great time.

Take it easy, swell that you're home, Pop.
Love and Kisses,
Charlie

Sunday, February 3, 1946 - Montfort L' Amaury, France

Hello Folks,

Here I am back in Montfort, France for a brief visit with my butcher friend and the family. Here is where I spent close to three weeks on that Red Ball business back in September - October 1944.

I arrived in Paris after a nice trip and yesterday morning I went to Versailles. It happened to be the day when no cars go to Montfort, so I was in a fix. I had some Frenchman call up the Desbrosses and they told me they would come to Versailles in their car, thank God they have one. So while waiting for them, I had a nice dinner and looked around Versailles - I have been there before. My friends finally arrived and sped me to Montfort where I saw the family and chatted with everyone. I was shown the guest room and it is a very nice place, strictly European bed and style and extremely comfortable.

In typical French fashion, we visited a café late in the afternoon, had a little wine, shot some pool (billiards) and then came home for dinner. These people have dinner at 8 o'clock all their lives, like clockwork. We had delicious soup, ham, pork (it pays to know a butcher), cake, jam, and of course wine. Water has no place in this country. Sat around the fire until late and boy, did I sleep well.

Got up at 10, had some sort of meatloaf for breakfast, read "Daddy Long Legs" (one of the novels my friend, George, has) and for lunch had delicious cold cuts, potatoes and veal (boy, it was swell) beer and cheese. This afternoon we went driving and I saw a lot of the countryside. I'm afraid I'll have to leave early tomorrow morning as The Rainbow Corner, where I am staying, is closing up and all my stuff is there. In addition, I have to get on to Holland. On Saturday I looked up the cousin of the Bialos, but they don't work on Saturdays and I had no way of finding out where she lives. I'll try to see her tomorrow.

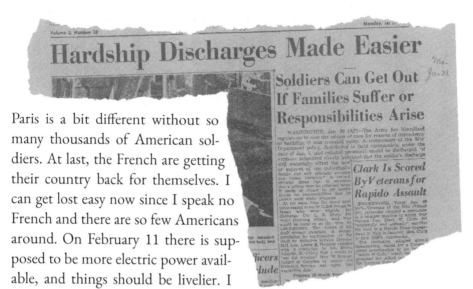

Paris is a bit different without so many thousands of American soldiers. At last, the French are getting their country back for themselves. I can get lost easy now since I speak no French and there are so few Americans around. On February 11 there is supposed to be more electric power available, and things should be livelier. I may be able to spend a day or two in Paris on my return trip. Before I leave Paris, I'm going to call Bad Tölz and find out whether anything has come through on my request for an emergency return.

I'm having loads of fun, taking it easy, seeing Europe.

Love and Kisses,
Charlie

The Desbrosses, family of Montfort, send their best regards to the Fletcher family of New York. Small world, eh?

Wednesday, February 6, 1946

Friday, February 8, 1946 - Brussels, Belgium

Dear Mom and Dad,

Had a pleasant 6-hour train ride up here from Paris and arrived at 6:30 Wednesday evening. This place is a small-scale Paris and is preferred by many Americans; for myself, I think I'd take Paris.

Without a doubt, Belgium has recovered from the War the fastest of any of the countries occupied by the Germans. There is everything to be had and although the price of goods has risen 400%, wages have increased 300% so the people do okay. Lights are on all evening, store windows are packed, nightclubs

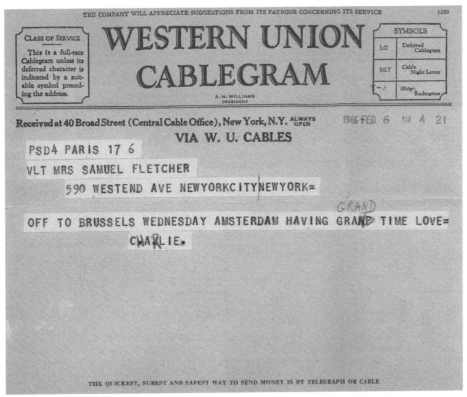

are numerous and it all goes to make a nice place to spend a few days.

I was going to the Hague today, but "Aida" is on tonight at the Opera and I decided to stay until tomorrow. I think I told you I saw "*La Tosca*" in Paris. The Brussels Opera rates with the best and "Aida" should be excellent.

This trip is turning out splendidly. First, four days in Paris, now three in Brussels and Amsterdam and perhaps Rotterdam coming up. On my return trip I plan to visit Antwerp for a few hours, I even may go early tomorrow. My train for the Hague leaves at 1:30 and it only takes 30 minutes by train to Antwerp.

After this letter, don't except mail for a week or so, this is the last APO I hit until I return. There are no US units in Holland. The weather here has been miserable. That's my only kick. So far on the trip I've had terrible weather, rain, rain.

Mom, I sent you two nice bottles of perfume from Paris. The Prince Matchibelli is for yourself. If you think I should send one to Anna or Stellie then give them the other box (three little bottles) and tell them I sent it. If you don't think they "deserve" it, give it to E, Mimi or keep it yourself. I sent Aunt Rose a bottle recently and today I sent her a few nice hankies made in Switzerland. I still have a couple of bottles in Germany.

I can't buy much stuff here because I'm rationed on my Belgium money. As it is, this is a rich man's trip. Had a delicious steak dinner with French fries yesterday and it cost 100 francs, a little over $2.00. Gosh, it was good and what a generous portion I had. The women here are a lot like the French, but I think the Parisians are more chic.

That's all now. Take it easy and take care of yourselves.

God Bless you,
Love,
Charlie

Tuesday, February 12, 1946 - Brussels, Belgium

Hi Mom and Dad,

Was in Holland Saturday night until this morning. Was in the Hague and Amsterdam and also saw Rotterdam, Haarlem, Breda, etc. The transportation to Heerlen is so bad from Amsterdam that I decided to come back here and go to Liege and then to Heerlen. I came down in a British truck and it was a three-hour trip. Northern Holland was swell and I had a great time.

By now you probably received my cable. As you know, the moment I received the letters from the doctor, I put in a request for an emergency return. They had just changed the rules, for the two previous months it had to go through Washington. Well, I told the boys back in Tölz to cable me at the Hague if anything came through. When I reported yesterday, there was a message stating that furlough was granted. So, I'm going to make this trip snappy and I expect to be leaving Munich for the Portno[384] later than the 22nd of February. I go direct by myself and I'll probably have top water priority. I should be home around the 10th of March, give or take a day. I'll call up as soon as I hit Ft. Dix, so don't get excited.

---

[384] The Port of Le Havre, France.

I'm glad that I worked things this way. It'll be a nice way to travel home and it speeds things up about six weeks or so.

Be good, see you soon.
Love and Kisses,
Charlie

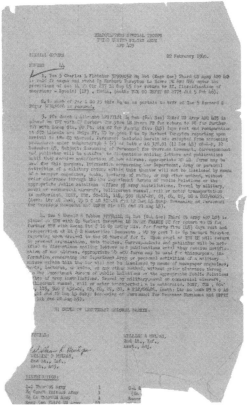

Charlie's orders attaching him for transport back to the United States.

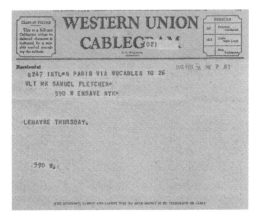

Charlie's final telegram from Europe, when leaving from Le Havre Port in France.

Chapter 13:

Epilogue – A Homecoming

Honorable Discharge

This is to certify that

CHARLES L FLETCHER   32 999 032   TECHNICIAN THIRD GRADE

HEADQUARTERS BATTERY – 102ND DIVISION ARTILLERY

Army of the United States

hereby Honorably Discharged from the military

service of the United States of America.

This certificate is awarded as a testimonial of Honest

and Faithful Service to this country.

Given at   SEPARATION CENTER
FORT DIX, NJ

Date   18 MARCH 1946

JAMES R. PHILBROOK
MAJOR INFANTRY

After one year, six months, and two days in Europe, Charlie departed from the port of Le Havre, France on Thursday, February 28, 1946. Upon his arrival Stateside, he received an Honorable Discharge on March 18, 1946, as well as the following in recognition for his service: The American Service Medal, European-African-Middle Eastern Service Medal, Good Conduct Medal, and World War II Victory Medal. Additionally, with its establishment in April 1946, he was awarded The Army of Occupation Medal for his post-war Garrison Duty in Germany.

Fulfilling his desire to attend college while transitioning back to civilian life, Charlie enrolled in NYU's Graduate School of Education in 1946. After the completion of the Spring and Summer semesters, and at the encouragement of his friend Irwin D. Schoen, Charlie moved to Allentown, Pennsylvania in 1947 to join Irwin's furniture business, Schoen Furniture Inc. Over the course of the next four decades, Charles L. Fletcher's professional career was with Schoen's Furniture, first as a partner and Secretary Treasurer and then taking over the company as the President and Chief Executive Officer in 1977. He remained in that post until his retirement and the business closure in 1990. As Charles remarked in a newspaper interview at the time, "Everything has to come to an end. I've had 43 wonderful years in business, but the time has come to take it a little easy."[385]

As Charles was establishing his professional career in Allentown, he was introduced by mutual friends to Allentown native, Bernice "Peeps" Rickel, and they were married on Sunday, June 19, 1949. Reflecting later in life on their first date he recounted with a grin, "I bought a pitcher of beer and ordered a plate of French fries; I was a big-time spender."[386] Charles treated Peeps as a queen and felt that she was the best at everything she did, and he wasn't shy about sharing this opinion with others. Together, they enjoyed 38 years of devoted marriage and lovingly raised their three daughters: Nancy, JoAnn, and Sally.

Throughout his adult life, Charles was a man of many interests and was constantly giving of his time and resources to numerous community causes. As he was quoted in an interview with The Sunday Globe, "I feel a sense of obligation to serve, a responsibility you might say. I believe everyone should serve

---

[385] "Schoen's Closing Its Doors" The Morning Call - Allentown, Pennsylvania, July 3, 1990.

[386] "Merchant Feels Obligation to Serve" The Sunday Globe - Bethlehem, Pennsylvania, December 15, 1985

where he has the capacity."[387] To this end, he was an active participant of the Allentown Jewish community through his membership in Congregation Brit Shalom, Temple Beth El and Sons of Israel. Additionally, Charles served for two years as the President of the Jewish Family Service and for three years as President of The Jewish Federation of Allentown, as well as an Honorary Board Member of the Allentown Jewish Community Center. While serving as President of the Jewish Federation from 1973-1976, Charles initiated and expanded the follow-

Charles and Peeps

ing social programs: The Jewish Federation Endowment Fund, The Community Relations Council, The George Feldman Achievement Award, a scholarship fund for high school seniors to attend a nine-week semester of study in Israel, and a course of Hebrew-content study for children with learning disabilities. Furthermore, he lent his talents to the broader Allentown community as a faithful member of The Lions Club, Cedar Crest College Association and as President of the Center City Association and Parking Authority.

Following Peeps's untimely death, Charles remarried Eleanor Denitz Wiener and spent this next chapter of his life in warm companionship together with her and their blended families. All told, Charles was a loving father and grandfather to his three daughters, two stepsons Alan and Steven Wiener, and eleven grandchildren. Today, Charles's family continues to grow with great-grandchildren living both in the United States and Israel.

Charles passed away peacefully on March 12, 2005, at the age of 81. Throughout his life, it can be said that Charles was a bit of a character, but he was also

---

[387] Ibid.

surely a man of great character. Perhaps the best way to end this book of tribute is to quote from Charles's own Bar Mitzvah speech, which he delivered at Congregation Adereth El on November 28, 1936. This excerpt, together with the full speech, is still carefully preserved. It stands as a testament to the values and principles that shaped his life, and precisely encapsulates the extraordinary man he would become.

> *"I promise you faithfully and sincerely that I shall strive to make myself the realization of your cherished hopes and dreams. I pray that I may grow up to be an upright man, loyal to the Jewish faith and to my country. I shall conduct myself to be pleasing in the sight of God and man...I pray to God that He may help me grow up to be the pride of my family, an honor to the house of Israel, and a credit to all mankind."*

Acknowledgments

From its very inception, this work has been a collaborative family endeavor. It reflects the coalescence of wonderful people who gave of their time and talents so that Charlie's story could be shared with others.

Firstly, I wish to thank my mother, Sally (Fletcher) Gerstein, for the endless encouragement and material support that she lent to this project. Without question, my enthusiasm to delve into this project was in large part the result of the conscious effort she invested so that Pop-Pop and I could develop a warm and loving relationship during my childhood years. I am also grateful to my aunts, Nancy (Fletcher) Cummings and JoAnn (Fletcher) Steele, for carefully preserving and sharing with me the letters and photographs which subsequently became the focused content of this book. Many thanks as well to Lauren (Marshak) Korman for providing the family history of her parents, Artie and Edith (Fletcher) Marshak.

Additionally, much appreciation to my wife Devora, whose attention to detail and skillful editorial touch can be seen on every page. It elevated the project from a stack of old letters to the beautiful book that it is today. I am incredibly fortunate that my life partner and writing partner are one and the same. Though the two of you never had the chance to meet, I am grateful that at least you had the opportunity to get to know Charlie through his letters.

And finally, dear reader, thank you for welcoming this story into your life. May it inspire you to discover the first chapter of your own story, one that follows in Charlie's legacy of upstanding responsibility, communal friendship, and faithful service.

References

(n.d.). Retrieved from Wolrd War Two USO Preservation Association: http://www.ww2uso.org/

Adler, C. (1938). THE JEWISH WELFARE BOARD—TWENTY YEARS OLD. *The American Jewish Year Book*, 149-177.

Bamford, T. (2020, August 27). *The Points Were All That Mattered: The US Army's Demobilization After World War II.* Retrieved from The National World War Two Museum: https://www.nationalww2museum.org/war/articles/points-system-us-armys-demobilization

Bamford, T. (2021, February 1). *"Keep 'em Rolling": 82 Days on the Red Ball Express.* Retrieved from The National World War Two Muesum: https://www.nationalww2museum.org/war/articles/red-ball-express

Camp Kilmer. (n.d.). Retrieved from National Archives & Records Administration Northeast Region: https://www.archives.gov/files/nyc/public/camp-kilmer.pdf

Creation of the Women's Army Corps. (n.d.). Retrieved from US Army : https://www.army.mil/women/history/wac.html

Frederiksen, O. J. (1953). *The American Military Occupation of Germany 1945-1953.* Historical Division, Headquarters, United States Army, Europe.

Gaerlan, C. I. (2020). *Liberation of the Philippines 1945.* Retrieved from The National World War Two Museum : https://www.nationalww2museum.org/war/articles/liberation-of-philippines-cecilia-gaerlan

Grathwol, R. P. (2005). *Building For Peace, U.S. Army Engineers in Europe 1945-1991.* Washington D.C.: Center of Military History and Corps of Engineers.

How to Plan, Organize and Promote an Off-duty Education Program, -Headquarters, Army Service Forces, . (1945). Washington D.C. : United States Government Printing Office .

MacDonald, C. (1993). *The Siegfried Line Campaign* . Washington D.C.: Center of Military History, United States Army.

Mick, A. H. (1947). *With the 102nd Infantry Division Through Germany* . Washington D.C.: Infantry Journal Press.

Order of Battle of the US Army - WWII - ETO 102nd Infantry Division. (n.d.). Retrieved from U.S. Army Center of Military History: https://history.army.mil/documents/eto-ob/102id-eto.htm

Palmer, R. (1991). *United States Army in World War II-The Procurement and Training of Ground Combat Troops.* Washington D.C. : Center of Military History United States Army.

TELLER, C. (1919). THE JEWISH WELFARE BOARD. *The American Jewish Year Book,* 88-102.

Training the American GI. (n.d.). Retrieved from The National World War II Museum: https://www.nationalww2museum.org/war/articles/training-american-gi

United States Holocaust Memorial Museum, W. D. (n.d.). *GARDELEGEN.* Retrieved from Holocaust Encyclopedia: https://encyclopedia.ushmm.org/content/en/article/gardelegen

World War II Core Area. (n.d.). Retrieved from U.S. Army Heritage and Education Center : https://ahec.armywarcollege.edu/trail/WWII/index.cfm

Ziemke, E. F. (1990). *The U.S. Army in the Occupation of Germany 1944-1946.* Washington D.C.: U.S. Government Printing Office.

About the Author

RABBI JOSHUA GERSTEIN currently serves as a Captain in the IDF Military Rabbinate. He holds Rabbinical Ordination, as well as a Bachelor's degree in Psychology from Touro College and a Master's degree in Jewish Education from the Hebrew University of Jerusalem. His other published works include "*A People, A Country, A Heritage*," two-volumes of original essays on the weekly Torah portion.

Originally from Lancaster, Pennsylvania, Rabbi Gerstein immigrated to the State of Israel in 2007. He lives in Jerusalem with his wife and family.

Made in United States
Orlando, FL
05 May 2023

32823463R00346